# THE CRISIS OF REASON

# The Yale Intellectual History of the West

*General Editors:*
J. W. Burrow (University of Oxford)
William J. Bouwsma (University of California, Berkeley)
Frank M. Turner (Yale University)

*Executive Editor:*
Robert Baldock

This series seeks to provide a chronological account of the intellectual life and the development of ideas in Western Europe from the early medieval period to the present day.

Now available:

*Medieval Foundations of the Western Intellectual Tradition, 400–1400*

by Marcia L. Colish

Forthcoming:

*The Intellectual Renaissance, 1400–1550* by Ronald Witt

*The Waning of the Renaissance, 1550–1640* by William J. Bouwsma

*The World of Knowledge, 1640–1720* by Peter N. Miller

*Reason's Empire: The European Enlightenment, 1710–1790* by Anthony Pagden

*Intellectuals in a Revolutionary Age, 1750–1860* by Frank M. Turner

# The Crisis of Reason
# European Thought, 1848–1914

J. W. Burrow

Yale University Press
New Haven and London

Set in Ehrhardt by Printline, New Delhi
Printed in Great Britain by St Edmundsbury Press

**Library of Congress Cataloging-in-Publication Data**

Burrow, J. W. (John Wyon), 1935–
    The crisis of reason : European thought, 1848–1914/J.W. Burrow.
        p. cm.—(Yale intellectual history of the West)
    Includes bibliographical references and index.
    ISBN 0–300–08390–4 (cloth : alk. paper)
    1. Europe—Intellectual life—19th century. 2. Europe—Intellectual life—20th century.
    3. Philosophy, Modern—19th century. 4. Philosophy, Modern—20th century I. Title. II.
    Series.
CB204 B87 2000
940.'8—DC21
                                                                                    99–059165

A catalogue record for this book is available from the British Library.

10 9 8 7 6 5 4 3 2 1

*For*
*Bob Johnson*
*in gratitude*

# Contents

# Illustrations

1. Proclamation of the French Republic. Lithograph. © Bibliothèque Nationale de France, Paris.
2. *George Sand.* Engraving after Delacroix. © Bibliothèque Nationale de France, Paris.
3. Italian Conspirators. Museo della Risorgimento, Rome.
4. Proclamation of the Roman Republic, February 1849. Museo della Risorgimento, Rome. Photo: Scala.
5. Ernest Meissonier, *The Barricade*, 1849. Musée du Louvre, Paris. © Photo: RMN.
6. *Genealogical Tree of Humanity.* From Ernest Haeckel, *The Evolution of Man*, vol. 2 (London, 1910).
7. The Natural History Museum. *Graphic*, 27 March 1880.
8. Central Hall of the Natural History Museum. From W. H. Flower, *A General Guide to the British Museum (Natural History)* (London, 1887).
9. The Reading Room of the Bibliothèque Nationale, 1862. © Bibliothèque Nationale de France, Paris.
10a and b. Illustrations from Charles Darwin, *The Expressions and the Emotions in Man and Animals* (London, 1872). British Library, London.
11a and b. Illustrations from Gina Lombroso Ferrero, *Criminal Man According to the Classification of Cesare Lombroso* (New York and London, 1911). British Library, London.
12. Félicien Rops, *Mors Syphilitica*. Etching, *c.* 1892. Private collection.
13. Fedor Vassilyev, *The Village Street*, 1868. State Tretyakov Gallery, Moscow.
14. Degradation of Captain Dreyfus. Mansell Collection.
15. Ludwig Meidner, *Revolution*, *c.* 1913. Nationalgalerie, Berlin. © Bildarchiv Preussischer Kulturbesitz. Photo: Klaus Göken.
16. Gabriel Ferrier, *Salammbô, c.* 1881. From Armand Silvestre, *Le Nu au salon: Champs des Mars*, Paris, 1889.
17. Giovanni Boldoni, *Portrait of Robert de Montesquiou*, 1897. Musée d'Orsay, Paris. © Photo: RMN.
18. Assassination of Tsar Alexander II. *Illustrated London News*, 1 March 1881.
19. A Nihilist Meeting Surprised. *Illustrated London News*, 20 November 1880.
20. William Holman Hunt, *The Shadow of Death*. © Manchester City Art Galleries.
21. Georg Unger as Siegfried. *Siegfried*, Bayreuth, 1876. Richard-Wagner-Stiftung, Bayreuth.
22. The Temple of the Graal. *Parsifal*, Bayreuth, 1930. Richard-Wagner-Stiftung, Bayreuth.
23. Ludwig Fahrenkrog, *The Holy Hour*, *c.* 1912. *Die Kunst*, 25, 1911–12.
24. Gustav Klimt, *Jurisprudence* (final version), 1903–7. Galerie Welz, Salzburg.
25. Umberto Boccioni, *The Street Enters the House*, 1911. Niedersächsische Landesgalerie, Hanover.
26. Oskar Kokoshka, poster for *Murderer, Hope of Women*. © DACS 2000.
27. Wassily Kandinsky, cover of the *Almanach der Blaue Reiter*, 1911. © ADAGP, Paris and DACS, London 2000.
28. Page from the first issue of *Blast*, 1914.
29. The Steiner House, Vienna, designed by Adolf Loos, 1910.

# *Preface*

This book is concerned with the history of ideas in Europe in a particular period. Obviously this formula can do with some expansion. What it is meant to indicate is that the intention throughout has been an historical one: to place the reader in the position of an informed eavesdropper on the intellectual conversations of the past. The book's obligation, that is, is not so much to what we now think important in the period as to what was then found important, among educated but not narrowly specialized readerships with a taste or even craving for ideas. I have not paid statistical attention to questions of sales, numbers of editions and so on, though I have tried to alert the reader to cases of extreme popularity and influence or temporary neglect. But intellectual dead-ends which made a stir in the world have counted for more with me than portentous moments which were then not recognized as such. The former are part – cynics might wish to say the major part – of the texture of the intellectual life of the past.

By speaking initially of 'conversations', however, I mean to issue a caveat against too ready an assumption of an overall coherence, perhaps fostered by the word 'period'. The latter, it seems to me, is best thought of as thematically overlapping circles in which are generated and invested contemporary intellectual excitement, aspirations, hopes, bitterness and dread. It must be a rare autodidact who seeks to inhabit all of them, though many inhabit more than one, while ideas, suitably transmuted, and the concerns they express, are able as it were to bounce from one circle to another. That is why a purely disciplinary approach to the intellectual life of the past is too limiting. Conversations, even arguments, flowed beyond the boundaries we, up to a point arbitrarily, set for them. So, while not presupposing coherence, as we do when we speak of '*Zeitgeist*', 'world-view', 'ideology', 'hegemony' and other terms from the same self-confident semantic family, I have tried to be alert to the occurrence of transfers and analogues.

These analogues and recurrences derived partly from a complex intellectual heritage and partly from an understandable desire to test the limits of powerful and fashionable concepts developed in particular fields: scientific law, evolution, the division of labour, competition, the work of art, myth and the unconscious mind are obvious examples. The correspondences derive also, however, from the perceived importance of three associated contexts, political, social and cultural, on which contemporary awareness was concentrated. The political was the advent of democracy, in the sense of representative institutions based on a wide though not necessarily universal adult male suffrage. This became a common phenomenon in all the weightier European states except Russia, from the 1870s onwards, after the unification of Italy and Germany, the establishment of the Third Republic in France, and the adoption of an urban working-class franchise in Britain after 1867. To speak of the achievement of popular sovereignty would be an oversimplification, but the perception that this was now the reality, or at least the destiny, of the modern state, with the associated rise of socialist political parties, was a powerful conditioner of middle-class anxiety, pessimism and fastidiousness.

The anxiety was enhanced by the other two contexts. The first was the growth of great cities with mass populations, of which London was the precursor, Paris in many ways the archetype, and Berlin the prodigy of the age. The great city and its teeming population was the dominant social image of the period: its excitement, its horrors, its threat to social order and decency, its physical and moral squalor and unhealthiness, its dwarfing impersonality. It was in the great city that the new democracy lurked, perhaps beyond the reach of civilizing influence.

This kind of concern was linked also to the third condition, the moral and cultural vacuum of an age which was now beginning to be thought of as post-Christian, among the masses as well as among the educated. This development had, of course, a long history, stretching back to the eighteenth-century Enlightenment, though after the French Revolution there was something of a religious revival and it was not until the 1840s and 1850s that alternatives to Christianity began to be widely and confidently entertained. Initially these tended towards a social humanitarianism (considered below in the Prologue) and pious contemplation of nature as conceived by the natural sciences (Chapter 1). Later the humanitarian internationalism of socialism acquired a powerful rival in popular nationalism, while for many intellectuals science seemed less the remedy for a spiritual void than its leading symptom. Confronted, too, by the possible consequences of mass irreligion, even some atheists came to see the problem less as the persisting grip of a decaying Christianity than as the need to replace it and, for the individual, the need to fashion out of spare and questionable post-Christian materials a self that would not be overwhelmed by the freedom secured to it by a fulfilled liberal agenda, by the social coerciveness of democratic society and by the pressures and solicitations of modern urban life.

A certain amount of repetition between chapters has therefore sometimes been necessary, and I hope it will be found useful rather than irritating because it is what holds the book together and makes it more than a series of separate studies. The first section and the last are untypical and to indicate this I have referred to them as 'Prologue' and 'Epilogue'. To begin and round off the book, each takes a loosely-bound sample from a narrow band of time, the later 1840s and early 1850s and the 1900s respectively. Each of the remaining chapters takes a particular genre or theme and traces it roughly from the beginning to the end of the period; each is therefore thematically selective but chronologically extended. It may be helpful here to give some indication of their contents.

The Prologue focuses on the beginning of the period and on a political and social project vaguely epitomized as 'revolution': the inauguration of a new era of liberty and fraternity, the unfulfilled project of the first French Revolution without its attendant horrors. The Prologue also registers the kinds of disillusionment which, from the middle of 1848 onwards, were evoked by the collapse of the European revolutions and still more by the internecine conflicts and even bloodshed among those who had initially supported them.

Chapters 1 and 2 announce another kind of project, equally optimistic but more long-term and therefore less vulnerable to refutation by immediate events. For some it is clear that it was a kind of continuation of revolution by other means, or at least a substitute for it. It was the pursuit, with a renewed intensity and confidence, of the long-standing ambition to unify human thought by the extension to all phenomena, including those of human life and consciousness, of the methods, the certainty and the objectivity of the natural sciences. This renewed impulse to the scientific conquest of the mental as well as the physical world was not exclusively derived from the theory of evolution but the latter played a significant role. It also provided, sometimes in a complex association with older, metaphysically grounded notions of human history as the self-education of mankind, a view of history as a teleological process from which a higher, perhaps ultimately perfected, form of human consciousness was emerging. The latter would attain a comprehensive awareness of the laws governing the world and of its own place in it, including the laws of its own development. Nature, the universal matrix, had hitherto travailed blindly in struggle and uncomprehended suffering, but in an evolved humanity it would have produced a being capable of comprehending the conditions of its own existence.

The universal scope and profound optimism of this aspiration inevitably brought its own kinds of disillusionment or at least discouragement, as in various fields, despite the immense achievements of science, its reach continued to exceed its grasp, especially in the realm of human action, and as faith in humanity's ability as a species to fulfil its great destiny accordingly wavered. Perhaps, it was felt, history and biology issued threats as well as promises; the counterpart of evolution might be degeneration. There had, in any case, always been some for whom the scientific project, or what it seemed to be, was itself the threat and for whom the extension of the idea of scientific law to psychology and history seemed to restrict or abolish human freedom, to empty life of meaning and the natural world of mystery and poetry. Such responses are considered chiefly in the later chapters of the book.

There had for long been, also, critics of the idea of social progress. The latter, in its liberal form, as increasing human emancipation, could also be viewed as isolating and desiccating, reducing human relations to their thinnest, least satisfying terms in the rational calculation and impersonality of capitalism or bureaucracy or both, and displacing an older experience of community and human wholeness. This is the theme considered in Chapter 3. The question of individual wholeness in the modern world is taken up again in Chapters 4 and 5. On some views the modern, autonomous, rational, self-conscious individual was hollow at the core, and his (and increasingly also her) freedom was essentially an emptiness or absence of identity. These responses to the predicaments and aspirations of modernity prompted attempts at restoring mystery and a sense of apocalyptic possibilities to the world through some new movement of the human spirit seen rather as the counteraction than the fulfilment of science and progress (see Chapter 3 and especially Chapter 6). As in Romanticism earlier, there was a yearning towards a source of inner, profound, immediately experienced knowledge, prior to and beyond rationality, which came increasingly to be referred to (before Freud) as

'The Unconscious' or, among the disparate disciples of Nietzsche, as 'the Dionysiac' (Chapters 4 and 5). From around 1900 some form of irrationalism – the surrender of the rational, social self to energizing unconscious forces, seen as the source of true freedom and creativity, at any cost – became a mark of the intellectual avant-garde.

This thematic treatment of the chapters, with their overlaps and recapitulations, constitutes the book's *raison d'être*. There are, however, costs to every strategic decision. In this case they include the fact that the book will not be an ideally convenient source of rounded, comprehensive summaries or thumbnail sketches of the ideas of the great European thinkers of the period. Not only are many figures introduced who are certainly less than great, or who are not now famous, but the nature of the book means that even those who are both tend to be discussed in different aspects in different chapters, as the intellectual context requires. A book of this kind does not therefore lend itself to rounded intellectual portraiture or definitive interpretation and appraisal of overall intellectual achievements, though I have naturally tried to avoid travestying them. One of the functions of a book such as this is to provide a context for more specialized studies; it is not intended as a substitute for them.

I have also been led by the book's historical intentions to inclusions and exclusions which a more present-minded perspective will find perverse: to speak a good deal about Herbert Spencer, Taine, Renan, Haeckel, but not about Mendel, Einstein or the pioneers in genetics at the beginning of the twentieth century, who occupy much higher places as makers of the modern intellectual world. The justification for the exclusion of the latter is that their work only really emerged from the confines of their specialisms, and made its way into the general culture, at or after the end of the period, and therefore belongs in the next volume in this series. This does not mean that all the influential figures of the period have been included. Neglected names which tug at my conscience include – in no particular order – Gabriel Tarde, August Strindberg, Albert Fouillée, Paul Renouvier, Wilhelm Rickert, Karl Lamprecht, W. S. Jevons, J. A. Hobson, Vilfredo Pareto, V. I. Lenin, Peter Kropotkin, Benedetto Croce, Heinrich von Sybel, Hugo von Hofmannsthal . . . and many others. But a line has to be drawn and it has been dictated here, I am sure not uncontroversially, by the need to keep a balance between thematic discussion and examples, making the choice of the latter a partly arbitrary one.

A final caveat is called for by the word 'European'. I have used advisedly the phrase 'European Thought' rather than 'European intellectual life'.

'Europe' here, with apologies to the neglected, effectively means France, Germany,[1] Austria, Britain, Russia and, too briefly, Italy. I have made, that is to say, no attempt at equitable representation of the many countries which participated in European intellectual life. This reflects partly my own cultural limitations, but also the chosen nature of the book. I have made, that is, no attempt at the comprehensiveness of a textbook or a work of reference. To have been more inclusive in a work of this scale would have produced an inert list of names and achievements, and the book would have sunk under the weight of its own conscientiousness. On the other hand I have tried to avoid a merely idiosyncratic choice of topics for attention. I have chosen these, rather, for what seems to have been their then dominance and pervasiveness. The result is necessarily in a sense impressionistic, but I hope that it is an informed and, given the book's intentions, a balanced impressionism.

[1] In writing on German (and Austrian) ideas of the *Volk* I have followed other authors in using the anglicized form 'volkish' instead of the German *völkisch*. The latter occurs so often in places as to be intrusive and no existing English word is adequate.

## Acknowledgements

My first debt to acknowledge in connection with this book is to Robert Baldock. As Editor at Yale University Press it was he who conceived the idea of the series to which the book belongs (the Yale Intellectual History of Europe) and was responsible for inviting me to write this volume. The measure of my debt is that without him the book would not exist; he has won my further gratitude by his patience and kindness during its gestation.

Some other debts are academic. I have tried to read all of what seemed the most important primary sources, but I have inevitably also relied in many places on the work of modern scholars. I have acknowledged these debts in the bibliographical note and in a few cases also in the text. I hope those whose work I have used will find this an adequate expression of my indebtedness and gratitude. I am also grateful to the universities of Sussex and Oxford for granting me periods of leave, without which the book would have been much longer in preparation. I thank their authorities for their tolerance of the less than impressive figure I have made in their returns for several Research Reviews while I have been working on the book. I would also like to thank the Warden and Fellows of All Souls College, Oxford, for electing me to a Visiting Fellowship in 1994–5 and for their great kindness and hospitality during my tenure.

Other debts are more personal. I am very grateful to Jane Wyatt, who has typed the book from a slovenly manuscript and borne, with characteristic patience and cheerfulness, my changes of mind. To the following I owe a great debt for reading and criticizing the typescript and saving me in a number of places from serious errors: Stefan Collini, John Thompson, Bernard Williams, Patricia Williams, Donald Winch. Finally, I welcome this chance to express my deep sense of gratitude to Bob Johnson for his generous support for the Chair of European Thought at Oxford during my tenure of it. I can only hope that others of similar generosity may be found to ensure its continuation.

# *Prologue*
# *1848–49: The Disillusionment of the Intellectuals*

Among the revolutions which swept across Europe in the years 1848 and 1849 the revolution in Dresden in May of the latter year was belated and not very significant. When the people of the Saxon capital rose against their king, the revolutions in the more important centres, notably Berlin and Vienna, had already collapsed. Barricades were set up in the streets and a provisional government established, but the king of Saxony could call on the aid of the other German powers which, with their own houses now in order, were able to send it. Prussian troops were soon advancing on Dresden. For a few days there was fierce, ineffectual resistance. It was not so much the last act of the German revolutions of 1848–9 as their epilogue.

The Dresden rising has, however, a symbolic interest in the intellectual history of nineteenth-century Europe. It is not without reason that the years 1848–9 in Europe have been called 'the revolution of the intellectuals'. Two prominent figures in the defence of Dresden were men who were to exercise, in different ways, a profound influence on the intellectual life of Europe in the later nineteenth century and beyond. One was Richard Wagner (1813–83), the discontented second *Kapellmeister* (musical director) of the Royal Dresden Opera House (which was burnt down in the rising). The other was the Russian revolutionist, to be known in the future as one of the fathers of European anarchism, Mikhail Bakunin (1814–76). The latter was in Dresden as a refuge, and not, as was already his custom, looking for a revolution to participate in. Bakunin's normal reaction on hearing of a promising revolutionary situation somewhere was to borrow the money to buy a train ticket to it (one of the remarkable features of his admittedly brief acquaintance with Wagner is that neither seems to have borrowed money from the other). He was in Dresden temporarily, having been obliged by the authorities to leave Prague, where he had been attempting to foment a revolution among the Slavs.

Wagner, frustrated in his grandiose dreams for German art and the staging of his own operas, was drawn, as many people were, to the fiery, immensely energetic, voluble and gigantic Russian exile. Both were titanic, towering figures, though in Wagner's case only metaphorically: dictatorial, arrogant visionaries, born to master others by the power of personality and will, and the intensity of their megalomaniac dedication. Bakunin was also credited with a quality of childlike innocence which no one attributed to Wagner or, for that matter, to the third figure to whom it is tempting to compare them, their contemporary and Bakunin's future political antagonist, Karl Marx (1818–83). The similarities in personality, which helped to set Bakunin and Marx bitterly at odds, seem at this point to have drawn Wagner and Bakunin to each other.

The qualities all three possessed in common, it is worth remembering, though personal, also have a wider cultural significance. The manner in which these powerful personalities saw themselves and acted out their roles was the manner of European Romanticism. The French composer Hector Berlioz (1803–69) and the poet Victor Hugo (1802–85) are in the same prophetic, megalomaniac mould. The cult of the titanic in art produced the symphonic poems of Berlioz, which called, as Wagner's operas were to do, for vast new orchestral resources; it produced also the apocalyptic canvases of Turner; and the monsters of will and passion, the Napoleons of the drawing room and the counting house, created by the supreme social chronicler of the 1820s and 1830s and the novelist Marx admired most, Honoré de Balzac (1799–1850). In the same quiz in which Marx named Balzac as his favourite novelist he was asked the name of his favourite mythological figure. He answered 'Prometheus', who in Greek mythology had defied Zeus the president of the gods by teaching men to make fire, thereby making them independent. Prometheus was a central mythological figure for the Romantics. Shelley made him the subject of a poem; Mary Shelley subtitled her novel *Frankenstein* 'The Modern Prometheus'; Beethoven named an overture for him. Bakunin, who wrote ecstatically of fire as an instrument of revolution, seems an even clearer case of the Promethean as revolutionary than Marx himself, while Wagner was to write fire music as no one had done before, and in his Siegfried created a hero whose role was not merely to challenge the chief of the gods but to overcome him, and thus to bring about the end of the era of the gods and to inaugurate that of mankind.

In an anonymous newspaper article Wagner published, while still Royal *Kapellmeister*, in the spring of 1849, he hailed the advent of revolution in authentically Promethean and apocalyptic terms. Revolution speaks as both destroyer and regenerator, Messiah and Phoenix, political and cosmic. 'I am the dream, the balm, the hope of all who suffer . . . I will destroy every illusion that has power over men. I will destroy the domination of one over many, of the dead over the living, of matter over spirit . . . I am the ever-creating life. I am the one God whom all creation acknowledges.'[1] To write of revolution in those terms was not uncommon. Thomas Carlyle (1795–1881) – steeped, incidentally, in German literature as well as in the Old Testament and in the history of the French Revolution – wrote of it as the 'World-Phoenix' and the burning up of imposture in a universal conflagration: 'Imposture is in flames, Imposture is burnt up: one Red-sea of Fire, wild bellowing enwraps the world.'[2] Bakunin, in an 1842 article proclaiming the coming of democracy, wrote almost soberly by comparison, concluding with a sentence that was to be much quoted: 'Let us put our trust in the eternal spirit which destroys and annihilates only because it is the unsearchable and eternally creative source of all life. The passion for destruction is also a creative passion.'[3]

The intellectual paths of Bakunin and Wagner were bound, of course, to diverge. Bakunin was an intensely political animal. For Wagner, even in 1849, politics was the handmaid of his art, and his opposition to the established order – the king was his employer as well as his ruler – was born largely of frustration with the obstacles it placed in his way as an artist, which prevented his redemptive message – expressed, as it had to be, through a new kind of music drama – from being staged and appreciated. Bakunin would go on to battle with Marx for the allegiance of the revolutionary working class. Wagner was to become, for the later nineteenth century, the supreme exemplar of the notion of art as transcendence, a kind of religion for modern man. Yet their conjunction in 1849 was more than just accidental, or a matter simply of personal affinity. They were drawn into the Dresden revolution by the common intellectual enthusiasms, hopes and illusions of their generation (Wagner in 1849 was thirty-six, Bakunin thirty-five). It is impossible properly to understand the paths they and others subsequently took without some understanding of those hopes and

[1] Ernest Newman, *The Life of Richard Wagner* (4 vols, London, 1933–46), ii, pp. 55–6.
[2] Thomas Carlyle, *The French Revolution*, in *Thomas Carlyle's Works* (17 vols, London, 1841), i, p. 245.
[3] Translation from E. H. Carr, *Michael Bakunin* (London, 1975), p. 110.

enthusiasms and their transmutation under the pressure of disappointment or disillusion.

For both men the immediate results of their part in the Dresden rising were drastic: prison and exile respectively. Bakunin was handed over to the Russian authorities and spent many years in prison in Russia and subsequently in exile in Siberia. Wagner fled to Zurich and to a poverty-stricken and wandering exile from which he was eventually rescued by the intervention of King Ludwig II of Bavaria, who was to become his patron and to make possible the realization of all his artistic dreams. Bakunin's fate was exceptionally harsh, but exile, voluntary or enforced, was a common experience of European intellectuals, especially Russians and Germans, in the 1840s. The counter-revolutions of 1848 and the *coup d'état* which brought an end to the French Republic in 1851 only added to the number of exiles; or sent them, reluctantly, further afield, usually to London. There were Poles, Hungarians, Italians, exiled by alien domination of their countries; Russians escaping the intellectual oppressiveness of their homeland or seeking education in the West; Germans who, like Karl Marx, had made the various German states, and eventually even Paris and Brussels, too hot for them. Their tracks in the 1840s had criss-crossed Europe, in search of self-education or freedom of expression. Circles of intellectuals briefly formed, and attracted others – often by the production of a journal, which offered a platform and even a source of income. Journals and cafés could be to the nineteenth-century intellectual, as means of making contacts, what salons or clubs were in more settled social circumstances. Then they broke up again, under pressure from the censor or the police.

But migration was attractive as well as often enforced. Many were drawn, in and before 1848, by the cultural and political magnet of Paris. For Russians a decade earlier the magnet had often been Berlin, and the reason was educational rather than political. There the philosophy of Hegel (1770–1831), which was eagerly discussed among the students in the University of Moscow, could be studied with Hegel's immediate academic heirs. It was this that had drawn Bakunin there in 1840, where he and the future novelist Turgenev (1818–83) were friends and fellow students. The journey further west could be a sign, or an occasion, as it had been for Bakunin, of political radicalization, for if Germany was the home of philosophy, France was not merely the mother of revolutions but the home of what was beginning to be called socialism: utopian plans for the reconstruction of the social order. Young Germans were often for a time able to take advantage of the plurality of Germany's states, moving easily across state borders which involved no change of language when the censor became oppressive.

Switzerland too was available, and Zurich, which gave Wagner refuge after 1849, was a port of call for exiles, but the migration to France or even Belgium was sometimes a sign that the patience of the German or even Swiss authorities was exhausted. The France of King Louis Philippe was not always impressively liberal but it was more so than the German states. The career of the German Left-Hegelian journal edited by Arnold Ruge (1802–80) seems symbolic. It began in Halle as the *Hallische Jahrbücher* in 1838. The Prussian authorities closed it down, whereupon it and Ruge migrated to Dresden, as the *Deutsche Jahrbücher*, where Bakunin contributed to it. Saxony in turn having become unwelcoming, it achieved one number in Paris as the *Deutsch-Französische Jahrbücher*, with contributions from Marx and the poet Heinrich Heine (1797–1856). Ruge himself was eventually obliged to migrate to England, where he lived in respectable retirement in Brighton.·

Wagner scarcely participated in this exilic culture, not only because politics meant far less to him than music but also because he was hostile to France. Germany remained his spiritual and linguistic home. For others Paris was a Mecca. Towards the end of the 1840s there were in Paris the Russians Bakunin, Turgenev, Alexander Herzen (1812–70) and the critic Belinsky (1811–48), the German poets Heine (a resident since 1831) and Georg Herwegh (1817–75), and Karl Marx. Herwegh was then famous as a leading poet of the 'Young Germany' movement and led a force of German exiles in a somewhat ignominiously abortive invasion of the Duchy of Baden in 1848; Bakunin was later to try to organize a similar, and equally abortive, invasion of Russian-held Poland by Slav exiles.

Herwegh, now largely forgotten, was ubiquitous in the 1840s and early 1850s. He shared lodgings with Turgenev and Bakunin in Berlin in 1842. We find him again, this time in Paris in 1843–4, as an associate of Marx and Heine. He acquired as a mistress the Comtesse Marie d'Agoult, the mother of Wagner's future wife. In Geneva in 1849 we find him involved in an ill-fated love-affair with Herzen's wife Natalie. In the early 1850s he was in Zurich providing Wagner with companionship in exile and, perhaps momentously, introducing him to the philosophy of Schopenhauer. It was in many ways a small world, though peripatetic, like that of international conferences today.

Not all these men were revolutionaries. But ideas of revolution, in the sense of some great transformation, were natural in the circumstances. Generally lacking any experience except of a wandering student-like existence, lacking political experience unless it were of agitation, with their attempts at journalism checked and blocked by censorship, oppressed either by the rigid conformities and police-state of Tsar Nicholas I or by the servility, parochialism and petty persecution of the authoritarian German states (from which Wagner suffered in Dresden), it was natural for these men to indulge in grandiose hopes and to see society and politics in apocalyptic terms – a tendency, as we have seen, that Wagner fully shared. In his own sphere of music he had reasons not only for his Francophobia but for his revolutionary hatred of the power of money, which finds expression in *The Ring* and also, it has to be said, in his anti-Semitism, from which Marx too was not free. The commercialism of the Paris theatre, which had thwarted Wagner's ambitions for the staging of his operas, fed his revolutionary impulses just as did the restrictions of his post in Dresden in the archaic role of court servant.

His practical political zeal, however, such as it was, was a brief creation of the excitements of 1848–9. For the more conscientious revolutionaries, Marx, Bakunin, Herzen and a host of lesser figures, the road of exile was to lead beyond Paris in 1848 to bleak, unwelcoming, tolerant London, where in the 1850s the exiles formed their national coteries and devoted themselves to the personal and ideological squabbles and false hopes which Herzen, in his incomparable autobiography *My Past and Thoughts* (1861–7), observed with the eye of a disillusioned connoisseur. The 1840s, by comparison, had been a period of peripatetic self-education, of exciting cultural and personal contacts across the borders of nationality; their places of exile were bases for further advance, intellectual and political. London was no more than a refuge, a hiatus, where Herzen, naturally sceptical, was to struggle to retain faith, from a distance, in the future of his country and to promote it through his journal-in-exile, *The Bell*, while Karl Marx, though never giving up hope, set himself to analyse the failure of the revolutions and, in the Reading Room of the British Museum, to rationalize the necessity of the long haul.

Bakunin reached London only in 1861, after his celebrated escape from Siberia, bursting into Herzen's house like a man returned from the dead. The years which had disillusioned others had left him, as Herzen said, intellectually untouched. Where others had soured, grown up or turned away, he had retained the naive, uncompromising hopes, the excited, apocalyptic sense of imminent possibilities, as well as the wandering, shiftless habits, of the 1840s. In many ways, though he was to exercise considerable influence over the growing working-class movements in Switzerland and southern Europe, and some intellectual influence in Russia, he was to be a kind of detached fragment of the culture of the 1840s, drifting around Europe in search of revolutions to participate in.

For Wagner, on the other hand, the 1850s, though years of frustration, were also to be years of immense creativity and development. Between 1849 and 1852 he wrote no music, but he completed the text of *The Ring*, loosely based on the old German epic the *Nibelungenlied*. In the same period he wrote his major prose essays *Art and Revolution* and *The Art-Work of the Future*. He wrote the music for the first opera of the Ring cycle, *Rheingold*, in 1853–4. These works and the operas which were to follow, were the products of cultural preoccupations with deep roots in the heritage of German Romanticism, informed for Wagner by a more contemporary kind of optimistic messianic humanism, which reached its peak in Germany in the 1840s. Karl Marx, in his early writings, absorbed and gave expression to the same influences, to which the counter-revolutions at the end of the decade were to be a shattering blow. They not merely, as we have seen, prompted Wagner's brief hopes of political revolution; they left abiding marks on his work, particularly in his conception of the hero Siegfried. It has been suggested that the figure of Siegfried, the fearless challenger of the Gods, may owe something to the impression made on Wagner by the reckless, fiery personality of Bakunin. This is certainly possible, but what is more in evidence is the intellectual influence – felt by Bakunin himself, and also, even more profoundly, by Marx – of the German philosopher by whom, above all, the humanist, anti-Christian, emancipatory enthusiasm of the 1840s was focused, Ludwig Feuerbach (1804–72).

It was Feuerbach's philosophy in which the shackles of religious authority and the Christian puritanical denial of the body seemed definitely to have been thrown off. In Feuerbach's theory of religion the relation of subject and object – to put it in the terms of German philosophy – had been inverted, or rather they had been set the right way round. Feuerbach's account has something in common with the later theory of Freud, in that God is man's creation, not vice versa. Man, objectifying his own higher qualities and endowing them with an independent existence, as God, has come to worship and sacrifice himself to his own creation. He has sacrificed his freedom by failing to recognize it, and in so doing sacrificed his own natural impulses. Christian repressiveness was man's self-torment, in the name of the God which, unknown to himself, he had created. The rational critique of religion, the revelation of its true source, would reveal its lack of necessity and hence its powerlessness. Philosophy was the way of emancipation; through it man would recover his freedom. The Feuerbachian critique of religion issued in that favourite project of nineteenth-century secularism, a religion of humanity. Man was naturally good. The love misdirected to a personification of abstracted human qualities called God must be redirected to its proper object, man. As Feuerbach's disciple, Marx, said, 'Man is the highest end for man.'

Wagner's essay *The Art-Work of the Future* is dedicated to Feuerbach. In *The Ring* Siegfried, the fearless natural man, untroubled by guilt or self-consciousness, is a very Feuerbachian hero. Yet Feuerbach's idea of humanist self-emancipation in a sense only gave philosophic form, for Wagner and others, to already powerful intellectual currents. Among Wagner's early literary enthusiasms were the authors of the Young Germany movement. We have already encountered one of them, as everyone seems to have done sooner or later, in Georg Herwegh. Another, Heinrich Laube (1806-84), the author of a novel characteristically called *Young Europe*, became a personal friend of Wagner and an influence on him: Laube became a member of the Frankfurt Parliament. The authors of Young Germany preached a form of humanism, free love and universal brotherhood. The notion of a kind of German neo-paganism was one which reached back to the later eighteenth century, but the Young Germany group were strongly influenced also by the ideas of the French writers and ideologists known as the Saint-Simonians after their intellectual father, Henri de Saint-Simon (1760–1825). Saint-Simonianism proclaimed a new religion of brotherly love and 'the rehabilitation of the flesh'. It is not surprising that the German Federal Diet's condemnation of the Young Germany group described them as unchristian and blasphemous: 'they trample under foot all morality, modesty and decency'. Wagner's testimony to his enthusiasm for these ideas is his early opera, his second in fact, *Das Liebesverbot* (*Forbidden Love*) (1834–5).

In passing it is worth pausing to consider for a moment names such as 'Young Germany', or Laube's 'Young Europe'. The 1830s and 1840s also saw movements called Young Italy, Young Ireland and even Young England. It was imitative, of course, but it also testified to the apocalyptic sense of renewal, of living at a critical historical juncture, whose redemption would have to come, and would come, from the new generation. Young Italy initially excluded men over forty. 'Youth is everything', said Benjamin Disraeli's Sidonia in his novel *Coningsby* (1842) to the young English aristocrat whose mentor he was to be, and who was supposedly to lead the regeneration of his country through a rediscovery of an aristocratic sense of social responsibility. It was not accidental that students played a prominent part in the revolutions in Vienna and Berlin as they had done, for the first time, in Paris in 1830. It was partly a matter of the increase in numbers. It has been estimated that there were 11,000 students in Paris in the 1840s. But it was also an attitude of mind. Wagner, when the cause of revolution in Dresden was lost, ran towards a fellow insurgent crying 'Nothing is lost! Youth, youth, youth will redeem everything, save everything.' Siegfried was a more considered product of the same assurance, the same hope.

We may think of Feuerbach, for Wagner, as a kind of philosophical culmination, not as the genesis, of the ideas which he poured into his Siegfried poem. For Bakunin, however, and still more for Marx, Feuerbach performed another and more vital function and was an emancipator in a further and more precise sense. It is perhaps a mark of the fact that Wagner never experienced a university education that he escaped the influence of the Hegelian philosophy, with its slogan 'the real is rational and the rational is real'. Hegelianism enthralled Marx and his contemporaries in Berlin; its impact on the students at the University of Moscow in the same period is graphically and ironically described by Herzen. By 'the real is rational' Hegel had meant something other than political conservatism. He was making a metaphysical claim which can be loosely rendered as an assertion perilously close to a tautology: only as rational is the world (rationally) comprehended and as it is comprehended it *is* rational. What constitutes the political conservatism is the principle, around which argument raged, that rationality in history is only comprehended when it is already embodied in the real. From this it seems to follow that the task of philosophy, of rationality, is essentially retrospective; it is to understand history, not to plan it. A radical group of Young Hegelians, known as Left Hegelians, of whom Marx became one, resisted this implication. The task of philosophy must be to criticize the actual by pointing out where it diverged from the rational. Even so, much of the Left Hegelians' criticism focused, like the ideas of Young Germany, on religion, and it was the critique of Christianity more than of the state as such which caused difficulties with the authorities.

For Marx, and for Bakunin, full emancipation from Hegel came, however, only with Feuerbach, in whom Marx found the genesis – though not the completion – of his own materialism. For Marx the relation of Feuerbach's 'man' to Hegel's '*Geist*', the Hegelian subject of history, mirrored the relation of man to God in Feuerbach's critique of religion.

Subject and object, in Hegel, had been inverted. History was not the working out of a central idea, a principle of active reason, with human beings as its imperfectly comprehending instruments. The subject of history was man and 'real, sensuous human activity'. Consciousness, ideas, were derivative, their form dictated by the forms assumed by man's activity in the satisfaction of his material needs. This was the theory of history, and of ideology, which Marx first fully worked out in his and Engels' unpublished *German Ideology* in 1845. The presiding genius of the book was in a sense Feuerbach, but it was Feuerbach taken two stages further. Feuerbach's materialism, according to Marx, failed fully to account for religion, which for Marx was the archetype of all distorting, self-mystifying 'ideology', because it was merely philosophical, not social and historical, and hence not truly revolutionary. It failed, that is, to see the causes of religious self-deception in the dislocations of man's social condition, and it therefore failed to see that philosophical critiques could produce only an emancipation in the mind, while the real world of social activity remained unredeemed and the real man, as opposed to merely speculative philosophical man, remained unemancipated. Religion would be destroyed not by philosophy but only by social revolution, destroying its underlying causes and the need for other-worldly consolation they created. And social revolution would arrive, as Marx came to stress, not because the need for it was proclaimed but because the contradictions in the existing state of society had reached breaking-point.

In one sense, therefore, Hegel was right; history was a sequence of contradictions and their resolutions, working itself out to completion by its own inner logic. Hegel could hold this because he assumed that the historical process was like the stages of a logical argument, successively working out the implications of its initial premise, which was its rationality. Whether, on the new Feuerbachian, materialist premises one could any longer have an assurance that history was like a puzzle which solved itself – why should it be like that? – Marx did not ask. Rather he concentrated on illustrating it, using history, above all contemporary history, to demonstrate that it was so. 'All previous history is the history of class struggles'; the declaration he and Friedrich Engels (1820–95) pronounced at the opening of *The Communist Manifesto* they published at the beginning of 1848, is as much a tautology, a definition, as Hegel's 'The rational is real'. *The Communist Manifesto* concluded that the outcome of the latest struggle would be the social revolution and human emancipation in general. In speaking of a general revolution, *the* revolution rather than just of particular revolutions in particular countries, the *Manifesto* was speaking thoroughly in the spirit of 1848 as well as of Marxism subsequently.

In criticizing Hegelian and Feuerbachian philosophy from the standpoint of the necessity of social revolution and the abolition of private property, Marx was in a sense stepping from the German cultural climate, dominated by the idea of the philosophical critique as the agent of reformation, to that of France. Bakunin made much the same kind of move, though he did not argue it through rigorously and systematically as Marx did. Paris was the home of the various forms of 'socialism', utopian schemes for complete social reconstruction. The most widespread of the French social doctrines was that of the followers of Henri de Saint-Simon. The ideas of French socialism were chiefly introduced in Germany through Lorenz von Stein's book *The Socialism and Communism of Present-Day France* (1844). Marx went to Paris in 1843, when he met some of the French socialists and was impressed by the evidence of working-class political activity. The influence of Saint-Simonianism, to which Marx was exposed, was extraordinarily ramifying, for it was a protean movement with many aspects. For the authors of the Young Germany movement it had meant, as we have seen, primarily the doctrine of free love and human brotherhood, a kind of secular religion, seen as the successor to Christianity. In England it left marks, chiefly through its ideas about history, on the thinking of Thomas Carlyle and John Stuart Mill (1806–73). Together with the work of other French socialists it helped to turn Marx and Bakunin towards ideas of social revolution. In France itself it formed part of the utopian 'socialist' ideas of the period, along with the writings of Charles Fourier (1772–1837) and Etienne Cabet (1788–1856). Through the teaching of Saint-Simon's secretary Auguste Comte (1798–1857) its central ideas were to be embodied, with extraordinary embellishments, in a new cult, the fusion of science with the religion of universal love of mankind: the Comtean Positivist Religion of Humanity. All these thinkers preached ultimate social harmony through peaceful social transformation – an idea Marx and Bakunin rejected. The French socialists taught class reconciliation rather than class war, but they also drew attention to the vast disparities of wealth and poverty, and to the sufferings of the poor, as the most urgent contemporary social and political problem. The existing social order was indefensible and provisional, and would have to be replaced, with the agreement of all people of goodwill. Marx accepted the diagnosis if not the solution.

Saint-Simonianism, and French socialism generally, incorporated the ideas of brotherly love and the natural goodness of man which we have seen present in the authors of Young Germany. Both these principles pointed to the reconciliation of classes in a new, just and harmonious social order, and to the emancipation of human nature, above all of the sacred passion of love, and, in some cases, to the emancipation of women. They implied also a recognition, in forms which to later generations seem cloyingly sentimental, of the sufferings and the virtues of – we have here to use the capital letter – the People. The cult of the People was partly an aspect of the idea of natural goodness. The French idea of the People – though one finds it also in Carlyle – was not quite the German *Volk*, the nation as anonymous creator and poet, though it could come very close to it. It was more like the Marxist notion of the proletariat, seen as the essence of humanity itself, though more sentimentally conceived. It was a conception which found many forms of expression. In painting, for example, there were the haggard but dauntless insurrectionists of Eugène Delacroix's *Liberty Leading the People at the Barricades* (a celebration of the revolution of 1830, with Liberty as a bare-breasted young woman), and the bowed toilers represented in Gustave Courbet's 'realist' paintings of the 1850s. The novelist Eugène Sue (1804–57), admired by Karl Marx, explored the underworld of the Parisian poor, as Charles Dickens (1812–70), with greater art, did that of London, in terms of popular melodrama. The poet Béranger (1780–1857) was thought by contemporaries to articulate the voice of the People, and was hailed as the French Robert Burns, while the historian Jules Michelet (1798–1874) rewrote the history of France with the People as its protagonist.

The confidence that the French, unlike the Germans, possessed in their own centrality in the life of Europe meant that they felt little need to distinguish sharply between a nationalist (volkish, one might say) and a universal conception of the People. Michelet, for example, compiled a Bible of Humanity, uplifting texts designed to promote the new worship of mankind. The socialist Pierre Leroux (1797–1871), a breakaway Saint Simonian who preached Saint Simonian ideas in the influential journal *The Globe*, teaching cooperation and the gradual, peaceful takeover of the government by the People, published a book in 1840 characteristically entitled *On Humanity*.

Leroux was the friend and mentor of the most famous French novelist in the 1840s and 1850s and perhaps the most influential, because the most widely read, of all the disseminators of ideas of emancipation, free love and a populist humanitarianism and sympathy with the poor,

George Sand (1804–76). A notoriously emancipated woman herself (George Sand was a pseudonym), she was in life the heroine of famous love affairs and in her novels the prophet of the absolute rights of love, whatever social barriers it might transgress. She was also known, through her pastoral novels of rural life, as the celebrator of simplicity, of the life of the People.

The vogue for George Sand's novels was extraordinary; it is hard to resist the impression that they were among the formative influences of the period. Young people read her with a sense almost of receiving a religious revelation, and a common enthusiasm for her novels formed a bond. Bakunin thought of her as a prophetess of humanity and said that reading her made him feel a better man. Natalie Herzen and Georg Herwegh conducted their love affair, as E. H. Carr showed in his masterly and sardonic study of the mentality of the 1840s, *The Romantic Exiles*, which is focused on the Herzen family, through notions of the absolute rights and cosmic sublimity of passion derived from George Sand. In England, of course, her 'shocking' reputation both as a novelist and a woman was against her, but she had many notable English admirers. Elizabeth Barrett (Browning) (1806–61) was influenced by her. John Chapman, the editor of the *Westminster Review* and G. H. Lewes, the editor of the *Fortnightly Review*, both radical journals, admired her. Chapman (1822–94) was George Eliot's first literary patron, Lewes (1817–78) her adviser and consort. Lewes' circle, in the 1840s, was touched by French socialist ideas and practised an unusually open sexual freedom. More surprisingly it may seem, Matthew Arnold (1822–88), England's leading critic in the second half of the century, was a reader of George Sand all his life and spoke of her as 'the greatest spirit in our European world from the time that Goethe departed'. Probably her most acclaimed novel, *Consuelo*, whose heroine was said to have been inspired by the singer Pauline Viardot, to whom Turgenev gave a lifetime's devotion, was described by Queen Victoria (1819–1901) as '*dreadfully* interesting'. George Sand's fame was European-wide and expressed perhaps better than anything else the cravings for a new religion of universal brotherhood and love combined with individual self-fulfilment through sexual passion, in terms which posterity has on the whole found unbearably declamatory and sentimental.

But George Sand represented only one strand of French intellectual life in the 1840s. There was, for example, also a scientific, 'positivist' strain, sometimes fused, as in the work of Comte, with the cult of humanity, but also extending to a self-consciously tough-minded materialist determinism;

we shall have to consider some of these developments in the next chapter. France, moreover, was already old in the ways of revolution. If the apocalyptic utopian mentality still flourished there, more perhaps than anywhere else, so too did a sense of *déjà vu*, of the oppressiveness of a past in which everything had been tried, a kind of weariness and even cynicism which, even if sometimes not impervious to the excitement of the February insurrection which overthrew the monarchy, was intensified by the disillusionment with the republic which followed and the bloody suppression of the workers' rising in June. The Italian Mazzini (1805–72) was the least cynical of men and one of the most ardent of the revolutionary lovers of humanity, but even he felt the French revolutionary tradition as a kind of oppression rather than an inspiration, a channelling of the revolutionary impulse into the well-known patterns of French revolutions. The French revolution crushes us, he wrote: 'We expect its programme to furnish us with both men and things: we strive to copy Robespierre and St. Just.' Others spoke of the same thing with weariness or sardonic amusement, as Herzen wrote of the revolutionary imitativeness of the Germans, where each town made its 'attempt at a "Committee of public safety" with its principal actors, with a frigid youth as Saint Just, with sombre terrorists, and a military genius representing Carnot. I knew two or three Robespierres personally; they always wore clean shirts, washed their hands and cleaned their nails.'

Theatrical metaphors had been applied to revolutionary activity ever since the first French revolution, notably by Edmund Burke. Now in France, three revolutions later, counting the first, they had a particular satirical force. Alexis de Tocqueville (1805–59), famous as the analyst of democracy in America, who was a minister in the short-lived new republic, wrote in his *Recollections*: 'I had the feeling that we had staged a play about the French Revolution rather than that we were continuing it.' Heinrich Heine, a Parisian resident since just after the revolution of 1830, put the point as a question: 'Is the great author repeating himself?' Marx ironically christened the *coup d'état* by which the President of the Republic, Napoleon's nephew Louis Napoleon, put an end to the Republican constitution in 1851 and subsequently made himself emperor, 'The Eighteenth Brumaire of Louis Napoleon Bonaparte', after the episode in the first French Revolution when Napoleon with his troops had crushed a rising of the Paris populace. Marx began his essay with a citation of Hegel's assertion that great events happen twice; he forgot to add, Marx said, first as tragedy, then as farce. Obviously with Louis Napoleon's *coup* in mind, the brothers

Edmond (1822–96) and Jules (1830–70) de Goncourt, writing during the Second Empire the diary that made them famous, commented cynically that '*coups d'état* would go off so much better if there were seats, boxes and stalls, so that one could see what was happening and not miss anything'.

The Goncourts became specialists in a literary theme which was explored again and again by authors in France in the next four decades, above all in the novels of Gustave Flaubert (1821–80): the unsatisfactoriness, staleness and tedium of experience and the disillusion it necessarily brings. It is a mood which, though, of course, it can be paralleled earlier, it is tempting to call post-revolutionary. As the Goncourts put it, 'our minds and bodies have mornings-after of an indescribable greyness'. The 1850s were a morning after. There was an orgiastic quality to revolution which some writers – Heine, for example – recognized. The poet Charles Baudelaire (1821–67), then best known as an art critic, who had hitherto been politically indifferent, was one who was caught up in the excitement of violence in the streets. He had stood with his friend the painter Gustave Courbet (1819–77) at the corner of the Place de la Concorde during the riot of 22 February, and a friend's report of his reaction employs the almost obligatory theatrical metaphor: 'The opening act of the drama he had found most interesting, though he felt dissatisfied with the conclusion, reckoning that the curtain had fallen too soon.' By the 24th he was joining in and calling for blood, though in his cry of 'General Aupick must be killed' the aspect of generational conflict characteristic of liberal revolutions was more than usually blatantly displayed; General Aupick was his step-father. Writing later in his journal of 'My intoxication in 1848', Baudelaire diagnosed it as 'literary intoxication; memories of what I had read'.

Flaubert played a less active part, though he joined the republican National Guard, but he, above all, in the central part of his novel *Sentimental Education* (1869), which he called 'the moral history . . . of the men of my generation', became the chronicler of the revolution of 1848 in Paris and of its disillusionments. Flaubert had been himself a discontented law student in Paris in the early 1840s, nursing a typical hatred of the bourgeoisie that was moral and aesthetic rather than political. In *Sentimental Education* he caught the frustrations of his contemporaries and depicted their futility. The types listed by Herzen as the raw material of the February revolution perfectly identify a large part of the cast of Flaubert's novel: 'naive people and revolutionary doctrinaires, the unappreciated artists, unsuccessful literary men, students who did not complete their studies, briefless lawyers, actors without talent, persons of great vanity but small capability, with huge pretensions but no perseverance or powers of work'. The last description exactly describes the hero, or anti-hero, of Flaubert's novel. But Flaubert expresses disillusionment with the people too, the real workers, brave but stupid, rather than the idealized 'People', just as his novel *Madame Bovary* (1856) set in Normandy offered a bleak realism far removed from the sentimental pastorals of George Sand.

Some intellectuals in 1848, as we have seen, experienced the Parisian revolution as a literary or theatrical event, with a sense of observing or playing parts already written. This sense also pervades, though at first joyfully, the provincial romanticism of Flaubert's heroine Madame Bovary. For Flaubert himself the weight of literariness, the sense of using words already soiled and debased by use, and the attempt to escape from it, through an endeavour to render reality and to do so with an intense verbal fastidiousness, became central to his conception of the novelist's task. If there was pathos in Madame Bovary's experiencing her first adultery as an essentially 'literary' event, placing her in a novel of her life written, as it were, by herself, there was also vulgarity in the lived cliché. For Flaubert, instead of the apocalyptic confidence, or at least hope, in a whole new collective future, entertained by many of his contemporaries before 1848, the attainment of anything new at all, anything not already a cliché, in feeling, experience or expression, became a purely personal and desperate matter, requiring the most intense honesty and aesthetic self-discipline and a kind of monastic dedication. It was a move which we shall have to consider further in Chapter 5 (pp. 173–4), prophetic of much of the artistic endeavour and aesthetic prescriptions of the latter part of the nineteenth century and the earlier part of the twentieth. Parenthetically, it is tempting to add that it was because musical novelty came so readily to Wagner that he was able, almost uniquely, to carry into the later nineteenth century so much of the expansiveness, the unabashed prophetic grandeur and vast moral, political and spiritual concerns, characteristic of Romanticism. Even so, of course, eventually the Wagnerian heritage, for composers, became itself a burden and a cliché, to be cast off by a more austere and minimalist approach to their art.

World-weariness, a sense of a world grown old and of belonging to a prematurely exhausted, post-Romantic generation, were also themes, though differently handled, in English literature, or at least in English poetry, at the end of the 1840s and in the early 1850s. The particular adepts of this intellectual melancholy and of the exploration of their generation's supposedly suspended intellectual and emotional animation were two friends, products of the same school, Rugby, and the same Oxford college, respectively in their middle and late twenties in 1849, Matthew Arnold (1822–88) and Arthur Hugh Clough (1819–61). Clough was sufficiently touched by the revolutionary excitement to go to Paris in the spring of that year, where a letter he wrote in May shows that he had retained a sense of ironic distance, and had, like others we have considered, an eye for the contrived, theatrical character of some of its events. (It is only fair to add that he arrived after the insurrection in February and left before that of June.) The 21 May saw a grand revolutionary fête, reminiscent of the first revolution, complete with girls in classical costumes with oak wreaths in their hair. 'It was funny,' Clough wrote, 'in the afternoon to see the classical virgins walking about with their papas and mamas.'

Clough was certainly not, as he knew well himself, cast in the mould of a revolutionary, but he, like a number of his university contemporaries, was disaffected, uneasy, at odds with the rigidities of his society. Young Englishmen of Clough's type and generation had their own form of rebelliousness, not altogether unconnected with those of the continent, and sometimes paid a price for them. When Clough went to Paris in 1848 he had just resigned his fellowship at Oriel College, Oxford, and was without occupation. He had chafed under the restraints and narrow-mindedness of Oxford rather as Wagner chafed in his post as Royal *Kapellmeister* in Dresden. Essentially the situation in Oxford in the 1840s offered a version of the conflict of generations evident also in France and Germany, though it took a rather different form. The oppressors were not court officials, policemen or state censors, but the academic seniors, the university authorities who sometimes behaved like censors. Enthusiasm for French political ideas, like the kindred vogue at both Oxford and Cambridge for the ideas of the Italian Mazzini and the cause of Italian liberation, were in part an oblique reflection of that conflict. Clough's friend and contemporary James Anthony Froude (1818–94) said of Oxford at this point, 'French socialism was in the air. We had read Rousseau and Louis Blanc and Madame Sand.' Froude's own enthusiasm took the form of sending a band to play the revolutionary anthem, the Marseillaise, under the Vice-Chancellor's window.

The central cause of friction with the university authorities, for Clough and Froude and other young men in their situation, was religious belief, but as in Germany it was entangled with other issues of personal morality, emancipation and self-expression. Froude resigned his fellowship, under duress, in 1849, after the publication of his scandalous novel *The Nemesis of Faith* (see below Chapter 4, p. 151), which was publicly burnt in his College hall by the senior tutor. Although the hero's lapse from Christian faith and the author's apparent defence of him, was the chief cause of scandal, his adulterous love affair was another. Clough's rather George Sandian long narrative poem, *The Bothie of Tober-na-vuolich*, written in the autumn of 1848, also caused adverse comment for the frankness of its acceptance of the physical and for the bare legs of its Scottish peasant heroine; the head of Clough's former College found it 'indelicate'. To understand the reactions we have to recall not only Victorian reticence but also the special character of Oxford and Cambridge. Both were closed religious corporations, their degrees available only to professed members of the Church of England. Not all, but a good many, of their undergraduates were headed for careers in the Church. Fellows of Colleges were required to be celibate and most were required after a time to take clerical orders – a step Froude, to his lasting regret, took. It was this requirement which led directly to Clough's resignation. To the university authorities it was almost as though Clough and Froude's scandalous books had been published by renegade priests who had been teaching in a seminary.

For it was religious belief, above all, which was coming to constitute the fault line between generations in Oxford and Cambridge. Much more disturbing in the context of a clerical establishment than the rather lightly worn influence of French 'socialism' was that of German biblical scholarship, the so-called Higher Criticism. It was not so much Feuerbach whose materialism was less congenial to the English, as the scholarly critique of the New Testament by David Friedrich Strauss (1808–74) which undermined the faith of earnest young Englishmen in the mid-nineteenth century. Essentially Strauss had dismissed the miraculous elements in Christianity, including the virgin birth and the resurrection, as legendary, a product of the messianic *Volk*-consciousness of the early Christians. Strauss's *Life of Jesus* (1834–5) and Feuerbach's *The Essence of Christianity* (1844) were translated into English, in 1846 and 1854 respectively, by Mary Ann Evans, the future George Eliot (1819–80). Partly through the influence of Thomas Carlyle, young English people were beginning to take an interest in German literature, above all in Goethe, and to learn German. A knowledge of German culture was beginning to be taken for granted in the circle of Arnold, Clough and Froude, and to the Oxford authorities it was a poisoned gift because it carried with it the Straussian infection.

Though there was, in a work like Clough's *Bothie*, an exhilarated, emancipated quality, English intellectuals like Clough took their prising loose from Christianity less as opportunity than as loss; the poems Clough, in particular, wrote in 1849 and 1850 on the abandonment of his Christian faith are anguished dialogues and laments. Froude too, though he found his way to a kind of solution, was psychologically scarred, and Matthew Arnold in his poetry reacted with a characteristic wistfulness and melancholy. The consequences of the loss of faith could be disorienting in a practical as well as a psychological sense. The older generation could be intransigent; Froude's clerical father virtually cut him off. Resignation of fellowships meant loss of profession and financial security. Public school or university teaching, like the clergyman's parish, were virtually barred, while the other traditional professions, law and medicine, were overcrowded and sometimes unappealing to men who had enjoyed a liberal education, as well as requiring further preparation and expense. Emigration was one resort sometimes canvassed. The hero and heroine of Clough's *Bothie* set off after their marriage for a new life in New Zealand where the class difference between them would not matter. Clough and Froude both contemplated the same step for themselves, and Matthew Arnold's younger brother Tom actually took it.

Inner emigration was a less drastic response to the sense of dislocation and its accompanying hatred of the comfortable bourgeoisie (in England 'the Philistines', the phrase Matthew Arnold borrowed from Germany, where it was used also by Marx). One, supposedly high-spirited, version was what came to be called 'bohemianism', the carefree, student-and-artist existence celebrated in Henri Murger's novel *Bohemian Life* (*La Vie de Boheme*) (1845). The Latin Quarter in Paris was the home of artistic and student Bohemia; on a smaller scale, university life in Germany, as lived, for example, by Marx in Berlin in the 1830s, offered parallels. Bakunin was a natural bohemian all his life, though for most men bohemianism was a stage, and recognized as such, on the way to professional and familial respectability. In England, Oxford and Cambridge, with their imposed celibacy, collegiate residence and stricter university discipline, offered a rather different model of student life and restricted possibilities of bohemianism; drunkenness was necessarily tolerated, females were not.

There was a university in London. University College had been founded in the late 1820s as a place of education free from religious tests and constraints. But it, and later King's College, in no sense played the same role as the Sorbonne or the University of Berlin; the magnet of the older universities was too powerful. In the arts, however, just as in France, the capital held the key to successful careers. The Royal Academy, established in the later eighteenth century, played much the same role as the Institute in France, and provided the same battleground for the clash of generations. The judgement of which pictures to accept and which new members to elect gave great power to older men and provided an appropriate focus for hostility, with the Academy standing in the minds of its critics, embittered or merely young, for everything that was stale, old-fashioned, unadventurous. It was the contact of three students at the Royal Academy, in something of this frame of mind, that gave birth in 1848 to the Pre-Raphaelite Brotherhood. The three founder members (there were only four others and the Brotherhood as such lasted only a few years) were John Everett Millais (1829–96), William Holman Hunt (1827–1910) and the son of an Italian political émigré, Dante Gabriel Rossetti (1828–82), whose life, more than that of any of the others, came to resemble that of the typical 'bohemian'.

The Brotherhood seems to bear in its conception marks of Rossetti's Italian heritage, though the most obvious model was the quasi-monastic group of German painters known as the Nazarenes. The tradition of the secret societies, the Carbonari, was strong in Italian liberal nationalism; Rossetti's father, who had found a refuge as professor of Italian at King's College, was an old Carbonaro. Mazzini's Young Italy was another offshoot of the same tradition. Pre-Raphaelite art was essentially apolitical, even escapist, and there was always an air of parody or playfulness about the Brotherhood itself, but in their art they were intensely in earnest. They were not untouched by the political mood of 1848: Hunt and Millais joined the march to the Chartist mass demonstration on Kennington Common, the distant English echo of the events on the continent. In 1848 Hunt was engaged on a painting of Rienzi, the medieval hero of a revived Roman republicanism, a subject also taken by Wagner for his early opera of that name; both works were inspired by a novel about Rienzi by Edward Bulwer Lytton (1803–73). There were, coincidentally, to be other parallels when the Pre-Raphaelites, including their slightly younger adherents William Morris (1834–96) and Edward Burne-Jones (1833–98), turned under the influence of Tennyson's poetry to the Arthurian cycle of legends from which Wagner was to derive his *Tristan* and *Parsifal*, which they invested with a similar quality of brooding mystery and sexuality. When Millais was elected an associate of the Royal Academy in 1853 Rossetti announced parodically, 'See how the whole Round Table is dissolved.'

The Pre-Raphaelites' aesthetic slogan, 'truth to nature', sounds superficially similar to that which later, in France, inspired the Impressionists in their own revolt against academicism, though it issued in a very different kind of art. But it was the Pre-Raphaelites' champion, the critic John Ruskin (1819–1900), who was to make their stance, or what he took it to be, doctrinaire beyond anything they themselves articulated. Ruskin was already known as an art critic and defender of the paintings of Turner, and he shared with the Pre-Raphaelites a detestation of the eighteenth-century founder-President of the Academy, Sir Joshua Reynolds, and all he represented. His own major work in 1849 was on architecture, where some of the wider themes of his later social as well as aesthetic doctrines were foreshadowed. In *Seven Lamps of Architecture* (1849) Ruskin took up the cause of the revival of Gothic architecture in England, which was already well under way, and already associated with a repudiation of what was considered the soullessness and commercialism of modern post-Renaissance building. As the Pre-Raphaelites sought to revive what they thought of as the purer painting techniques of the early masters, and took refuge from the modern world in Arthurian legend, Ruskin saw in the earnest and, as he would have said, 'truthful' adoption of Gothic as the common architectural language of the nineteenth century a means of national spiritual renewal. His condemnations of Renaissance and modern architecture as heartless and frivolous have a good deal in common with Wagner's parallel feelings about French and Italian opera.

Ruskin has sometimes been compared with Marx, and in fact there is much in Ruskin's denunciations of the mechanical nature of modern production, which reduces the worker to a mere tool, that is similar to Marx's concept of the alienation of the worker from his labour and its product. But the parallels between Ruskin and Wagner are even more extensive. Both denounced modern commercialism and money-worship and called, often violently, for a redemption of the modern world through art, while also sometimes speaking, earlier in Wagner's career, later in Ruskin's, of social transformation as the precondition of healthy and joyful artistic creation; both dwelt on the virtues of the medieval guilds and the medieval craftsman-artist. In Ruskin's conception of the medieval cathedral as both a collective creation and a fusion of all the arts we have a resemblance to Wagner's concept of music drama as a total work of art and the focus of the life of a society. The two men worked quite independently. The similarities are testimony to the prevalence of certain basic ideas in the European culture of their time (Ruskin was born in 1819, Wagner in 1813): hostility to commercial values; the idea of the creative *Volk* and of art as the index of the spiritual life of a people. For the origins of these ideas we would have to look back beyond the lifetime of either man and beyond the scope of this book.

One immediate source of inspiration for Ruskin, however, leads back ultimately and in part to Germany: the influence of Thomas Carlyle, in the formation of whose mind some of the key concepts of German Romanticism and German metaphysics, as well as of Saint-Simonianism, had played a major part. Carlyle was fifty-three in 1848, and although he was to live more than thirty years longer his best work, on which his immense influence rested, was already behind him. Intellectually he belongs to the first half of the century, but no survey of English intellectual life at the beginning of the second can avoid the evidence of the mark he had already left. It is true that the philosopher of English liberalism, John Stuart Mill, who as a young man had undergone his own period of enthusiasm for Carlyle, had shed it when the period we are concerned with opens, but there were by this time many other enthusiasts. Ruskin and William Morris felt his influence. Disraeli's philosophy for Young England had owed something to it. Clough turned to him and so, much more emphatically, did Froude.

Clough's contribution to the literature of the 1848–9 revolution was his poem *Amours de Voyage*. It shows us, through the letters of its cast, an unrealized love affair between young English people travelling in Italy, as Clough himself did, in 1849. It is the kind of story which might later have provided the plot of one of Henry James's tales. The title and the inconsequential continental wanderings of a leisured class and their glancing encounters seem to epitomize the rootlessness and absence of a sense of purpose which is one of the chief preoccupations of the main character. In Rome, where the story comes to its anti-climax, the desultory life of the idle English visitors is set against the backdrop of the Roman revolution. Rome was almost the last outpost of the liberal conquests of 1848 to hold out, and in 1849 the Romans were heroically defending their revolution against, ironically enough, the troops of the country where the revolutions had begun in the previous year, France. There had been risings all over Italy in 1848, but the republic was not proclaimed in Rome until February 1849. The Pope, who had fled, called on France, by now under the presidency of Louis Napoleon, for help in reconquering his territory. The resistance of the city was organized by Mazzini. This was the setting for the Roman episode in Clough's poem, with its self-consciousness about the absurdity of foreign tourists in the midst of a revolution and a siege. If Clough had sometimes seen the republic in Paris in the previous year with an ironic eye, here the irony was directed at himself, and at the expense too of the creeds and slogans in which his contemporaries found alleviation for their fundamental scepticism and indecision.

Clough's ironic scepticism was not an altogether unsounded note in 1849, but it can come to seem so after dwelling for any length of time among the terrible certainties of the leading revolutionaries. It was nowhere more alien than in the world of Mazzini. He and Clough possessed a mutual friend in Carlyle, but little else in common, and it seems appropriate that Clough should have put, through his protagonist, his own self-consciousness and aversion to heroic role-playing to the test of possible participation in a Mazzinian revolution. Mazzini was a hero and potential martyr, entirely devoid of irony. His form of democratic, populist nationalism was the revolutionary spirit of 1848–9 at its most idealistic and innocent: a nationalism which asked only fraternally to embrace other nationalities; an exaltation of 'the People' with no implication of class war. It was a kind of innocence for which the continuation of foreign oppression was a necessary condition. Carlyle, who liked Mazzini's courage and sincerity, said he was 'to me very wearisome, with his incoherent Jacobinisms, George-Sandisms, in spite of all my love and regard for him'.

The core of Mazzini's creed was the idea of love of humanity; the principle of nationality to which he dedicated his life was for him an indispensable aspect, not the cancellation, of it. He inherited an idea of the later eighteenth century, one of the earliest concepts of German cultural self-assertion in that period, that each nation possessed a special mission, a unique contribution to the development of mankind. It was an idea with an appeal to other nationalities besides the Germans, above all to those who felt their national identity and self-expression to be thwarted, stifled and hitherto unexpressed. It had a strong appeal for Russian thinkers brooding on the relation of their country to Western civilization; one can see it even in Herzen. 'Humanity,' Mazzini wrote 'is the association of Nationalities, the alliance of the peoples in order to work out their missions in peace and love.' The vehicle of the national mission was the People, and in order to carry it out it must first forge its own identity as the Nation (there is an analogy here with Marx's concept of the proletariat creating itself as a class in order to carry out its – unique – historic mission of emancipating humanity). But, as also in some early forms of communism, there was a role for a dedicated élite, 'a living apostolate . . . a nucleus of men strong in determination and constancy'.

This was how Mazzini conceived Young Italy, which he had inaugurated in 1831. He shared a common enthusiasm of the time for dedicated, secret or semi-secret brotherhoods bound together by oaths and symbolism. The underlying model was of course Freemasonry, which had sometimes been credited with manipulating the first French Revolution. English Trades Unionism during its years of suppression had developed something of this character. Disraeli (1804–81), as a young man, was fascinated by the idea of powerful or omnipotent secret societies. It was one of the intellectual fashions of the 1840s to which Bakunin was to remain faithful for the rest of his life. The idea of a chivalric political or artistic brotherhood was, as we have seen, present in Young England and the Pre-Raphaelite Brotherhood. It provided the central theme for Laube's novel *Young Europe* (Mazzini tried to inaugurate a 'Young Europe' movement in actuality in the mid-1830s); it is an idea which finds echoes in Wagner's *Tannhäuser, Mastersingers* and *Parsifal*. For Young Italy, Mazzini says, we devised 'secret rules for the affiliation of members, decided upon the formula of oath to be taken, and chose – as the common symbol – an ivy leaf'. There was also a uniform: green blouse, red belt, white trousers, and a beret. The Saint-Simonians in France too, whose creed and Mazzini's had a good deal in common, also devised a uniform for themselves: blue tunic, red waistcoat, more white trousers; the waistcoat buttoned at the back as a symbol of mutual dependence. The Pre-Raphaelites were modest in confining themselves to the initials 'P. R. B.' as their badge of solidarity.

The outcome of the revolutions of 1848–9 was cruel to Saint-Simonian idealism, based as it was on ideas of love, cooperation and universal brotherhood; the revolutions' success would have been as fatal to it as their failure. As it was, younger Italian democrats condemned Mazzini's refusal to accept the notion of class struggle and called for a social revolution, rejecting the idea of secret societies and conspiracies in favour of cultivating the masses. The movement for Italian liberation seemed forced to choose between class war on the one hand or a constitutional monarchy under the King of Sardinia on the other, both equally inimical to Mazzini. A similar choice seemed imposed on the Germans between 1849 and 1871: unification under Prussian or Austrian imperial rule or, for some, faith in an apparently distant social revolution through class struggle. The limited success of liberal republicanism in 1848–9 had been as disillusioning as its defeats, if not more so: the establishment of the French republic and the calling of the Frankfurt Parliament had uncovered class and ethnic tensions hitherto masked by common opposition to what could be seen as archaic tyrannies.

In France the republican government crushing the workers' rising in June was a plausible version of what Marx and others could represent as the dictatorship of the bourgeoisie; subsequent national elections showed that even the liberalism of Paris was unrepresentative and the votes of the Catholic peasantry helped to bring an end to the republic and inaugurate the Second Empire. In Germany and Austria the same divisions were complicated by the issue of nationality. Polish peasants were hostile to the gentry who were the spearhead of Polish nationalism, and struggling to throw off alien rule. The apparent advance of Hungary to full nationhood aroused the hostility of the smaller nationalities within the Austrian empire. In the liberal-dominated Frankfurt Parliament the aspiration to unite the various German states in more or less their existing form clashed with the national aspirations of the Slav peoples under Austrian rule, notably the Czechs. Almost everywhere conflicts along class lines, between bourgeois and workers, gentry and peasantry, city and country, became to a lesser or greater degree apparent. All Europe seemed engaged in verifying Marx's view of history: that liberal-democratic and national revolutions temporarily obscured but could not permanently stifle the reality of class-struggle. Marx and Engels worked out their diagnosis in retrospective dissection of the revolutions and their failure.

Some liberal democrats and socialist humanitarians clung to their hopes. The most impressive of such attempts, because marked by a struggle with a strong, sceptical realism, is Alexander Herzen's *From the Other Shore*, published in Germany in 1850 with two open letters addressed to Herwegh and to Mazzini. Herzen said in his autobiography that the suppression of the insurrection in Paris in June 1849 'drew a line across my life'. *From the Other Shore*, much of which is in the form of dialogue, was in fact a kind of dialogue of Herzen with himself on the reasons for the failure and for the persistence of hope. Dedicated to his small son Alexander, it was a plea, to himself rather than the boy, to go on in the face of disillusionment: 'Do not, I beg, remain on *this* shore . . . better to perish with the revolution than to seek refuge in the almshouse of reaction.' Much of *From the Other Shore* is impassioned and declamatory in the manner of the 1840s, but Herzen, as we have seen, was an ironic observer of revolutionary manners and he did not exclude himself. He mourned over his not quite renounced revolutionary faith like Clough and Arnold over their lost Christianity, and like them identified his own generation as one cast into the limbo of an historical hiatus, 'having lived too much by fantasy and ideals to fit into the age of American good sense'. Herzen struggled to retain, even masochistically, a sense of an historical role for his own revolutionary generation: 'by means of us humanity is regaining sobriety; we are its head-ache the next morning; we are its birth pangs'.

But for Herzen history gave no built-in assurances, an inference Marx continued to refuse to draw. Marx too dealt with the failure of the revolutions with irony, most effectively in *The Eighteenth Brumaire*, and verbally scourged his fellow revolutionaries for their lack of realism, but he retained his Hegelian belief that history worked out its contradictions to a predestined consummation. Herzen, who had also been exposed as a student to the predominance of Hegelian metaphysics, retained no such faith. 'Irony,' he wrote, 'gives expression to the reaction aroused by the fact that logical truth is not the same as the truth of history.' In this he spoke the epitaph of a powerful and central nineteenth-century belief, though many in the nineteenth and twentieth centuries continued to affirm it – that, though creeds and dogmas were relative and provisional when seen in the perspective of history, history itself might be trusted: the rational is ultimately the real and history is a riddle which solves itself. The loss of that belief is, if we may speak so, one of the marks distinguishing the twentieth-century mind from that of the earlier nineteenth century, and it is a loss which has found its characteristic mode of expression in irony. In that sense Herzen's is more like a twentieth-century mind than Marx's, Clough's than Carlyle's. The lesson Herzen most immediately drew was a kind of empiricist humility which was to find many echoes, more and less confident and affirmative, among those to whom faith of any other kind had become an impossibility: 'meekness before the truth'. T. H. Huxley, Darwin's champion, was to use almost exactly the same form of words.

For some, as for Herzen, the years 1848–9 marked a kind of watershed in their intellectual and sometimes their personal lives. They turned the historian Michelet, for example, temporarily away from history and mankind to strange works in which he celebrated the immensities of the earth and sea in a kind of idiosyncratic nature-mysticism. The public and personal catastrophes of these years turned the sick Heine from his Young German Hellenism and Saint-Simonianism (always, in his case, touched with irony) back to thoughts of God: 'in such hideous moments,' he wrote, 'Pantheism is not enough'. Men swung, as always at moments of crisis, further towards the left or the right, or gave their allegiances new forms. The painter Courbet (1819–77) moved from detachment to a committed socialism and republicanism which found expression in the early 1850s in his realist studies of the life of the poor. His friend Baudelaire, with whom he had seen the outbreak of the February revolution in Paris, quickly recovered from his temporary intoxication for revolution; in the

1850s, in so far as he had any political views they were of the right, and he read admiringly the work of the intellectual master of French royalism and reaction, Joseph de Maistre (1753–1821). The ideas of another Frenchman, Arthur de Gobineau (1816–82), already a man of the right and a contributor to the royalist press, took a new and portentous turning. In the midst of the revolutionary years, in the long narrative poem Gobineau was writing, there appeared for the first time in his work the ideas of Aryan and Teutonic racial pre-eminence by which, expressed in his book *On the Inequality of the Races of Man* (1855), he was to exercise a major influence on the racialist thought of the latter part of the century. Another notable figure of the second half of the century began, as it were accidentally, in 1849, his journey towards his advocacy of autocracy and Orthodox Christianity and his violently anti-liberal and anti-Western form of Russian messianism. Fyodor Dostoevsky (1821–81) was arrested as a member of a circle of young Moscow liberals, the so-called Petrashevsky circle; he was condemned to death, subjected to a mock execution and then sent to Siberia. Psychologically it was a turning-point, moving him not to further dissidence but to a distinctly Russian form of Christianity.

Another for whom the years 1849–51 was a kind of watershed was Carlyle (the *coup d'état* of Louis Napoleon in the latter year was in a sense the conclusion of the revolutionary episode and had its own impact). The diatribe on the state of Europe and England which he published in 1851 as *Latter-Day Pamphlets* is, perhaps not altogether coincidentally, the last of his works to exhibit, intermittently, the immense imaginative vitality of his earlier ones. Carlyle was not a revolutionary or even, in any directly political sense, a democrat, but he had lived his earlier life in an atmosphere tense with the expectation of revolution and he had made prophesying it and preparing to meet it a kind of vocation; it fitted his conception of history, founded on notions, Biblical, Saint-Simonian and German metaphysical, of retribution and renewal. The prospect of a sort of baulked apocalypse threw him into a, for him, new kind of gloom and frenzy. The fiery reign of revolution, exhilarating though fearful, seemed quenched in a morass of mud, and worse than mud, which was how he saw the contemporary world. The imagery of *Latter-Day Pamphlets*, is excremental; the contemporary English preoccupation with sanitation provided Carlyle's impatience with pictures of almost Dantean force, of clogged immobility and dismal, squalid repetition, like the dead dog rolled up and down the filthy Thames with the tide. It seems appropriate that the book ends, with Carlyle's full endorsement, with a description of the prison yard as a place of punishment and discipline. Images of imprisonment had been common emblems of despotism ever since the fall of the Bastille, and particularly since the Congress of Vienna in 1815 had restored the European monarchies, when, as Heine said referring to the caged Napoleon, 'all Europe became a St Helena'. But they had often, as in Beethoven's opera *Fidelio*, been accompanied by stirring images of liberation. Carlyle, always drawn to ideas of vigorous, as distinct from effete, authority, had learned to kiss the rod.

How far the events of 1848–51 may be thought of as a cultural watershed generally is debatable. The Marxist critic Georg Lukács (1885–1971), for example, later saw the genre of the historical novel as embodying the relation of middle-class consciousness to the processes of history. In the historical novel as practised in the second half of the century he saw a retreat into sensationalism and exotic and archaeological detail which it had not exhibited in the earlier period, when, in the tradition of Walter Scott, the novel had been used to identify and explore the real forces of historical transformation in European society. Lukács took 1848 to mark the transition, because it marked the loss of the bourgeoisie's sense of control of and participation in that transformation. The year 1848 was its climacteric. Afterwards 'History is no longer felt or understood by it, and so it becomes a collection of exotic anecdotes. At the same time, and again inevitably, as real historical relations are less and less understood, wild, sensual, even bestial features come to occupy the foreground.' He instanced particularly Flaubert's novel of ancient Carthage, *Salammbô* (1862), to which such adjectives are not unfairly applicable. Lukács' argument is overstated and his characterization of the 'bourgeois' historical thought of the second half of the century is partial as well as unsympathetic, but there is some truth in it. The historian Jacob Burkhardt (1818–97), for example, was clearly, and indeed self-consciously, to invest in his celebration of the counter-example of Renaissance Italy his rejection of nineteenth-century democracy and mass civilization, though it also has to be said that history as a refuge from political disillusionment and cultural distaste was hardly a new development.

Other genres mark a transition around the mid-century more strikingly than the presentation of history. Philosophy certainly did. The vogue for Feuerbach's optimistic, humanist philosophy of emancipation was to prove as brief as it was intense, confined, in fact, to the 1840s. The new vogue, at least among artists and men of letters, in the 1850s and 1860s, was for the pessimistic philosophy of renunciation of Arthur

Schopenhauer (1788–1860). But the enthusiasm for Schopenhauer too was a trick of the *Zeitgeist*, for his chief work, *The World as Will and Representation*, had been written as long ago as 1818, when it had made little headway against the then dominant Hegelianism. Schopenhauer had to wait for the very last years of his life to enjoy fame, and it is tempting to see his philosophy of rejection of the world, which is seen as essentially evil, as being carried into fashion in the backwash of the revolutionary tide. Wagner and Flaubert were both deeply influenced by it (Baudelaire preferred the mysticism of Swedenborg (1688–1772)). How far, in either case, political disillusionment played a part in preparing their minds for Schopenhauer's ideas is arguable. Flaubert's observation of the revolution intensified rather than created his disillusionment not just with politics and people but with life itself; his was the disillusionment of the Romantic who perpetually finds life colourless and unsatisfying because it can never match the world of his fantasy. In *Salammbô* and elsewhere it is possible to see the mature Flaubert deliberately indulging the fantasies in a spirit of revenge. In Wagner's case the shift in the text of the *Ring*, from a Feuerbachian affirmation, embodied in Siegfried, to a kind of Schopenhauerian renunciation embodied in Wotan and in Brünnhilde's self-immolation, is very marked and, as Ernest Newman showed, even makes for a certain incoherence. But Wagner read Schopenhauer's work, introduced to him by the ubiquitous Herwegh, only in 1854, after the first private printing of the poem of the *Ring*. Schopenhauer's philosophy was to remain a powerful influence, above all in *Tristan*, but so far as the *Ring* was concerned Wagner saw it as providing retrospective illumination: 'Only now,' after reading Schopenhauer, he wrote, 'did I understand my Wotan.' The defeat of Wagner's political hopes certainly played a part in the transition, very evident in his work, from social optimism to world-renunciation, but the latter, as an indulged death-wish, lay deeper and earlier in Wagner's mind than the political excitement of 1848–9. The idea of renunciation is powerfully present in *The Flying Dutchman*, *Tannhäuser* and *Lohengrin*, all written by Wagner before 1849.

This no doubt only illustrates the obvious: that individuals brought their own psychological bent, however shaped by the culture of the time, to the ways they approached the idea of revolution and accommodated themselves to its defeat. It is well, too, to bear in mind that for some thinkers, profoundly concentrated on their own intellectual concerns, the issues considered in this chapter were at most a background noise. A survey of the mind of Europe, above all of young Europe – that is, of the people whose achievements, mostly still in the future, were to dominate the intellectual life of the second half of the century – which is focused on the revolutionary years 1848–49 and their antecedents and aftermath, is one way of beginning to consider those achievements and the influences that lay behind them. But it is not, obviously, the only way. In the spring of 1848, for example, the main excitement for Charles Darwin (1809–82) was his discovery of the existence of bisexualism in barnacles. In context, which Darwin by then was able to supply, it was a concern as portentous as any of those, often so portentously proclaimed, that we have considered so far.

# CHAPTER 1

## The Stuff of the World and the Promises of Science

### 1.1 The New Generation

One of the distinctive intellectual features of the early and mid-nineteenth century is a cultivated awareness of intellectual transition and changing cultural mood, considered not just, as earlier, as the succession of great epochs in the history of mind but in the fine grain of the transition of generations and even decades. Contemporaries, that is, began to see themselves under the sign of continuous intellectual history. John Stuart Mill, in his *Autobiography*, published in the 1870s, saw his younger self in the 1820s, as a microcosm of the intellectual tendencies of the age – utilitarian, Saint-Simonian, Coleridgean, Hellenic and Romantic – and dramatized his early conflicts as the battle between 'the eighteenth century' and 'the nineteenth century'. Carlyle constructed a rather similar but more complex cultural predicament for his fictional alter ego in *Sartor Resartus* (1834). For young French intellectuals of that period, understandably, the Restoration, the closing of the Revolutionary and Napoleonic era, drew a line across their lives and across the cultural life of Europe. Alfred de Musset's exercise in historical self-consciousness, *Confessions of a Child of the Age* (1836), Stendhal's novel *The Red and the Black* (1830) and Chateaubriand's posthumous memoirs stand as monuments to that generational self-consciousness. Later, post-Romanticism, too, became a diagnosed condition and predicament, expressed, for example, in Matthew Arnold's poem 'Stanzas from the Grande Chartreuse' (1855), which shifts significantly from first person singular to plural as the poet takes on the role of spokesman for his generation. It is pointless now to emulate the passion and outcry of the 'fathers', the Romantics, Byron and Shelley, yet the new world of science and industrial bustle cannot claim them as its own:

> Too late for us your call ye blow
> Whose bent was taken long ago.

Young Russians, already conscious of getting their culture at second hand, predictably showed this historical self-consciousness, epitomized in the title of Lermontov's novel *A Hero of our Time* (1839), and entered into the intellectual collisions of the generations with the eagerness of parvenus. In Moscow and St Petersburg, from the 1830s onwards, Romanticism and high philosophical Idealism, inspired by Schiller, Byron, Schelling, Fichte and ultimately Hegel, gave way first to Feuerbachian de-mystification and Saint-Simonian or Fourierist humanistic 'socialism' and then, in the 1850s and 1860s, to the self-consciously hard-headed, even ruthless practicality and rejection of all Romantic idealism in favour of a 'scientific' reductionism which came rather inappropriately to be termed Nihilism. Herzen charted these transitions in his *My Past and Thoughts*; but, reaching the end of his personal intellectual odyssey, was repelled and baffled by the last of them. Its chief chronicler became Turgenev, above all in his novel *Fathers and Sons* (1865) with its classic portrait of the Nihilist as the new man, the young doctor Bazarov, who scorns idealism and polite etiquette, who dissects frogs and whose rooms 'have a sort of medical-surgical smell, mixed with cheap tobacco'. Bazarov carried a blunt, materialist and utilitarian realism and rejection of convention to the point of brutality, while retaining a humane dedication to healing the sick. As a cultural type, and emblem of a generation, he stands as accuser of an older generation which has overdosed on an ineffectual Romanticism and a heady but futile metaphysics; as its chief representative in the novel remarks, modernity used to be Hegelian and now it is Nihilist – and frogs. The new mentors, still German, are not poets and philosophers but chemists and physiologists.

Turgenev himself was firmly on the side of those who held that Russia needed above all to learn from the West – the so-called Westernizers – but he noted ironically the garbled hyper-enthusiasm to which this could give rise. In his novel *Smoke* (1863), set in the cosmopolitan meeting place of Baden-Baden, he presents a young Russian enthusiast: 'in a single breath, almost choking himself, he mentioned Draper, Virchow, Shelgunov, Bichat, Helmholtz, Star, St Raymund, Johann Müller the physiologist and Johann Müller the historian . . . obviously confusing them, Taine, Renan . . . ' Voroshilov's list of mentors, though garbled, and made comic by the addition at the end of three Elizabethan dramatists, is worth some scrutiny. It has Turgenev's usual strong awareness of such matters, and is in fact a good deal less heterogeneous and random than it looks. Johannes Müller (1801–58), (the physiologist not the historian) is the chief clue. Two of the others, Rudolf von Virchow (1821–1902) and Hermann Helmholtz (1821–94), were Müller's pupils and had worked in his famous laboratory in Berlin; if the mysterious St Raymund is in fact the physiologist Emil Du Bois Reymond (1818–96), German despite his name, then he too had worked with Müller. Bichat (1771–1802) was a French physiologist of an earlier generation; Auguste Comte had made him retrospectively one of the twelve 'saints' of the Positivist Religion. William Draper (1811–82) was an American chemist and physiologist who had published *Human Physiology, Statical and Dynamical* (1856). He had become mildly notorious in 1860 as the unappreciated warm-up act to the T. H. Huxley–Bishop Wilberforce debate on Evolution at the Oxford meeting of the British Association for the Advancement of Science, when he had given an address on 'The History of the Conflict of Science with Religion', subsequently turned into a book in 1874. In the year of *Smoke*, 1863, he published *A History of the Intellectual Development of Europe* on the same lines: just the thing to appeal to Voroshilov. Shelgunov was presumably a name of Russian resonance; 'Star' seems garbled beyond identification. Hippolyte Taine and Ernest Renan we shall have to consider shortly.

Experiment (as in Bazarov's case) is clearly one important key, and Müller's Berlin laboratory was an intellectual power-house of the mid-century. The ramifying European intellectual influence of chemistry and physiology at this point marks in a sense a return, after decades of the dominance of Idealist philosophy and the speculative, teleological *Naturphilosophie* which was its German biological counterpart, to the 'mechanistic' ideas of the late eighteenth and early nineteenth centuries in France, themselves the outcome of a long history of speculative attempts to resolve the Cartesian dualism of mind and matter into a materialist monism. Saint-Simon and later Comte had proclaimed the forthcoming hegemony of a unified world-view, grounded in physical science and extended to the social world, and the dominant social role of scientists. Coinciding with the disillusionment with philosophical and political idealism we glanced at towards the end of the last chapter, in the mid-century the physical sciences were feeding into the general culture, at what seemed an accelerating rate, a whole, related succession of concepts and experimental results, accompanied by able popularizations, which began to make such claims without the bizarre neo-Catholic embellishments in which Comte had sought to clothe the authority of science.

## 1.2 The Conservation of Matter and Energy; Materialist Reductionism

Let us return to Voroshilov's list. The first to claim attention is Helmholtz, because although also a distinguished physiologist and physio-psychologist he was one of the pioneers of what became the central, certainly the most generally known, physical concept of the middle of the century, the law of the conservation of energy. It is, of course, a simplification which makes Helmholtz pre-eminently responsible for its foundation, just as it is to take Müller's laboratory as epitomizing physiological and physio-psychological experiment, but at least in both cases no better single name could be found. A number of other names are associated with the law of the conservation of energy (Faraday, Joule, Carnot, Kelvin); but Helmholtz's 1847 paper, though little noticed immediately, was a foundational text for the theory. It is not surprising that a society growing dependent on coal-fired heat-engines should have been preoccupied with the relations of matter and energy and with finding the mathematical formulae for the transformations of motion, heat, light, magnetism and electricity. Initially the aim was to reduce all such phenomena ultimately to the mechanical laws governing the behaviour of matter and hence to integrate them with the account of the world given in Newtonian mechanics. The attempt was eventually given up, and the order of priority came to be revised, so that matter itself came to be regarded as expressible in terms of energy. The implications of the special case of heat, expressed in the second law of thermodynamics, according to which heat flows from a hotter to a colder place but never vice versa, was to introduce a prophetic gloom into perceptions of the world because of its implication of an ultimate state of inert equilibrium, a dead world devoid of life and motion, like that discovered by H. G. Wells' Time-Traveller. We shall have to consider responses to this later, but for the moment we are concerned with the general conception of the world as a closed energy-system to which nothing was ever added and from which nothing could be taken away, all of whose multifarious transformations could be seen as the various conversions of a fixed overall quantity of energy, all of which could be expressed scientifically, including certainly those of life and perhaps even those of consciousness.

For, after all, were not living bodies also heat engines and sites, through digestion, respiration and motion, of the conversion of matter and energy, and should not the recently acquired understanding of the functions of the nerves also be interpretable as modes of energy-conversion in a system of inputs and outputs, converted from one to the other through the spinal cortex and motions of brain matter? The function of the motor and sensory nerves was understood, the functioning of the parts of the brain were being experimentally mapped. Might these not prove the Ariadne's thread to the mystery of consciousness itself? Thus complementary discourses in physics, in the chemistry of life and in neurology seemed, optimistically regarded, to promise a whole series of reductions and derivations, from the ultimate laws of physics and chemistry to the functioning of living beings, and as part of that functioning not merely sentience but all the phenomena of consciousness. Animal experiments were crucial in many areas; Bazarov's frogs stood at several important interfaces, though we do not know what he made of them.

It was the promise of a wholly unified, scientific account of all existence that underlay some of the most aggressively confident 'materialist' pronouncements of the 1850s and 1860s, scandalizing to some, exhilarating to others. To the latter the key to the universe seemed only just out of reach and the route to it, physical science and particularly experiment, already laid out. This was the cultural significance of Voroshilov's list, and if he did not appreciate it he was presumably echoing others who did. Helmholtz, Virchow, Du Bois Reymond were notable guides to the promised land of a total, unified scientific conception of the world and of life. All were thorough reductionists as well as experimentalists, consciously at war with the older, speculative *Naturphilosophie*, which, with comparative anatomy, morphology, as its master-science, had tried to grasp the underlying patterns, the immanent Ideas, beneath the variety of material forms, and which was associated with the notion of a creative vital force, specific to living beings. Du Bois Reymond, for example, in the introduction to his *Researches in Animal Electricity* (1848) denounced Vitalism and *Naturphilosophie*.

Helmholtz was a polymath who worked experimentally on the physiology of the muscles, muscular motion being related to chemical reaction and heat production. He also conducted refined experiments, which became classic, on acoustics and vision which, incidentally, Taine was to make use of in his own, purely philosophical work on psychology and physiology, *On Intelligence* (1870). The researches of the graduates from Müller's laboratory were given direction and point by their determination to break down the barriers between the inorganic and the living and then between inner and outer life, body and mind. It was therefore on the interfaces that they focused. It was important, for example, that physiological heat could be reduced to physico-chemical processes. The organism was an energy-conversion machine. Nutrition is obviously such a bridge between chemistry and physiology, which drew the attention of pupils of the great chemist Justus Liebig, who was not himself a materialist reductionist. Nutrition in fact proved something of a blind alley, prompting over-enthusiastic claims about the relations between diet and disposition in human beings; work on it was hampered by the absence, until later in the century, of an understanding of the role of vitamins.

Much more immediate progress was made in cell-theory, of which Virchow was a pioneer. He was another scientific polymath who developed wide interests in general biology and in group as well as individual psychology, but his central experimental work was on cell-division. It derived from the search for the basic elements of living organisms, which depended crucially on work with the microscope. Bichat had been a pioneer in looking for what he regarded as the primal tissue of which organisms were constituted, but he had been hampered by the inadequate microscopes of his day. Virchow was the beneficiary of technical improvements in microscopy, the result of which was cell-theory. The concept of the cell as the basis of all organic life crossed another important interface, constituting the crucial conceptual link between plants and animals. There were also, naturally, hopes of demon-strating the reduction of cellular processes to physico-chemical ones. Virchow's contribution lay chiefly in establishing the cell as a self-perpetuating unit and cell-division as the thread of continuity of all life through time.

Germany was not only the seat of much, though by no means all, impor-tant work in chemistry and neurology in the 1840s and 1850s, it was also, in the latter decade, the theatre for the most vigorously assertive materialist polemics of the period, which of course drew authority and confidence from scientific research but which also constituted an outlet, in the years of reac-tion after 1848, for a radicalism which had found in that year, but not for years afterwards, a direct political expression. The overlap of reductionist science and its popularization with radical politics was unmistakable. As Frederick Gregory points out in his *Scientific Materialism in Nineteenth-century Germany*, many of its proponents had been caught up in the enthusiasm of 1848 and some were to pay the penalty of exile or blocked careers. Virchow's revolutionary sympathies had got him into trouble; later, after German unification, he was to become a leading spokesman for the advanced liber-als in the Reichstag. Carl Vogt (1817–1895), one of the most vehement of the materialist polemicists of the 1850s, had actually been a member of the abortive Frankfurt Parliament. Vogt, who like many others of his persuasion, came from a medical family background, studied chemistry under Liebig and also physiology, zoology and geology. In the 1840s his political radicalism had led to exile, initially to Switzerland. In Paris from 1844, he became a close associate of Bakunin and Georg Herwegh and also imbibed the French materialist tradition. Vogt's materialism was expressed in a work in 1855 entitled *Köhlerglaube und Wissenschaft*. The latter, of course means knowledge, but *Köhlerglaube* is virtually untranslatable, incorporating the double suggestion of 'implicit faith' and 'nonsense'. Vogt was convinced that the general laws of matter were exhibited in physiology while thoughts stood to the brain as gall to the liver or urine to the kidneys, as a kind of secretion. He later embraced Darwinism and devoted himself into the 1860s to palaeontology and anthropology. After 1848 he went again into Swiss exile, and eventually fell foul of Marx and Engels, who accused him of being a government spy and denounced him in a bitter pamphlet (*Herr Vogt*). He derived his notion of the inevitability of revolution from the 'catastrophist' geological theories now becoming somewhat out of date. It was a not uncommon idea: the weekly journal of popular science *Die Natur*, founded in 1852 and still appearing at the end of the century, carried on its cover a picture of a volcano in eruption as a subversive revolutionary emblem.

Vogt's career is quite closely paralleled by that of another of the materialist publicists of the 1850s, Jacob Moleschott. He too came from a medical (Dutch) family, was caught up in the fervour of 1848, endured Swiss exile and the friendship – as who seems not to have done? – of Georg Herwegh. Moleschott's reductionism found early expression in ideas of nutrition. It was in a review of Moleschott in 1850 that Feuerbach misrepresented his own philosophical empiricism by the famous, and one can see irresistible, German pun 'Man ist was er isst' (One is what one eats). How little theoretical weight he attached to this is indicated by the sentence which precedes it, which refers to the improvement of the people through better nutrition – also a practical concern of Moleschott's. The latter's *The Circulation of Life* (1852) was a more sophisticated exposition of materialism grounded in the concepts of matter and energy. Matter was eternal and energy a quality of it, while life was one of its states; life is matter in motion.

The most widely read of the materialist publicists was Ludwig Büchner (1824–99), younger brother of the radical dramatist Georg Büchner, author of *Wozzeck* and *Danton's Death*. We find in Ludwig Büchner the usual ingredients: enthusiasm for 1848, a medical degree with a thesis on the nervous system and work on reflex action. In the post-revolutionary period, he claimed, the public was turning to natural science as an alternative form of opposition. It has to be remembered, as in the case of the earlier preoccupation of the Left Young Hegelians with theology, that German conservatism was still legitimist in its principles; the concept of the divine, hereditary right of kings still underwrote the claims of autocracy; religious belief and the authority of the churches were the mainstay of absolutism. Büchner became famous through the most successful of all materialist manifestos, his *Force and Matter (Kraft und Stoff)* (1855), which went through 21 editions and was translated into 17 languages. It made the usual claims: the world is a closed system to which nothing can be added and from which nothing can be taken away. Activity of all kinds is a property of matter; thinking is an activity of the brain as much as digestion is that of the stomach. Some of Büchner's later thoughts are more complex and we shall have to return to them. In politics he became involved with the state socialism of Lassalle and, seeing knowledge of science as an instrument of workers' self-education, he turned to wider forms of popularization, forming the German Freethinking Association, which had counterparts in Britain in the Secularist Society and later the Rationalist Press Association and other groups.

We have been running the danger of speaking as though Germany was the only centre of crucial scientific research and politically accented materialist polemics and popularized science. It was the vehemence of the reaction against central German intellectual traditions, *Naturphilosophie*, pantheistic Vitalism and philosophical Idealism that caught attention. In France the educational climate of the 1850s in the early years of the Second Empire, depending as the latter did on clerical support, was repressive, and young Frenchmen like Taine and Renan tended, as we shall see, to an intensely cerebral kind of inner emigration and a fastidious elitism, both under the watch word 'science', rather than to manifestos or exile. Renan did not publish the manifesto of faith in science, *The Future of Science*, to which he was prompted by the events of 1848, until 1890; while Taine abandoned for a while the philosophy of mind, where his rejection of the officially approved 'spiritualist' ideas of the so-called 'Eclectics' brought him into conflict with the educational authorities and blighted his career. To a French intellectual, the exile to the French provinces to which Taine was condemned was scarcely better than Siberia. He turned instead to the rather safer ground of psychology in literature and the arts.

In France anti-clericalism and the exaltation of 'science' were an increasingly prominent part of the French republican tradition, though it was an association which went back, of course, to the first French Revolution. But materialism, though a strong tradition, had for that reason hardly the claim of novelty that it had in Germany in the mid-century. Materialist claims were somewhat inhibited, too, by the influential ban that Comtist Positivism, though it exalted the authority of science, had placed on all metaphysics, on any quest for ultimate causes: science's business was only with correlations of phenomena. In Germany, on the contrary, the national bent for metaphysics was not so much extinguished as re-housed in Materialism, which inherited much of the tradition of nature-worship and the impulse to total comprehension of the world found in *Naturphilosophie* even while displacing it.

Britain had experienced the impact of the new geology, with its insistence on purely natural causes and its incompatibility with the Biblical time-scale, from the 1830s onwards, and the furore over the evolutionist *Vestiges of Creation* by Robert Chambers in 1844. It was, however, to be the 1860s and 1870s, after the publication of Darwin's *Origin of Species* (1859) followed by his *Descent of Man* (1871) and T. H. Huxley's *Man's Place in Nature* in 1863, which were to be the high point of the 'the warfare of science with religion', to use Draper's title. Attacks were made by the propagandists of science (Huxley, John Tyndall, Herbert Spencer) on all claims for the authority of dogma and all limits to free inquiry. The polemicists for science were liberals, even radicals, and to attack dogma, and sometimes humanistic learning also, in the name of science and natural laws was necessarily a bid to replace the authority of the clerical and educational establishments – still closely connected – by that of physical science and its practitioners. However, political conditions in England, though still aristocratically dominated, were not such as to foster the revolutionary hopes which German materialist propagandists often embraced and wished to promote. In Germany it was after 1871, with political unification and the adoption of a federal constitution, that some leading scientists began to turn perceptibly to the right, and to justify hierarchy and national self-assertion in terms borrowed from science.

Of course neither fundamental research nor the reductionist programme was anything like the German near-monopolies that, under the suspect influence of Voroshilov, we may have made them seem. He might, for example, have included Claude Bernard (1813–78), the leading French physiologist and biochemist, along with the more conservative Louis

Pasteur (1822–95). Bernard also placed cell-theory at the centre of his conception of organic life. Bernard criticized Vitalism and worked experimentally on animal chemistry, on digestion and respiration, and on neurophysiology. He held aloof, on positivist grounds, from materialist metaphysics, but embraced determinism and regarded the human will as a fact of nature. He also provided, at least in France, what became the classic account for its period of the disciplines and aims of experimental method. In France, too, there was a tradition of experimental psychology centred on the eminent figure of Pierre Flourens (1838–71), Professor of Physiology at the Collège de France who, however, retained vitalist assumptions.

In Britain, besides work in physics, geology, palaeontology and morphology, and of course the advent of Darwin's and Wallace's evolutionism following their papers to the Linnaean Society in 1858, another major contribution was to neurophysiology, mostly initially in medical circles. There were, as we have noted, eloquent spokesmen for the reductionist enterprise, whether or not employing an emphatically materialist terminology. Some of the most lucid and economical accounts of it were provided by John Tyndall (1820–93) in addresses to the British Association, which, founded in 1833, gave in this way a platform, as also did the Royal Institution, for publicly propounding the goals and methods of science as well as presenting particular results. Tyndall's lecture in 1868 entitled 'Scientific Materialism' became notorious on account of its title, but its arguments were more fully put in what became known, from the place of the meeting, as his 'Belfast Address' in 1874. Tyndall was there speaking, of course, more than a decade after the publication of Darwin's *Origin*, and evolution is an important presence in the address, but the latter offers an extensive survey, beginning with a history of the progress of the scientific outlook, manifested in atomic theory from Democritus onwards. Matter and activity are crucially linked. Tyndall ranges up and down the scale of molecular activity, of the inorganic, the organic to the structuring of consciousness through repeated nervous responses, finding continuity everywhere until he comes to the top and bottom of the scale. Darwin seems censured for believing in an original creative act or acts, but Tyndall argues that we must reject this or else change our notions of matter. Tracing 'the line of life' backwards, he says we find it more and more approaching the purely physical.

Believing, as I do, in the continuity of nature I cannot stop abruptly where our microscopes cease to be of use. Here the vision of the mind authoritatively supplements the vision of the eye. By a necessity engendered and justified by science I cross the boundary of the experimental evidence, and discern in that Matter which we, in our ignorance of its latent powers, and notwithstanding our professed reverence for its Creator, here hitherto covered with opprobrium, the promise and potency of all terrestrial life.[1]

Tyndall takes heart for his belief in the potency of matter to create life in 'the structural power of matter as evinced in the phenomena of crystallization', but his faith in the 'necessity' he invokes is really grounded, as he makes clear, in the law of conservation of energy. Among the 'grand generalizations' reached by science at the present time, the theory of the origin of species is one, but

> Another of still wider grasp and more radical significance, is the doctrine of the Conservation of Energy, the ultimate philosophical issues of which are as yet but dimly seen ... exactly from every antecedent its equivalent consequent, from every consequent its equivalent antecedent, and bringing vital as well as physical phenomena under the dominion of that law of causal connection which, so far as the human understanding has yet pierced, asserts itself everywhere in nature.[2]

T. H. Huxley (1825–95), in his essay on 'The Physical Basis of Life' in 1868, summed up the argument for continuity: 'Protoplasm [the new term emerging from the investigation of cells], simple or nucleated, is the formal basis of all life.' The elements of which life is built, carbon, hydrogen, oxygen and nitrogen, and their components, are lifeless, 'But when they are brought together, under certain circumstances, they give rise to ... protoplasm, and this protoplasm exhibits the phenomena of life. I see no break in this series of molecular complication.' Huxley always denied being a materialist; materialism was metaphysics. But the progress of science 'has in all ages meant, and now more than ever means, the extension of the province of what we call matter and causation, and the concomitant gradual banishment from all regions of known thought of what we call spirit and spontaneity'.

---

[1] John Tyndall, *Fragments of Science* (2 vols, London, 1899), ii, p. 191.
[2] Tyndall, *Fragments*, ii, pp. 180–1.

## *1.3  The Enigma of Consciousness and the Impact of Evolution*

Apart from the origin of life, the final and most formidable barrier to the reductive enterprise was generally acknowledged to be that of consciousness. Tyndall, in a meditation entitled 'Musings on the Matterhorn' in 1868, gave vivid expression to the notion of consciousness as the last frontier, taking as a microcosm of all existence the Matterhorn, and the reflections it had aroused in him on a climbing expedition on 27 July 1868. He reflected, he said, with melancholy on the mortality of the great mountain, constantly undergoing erosion and decay by the action of wind and water. This led in turn to the thought of its formation and to 'that nebulous haze which philosophers have regarded, and with good reason, as the proximate source of all material things'. The potential Matterhorn, the materials of which it is composed, had unquestionably been already contained in it. But there was a further question: 'did that formless fog contain potentially the *sadness* with which I regarded the Matterhorn? Did the *thought* which now ran back to it simply return to its final home?' Were consciousness and emotion continuous with the physical world or extraneous to it? Tyndall left the question hanging, having ingeniously implied for materialism the comfort of a return to the womb, but it was being increasingly thought, as he well knew, that the answer might lie in neurology.

Physiologically based psychology had had to shed the legacy of a premature materialism, once widely appealing but subsequently embarrassing, in the form of phrenology, the discipline which, in the earlier part of the century, had professed to locate character and disposition in the conformation of the skull. Phrenology had been taken up very seriously by some: Comte had believed in it, Spencer had dabbled in it, but it had been subjected to a devastating demolition by Flourens. The physio-psychologists of the mid-century were inheritors of more usable ideas than those of phrenology. Flourens had pioneered systematic experiments on the location of brain functions; the distinction between sensory and motor nerves, dating from the 1830s, was known as the Bell–Magendie function after its joint discoverers, respectively English and French. The English physiologist Marshall Hall, in 1833, had drawn the crucial distinction between voluntary and reflex action, launching the nineteenth century on its long and intense preoccupation with the latter as the matrix from which the former had perhaps developed, and perhaps also in some way for the deliberation which in human beings preceded voluntary action. Reflex action came to be seen as the effect of physiologically stored memory of earlier experiences and response to them, made habitual over time, and heritable. Reflex was clearly physical because it could be produced at will by artificial stimulation of the nerves as well as by the appearance of the psychological or instinctual trigger. It was therefore a point of intersection between the effects of life experiences and mechanical stimuli. If the formation of reflexes and their inheritance formed the key to instinct, and if the higher functions of consciousness could be seen as self-correcting instinct, perhaps this process might be mapped physiologically in the development of the cerebral cortex and the hemispheres of the brain, though admittedly, for the moment, the latter remained a long shot.

The assumed process must clearly be a developmental one. Darwin, in *The Origin*, wrote that if evolution were accepted 'Psychology will be based on a new foundation'. He was already a little late. It was Herbert Spencer (1820–1903), in his *Principles of Psychology* (1855), who most fully linked the physiological approach to consciousness to the idea of biological evolution. Evolution for him was at that point, and predominantly remained, J. B. Lamarck's conception of the direct adaptation of the living organism to its environment by the formation of new habits and organs, and the storage of the former in a physical form in which it could be inherited.

For Spencer, adaptation of all organic life to its environment was the key. Mind had gradually evolved out of life as a form of adaptation. Simple reflex motions were compounded, by repetition and inheritance, into instincts, in which lay the origins of conscious life. Instinct was the organization of memory. Spencer's Lamarckianism was combined with the English associationist tradition in psychology in a synthesis of environmental conditioning and instinct. According to associationist theory, the constant conjunction of two sensations or 'ideas' in individual experience ensured that the future occurrence of one would automatically evoke the other in the mind. In the new, physiological and Lamarckian version, the related images postulated by associationism were neurally stored as revivable stimuli and the reflex responses to these were inherited in the form of instinct. All that was left for consciousness was deliberately to adjudicate between different stimuli as triggers to action. The lower functions, however, did not necessarily disappear with the development of the higher but could co-exist with them and reappear as regression, a thought to which we shall have to return in a later chapter. There was, of course, in psychology no equivalent to the fossil record in tracing evolutionary sequences, but living animals and humans could be, and were, seen on an evolutionary scale provided by the increasing complexity of organs and functions. Spencer's overall psychological message was clear: the highest forms of consciousness 'are the effects of a complication that has arisen by insensible steps out of the simplest elements'.

It was in the later 1850s, after completing *Principles of Psychology*, that Spencer was to conceive the project of imaginative synthesis, his 'Synthetic Philosophy' which was to occupy the rest of his long life (he died in 1903) and to be embodied in a series of works from the 1860s to the 1890s, beginning with *First Principles* in 1862 and continuing with *Principles of Biology* in 1864. *Principles of Psychology*, of course, really belonged at the next point in the sequence but was already published; the 1870s were devoted to *Principles of Sociology* (1876–83), on which his subsequent reputation was chiefly to rest when the grand scientific synthesis had become outdated, and the last years were devoted to Ethics. No other contemporary monument to the belief in the continuity of matter, life and thought, and the laws governing them, could remotely equal it in volume and laboriousness of construction.

The 'Synthetic Philosophy', outlined in *First Principles*, derived from the fusion of Lamarckian evolutionism to which Spencer had subscribed since the 1840s, and in *Social Statics* (1851) had already begun to apply to human society, with the concept of the conservation of energy. This seems to have begun to preoccupy him around 1857, when, as he wrote in his *Autobiography*, 'the scientific world was becoming everywhere possessed by the general doctrine of the "Conservation of Force" as it was then called'. It formed the fundamental premiss of *First Principles* and therefore in a sense of all Spencer's subsequent work. The ultimate metaphysical question of the nature and cause of existence, which Spencer called 'the Unknowable', was beyond the reach of human understanding, but the phenomenal world was an unbreakable chain of transformations of matter and energy. This consciousness, as we would expect, made no gap in the chain:

> the law of metamorphosis which holds among the physical forces, holds equally between them and the mental forces. Those modes of the Unknowable which we call motion, heat, light, chemical affinity, etc., are alike transformable into each other and into those modes of the Unknowable which we distinguish as sensation, emotion, thought . . . How this metamorphosis takes place – how a force existing as motion, heat or light can become a mode of consciousness – how it is possible for aerial vibrations to generate the sensation we call sound, or for the forces liberated by chemical changes in the brain to give rise to emotion

– these are mysteries. But they are not profounder mysteries than the transformations of the physical forces into each other.[3]

But what was the form of this fundamental 'law of metamorphosis'? Spencer identified it as evolution, to which he gave the highest general sense possible, incorporating not only organisms but the inorganic and the social. Evolution ran from the formation of concentrations of matter out of an original gas cloud – Laplace's 'Nebular Hypothesis' on which Spencer had written – to the formation of social institutions and coherent forms of social life and cooperation out of primal, undifferentiated human hordes of asocial beings. It also, of course, incorporated species differentiation and the development of the adult organism from the fertilized embryo. In all of these manifestations Spencer saw a significant parallelism. Force acquired coherence as specific forms of integrated matter and dissipated itself as motion – 'the continuous redistribution of matter and motion'. Every change is in the direction either of Evolution – greater coherence – or Dissolution. Plants grow by concentrating elements previously diffused as gases, and animals grow by concentrating elements previously dispersed in surrounding plants and animals.

Evolution in its most abstract sense, then, was this increasing coherence – integration – but also, concomitantly, differentiation, the development of heterogeneity out of an original homogeneity, as exemplified in the creation of planetary systems and the evolution of diverging species. The controlling explanatory concept was that of adaptation, broadened from its Lamarckian application in the organic world to govern the behaviour of matter as such by the analogy that Force always follows the line of least resistance. This was the key to all development of cosmic heterogeneity. It had for some time been claimed that the line of evolution (or 'transmutation') was from simple to complex. Spencer made this a derivation from the fundamental laws governing matter and motion. Greater heterogeneity, as Spencer saw, also implied greater coherence, as, in the organic world, a highly differentiated organism, with different organs performing special-ist functions, would require a central nervous system and even a brain to co-ordinate the functioning of the parts. In the next chapter we shall have to consider the influence in social thought of Spencer's concept of Evolu-tion as differentiation or the social division of labour, which he saw (picking up the phrase of the physiologist Milne-Edwards, 'the physiological divi-sion of labour') as both physiological and social. Evolution as differentiation

[3] Herbert Spencer, *First Principles* (5th edn, London, 1884), p. 217.

and integration was universal, except that it stood in a constant, antagonistic relation to the reverse process, Dissolution.

There is a temptation to regard Spencer's concept of the Unknowable as simply a kind of ground-clearing, a hurrying off the stage of the ultimate questions of the nature and cause of existence itself, akin to Kant's 'thing in itself' unknowable through the representations of the senses, but also consistent with the Comtean positivist declaration that science deals only with phenomena. As Spencer put it, 'the connection between the phenomenal order and the ontological order is for ever inscrutable'. Yet it was also much more than an epistemological convenience; it was, if the text is any guide, conceived as a real replacement for the traditional conception of God, in which 'personal superintendence becomes merged in universal immanence'. Spencer speaks in what seem like genuinely religious accents of 'a Power of which the nature remains for ever inconceivable and to which no limits in Time or Space can be imagined [which] works in us certain effects', declaring that belief in such a power 'is that fundamental element in religion which survives all its changes of form'.

It was a not uncommon kind of reverence. Spencer's 'universal immanence' seems to point to a kind of pantheism, while his combination of 'the unknowable' with the scientific *hubris* which dreamt of some future 'total and specific interpretation of each phenomenon in its entirety, as well as of phenomena in general', incorporates both the aspiration to a total conception of life and the world and a cultivated awe before ultimate incomprehensibility. Both piety before the universe and the conception of universal law and the possibility therefore of an omni-comprehensive knowledge of it, in which consciousness, a phenomenal product, should as it were master all phenomena, were common in the third quarter of the century. They help to explain some of the interpretations and distortions to which Darwin's more limited and cautious version of evolution, bold though it was in strictly biological terms, was subject in the decades after the publication of *The Origin of Species* in 1859.

Contemporaries inevitably assimilated Darwinian evolution to their own contexts of thought and emotional response: defensive, embattled, optimistic, hubristic, polemically materialist, latently or explicitly pantheistic. In the history of biology Darwin (1809–82), with A. R. Wallace, stands out above all in the establishment of the theory of natural selection, making redundant, though this was a slow process, the undemonstrable Lamarckian assumption of permanent modification of the organism and the species by use and inheritance. Darwin focused instead on the random variations observable in offspring and the utility of some of these in a given environment, by conferring an advantage in survival and successful breeding on their possessors, ensuring the passing on of advantageous variations to future generations. The constant environmental pressure on populations, and the elimination of those less equipped to fill the niche offered by the environment, would ensure the accumulation and successive improvement, relative to an environment, of the favourable variation until new species were, after a long period of time, produced.

The acceptance of Darwin's theory by a number – not all – of the eminent 'men of science' in the course of the 1860s was a crucial aspect of the authority the theory of evolution came to acquire, though this may have owed as much to Darwin's impressive marshalling of the corroborating evidence, and his painstaking explanations of its lacunae, as to the theory itself. Natural selection was sometimes rejected, often sidelined, sometimes distorted by those who accepted the evidence for evolution; even Darwin himself continued to use the Lamarckian notion of the inheritance of acquired characters, as well as his own subsidiary principle of Sexual Selection, and came to do so more freely in the successive editions of *The Origin*, as criticisms of his theory mounted. The most troublesome objections, leading to something like a trough in Darwin's reputation around the turn of the century, were two: first, that (in the absence of the genetic concepts later to be grounded in the rediscovery of the ideas of Mendel) there seemed no answer to the accusation that the chance of a particular variation being inherited would be halved in each generation, eventually being 'blended out'; second, that a revised estimate of the age of the earth, based on its supposed rate of cooling, allowed too little time for Darwinian evolution to produce the complexity and variety of the earth's species.

There was also, of course, the simpler option of rejection of evolution from the standpoint of Christian orthodoxy: Bishop Wilberforce (1805–73) had perhaps a stronger theological point than he has been credited with when, in his hostile review of *The Origin*, he pointed to the incongruity between evolution and an incarnational religion, in the former's implications for the Saviour's remoter ancestry in the female line. Initial responses in Britain to Darwinian evolution focused immediately and emphatically on something Darwin had deliberately avoided, though he dealt with it later, in *The Descent of Man* (1871): the question of human evolution. This was the crux of the famous Wilberforce–Huxley debate at the 1860 Oxford meeting of the British Association and of Huxley's extension of it, three years later, in his anatomical account placing man in the order of apes, in

*Man's Place in Nature.* One of the points of greatest sensitivity for contemporaries, also raised by materialism, was that which had earlier focused shocked attention in Britain, from the 1830s onwards, on the scholarly critique by David Friedrich Strauss and his followers of the gospel accounts of the Resurrection: the implication for the doctrine of immortality. If, as Darwin had written in his notebooks, speaking of the animal kingdom, 'we may be all netted together', at what point in evolution might the immortal soul have made its debut and how?

Strauss, in his 1835 *Life of Jesus*, while denying the historicity of Jesus' miracles, and treating the accounts of his life as myth, had none the less treated Christianity with some reverence: it expressed in mythic form a leap of human consciousness, as the vehicle of the World-Spirit manifesting itself, as taught by Hegel, in human history. In Strauss's last work, however, *The Old Belief and the New* (1872), residual piety towards Christianity was decisively replaced by the gospel of science, including Darwinism, and reverence was redirected towards the natural laws governing the universe, as revealed by science. While Hegel's concept of the self-revelation of the World-Spirit had stood godfather to Strauss's old faith, Darwin was invoked to occupy something like the same role in the new, though Strauss was a considerably better Hegelian than he became a Darwinian, for the new faith was little less than nature worship. Strauss's book was intended as, and in some respects was, an optimistic summation of the new outlook prompted and sanctioned by science. Nietzsche attacked it in his *Untimely Reflections* as smug, philistine and philosophically naive.

Christianity, Strauss proclaimed, was now incredible to the educated. The Book of Genesis and science were incompatible and the idea of Atonement was a primitive one. So little was known about Jesus that he could not be taken as a moral example; the Christ of faith was legendary. Darwin had demonstrated the absence of design or purpose in the universe. What was left? Strauss's answer seemed largely to ignore the Darwinian lesson he claimed to have learnt. The universe itself was the 'highest idea', and in it we recognize order and goodness and rationality, and we surrender ourselves to it 'in loving trust'. Though purpose is denied there is a strong Hegelian echo in the idea of a human mission to 'ennoble' nature; nature 'willed to surpass itself'. Strauss's book, for all its incoherences, went through six editions in as many months. The orthodox were naturally outraged, and sophisticated minds were repelled by Strauss's simplicities, but it became common, most particularly it seems in Germany, having expelled God and even, ostensibly, teleology from nature, to invest nature itself with at least some of the attributes of divinity.

In Britain inspiriting, teleologizing versions of evolution were certainly not lacking, but the damage done by Darwinism to the English tradition of Natural Theology was long to heal. Natural Theology purported to find evidence of God's benevolence in all the ingenious contrivances of nature, which Darwin now explained as consequences of natural selection. Even before Darwin's *Origin* the ruthlessness apparently revealed in the fossil record, with large-scale and unscriptural extinctions of species, was felt and found eloquent expression in Alfred Tennyson's *In Memoriam* (1850). Tennyson (1809–1892) there lamented the indifference of nature not only to the individual life but to the elimination of whole species. Waste seemed everywhere. Tennyson's famous line 'Nature red in tooth and claw' is pre-Darwinian. The apparently inexplicable disappearance of species – far too spread through time to be explained by the Biblical Flood, even if one allowed the unorthodoxy of a design-fault in the dimensions of the ark, were perturbing in a context still set by creationism. Either the creator had built eliminations of species into the plan for creation or he had experienced second thoughts. It seemed possible to vindicate his benevolence only at the cost of his omniscience or vice versa. Contemplating the ruins of Natural Theology rather than biblical literalism Tennyson saw man confounded

> Who trusted God was love indeed
> And love Creation's final law.[4]

The natural world, once 'the great world's altar-stairs', no longer offered steps to the mind of God. The poetry of wistfully reluctant unbelief, prompted by Strauss's mythologizing of Jesus or by the harshness of a Godless natural world, became something of an English genre, from Tennyson through Matthew Arnold and Clough and, with Thomas Hardy (1840–1928), even into the early twentieth century.

Darwinism, in a sense, came to the rescue in the dilemma proclaimed in *In Memoriam*. Natural ruthlessness, as natural selection, was also in a sense creative, if not exactly purposive. But it remained ruthlessness. Hardy expressed a post-Darwinian sensibility particularly uncompromisingly. In his novel *The Woodlanders* (1887) the trees in the forest jostle and choke each other like 'the depraved crowds of a city slum. The leaf was deformed, the

[4] Alfred Tennyson, 'In Memoriam', LVI, in *The Poems of Tennyson*, ed. Christopher Ricks (London, 1969), p. 417.

curve was crippled, the taper was interrupted; the lichen ate the vigour of the stalk and the ivy slowly strangled to death the promising sapling.' Elsewhere in the novel the coming of a sylvan dawn becomes the signal for the retirement of 'Owls that had been catching mice in the outhouses, rabbits that had been eating the winter green in the gardens, and stoats that had been sucking the blood of the rabbits'. In Natural Theology, the front teeth of rabbits, so perfectly adapted to their requirements, had been a mark of the divine benevolence and care. Hardy wrote his epitaphs for a benign creator and for Christian belief with a frank nostalgia. On Christmas Eve

> We pictured the meek mild creatures where
> They dwelt in their strawy pen,
> Nor did it occur to one of us there
> To doubt they were kneeling then.[5]

Another source of gloom in the contemplation of nature was, by the end of the century, the second law of thermodynamics, which seemed to predict the inexorable approach of a steady-state solar system, a dead world and an extinguished sun, which the equalization of energy had deprived of all motion. Rudolf Clausius (1822–88) had restated the second law in 1854 in terms of entropy. The universe was tending to a state of 'thermal death'. In Britain William Thompson, Lord Kelvin (1824–1907), predicted with the authority of science a world eventually unfit for habitation. Literary imagination responded.

Tennyson, doing his duty by contemporary science in his second *Locksley Hall* poem (1886), wrote that

> The moon, astronomy tells us, is dead:
> Dead, but how her glory lights the hall, the dune, the grass!
> Yet the moonlight is the sunlight and the sun herself will pass.

But perhaps the most powerful evocation of a dying world is the experience of H. G. Wells' Time-Traveller:

> I cannot convey the sense of abominable desolation that hung over the world. The red eastern sky, the northward blackness, the salt Dead Sea, the stony beach crawling with these foul, slow-stirring monsters, the uniform, poisonous-looking green of the lichenous plants, the thin air that hurt one's lungs, all contributed to an appalling effect.[6]

[5] Thomas Hardy, 'The Oxen', in *The Complete Poetical Works of Thomas Hardy*, ed. Samuel Hynes (5 vols, Oxford, 1982–95), ii, p. 206.

[6] H. G. Wells, *The Time Machine* in, *The Short Stories of H. G. Wells* (London, 1952), p. 83.

Native traditions and interests naturally shaped responses to implications of science, including Darwinism, for long-standing beliefs. In England they were influenced by the strength of the religious traditions of the earlier part of the century, the uncritical Evangelical use of the Bible, and Natural Theology. In France neither evolution nor the materialism often treated as an inference from it was new. Darwin was disappointed by the reception of his book there and Lamarck (1744–1829) for long remained the predominant influence in French biology. Some of its leading figures like Bernard and Pasteur ignored Darwinism or remained agnostic. The issue of evolution became entangled with the contemporary preoccupation with the spontaneous generation of life, in which many wished to believe though Pasteur had demolished the evidence. Flourens, for example, drew the inference that since spontaneous generation was disproved, creationism was vindicated. Elsewhere Darwin was assimilated to the materialist traditions of militant French anti-clericalism, notably (to his annoyance), by his idiosyncratic and intrusive translator, the formidable Clémence Royer. In general the impact of Darwin in France was much less than in Britain, Germany or Russia, while the concept of evolution itself was pervasive.

In Germany, though the assertive materialism of the 1850s had not been evolutionist it had in a sense prepared the ground. Darwinism made rapid headway in the scientific community. Carl Vogt became one of its leading proponents, though Virchow rejected it. Some materialists found it insufficiently rigorous and far-reaching. Moleschott and Büchner tended to prefer the directly modifying influence of the environment to natural selection, as more mechanical, and Büchner regretted that Darwin had not traced the origin of life to a single, spontaneously generated form; he had remained too creationist. Everywhere Darwin's achievement in eliminating teleology from evolution through the concept of natural selection was widely ignored or misunderstood. The divergent, branching tree with which Darwin had illustrated his conception of evolution in *The Origin* was tacitly, or even explicitly, replaced by an image of a single, central line of the development of life, culminating in humanity. Darwinian evolution was assimilated to pre-existing notions of teleology and progress, either implicitly or by interpreting 'Natural Selection' in purposive terms. Even in English the phrase gave trouble; in German *Zuchtverwahl* sounded even more purposive. '*Zucht*' means 'breeding' or even 'good breeding', and '*Wahl*' means 'choice'.

As the supposed scientific endorsement of progress, a teleologized version of evolution – which could, as always, be interpreted pantheistically, or as the specific form assumed by the divine plan – was well placed to become an optimistic creed for the *bien pensant* and enlightened, in which the elements of randomness and ruthlessness which troubled sensitive souls could be discreetly submerged. In Germany in particular, the heritage of *Naturphilosophie*, which had interpreted transformism as the working out of an immanent Idea and had fostered a materialistic or even pantheistic form of piety, cast its shadow over the reception of Darwinian evolution as a comprehensive vision of nature. Darwin's leading German champion and popularizer Ernst Haeckel (1834–1919), for example, spoke of himself as a materialist, but increasingly professed, under the name of Monism, a kind of enthusiastic, vitalist nature-religion of sentimental awe in contemplation of the All. What he found in Darwin, he said, was 'a great unified conception of nature' and 'the universal theory of development'; Haeckel was one of those, as one of his illustrations (he was a passionate morphologist) showed, for whom the evolutionary tree had one central trunk to the very top. Evolution was reified by Haeckel as 'a cosmic force' and, conversely, spoken of as 'a manifestation of the creative energy of nature'.

Haeckel, a vehement anti-Christian who proclaimed his own evolutionist nature-religion as its successor, was not only a great morphologist but a highly successful polemicist and popularizer; his *Riddle of the World* (1899) sold 100,000 copies in its first year. What Haeckel popularized in the form of evolution was the World-Soul. All matter was alive and possessed mental attributes: 'Desire and dislike, lust and antipathy, attraction and repulsion, are common to all atoms'. It was not a new thought – one finds something like it in Saint-Simon, but it is as though matter was paying for having had the presumption to subsume human beings by being, in its turn, anthropomorphized. Haeckel's Monism was in one sense a high point of the scientific outlook, but how much of it remained in any recognizable sense scientific was obviously questionable. This is the paradox of the mid-nineteenth-century materialist bid to take over the world. The more matter assumed the properties of everything in existence, the less like matter it looked; the more the scientific view of the world seemed to replace religion, the more of its predecessor's metaphysical and emotional and even ethical responsibilities it seemed to have to assume.

## 1.4 The Claims of Science; Science as Vocation

To speak of aspirations to intellectual hegemony and to replace religion is not, in some cases, an exaggeration. Rivalry with the authority of churches and pastors was entirely conscious, and it became a cliché to speak, like

Draper, of the warfare of science with religion; that the war was possible was due at least as much to the metaphysical and moral claims made on behalf of the former as to any residual cosmological meddling of the latter. Tyndall said, 'We claim, and shall wrest from theology, the entire domain of cosmological theory'; and Huxley that '[science] is teaching the world that the ultimate court of appeal is observation and experiment, and not authority; she is . . . creating a firm and living faith in the existence of immutable moral and physical laws, perfect obedience to which is the highest possible aim of an intelligent being'. Huxley was a considerable prose artist who can hardly have been unaware of the religiosity of the diction 'firm and living faith' and 'perfect obedience'. His writings are said to have provided assurance to young Russian Nihilists like Bazarov that natural science provided the key to the good life and the improvement of the human lot. The writ of the scientist was to run, as Comte had envisaged, in the realm of human society. As Moleschott, no Comtean, put it, the solution of 'the social problem' (essentially poverty) lay in the hands of the scientists. Science – often as 'evolution' or the requirements of 'development' – was to provide the basis for ethics. Haeckel produced out of his Monist creed a decidedly hierarchical and strenuous set of social prescriptions. Leslie Stephen (1832–1904), on the basis of evolution, produced a voluminous though unread work *The Science of Ethics* (1882). Spencer devoted the latter part of his life to establishing the authority of his own laissez-faire version of evolutionary science in sociology and ethics, while one of his leading critics – Huxley was another – the French sociologist Emile Durkheim, never doubted that it was to the scientist, in his role as sociologist, that the shaky French Third Republic must look to establish the ethical foundations of a secure civic republicanism, though he refused, unlike Spencer, to accept that its fundamental concepts would be derived from biology.

But science was not only to provide the ground of social ethics; its practice and principles were themselves an ethic – the highest, prescribing duties and claiming undeviating allegiance, like a religious vocation. Stephen, actually one of its drier exponents, wrote in his essay 'An Agnostic's Apology', 'where is the shame of ignorance in matters still involved in endless and hopeless controversy? Is it not rather a duty?' This came close to making unfounded belief a kind of sin. W. K. Clifford (1845–79), Professor of Mathematics at University College, London, went much further. Clifford, who also wrote an article entitled 'On the Scientific Basis of Morals', planned a book called *The Creed of Science*, which under the heading of 'What Ought we to Believe' spoke of 'the duty of inquiry and the sin of credulity'. In an essay on 'The Ethics of Belief' he wrote that 'No sympathy of mind, no obscurity of station, can escape the universal duty of questioning all that we believe' and 'it is wrong always and everywhere, and for anyone, to believe anything upon insufficient evidence'. The method of science was the condition of virtue, the one thing necessary. Some Victorian domestic employers took an interest in the religious principles of applicants; it is irresistible to think of Clifford setting tests of agnosticism for prospective housemaids.

In Germany in the 1850s scientific inquiry seems to have taken over from post-Hegelian philosophy the crucial role in human emancipation; Carl Vogt, championing its right of unfettered investigation, wrote that every church was a restriction of the free development of the human spirit. But nowhere perhaps did the idea of scientists and scholars as the new, dedicated elite, heroes of the spirit, the priesthood of the religion of the pursuit of truth, and the vanguard of humanity, receive more ascetic yet enthusiastic expression than in France after 1848 and in the stifling intellectual atmosphere of the early Second Empire. Ernest Renan (1823–92) and Hippolyte Taine (1828–93) are exemplary in this respect. In their case, of course, the interpolation of 'and scholars' after 'scientists' is essential if we are not to interpret what they say in too physical a fashion. For Renan it was the ideal scholar who was at the centre of his concern, though the rigorous employment of scientific methods, disciplined empirical inquiry and criticism of sources, was part of his characterization; Renan's work, under the rubric of 'science', belonged wholly in the humanities. So for the most part did Taine's, though in *On Intelligence* (1870) he tried to synthesize philosophical and physiological approaches to psychology. However, his belief in the universal empire of causality in human affairs as in nature forbade the erection of any crucial barrier between the human and physical sciences. We shall have therefore to consider them both in the next chapter.

What makes it indispensable to consider them here, apart from their key roles in French intellectual life from the 1860s to the 1880s, when they enjoyed an almost unchallenged general pre-eminence, is the eloquence and deep feeling with which they articulated the ideal of science, in the widest sense, as a vocation, extolling its ethic and its rewards. The German materialists, as we have seen, regarded science as the pursuit of revolutionary activity by other means. In France, though there was the same sense of a stifled or suspended public life from 1851 to 1870, the shock of Revolution and still more of the subsequent violent repression of the Parisian workers by the Republic, and the *coup d'état* of 1851 which destroyed it, inflicted psychological wounds too deep for any optimistic sense of the merely temporary postponement of emancipation. Revolution and democracy had themselves become Janus-faced. Hopes for humanity in the mass became more tentative and long-term and even tinged with disgust. There was in Renan's and Taine's notion of the vocation of science a cloistral character quite alien to the British or the Germans, an interior emigration akin to aestheticism, into a kind of Platonic world of untroubled rationality and freedom from compromise and vicissitude, though the method itself was to be empirical. Science was the one goddess who would never betray her worshippers. Humanity might still be a deity, but for the moment one in heavy, not to say grubby, disguise, whose transfiguring apotheosis might be a long way off; alas for the hopes of the Saint-Simonians, of Pierre Leroux and George Sand.

This was one of the messages of *The Future of Science*, the manifesto that Renan wrote but did not publish in the wake of 1848. It was a reaffirmation of faith in progress, but it was also one of those works, like some of Marx's writing after 1848, in which the writer seems to be reconciling himself to the long haul after the dashing of apocalyptic expectations. Even so, in a preface written long afterwards, the old Renan found it over-optimistic. But 'science' was not only the long-term hope of human perfection, it was also, in itself, beyond the reach of social upheavals, so that he personally in 1848 and after was , he says, 'solitary and calm in the midst of universal agitation', because 'living solely in the intellect and believing frenetically in truth'.

Taine, who was a little younger, entered the Ecole Normale Supérieure in 1848. His letters in this period and in the early 1850s are much given to the theme of withdrawal from a chaotic and distasteful external life, and the private pursuit of perfection in the search for truth and what he saw as consciousness of the universal. A commentator speaks of his 'metaphysical intoxication' at this point, when his guiding lights were Spinoza and Hegel. Like Renan he explicitly compared science to religion: 'science is infallible' and offers a sight of the universal, 'the logical connection and necessity of things'. The task of the self he described in Hegelian-sounding phrases as being 'to individualize the universal and to universalize the individual', but the instrument of metaphysical ambition had become, for him, empirical science. The ambition was combined with a considerable self-pity; 'real life,' he wrote in 1848, 'is so full of disgust and suffering that one must retreat into oneself'; and in 1851, speaking for the élite of his generation (for him more or less co-extensive with the graduates of the Ecole Normale Supérieure), he said 'We must keep silent, obey, live in silence.' He lamented his academic relegation from Paris to Poitiers as vocally as any exile of the early 1850s. The exaltation of the vocation of science for him derived, intellectually, from the Idealist metaphysics of the first half of the century, despite the fact that in philosophy he was becoming an empiricist who dissolved the Ego into its passing sensations. It was also a strategy of self-preservation.

The emotional costs of the scientific enterprise, however, were sometimes dwelt on by its devotees in a spirit of conscious heroism and sacrifice for truth. Renan feared the eradication of 'poetry' from the world – his word for the emotional dimension of religion. Büchner fell for a while into deep depression, but asserted that truth must be acknowledged even if it were ugly. Clifford, incidentally another enthusiast for Spinoza, resolved 'to accept the facts as they are, however bitter' and looked to future consolation, speaking of science as more politically inclined Europeans sometimes spoke of Revolution: 'Without mercy and without resentment she plows up weed and briar; from her footsteps behind her grow up corn and healing flowers.' The great prize, as we have seen in the case of Taine, was often envisaged as no less than the complete, comprehensive vision of the universe as a set of comprehensible relations, and the individual's submission, joyful or stoic, to its laws. Moleschott, referring to the endless recycling of energy, death always in life, life in death, wrote of 'cherishing joyously the feeling of relationship one has with the universe', while Büchner emerged from his depression with 'a feeling of the eternal, invisible spirit of the All permeating me'. We have already seen similar feelings in Haeckel and Taine. Spencer, in *First Principles*, spoke of his adumbration of a totally integrated knowledge of all the phenomena of the universe as his 'Philosophico-Religious doctrine'.

### 1.5 The Reaction against Materialism: Phenomenalism, Pragmatism and Pan-psychism

But if knowledge of the All and the sense of one's identification with it was the ultimate goal, what exactly was it knowledge of? Laws, certainly, but laws governing the behaviour of what? Kantians (and Positivists) held aloof from ultimate questions of ontology; phenomena, mediated through the senses, would have to do. Huxley, whose mentor in epistemology seems unfashionably to have been David Hume rather than Kant, was clear: 'all our knowledge is knowledge of states of consciousness'. Others, as we have seen, were less metaphysically reticent; the scientific view of the world and the reductionist project were obviously most challenging when proclaimed as 'materialism', and it was as 'materialism' that they were usually denounced. Increasingly, however, there was a tendency to declare that the conflict between 'materialism' and 'spiritualism' was none of science's business, a mere matter of words, and to proclaim a kind of equivalence.

Even Büchner wrote in his *Nature and Spirit* (1857), only two years after the great materialist *coup* of his *Force and Matter*, a dialogue between a Materialist and an Idealist, in which the latter claimed that one could as easily make *Kraft* (force) primary and *Stoff* (Matter) secondary; Büchner, like a number of others, began to replace 'materialism' by the increasingly fashionable, non-committal term 'Monism'. The distinctions were often elusive and much might depend on tone and diction; an emotional tremor in the prose, a fit of unguarded exaltation, could turn a reductive material-ism into a vitalist monism or even an enthusiastic pantheism, just as an incautious phrase, a spasm of metaphysical *hubris*, could turn a Positivist phenomenalism into a materialist ontology. The challenge of Materialism depended on making all activity a property of matter, but one could as eas-ily, it seemed, regard matter as simply particular concentrations of energy, and physics seemed increasingly to encourage one to do so. The more that was invested in the attributes of matter, including sometimes conscious-ness, the less it looked merely material; if matter could assume the properties of spirit then might one not as easily say that spirit assumed the properties of matter, rather as Schelling and Hegel had done? Marx claimed to have stood Hegel the right way up, but which was the right way up to stand the universe?

Spencer ended *First Principles* in this even-handed fashion. Claiming that the position he had outlined was 'not a degradation of the so-called higher, but an elevation of the so-called lower', he pointed out that 'the establishment of correlation and equivalence between the forces of the outer and inner world, may be used to assimilate either to the other'. There is a rather startlingly twentieth-century air about his suggestion that it is only the grammar of subject and object that seems to oblige us to choose between Spirit and Matter. Taine made a rather similar point in *On Intelli-gence*, in which he attempted to integrate philosophical and physiological psychology, arguing, like a good Spinozan, that sensation and the internal movement of the nervous centres may be at bottom one and the same unique event, 'condemned by the two ways in which it is known, always and irre-mediably to appear double', and he drew the analogy of the ways we can experience an electrical charge, either perceptually as light or heat or as a blow. He concluded that there is really neither substance nor force, only events; 'all else is metaphysics'.

Spencer, Taine, Huxley always denied that they were materialists. Of course there could be costs to a proclaimed materialism, if only in arousing unnecessary opposition, and opponents may have regarded their disclaimers as mere prevarication, but there was plenty of evidence that they would have been wrong. Taine was particularly vehement in his denial of materialism when he was lobbying to be elected to the Académie Française, but he had always denied it, even as a young man in the 1850s. Perhaps his best-known pronouncement, that virtue and vice are products, like sugar and vitriol, was as misleading as Feuerbach's 'Man ist was er isst'. Taine did not mean that virtue and vice were products like sugar or vitriol; he meant that like sugar and vitriol, virtue and vice were products. He was endorsing something from which he never receded (as Spencer did not), the universal reign of causality. Taine may not have been a materialist but he certainly proclaimed himself a determinist.

It was determinism as well as materialism which eventually came increasingly under attack. The power of the challenge of materialism had owed much to the supposed elaboration of the more complex laws of life and mind on the basis of Newtonian mechanics. Science was uniform. As Huxley said, 'the universe is one and the same throughout', and Tyndall spoke of science as 'organized common sense'. Much of the wider plausibility of the reductive enterprise derived from this continuity between science and common sense. Proselytes for common sense ought perhaps always to prefer Aristotle, but more than a century of acceptance had established the common-sense credentials of Newtonian mechanics, which, in turn, helped to make its extension seem irresistible. Tyndall, while conceding the point about convertibility being able to be run either way, seemed to make the case for materialism on methodological rather than metaphysical grounds: 'matter may be regarded as a form of thought, thought may be regarded as a property of matter. But with a view to the progress of science the materialistic tendency is in every way to be preferred. For it connects thought with the other phenomena of the universe.' What it in fact tried to connect thought with was Newtonian mechanics, which was also continuous with a 'common-sense' conception of explanation. But it was precisely this continuity with Newtonian mechanics that new fundamental work in physics in the latter part of the century increasingly made untenable. It is presumably a long time now since anyone described physics as common sense.

Materialist reductionism and determinism based on a supposed unbroken chain of causality both came to be challenged in the last decades of the century, on several grounds: supposed naïveté in propounding an arbitrary metaphysics, a naïveté which seemed all the more glaring as a powerful Kantian revival in epistemology occurred in Germany and France (in Britain it was neo-Hegelian); their incongruity with new developments in physics, as energy increasingly took centre stage from matter, and physical reality was identified simply as events describable in mathematical terms. Theories were developed for ranges of phenomena, beginning with the electro-magnetic field, which were hard to interpret in terms of Newtonian mechanics. However powerful in their own spheres the new theories might be, they ensured that 'science' presented a less homogeneous face to the world. Theoretical pluralism and the increasing disposition to treat theories as working hypotheses made untenable the naïve assumption that science provided a literal picture or copy of how the world 'really' was. The early twentieth century was entering the subatomic world, not at this point microscopically examinable, to which the hard, deterministic laws of Newtonian mechanics and earlier atomic theory seemed inapplicable.

'Science' had manifestly not, moreover, resolved the mysteries of consciousness and volition, nor had it unambiguously established its empire over the fundamental principles governing human life and society, though the ability to draw on the authority of science for any moral and political view was much coveted and claimed. But the bid for a comprehensive, unified scientific understanding of the universe, including the human mind, had, temporarily at least, failed, and the intellectual climate of the turn of the century was crucially shaped by that perceived failure, whether experienced with disillusionment or relief. Science was a powerful and much solicited voice rather than an unchallenged hegemony. It remained, however, at the popular level the chief guarantee of an optimistic belief in progress, while, on the other hand, the intellectual authority of the churches had perceptibly diminished by the end of the century.

Of course it is only by contrast with the enormity of the initial ambitions entertained that one can speak of failure; the achievements had been great, in the chemistry of life, in cell theory, in neurology, and major advances were about to be made in theoretical physics and in genetics. The impact of technological applications, of electricity, in particular, was clearly great and increasing. The authority of the collective voice of scientists in their proper domains was undeniable, though boundaries remained heatedly contested. But it had not quite replaced the authority of religion;

the boundaries, for most people, did not extend so far. Even in the realm of empirical knowledge, the humanities and even the social sciences had not been subsumed; their methodological independence was increasingly proclaimed in such concepts as *Geistesgeschichte* (History of Spirit) or *Verstehen* (inner understanding). By the end of the century it was becoming both a cliché and a mark of some intellectual sophistication to speak of the limitations of scientific method and even, fostered by Nietzsche, of the obstacle the cult of scientific detachment presented to 'life'. The phrase 'revolt against science' became common as a mark of the avant-garde. The arts, repudiating Taine's attempt to explain them causally, sought an escape under the rubric of creative imagination. Even theologians began to strut a little, on ground cleared by Idealist philosophy or in an enclave of inner personal experience of the divine which might reasonably – not anticipating Freud – seem immune from scientific tampering. Even the ethic of scientific dedication, of the supreme value of the scientist's exalted immolation of self, was made by Nietzsche to seem smug and unhealthy. Taine's follower Paul Bourget (1852–1935) pilloried his mentor in a novel, *The Disciple* (1889), as the epitome of desiccated, ineffectual intellect. To some the crumbling of materialism and determinism seemed to license or even require a deliberate irrationalism. The Italian philosopher Antonio Aliotta (1881–1964), in a book entitled *The Idealist Reaction against Science* (1912), complained that 'One of the essential characteristics of contemporary thought is undoubtedly the reaction from intellectualism in all its forms. Reaction against scientific naturalism has gone too far.'

Subsequent chapters will lead us to consider many forms of turn-of-the-century anti-rationalism and anti-intellectualism. I want to conclude the present chapter, however, with two developments which arose, as it were, within the matrix of science and the scientific outlook itself. They are an epistemological phenomenalism, purporting decisively to detach science from metaphysics; and a conventionalist or pragmatist version of what scientific theories are and what gives them their validity.

Just as the newer physics contributed to the undermining of materialism and determinism, so, inadvertently, as it were, and just as paradoxically, did the evolutionary biology, Lamarckian and Darwinian, which had been hailed as its crowning glory, the keystone of the arch for which chemistry and physiology had provided the foundations. For it was the biological concept of life as adaptation which underlay the new phenomenalism and the new pragmatism which were to leave materialism in ruins.

A central figure is the scientist and epistemologist Ernst Mach (1838–1916). Mach, seeking to rescue science from metaphysics and give it an unshakeable epistemological foundation, sought a unified view of the ground of all knowledge in the primacy of sensation. Sensation is all there is, whether considered as the basis of generalized knowledge or as subjective experience. The distinction between reality inner and outer thus has no foundation; reality for us, as the world and as consciousness, is an unstable sequence of sensory events; everything else is abstraction. Knowledge is not the impossible notion of correspondence to a reality external to us but the stabilizing and reconciling of sensation in concepts and theories governed by the scientific criterion of economy; in other words the creation of shorthands of maximum usefulness, abridging the actual memories of past sensations into something more easily retained and manageable. Theories are tools serving the needs of life; science is essentially abstraction from sensory experience, and the more general – economical and therefore useful – its concepts and theories, the further, the more abstracted, they were from the sensorial activity they abridged and organized. There could be no scientific 'picture' of the world, for the world was the sensory flux.

The idea of knowledge as ultimately knowledge of sensations, and of concepts as generalizations from them, was of course one with a long, ultimately Lockean, pedigree, just as the idea that consciousness had evolved from the needs of life as an instrument of adaptation was firmly located in, for example, Spencer's view of the world. What Mach and his generation added, under the influence both of new tendencies in physics and of the theory of evolution with its central idea of adaptation, was a pluralistic notion of concepts and theories essentially as tools, useful devices in the organism's struggle to maintain its existence. In Mach the long-employed criterion of economy in judging scientific theories and concepts was explicitly related to the notion of organic needs. Knowledge, in the newer version, was not a self-justifying ideal, the goal of humanity in its highest manifestation, as comprehension of the world in its totality, as in the neo-Hegelian conception of Renan and Taine; it was an organizing instrument in the struggle for life.

Clearly, a possible version of this idea was a practical, pragmatic version of the concept of truth, defined in terms of usefulness. This was the line of thought developed, under the influence of the idea of evolution, by the American Pragmatist William James (1842–1910), who in the early twentieth century was also to be an influential intellectual voice in European culture. James, as a professional psychologist, was interested in the psychological functions of belief; his *Varieties of Religious Experience* (1902) put religious beliefs and experiences to the test not of propositional truth in the sense of correspondence to an external reality but of their role in psychological health or morbidity. The concept of the *social* function of religion, irrespective of its truth-claims, was already current in the social sciences as the social and psychological vacuum its disappearance might leave was increasingly contemplated. In the initial evolutionary conception of consciousness it was self-evident that ideas were serviceable in so far as they gave reliable – one could easily say truthful – information about the environment to which the organism had to adapt. But what if this were not in all cases a necessary condition? There were also internal, psychological needs to be met. The will to live might, it seemed, falter. James was much interested in religious descriptions of the sick soul – an understandable preoccupation in a secularized child of New England Puritanism. Others were generalizing the condition to whole societies and speaking fashionably of 'decadence'. To these concerns the conception of truth in the sense of correspondence to external conditions was marginal or irrelevant. The needs of the organism might include something more than reliable information about the world.

In its broadest terms, and ignoring all individual subtleties of interpretation, pragmatic evaluation conducted in terms of serviceability for 'life' was a pervasive intellectual tendency at the turn of the century, with many variations and intersecting influences to which no single formula can do justice. Nietzsche's influence, for example, becoming powerful from the 1890s onwards, encouraged evaluation in terms of health and morbidity, life enhancement and life denial, and undermined the construction of grand schemes of comprehension based on ideas of truth grounded in either logical coherence or in systematic correspondence to the world in the form of scientific laws.

A summary of the ideas we have been considering was offered in the 1911 Preface to a book written more than thirty years earlier but not then published, *The Philosophy of As If* by the neo-Kantian Hans Vaihinger (1852–1913). In the earlier period it would have been strikingly original; in 1911 it followed a number of now well-worn paths with some variations. Vaihinger's book did not emulate Mach's sensationalism, though it did not contradict it, and it made the now customary references to adaptative utility. It addressed the question of scientific theory-construction while also including an interest in the possible beneficial functions of myths

and ethical ideas which had no serious claims to truth. Vaihinger distinguished, as he claimed Pragmatism did not, between hypotheses, which are
subject to confirmation and disconfirmation, and useful 'Fictions', which
are not. Among the latter were not only such things as the definitions of
Euclidean geometry or the idea of infinity but ethically desirable myths
such as God, immortality and Freewill. Vaihinger consciously tried to
straddle the philosophy of science and the requirements of the moral and
social world.

Another, more impressive and influential, version of the role of fictions
in social science, this time an explanatory one, was Max Weber's term 'the
ideal type': the ideal type was a fiction, like, for example, the assumption of
perfect rationality – on the analogy of the frictionless engine – from which
hypothetical consequences could be deduced which could then be compared
with actual outcomes. It was not, of course, an entirely new conception in
social science – J. S. Mill had said something similar about Political Economy
in the 1830s – but it marked a methodological break from comprehensive
schemes of social evolution like Spencer's which dominated sociology at
the end of the nineteenth century. Another term which to us seems to
mark the advent of modernity was 'model', which originated, in its scientific sense, in physics – it has been credited to James Clerk-Maxwell (1831–
1879) – and which was gaining currency there, though not yet with the
extensive application across virtually all fields of inquiry it has acquired
more recently. Among physicists themselves there seems to have been a
temperamental difference between those like William Thompson, Lord
Kelvin, whose cast of mind, as he said himself, inclined him always to think
in terms of a mechanical model, and those like Clerk-Maxwell who were
content with relations between physical events expressed mathematically,
over which physical hypotheses cast a kind of veil. The vital possible implication, however, in the term 'model' was that a model is provisional and dis-
pensable and that different models might be useful for different purposes.

Behind accounts of theory construction there was not only, often, a
biologically inspired notion of adaptive success but sometimes also, as we
see for example in Vaihinger, an emphasis on the active role of the mind of
the inquirer in the construction of knowledge, bringing it to the service of
life under the dominion of will. 'Ideas, judgements and conclusions, that is
to say thought, act as a means in the service of the Will to live and dominate.
Thought is originally only a means in the struggle for existence and to this
extent is only a biological function.' This formulation by Vaihinger echoes
not only Darwinism but also German philosophy in the Idealist tradition,

particularly, as Vaihinger is fully aware, Schopenhauer. If we then add to this Darwinian-Schopenhauerian *mélange*, which sees life as animated by the Will to exist, Mach's account of existence as an irreversible sensory flux, only artificially stabilized in the conceptual representation of things, we have the germs of a new (though to students of Schopenhauer, recognizable) vitalist, evolutionist metaphysics for the last part of the century, adumbrated in Eduard von Hartmann's very popular *The Philosophy of the Unconscious* (1868). Hartmann's 'Unconscious' was a world-pervading Unconscious Will clearly derived, as he acknowledged, from Schopenhauer, and elaborated physiologically. It reappeared eventually in the even more acclaimed and widely influential work of Henri Bergson at the end of the century, particularly his *Creative Evolution* (1905), which we shall have to consider later, in Chapter 4.

As we have seen, a consequence of the recession from materialism was a disposition to regard mind and matter as simply two ways of seeing the same thing. It is not surprising that the great metaphysicians of the seventeenth century, Leibniz and Spinoza, were sometimes invoked. Haeckel's term 'Monism' was intended to convey a metaphysical neutrality, but it proved much more obviously a bridge by which materialism was transformed back into a kind of vitalism and even into what has been called 'pan-psychism'. One of the nineteenth-century pioneers here was the anti-materialist physicist and experimental psychologist Gustav Fechner (1801–87), notably in his *Elements of Psychophysics* (1860). According to Fechner mind and body are identical; what to itself is psychical, to observers is physical. Phenomena are the external manifestations of the psychical reality, and existence is a spiritual hierarchy leading from atoms up to God, who includes all.

For the later Haeckel, who was influenced by Fechner, everything is a manifestation of the World-Soul. All was alive and possessed mental attributes. There was no difference between organic and inorganic. Nature, in fact, as though to pay for its presumption in subsuming human beings, was thoroughly anthropomorphized. Atoms experience lust and attraction, antipathy and repulsion. This thought was elaborated in even more anthropomorphic terms by another immensely successful popularizer of science, a member of Haeckel's Monist League, Wilhelm Boelsche. He was not, like Haeckel, a distinguished scientist but a propagandist for science and nature-worship, in an evolutionist but highly teleological and pan-psychist mode, to a wide audience which extended well into the working class. Boelsche wrote rhapsodically and devotionally, not merely of the World-Soul but of a cosmos permeated by a kind of universal eroticism.

Attraction was the law of the world – a thought which had also appealed to earlier 'socialists' like Saint-Simon and Fourier. For Boelsche, all nature, inorganic and organic, was steeped in love, and he wrote about it as though celebrating a kind of permanent cosmic orgasm.

Much more sober, philosophically sophisticated and bleak was an earlier product of pan-psychist ways of thinking, the work by Hartmann (1842–1906), influential in the 1870s and 1880s among intellectuals in both Germany and France, entitled *The Philosophy of the Unconscious* (1868, translated into French 1877). Hartmann managed to combine a teleologically evolutionist and pan-psychist vision of the world with a Schopenhauerian abhorrence for it. He became known, in fact, as the 'philosopher of pessimism'. Hartmann professes neutrality between Materialism and Idealism, but the effect of his work, which made use of Lamarckian evolutionism and modern physics, especially atomic theory, is to reconquer the physical world for a version of an immanentist philosophical Idealism. In this it is sometimes reminiscent of Schelling and Hegel, but most of all of Schopenhauer. Another influence, congruous with the latter, was the Hindu scriptures, now becoming more accessible (see Chapter 6 below), which also figured among the influences on Fechner. Hartmann explains his task in terms of achieving a synthesis of western and eastern philosophy and religion. 'Aryan' (see Chapters 3 and 6 below) Indian religion was Monist (Pantheist) but not, Hartmann says, historical. Christianity was traditionally dualist, but historical. The modern western problem, having rejected Christian transcendentalism, and embraced purposive evolution, is 'to unite historical consciousness with pantheistic Indian religion to produce, out of the spirit of our Aryan stock, a vivifying renewal of our irreligious age'.

For Hartmann, as for Fechner, the universe is a hierarchy of consciousness. 'The Unconscious' of his title is consciousness which has not achieved self-awareness. It is, in fact, Schopenhauer's striving, all-pervading cosmic Will. But Hartmann's version – he sometimes calls it 'the Unconscious Will' – is, unlike Schopenhauer's, teleological, which he justifies in Lamarckian terms. The manifestations of the universal will are purposive and conscious, but without knowing themselves to be so. Hartmann speaks of it as 'plastic energy' and 'unconscious formative activity'; he also speaks of 'the clairvoyance of the Unconscious', most obvious in instinct and in a teleological process like the growth of an embryo. To allow Darwinian explanations here would demolish Hartmann's argument, and he predictably repudiated them.

All will is devoted towards a future state and must therefore make for itself, unconsciously, a representation of it. Ideas as well as Will are therefore present in the World-Unconscious: 'the unconscious idea can be present to the ganglia even though not in the brain'. Consciousness develops, and self-consciousness is eventually attained, through what reminds the reader of Freud's 'reality principle', by wills encountering resistance to themselves, by the discovery of the not-self. The will is said to be 'stupefied' that an idea can exist without being willed. Consciousness develops through frustration and therefore in pain, and the higher the level of consciousness, the sensitivity, the greater the pain. But in the further development of consciousness is salvation: it lies in the selfless suspension of desire, and therefore of suffering, which Schopenhauer had found in aesthetic contemplation. The latter is made by Hartmann teleological and cosmic. Consciousness rises above itself, above its origins in Unconscious will: 'the salvation of the world depends upon the emancipation of the intellect from the will'. But in rising above its individual striving it also unites itself with the striving, teleological cosmic process as a whole. Recognizing the cosmic purpose, it can now selflessly identify with it.

Yet there is in Hartmann another kind of tension which it is not clear that he resolved. For though the development of conscious intellect seems the way of deliverance, of self-emancipation, it is also, it seems, as it was for the Romantics, the way of desiccation. Conscious intellect is self-corrective, but sterile when detached from will. If a man, Hartmann says, 'loses the faculty of hearing the inspirations of the Unconscious, he loses the springs of life'. The predicament of consciousness begins to sound like that of Thomas Mann's Gustav von Aschenbach in *Death in Venice*, for whom Eros presents itself both as the revitalization of a controlled but desiccated consciousness and also as 'the abyss' (see Chapter 5 below). The hope that Hartmann seems to be expressing is that hearing the intimations of the Unconscious will, and making a conscious identification with it at the cosmic level, is not the same as reverting to a mere blind striving. (For further discussion of the Unconscious see particularly Chapter 4 below, section 4.4).

The stories we have considered in the present chapter have been full of paradox: physical and metaphysical ideas turning into something like their opposites, not, generally, through refutation but more through the development of their latent potentialities – teleology, vitalism and pan-psychism. There is more here, however, than just the perpetual philosophical oscillation we might cynically like to assume between Materialism and Idealism. The intellectual world of the 1900s, though much in it now inevitably seems archaic, unacceptable, even ominous as well as portentous, is closer to ours in a number of ways, chiefly though the loss of various kinds of innocence, than is that of the 1850s. Yet we can of course also see it under the category of intellectual fashion, where much of it deserves to remain, in an oblivion only intellectual historians can be bothered to disturb. For the latter it is a useful hypothetical exercise to imagine the list of mentors we might have been offered, forty years on, by an eager young Russian autodidact, a Voroshilov of the early twentieth century; the type was surely not extinct. We can make some educated guesses, some more confident than others. Bergson would certainly have replaced Taine and Renan. Hartmann would be a possibility, as perhaps would Ibsen. Nietzsche would be by then inescapable; Haeckel too, as popularizer of evolution, as Social Darwinist and Eugenist; we shall have to return to these latter categories. In general, however, natural science would probably be less prominent than for his predecessor; chemists and physiologists would be far to seek and it would have been a bold autodidact to dip a toe into the world of Albert Einstein and Max Planck. It would be early for neo-Mendelian genetics, in any case perhaps too much a specialists' matter; early, too, for Freud, though psychology might well be represented, apart from James, by an heir of Taine, the crowd-psychologist and theorist of mass irrationality Gustave le Bon; we should expect also perhaps one of the acknowledged contemporary diagnosticians of 'decadence', now largely forgotten: Paul Bourget or Max Nordau. Tolstoy and Dostoevsky might figure, and if patriotism called for another Russian, promising candidates would be the Marxist Plekhanov or the anarchist Kropotkin, according to inclination.

Such a list – not, I hope, historically implausible – gives, compared with its predecessor, the impression of a more tense, febrile, fragmented and generally less optimistic and confident intellectual world, and certainly one more absorbed in various ways in the contemplation, sometimes with complicity, of the irrational and of the inevitability of conflict. It is the, in some cases now occult, preoccupations and anxieties represented by these names that we have to consider in subsequent chapters.

# CHAPTER 2

## Social Evolution and the Sciences of Culture

### 2.1  A Classified World

An under-acknowledged aspect of the history of science tends to be the vital importance of exhaustive, systematic classification: taxonomy. It seems a laborious, unglamorous and rather primitive expression of the scientific impulse, lacking the dash of theory-construction or crucial experimentation. Yet it is in some contexts basic. Confronted with the variety and geographical spread of the organic world, classification can only be the work of time and the cumulative efforts of field botanists and zoologists, of palaeontologists and morphologists. The foundation of a systematic taxonomy had been laid in the eighteenth century; in the first half of the nineteenth century some of the leading scientists of the age were engaged in essentially classificatory activities and the speculations about origins and relationships to which they gave rise. It could hardly be otherwise, before such sciences were quickened and brought together by an established evolutionary consensus. In a Creationist climate of thought, to collect and classify, to study morphology, was to be in touch with the thought of the creator.

Such activities were to be, sometimes contrary to the wishes of their leading practitioners, the precondition of an established concept of evolution. One has only to think of what is presupposed in the ability to declare confidently that a newly uncovered fossil was evidence for an extinct species belonging to an identifiable geological era, or to be able to assign a new living specimen, collected say by the young Charles Darwin in an Amazonian forest, precisely into its appropriate space on the map of life, present and past. Towards the mid-century 'the species question' and the theory of transmutation or transformism, as it was then called, gave such discoveries a peculiar excitement. The mapping of living and fossil species onto the geography of the areas he visited when on HMS *Beagle* as ship's naturalist (i.e. collector and classifier) in the 1830s was to provide Darwin with a crucial argument for the evolutionary hypothesis in *The Origin of Species* a quarter of a century later. In the first half of the century comparative anatomy had formed a prominent part of the general perception of what scientists were and could authoritatively pronounce on. A towering figure in the scientific world in this period was the French anatomist Georges Cuvier (1769–1832), who remained a firm anti-evolutionist. His younger English counterpart, the anatomist Richard Owen (1804–1892) was, along with the geologist Sir Charles Lyell (1797–1875), the most eminent English scientist at the time of the publication of Darwin's *Origin*, towards which he displayed more hostility than his own theoretical position really justified. Arguments between Creationists and Evolutionists (though there were intermediate positions) were essentially confrontations of rival explanations of the taxonomies painstakingly established over the previous century. Were the relations between species, and particularly between apparently closely allied groups of species, exhibiting greater and lesser degrees of complexity, the results of a universal, causally explicable evolutionary process, or the different manifestations, as German *Naturphilosophie* held, of a finite number of basic natural archetypes, or thoughts in the mind of God?

Owen presided over the establishment of the Natural History Museum in South Kensington which opened in 1881; the collection had previously been housed under Owen's supervision in the British Museum. The Natural History Museum was part of the development of museums and scientific institutions paid for from the proceeds of the Great Exhibition in Hyde Park in 1851, itself a kind of great though evanescent museum of contemporary arts from all over the world; the urge to collect, assemble and exhibit and usually possess could take more than one form. The second half of the nineteenth century was the great age (though not the pioneering one – that was the late eighteenth and early nineteenth centuries) of new museums, of arts and archaeology, palaeontology, natural history, ethnography and anthropology. Owen spent his whole professional life in museum curatorship and its associated activities; along with medicine, in which he received his training, it offered one of the few routes to a scientific career in England while opportunities in the universities were so meagre, though Edinburgh, like Germany and Paris, offered considerably more. A university career structure in modern subjects, including natural science, only began to emerge in the last quarter of the century.

The comprehensive, systematically arranged and catalogued museum collections, however, which later generations take for granted, offered an outlet not only for employment but for the aspiration to an ideal of totally comprehensive and systematized knowledge. There were some in England who deplored the separation of the natural history collection from its earlier home in the British Museum (opened in 1759), which seemed to drive a wedge between the sciences of nature and man. The author of the article on museums in the 1911 edition of the *Encyclopaedia Britannica* polemically asserted that 'The ideal museum should cover the whole field of human knowledge. It should teach the truth of all the sciences, including anthropology, the science which deals with man and all his works in every age. All the sciences and all the arts are correlated.' There was in this, of course, not only high aspiration but a large measure of cultural confidence in such declarations: confidence in a world intellectually as well as physically possessed and classified. It was a neat ironic touch of H. G. Wells (1866–1946) to make his Time-Traveller stumble in a remote, decayed future, on a museum, 'The Palace of Green Porcelain', in what he recognizes as 'the ruins of some latter day South Kensington' (where Wells himself had received his education under Huxley), with a library and Palaeontological, Technological and Ethnological sections. In an ironic inversion the scientific triumph over time in an archaeological and palaeontological museum has been replaced by the ultimate triumph of time over the museum, dust-covered and crumbling away. Wells had given a contemporary and scientific turn to an old literary and pictorial topos.

'Anthropology', mentioned by the *Encyclopaedia*, dates in something like its modern English sense – earlier it had tended to mean human comparative anatomy – from the 1860s. Ethnographic and anthropological museums proliferated in European capitals in the latter part of the century. By now museums had come to be regarded not just as repositories and aids to research but as instruments of popular education. The Great Exhibition too turned out to have established a precedent; the Paris Exhibition of 1867 was the first to include archaeological material as well as contemporary artefacts. Archaeology, the cultural equivalent of palaeontology, was another human science to become firmly established in the second half of the century, though its most basic taxonomic tool, the sequence of Stone, Bronze and Iron Ages, dated from much earlier in the century, in Denmark; 'Stone Age' was subdivided into Palaeolithic and Neolithic in the mid-century. Evidence of the antiquity of man in the conjunction of human artefacts and remains of extinct animals, which had been accumulating from excavations in France and England from the 1830s onwards, was finally accepted, after long scepticism, at the end of the 1850s.

Much conspired to make it natural to consider human cultures, even contemporary ones, in sequential terms rooted in archaeology and evolutionary biology, when many of the classics of evolutionary sociology and anthropology first appeared in the 1860s and 1870s. The supposed analogy with evolutionary biology was important, of course, but so was the need to provide context and imaginative depth and human meaning to the artefacts of the archaeological record, and also to bridge the gap, as Darwin tried to do from (as it were) the biological end, in his *The Descent of Man* (1871), between the evolution of human physique, faculties and instincts and the origins of social life and culture. Anthropology was inevitably a vogue-science of the period, organized equally inevitably in broadly evolutionary terms.

One of the pioneers of evolutionism in archaeology and ethnography was Augustus Lane-Fox (1827–1900) (who changed his name to Pitt-Rivers), founder of the Pitt-Rivers museum collection in Oxford. From 1851 he was arranging his collection of weapons of all kinds in developmental sequences, according to their degrees of complexity and sophistication, instead of the more obvious arrangement in terms of ethnic and geographical provenance. Pitt-Rivers, as it is easiest to call him, articulately justified the practice, including the interpolation of modern artefacts to fill gaps in the archaeological sequences, to provide 'a philosophy of progress'. As he said, 'every form takes its own place in sequence by its relative complexity or affinity to other allied forms'. It was a thought (not confined to Pitt-Rivers) capable of far-reaching application, which it was amply to receive, to forms of social organization, when it was generally called Sociology, and to the impalpable as well as the technological aspects of culture, including ritual and the hypothetical development of supernatural belief, when it tended to be called Anthropology; in both cases, in Britain, it was sometimes referred to just as the Comparative or Evolutionary method.

Pitt-Rivers' kind of arrangement contained a contestable, though in Britain for a while highly fashionable, assumption: that cultures are to be approached not primarily morphologically, as integrated wholes, but through the isolation of various practices and beliefs and the classification of these with those of the same apparent type from elsewhere, with no indication of contact or historical transmission, to constitute a stage in a hypothetical 'evolutionary' sequence. The use of evidence from contemporary 'sources' (i.e. 'primitive' or 'savage' societies) rested, of course, on the assumption that they represented cases of arrested development, and were in a sense contemporary with parts of the archaeological record. The historian W. E.

Lecky (1838–1903) wrote in 1869, 'There is still so great a diversity of civilization in existing nations that traversing tracts of space is almost like traversing tracts of time, for it brings us in contact with representatives of nearly every phase of past civilization.'[1] Space travelling was like time travelling because hierarchical classifications were convertible into hypothetical developmental sequences. That, after all, was what had happened to biological taxonomies in the theory of evolution.

## 2.2 Social Evolution as the Division of Labour

Biological classification was, admittedly, a good deal easier to make rigorous than social. Darwin, moreover, had emphasized that evolution was essentially a branching process, the creation of variety, rather than a main line of development with subsidiary ones. His expositors, notably Haeckel, had not heeded him and still less did the enthusiasts for 'evolutionary' sociology and anthropology. A central serial arrangement, at least implied, was for the most part irresistible in Britain – Germany, as we shall see, was another matter – despite occasional disclaimers and almost ritual gestures in the direction of multiple or divergent lines of development. Such gestures can easily be found in the most systematic, comprehensive and widely influential of social evolutionists, Herbert Spencer, but the divergences he allowed still to count as evolutionary seem minor.

In *The Principles of Sociology* (1876–95), however, Spencer insisted, with exhaustive demonstration, that the concepts specified in his general concept of evolution, and applied to other areas in the earlier volumes of the Synthetic Philosophy, were to be applied also to what he called social, or more strictly, 'Super-Organic' evolution (Chapter 1 above). In organisms evolution occurs as 'the physiological division of labour', under the environmental pressure to further adaptation. Exactly the same requirements were faced by the social organism, and the same concepts were applied in considering its evolution: structure, function and adaptive differentiation, in the form of the social division of labour. Structures were institutions and co-ordinated social practices; functions were their role in sustaining and integrating the society. Their successive elaborations, as societies found more specialized and therefore more efficient ways of meeting their needs for sustenance and integration, were a case of the general

---

[1] W. E. Lecky, *History of European Morals* (2 vols, London, 1902), i, p. 148.

evolutionary 'law' of the development from homogeneity to heterogeneity
we considered earlier in *First Principles*.

Human society, in Spencer's version, began as an undifferentiated
horde, just as the organism began its embryological development –
embryology was an important influence on Spencer – as a virtually undifferentiated piece of biochemistry; in such a society almost all necessary
functions are performed by virtually everyone. Spencer, as Marx and
Engels had done in Part I of their (unpublished) *The German Ideology* (1845),
saw the beginning of human society as the division of labour, though they
would have added that it was also the beginning of class-divided society.
The social division of labour was more efficient, according to Spencer,
and therefore made for survival; in that sense there was an analogy with
Darwinian favourable mutations. But division also implied integration.
The activities of the organs needed to be co-ordinated. Chieftainship was
the earliest form of social regulation and direction: in fact, coercion. The
horde became, albeit precariously, a society. Gradually, however, the various functions of chieftainship, warlike, political, religious, ritual, legislative
and judicial, each acquired distinct organs (institutions) to perform them.
Spencer's use of the concept of the division of labour therefore extends far
beyond the economic, yet it is the latter which, for him, is in a sense the goal.
The need for coercion would gradually diminish until the structures and
functions of highly evolved human society would come to approximate
simply to those of the free market, while the functions of government
dwindled. This, for Spencer, was evolutionary social progress. Free contracts and the operation of the laws of Political Economy would be sufficient
to co-ordinate the activities of highly evolved societies exhibiting a high
degree of specialization, together with the exchanges of goods and services
implied by such specialization. Eventually, as with the evolutionary formation of reflexes and instinct in the human mind, the necessary responses
and disciplines of production and the market would become internalized
in human beings, no longer requiring coercion to produce them. As in Marx,
after the establishment of Communism, the state would wither away.
Spencer, born in 1820, had been reared in the period and in the milieu of
English provincial Nonconformity, in which hostility to the State, and still
more to an Ecclesiastical Establishment supported by it, was axiomatic, and
the hopes reposed in the principles of Free Trade and self-help to produce
perpetual peace and a society of the virtuously industrious were almost
millennial. Spencer's sociology made peace, Free Trade and the absence
of coercive regulation not merely the means and ultimate goal of social

progress but the inevitable terminus of Social Evolution itself; he was already predicting this in his first book, *Social Statics* (1851). He had inherited, and employed, the Saint-Simonian and Comtean antithetical categories of the Militant and Industrial (really Industrious) types of society, in which the latter was superseding the former. Spencer, especially in his younger and more optimistic days, saw this as a central fact of contemporary history which was also guaranteed by evolutionary laws; the later nineteenth century, into which he had the misfortune to live on, gave it less support: a new era of economic protection, state interference and militarism was the last thing Spencer had anticipated and it seemed to him merely perverse.

Spencer's organic analogy for human society did not produce quite the theoretical consequences one might have expected. It did not altogether save *The Principles of Sociology* from the methodological fragmentation characteristic of British social evolutionism generally. Although Spencer did undoubtedly have a conception of the functioning of a society as a whole, his focus on the differentiation of distinct institutions meant that the arrangement of examples in *The Principles of Sociology* corresponded more to those illustrations of the biological evolution of distinct organs, the wing, the hand and so on, than to the evolution of species as such. Moreover, his marriage of evolution with laissez-faire principles (though he disliked the phrase) was accomplished in the teeth of the most obvious implications of his organic analogy. Highly complex organisms, as he recognized, are, after all, highly *dirigiste*. The 'lower' functions – body chemistry, breathing, digestion – are spontaneous and self-regulating from the point of view of the organism, but the brain is a highly peremptory organ and the motor nerves, and the limbs they control, on the whole carry out orders; the model seems to be one for a strong, centralized government, with discussion allowed only in a kind of cerebral cabinet.

Spencer solved the problem essentially by resorting to another level of evolutionary explanation, to the Lamarckian evolutionary psychology with which he had in a sense begun. Adaptative responses, if repeated sufficiently often, become reflex or instinctive and are heritable; over a course of generations such adaptations are accentuated and become firmly established in species characteristics. In social evolution, as Spencer pointed out, there are really two environments, internal in the society itself as it presents itself to the individual, and the external and natural; the former, for the individual, becomes the more important. Human beings, originally asocial, become habituated to the disciplines of social life, these habits become in due course internalized, spontaneous and intensified, partly through the elimination of the maladapted, the anti-social. The acceptance of social rules, becoming unconscious, would eventually no longer need to be coercively reinforced. As he wrote in an article in 1854, 'consequent as all kinds of government are upon the unfitness of the aboriginal man for social life, and dwindling in coerciveness as they do in proportion as this unfitness dwindles, they must one and all come to an end as humanity acquires complete adaptation to its new conditions'.[2]

Inevitably Spencer had many critics as well as imitators. Indeed many critics were in some degree imitators, though T. H. Huxley, rather cancelling some of his own earlier pronouncements, later wrote an uncompromisingly independent critique of Spencer's evolutionary ethics and what he called 'Administrative Nihilism'. The leading German social organicist, Albert Schäffle (1831–1903), in his *Bau und Leben des Sozialen Körpers* (*Structure and Activity of the Social Body*, 1875–8) unsurprisingly drew out more the *dirigiste* potentialities implicit in the organic analogy. The most subtle of Spencer's critics, however, though he had clearly learnt a good deal from him, was the leading French sociologist of the end of the century, Emile Durkheim (1858–1917). His *The Rules of Sociological Method* (1895) was a bid for the methodological independence of sociology from biology, though still under the rubric of 'science', which required a running polemic against Spencer. His *The Division of Labour in Society* (1893) was essentially his own rival, but in some respects derivative, version of social evolution, from an original, undifferentiated state towards individual autonomy and self-consciousness and respect for individual rights. 'The rise of individualism' would not have been a misleading title, though for Durkheim it would have had the wrong, excessively egotistical resonances. As in the now traditional dichotomy of Militant and Industrial society, to which, however, his own bears only rather superficial resemblances, Durkheim's classification, which is also a sequence, is a binary one: a version of a common nineteenth-century historical dichotomy, under various names and naturally with variations. Walter Bagehot (1826–77), in his *Physics and Politics* (1866) called it 'the Yoke of Custom' and 'the Age of Discussion'; Henry Maine (1822–88), in *Ancient Law* (1861) spoke of the sequence as 'from Status to Contract'. Ferdinand Tönnies (1855–1936) classically christened it in the virtually untranslatable antithesis *Gemeinschaft* and *Gesellschaft*. Durkheim spoke of two kinds of what he called social solidarity, which he called Mechanical and Organic – a deliberate provocation one presumes

---

[2] Herbert Spencer, 'Manners and Fashion', *Essays Scientific, Political and Speculative* (3 vols, London, 1858), i, p. 137.

because it was common to speak of traditional societies as organic and modern ones as mechanical, and Durkheim inverts the order. His point is that the social pressure to conformity, through the operation of what he calls the 'collective consciousness' (*conscience collective*, in French) in the first type is rigid and automatic and in the second flexible. The two types of social solidarity are the means by which Durkheim tries to unite the structural and the moral features of social development.

His account of the nature of socialization is very different from Spencer's and in some respects inverts it: not the gradual taming and increasingly perfect integration of originally feral individuals through an unconscious, essentially biological, hereditary process which could be described as the formation of social instincts, but rather the gradual social creation of a consciousness of individuality out of an original state in which individuality, far from chafing at its social bonds, is scarcely conceivable. The individual is not primary but a social construction; society is formed not by the integration of independent human particles but by their differentiation – as Spencer himself might have said – from an original undifferentiated social mass. In his account of the structural changes which produce these moral effects Durkheim sounds, in fact, very like Spencer. Initially, for both, there is only a very low degree of the division of labour. Each small society is homogeneous and self-sufficient and at that stage can grow in mass, as Durkheim says, only segmentally, that is by the aggregation of a number of such undifferentiated local units: the mass may cover a larger area but is scarcely more integrated than before. An advanced society, however, can integrate a large mass not only by segmental adhesion but organically, through specialization and the exchange of different goods and services made possible by the division of labour. The explanation of the latter is offered in Darwinian rather than Smithian terms: the pressure of population and the need to alleviate the resulting intensification of competition leading to the discovery and exploitation of new kinds of economic production for which a demand can be found.

For Durkheim the moral consequence of structural differentiation is the creation of individual difference. In a segmental society in which the way of life for its members is essentially uniform, individual self-consciousness can hardly exist, and the individual units are prevented from challenging a highly constricting social code made up of specific injunctions and prohibitions, as in the Book of Leviticus, not purely by fear but by the virtual unthinkability of doing so. Naturally cases of deviance occur, some accidentally, but they are thought of not as moral or civil offences but as the breaking of a taboo. In a modern, 'organic' type of society, however, constituted by a high degree of the division of labour, the complexity of social circumstances requires laws which are thought of not simply in terms of discrete prohibitions but as general principles, applicable to diverse circumstances and hence open to interpretation, and, in the long run, conscious appraisal and modification. At the same time, individual human difference, being required by the division of labour to minister to society's now diverse wants, becomes acknowledged and even respected. The sense of an autonomous individual self, universalized as recognition of and respect for a similar autonomous self and individuality in others – the Kantian note here is in Durkheim's case not accidental – becomes the content of the modern form of the *conscience collective*, the moral consensus of society as respect for universal moral principles regarded as sacred: namely, individual freedom and equality of respect for it. While for Spencer social evolution culminates in the radical liberal individualism of mid-nineteenth-century provincial England, in Durkheim social development culminates in a civic morality for French secular republicanism, based on the Rights of Man and refined by the Kantianism then riding high in French philosophy, with the ethical injunction to treat every individual as an end not a means. For Durkheim sociology had the task and opportunity of replacing the dubious eighteenth-century Natural Law metaphysics underpinning the idea of the Rights of Man, making the latter, instead, the inevitable outcome of the structural process of social change; it was for Sociology, not Philosophy, to identify and in doing so justify, the social norms of a modern society.

## 2.3 Sciences of Religion and Culture: France, Britain, Germany

One feature of social differentiation as progress on which nineteenth-century writers sometimes understandably dwelt, though it is only lightly touched in Durkheim, is that the separating out into different structures and functions from a primitive unity is also a form of what we may call, though they did not, secularization. One of the first examples of fission in the Regulating system described by Spencer was the separation of political and military functions from ritual and religious ones. Similarly, but coincidentally, in Maine's *Ancient Law*, judgements thought of as divinely given develop through a long process into the reasoned interpretations of a professional class of lawyers and a distinction between *ad hoc* judgement and general legislation, the latter being justified in purely utilitarian terms. The alternative development, for Maine, was the monopolization of law by a theocracy, as by the Brahmins. Secularization and Western progress, theocracy and oriental ossification and stagnation were the two great alternatives for mankind. The appeal of this antithesis to English liberals was understandable, at a time when a large part of the content of political liberalism consisted in hostility to the privileges of the Anglican Church at home and to the dogmatic and temporal claims of the Papacy. Maine himself had to abandon his Fellowship at Trinity Hall, Cambridge, because its continuation depended on ordination to the Anglican priesthood. His was by no means a unique case: religious tests remained a *casus belli* until 1870.

The same concerns were present in France: Taine's academic career in the fifties suffered as much, fundamentally, from clerical as from political obstruction. Anti-clericalism was a defining characteristic of French Republicanism, whose roots went back to the Enlightenment and the first Revolution. But there was a difference between the two countries, epitomized (and exaggerated) in the ideas of Auguste Comte. Where English liberal demands for the ending of religious tests were virtually indistinguishable from those of Protestant Dissenters, Comte and Comtists aspired, as in Comte's *System of Positive Philosophy* (1854), not merely to eradicate Catholicism but to replace it with literally a new religion of science, progress and humanity, for religion human beings must have. The bizarre neo-Catholic rituals of the Comtist Religion of Humanity were extreme and not widely imitated, but the cultural contexts, Protestant and Catholic respectively, continued to exercise an influence on British and French liberalism, particularly in the disposition of the former to see religion in terms of individual belief, even when investigating it anthropologically, and in the latter to see it in terms of collective ritual and social function. The distinction cannot be applied rigidly, but Durkheim, whose personal background was Jewish (he was the son of a rabbi), is certainly a case, and in the long run a highly influential one, of the latter.

Durkheim's late work *Elementary Forms of the Religious Life* (1917) approached religion not so much as a system of belief but as a body of collective ritual practice. It focused on the totemic rituals of the Australian aborigines and attempted to decode the explanations offered by them. Durkheim's work came as something of a revelation to British anthropologists already in revolt against speculative evolutionism, though the first effect of this was a renewed emphasis on tracing actual cultural connection, spoken of as 'Diffusionism'. The British anthropological approach to religion in the later nineteenth century, with the notable exception of the Hebrew scholar William Robertson Smith (1846–94), who can be seen as a precursor of Durkheim, had been not only evolutionist but individualist, psychological and rationalistic, focusing on belief, magical or animistic, and explaining collective rituals, where they were noted, in terms of beliefs. Durkheim's approach, like that of his mentor at the Ecole Normale Supérieure, Fustel de Coulanges (1830–89), in his book on Roman religion and society, *The Ancient City* (1864), was essentially social. Religion was not speculative in origin, the consequence of savages' poor grasp of causality, it was a whole dimension of the life of a society – any society, not only those of savages, though Durkheim remained enough of an evolutionist to see the latter as providing insight into origins; religion was the realm of the sacred. Asking what the Australians were doing in their totemic collective rituals, Durkheim argued that they were enacting and paying worship to the most important and awe-inspiring feature of their world, the ordering of their own collective life, society itself.

·It is a description as applicable, clearly (sceptics might say more so), to singing the Marseillaise as to taking part in totemic dances. It is tempting to say that for Durkheim the religion of Humanity, in localized forms, was not, as for Comte, the culmination of the religious history of mankind but its origin and perennial meaning. There had always, since the early 1790s, been a cultic element in French Republicanism in its attitudes to 'the People', and to the Republic itself, 'one and indivisible': initially it had incorporated an entirely sensible and conscious attempt to appropriate the sanctity attached to kingship and royalty. On 14 July 1790, the first anniversary of the fall of the Bastille, representatives from all over France had gathered to take an oath, affirming their unity, their corporate existence, in the Champ-de-Mars on an 'altar of the fatherland'.

Not surprisingly given 'the warfare of science and religion', the explanation of religion was a central concern of Anthropology in Britain from its origins in the 1860s; its other main preoccupation was with the 'evolution' of kinship systems and hence of property rights. After more than half a century there was a revival of the interest in the psychological origins of religion which had been a feature of the eighteenth-century Enlightenment. To explain religion psychologically was, after all, to provide an alternative to the claim that it must derive from an original revelation, later corrupted by superstitions. Other explanations had been current in the eighteenth century, notably the idea of priestly conspiracies, but these had fallen away. From the 1860s until roughly the end of the century in Britain, however, not merely was the predominant explanation of religion conducted in terms of individual psychology as in the eighteenth century, but the psychology itself was still much the same, though now massively documented in examples from contemporary savagery; essentially it was the mechanism of the association of ideas, operating uncritically in simple minds under the impression of fear; religion was the result of an intellectual failure, a failure in the classification of phenomena. Misled by superficial resemblances the savage jumped to conclusions, attributing agency and intent to the consequences of natural laws, and misinterpreting the appearance of the dead in dreams and visions and hence feeling the need to propitiate them.

The latter was Spencer's main theory. The practice of propitiatory magic had been called in the eighteenth century the making of fetishes – a term taken up for different purposes by both Marx and Comte. Later the term 'animism' became current, for the peopling of the world with invisible spirits of incalculable powers and erratic disposition. This was the term used by both Spencer and Tylor (they quarrelled over priority). Edward Tylor (1832–1917), who became the first Professor of Anthropology at Oxford, was the leading British anthropologist in the 1870s and 1880s. He came of Quaker stock, an odd preparation perhaps for a discipline much concerned with the interpretation of ritual; there is evidence that the desire to eradicate surviving ritualism and superstition by exposing their savage origins was one source for Tylor's commitment to Anthropology. He made his name with his *The Early History of Mankind* (1865) and *Primitive Culture* (1871). He became particularly associated with the use of the concept of 'survivals' to underpin the claim that modern 'savages' represented past stages of culture. Characteristics found fully at work in modern savagery were also found in residual form in civilized societies, as superstition, ceremonies, folklore – in which Tylor also had an interest. The latter were 'survivals', the equivalent of vestigial organs which Darwin pointed to as evidence for the past of a species. Once functional but now redundant, they were gradually dwindling away. To identify superstition and ritual in civilized society in this way was to predict their eventual disappearance: the death of religion. The method required no direct historical transmission or ethnic connection between the societies concerned; as the folklorist Andrew Lang (1844–1912) wrote, 'similar conditions of mind produce similar practices, apart from borrowings of ideas and manners'. This was the evolutionist anthropologist's creed, just as detaching cultural features – myth, ritual, marriage and kinship – from the mostly contemporary cultural matrices in which they were observed, in order to arrange them in hypothetical evolutionary series, was his characteristic method.

This method reached its apogee in the eventual thirteen volumes of Sir James Frazer's *The Golden Bough* (1892–1913). Frazer's book was an amalgam of three types of source: ancient legends and mythologies, notably, of course, Graeco-Roman (Frazer (1854–1941) was a classicist by training) but also Norse and other myths; the research of folklorists, most notably the collection of the German scholar Wilhelm Mannhardt (1831–80), into contemporary rural customs, legends and superstitions, and folk rituals associated with the agricultural year, all treated as pagan 'survivals'; and finally, of course, contemporary savagery. Frazer primed travellers, colonial administrators and missionaries with questionnaires, the equivalent of the naturalist's collection of specimens. The work grew under his hand – it had originally been published as two volumes – as evidence piled up and the themes were elaborated. Frazer wove his sources together with conscious art but also with copious references to examples from a vast range of cultures, sometimes half a dozen on a page: ancient European mythologies and modern Central African rituals, Amazonian or Polynesian fetishes and the traditional holiday caperings of the European peasantry, authorized by the calendar and the solstices: 'In some parts of Melanesia ... ', 'The Huichal Indians admire ... ', 'If a South Slavonian has a mind to pilfer ... ', 'The Ancient Greeks thought ... '. *The Golden Bough* was, among other things, an anthology of global eccentricities. Anyone who has listened to 'Mad Dogs and Englishmen' will find Frazer's method of citing evidence familiar and, exceptionally, even its content: in Amboyna and Uliase 'The people make it a rule not to go out of the house at midday because they fancy that by doing so a man may lose the shadow of his soul.' Quite.

The logical adhesives which, according to Frazer, bound all these examples into an account of the prehistory of the human mind and the origins of religion are, when scrutinized, less impressive; it may have been ... we may conjecture that ... it is reasonable to assume. If the analogies and the explanatory logic were often more than doubtful, the quest which in another sense held the book together had an air of mystery and fascination. Frazer's mock-modest claim – certainly so by the time the work had swelled to its full thirteen volumes – was that the aim of all this accumulation was the interpretation of a particular ancient ritual, associated with the guardianship or 'kingship' of the wood beside the lake of Nemi, south of Rome. Each successor to the kingship was a fugitive seeking sanctuary, who could acquire it only by killing his predecessor, having first torn a branch from a particular tree, 'the golden bough'. Frazer's text and subtext ran in parallel, though both were often swamped by examples. In the generalizing subtext he developed in later editions primitive man was first a would-be magician, attempting to control nature through sympathetic and contagious magic, mimicking, or establishing physical contact with, the object to be controlled; he was a kind of misguided technologist. Religion, the gods, were born of the fact that magic does not work automatically but is disappointingly erratic in its achievements. Behind the appearances of phenomena, therefore, there must lie wills sometimes antagonistic to the magician's purpose, which must hence be propitiated. Failed magic, in other words, leads to a proliferation of spirits, and spirits, once they become more generally powerful and departmental rather than inhering in particular trees and streams, in the manner of subdeities like the classical dryads and naiads, fauns and nymphs, are gods.

The intellectual sequence is the same as Comte's: from fetishism to polytheism, and eventually to monotheism and science. The last two do not appear explicitly in Frazer, but Christianity is certainly implicit and science is, as it were, the frame: the book itself. The gods, in Frazer's account, are fertility deities, from which came the god-kings who were subject, in fertility cults, to being hanged on a tree and having their bodies afterwards strewn over the fields in order to ensure the spring resurrection of life. Autumn and spring, death and resurrection, Orpheus, Balder ... Frazer never completes the line, but the designation of the latest dying and resurrected god, whose flesh and blood are the source of perpetual life, is hardly mistakable. The conclusion of the book, written in the five-star prose of the *fin de siècle*, is at least symbolically explicit. As beginning and end come together, both for Frazer's book and for mankind, the conclusion becomes both elegiac and ironic:

> It is evening, and as we climb the long slope of the Appian Way up to the Alban Hills, we look back and see the sky aflame with sunset, its golden glory resting like the aureole of a dying saint over Rome and touching with a crest of fire the dome of St Peter's ... The King of the Wood no longer stands sentinel over the Golden Bough. But Nemi's woods are still green, and as the sunset fades above them in the west, there comes to us, borne on the swell of the wind, the sound of the church bells of Rome ringing the Angelus ... *Le roi est mort, vive le roi! Ave Maria.*[3]

[3] J. G. Frazer, *The Golden Bough: A Study in Magic and Religion* (abridged edn, London, 1950), p. 714.

Nature, Religion and Science, the dying and the successor king, the annunciation of the new reign, are here woven together into an extraordinary piece of scientific triumphalism, touched with just the right amount of gracious nostalgia for its dying adversary. It is a further irony that Frazer's conclusion was virtually the last word of Victorian evolutionist cultural anthropology.

In the collected works of Ernest Renan there is an unperformed play, dated 1885, entitled *The Priest of Nemi*. It is tempting to think that Frazer may have known of it, though perhaps he did not. It also deals with the dialectic of superstition and enlightenment, but it lacks Frazer's triumphalism. Renan had renounced his clerical vocation but his attitude to religion retained the wistfulness of others of his generation, Arthur Hugh Clough, James Anthony Froude, even Matthew Arnold, the 'failed priests', one might say, of the 1840s. Renan's play imagines a priest of Nemi who is an enlightened man, a religious reformer resisted by 'the crowd', wedded to their ancient superstitions. The self-identification is obvious, but Renan was never Tylor's and Frazer's kind of militant positivist rationalist. Religion to him was a human creation, but worthy of reverence and having cultural value. His conception of cultural history, accordingly, was not the positivist one, from fetishism to theology to science, but the Romantic one much more common in Germany – Renan was much open to German influences – derived ultimately from Vico and Herder. It too was a triad: an age of myth, when the human mind was essentially concrete and poetic, thinking in images; an age of scepticism and critical science, dry and prosaic, is the next stage; finally, in Renan's version, a longed-for synthesis of imagination, science and religious feeling. Further consideration of Renan's religious outlook is best left to Chapter 6 (below, pp. 198–200).

For the French, his younger contemporary, Taine, was Renan's only rival in what German philosophers called the world of objective mind or spirit, what Tylor and Matthew Arnold, borrowing another German term, called culture, and what Spencer, characteristically, called 'super-organic products'. Taine, in some respects more than Renan, because of his more unequivocal commitment to science and his determination to find causal explanations, was the French master of what for convenience we may call the science of culture. It was not at all like 'Mr Tylor's science', as Anthropology was for a while spoken of in Oxford. Taine's master science was also psychology, but of a more modern kind – modern in the 1860s, that is – and he took it in different directions. Taine's speciality was the scientific explanation of literature and art in their national and historical manifestations; he acknowledged privately the influence on him of the Hegelian tripartite division of the world of spirit or objective mind into Philosophy, Law and Politics, and Art. What Taine brought to the last, chiefly though not exclusively as literature, was a supposedly strict determinism and a quite un-Hegelian devotion to 'facts'. He also drew, as he well knew, on something like a French tradition in the application of psychology to literature and an interest in the influence of nationality. The latter went back to Madame de Staël's *On Germany* at the beginning of the century and to Stendhal's *Racine and Shakespeare* (1822–5), which Taine admired, and his *Life of Rossini* (1824). Apart from Stendhal (1783–1842), the precursor in the application of psychology to literature whom he most admiringly acknowledged was the critic Sainte-Beuve (1804–69). Taine also had an interest in the conditioning effect of climate, a theory which derived ultimately from the eighteenth century.

Some of Taine's preoccupations were present in England too, but nowhere so systematically pursued. Matthew Arnold touched on another of Taine's interests, the influence of race in literature, in his lecture on 'The Celtic Element in Literature'. Ruskin, England's most influential art critic in the same period, did not ignore nationality and climate but his emphasis was most of all on art as an index of the quality of life and the moral condition of its producers. *The Stones of Venice* (1851–3) was a 'Decline and Fall' for the nineteenth century: a story of moral and therefore artistic decline, in terms of pride, luxury, impiety and artistic dishonesty, all epitomized in the Renaissance; the book ends with an invocation of the fate of the Cities of the Plain. Walter Bagehot, who, though very different from Taine in his literary manner, offers in some respects the closest English parallels to him, dwelt in *Physics and Politics*, drawing on modern psychology, on the role of imitation and the creation of reflexes in the formation of national character, and used the latter freely elsewhere as an explanatory principle in politics and literature. But Bagehot was a journalist with neither the time, nor much inclination, for the creation of systems, and Taine, for all his professed regard for the significance of 'the little facts', a phrase he picked up from Sainte-Beuve, was deeply drawn to systematization.

The first expression of this in relation to literature was his *Critical and Historical Essays* (1858), with a second series in 1865, but its chief manifestation was his *History of English Literature* (1864), with its celebrated introductory remarks setting out the explanatory method to be followed in all such studies. Taine was an anglophile, but in his presentation of the climatic and racial factors determining the character of English literature

England is a country of almost eternal fog and rain, whose waterlogged inhabitants peer through the gloom rather like cattle in a field painted by a Dutch master in the rain (not his analogy). There is, of course, much truth in this, but it hurts rather that Taine came, not as one might suppose, from Provence, but from the Ardennes, where fog is hardly unknown. Taine's travel book *Notes on England* (1862) contains some more cheerful passages, with kind words for Oxford and cricket, though he compares the Thames at Westminster to the Styx. There are in nineteenth-century racial psychologies sometimes unconscious reminiscences of the theory of the four elements and the predominant humour. Taine seems to have taken the concept of the phlegmatic rather over-literally. The English, creatures of a cold, wet climate and adapted to it, are susceptible only to the most violent and shocking images. Their literature therefore has no place for nuance or finesse; it is the natural home of horrors, eccentricity, even dementia: Shakespeare's frenzied protagonists, presented by Taine as virtually all mad; the characters of Byron and Dickens in more recent times.

Of more interest here than this cameo in the history of Anglo-French mutual misunderstanding, however, is Taine's introductory manifesto on the methods of what we are calling the science of culture. It can be compared in some respects with J. S. Mill's *System of Logic* (1843), Book VI, with its call for a science of character-formation in all sets of circumstances. It was a work Taine knew well. Taine, however, aimed at ample demonstration through examples. Like Bagehot later, he believed in the possibility of determining the centre of gravity, so to speak, of a culture, 'the reigning model' and the '*idée maîtresse*'. He seems to have derived this in part from the physiological idea of the eminent biologist Geoffroy Saint-Hilaire (1779–1853), whose lectures he attended, that in an organism some characters are preponderant and determine the others. H. T. Buckle (1821–62) who in his *History of Civilization in England* (1857–61) was also trying to determine the dominant type in a culture, which like Taine he called by the older term 'civilization', related it instead to the idea of the statistical mean.

For Taine the reigning model was incarnate in great authors, so that to study the history of its literature was to study the psychology of a whole people and an age. The characterization of that psychology and its explanation was encapsulated in Taine's threefold formula: race, milieu, moment. The character of a race was 'a primitive disposition', linked to physiology and akin to instinct, but it must be remembered that Taine was, like Spencer, a Lamarckian as well as a Darwinian evolutionist, who saw character as modifiable by circumstances, and the modifications as heritable 'so that at any moment we may consider the character of a people as an abridgement of all its previous actions'. Race is therefore an element of modifiable continuity through time; it incorporates past experiences and is, in turn, mediated in its effects by the contemporary milieu. Milieu, the second factor, includes climate and such things as political constitutions and traditions; milieu 'is to nations what education, career and abode are to individuals'. But as well as the national milieu there is also the third factor, moment, the historical epoch. Epochs have their reigning models too, their *idées maîtresses*. In each era there is 'a certain ideal model of man', the medieval knight or monk, the Renaissance courtier, whose influence 'is displayed over the whole field of action or thought'. In other words (not Taine's) there is a *Zeitgeist* as well as a *Volksgeist* and the latter, besides being a primordial disposition, is modified and therefore in a sense constantly re-created through time.

So far, one may feel, so sensible, if not particularly startling. Part of Taine's fame or notoriety, however, and the authority he came to enjoy, derived from the hard, deterministic language he used for his formula, and the mechanical, anatomical and psychological analogies he applied to it. It is true that, recognizing that the entities he postulated could never be given the precision of those in the physical sciences, he in a sense gave only to take away again in qualification, but it was the initial characterization of his enterprise which arrested attention. In the psychology of peoples

> we have but a mechanical problem: the total effect is a result, depending entirely on the magnitude and direction of the producing causes. The only difference which separates these moral problems is, that the magnitude and direction cannot be valued or computed in the first as in the second ... [But, says Taine returning to the charge, being] equally made up of forces, magnitudes and directions, we may say that in both the final result is produced after the same method.[4]

Taine had a highly distinctive and in his view original conception of cause which, since it has never really established itself in philosophical discourse, is hard to explain briefly; as he explained in his critique of Mill's *System of Logic*, his idea was neither purely *a posteriori* (the positivist view of cause as a regular conjunction of an antecedent and a consequent phenomenon) nor was it a metaphysical *a priori* assumption, the animating Idea in Idealist metaphysics, but something between the two: an organizing idea inferred

[4] Hippolyte Taine, *History of English Literature*, trans. H. van Lann (4 vols, London, 1920), i, p. 23.

from the evidence but existing *in* the phenomena as well as in the mind of
the observer as an organizing principle. What can be said of it briefly is that
it seems particularly liable to produce circular, self-confirming arguments,
as in the use of the imputed '*idée maîtresse*' when offered not merely as gen-
eralization but as an explanation: the English literature of the Restoration,
for example, in Taine's account, not merely is not, but cannot be, really
English since it conflicts with his idea of the English character.

Taine's explorations of collective psychologies and their products – of
cultures, it is easier to say – differ, as we have now seen, notably from
English cultural anthropology, though less so from the ideas of some
English writers (Mill, Buckle, Bagehot) for whose interests in this respect
we have no collective name, though it might be convenient to coin one.
Taine is concerned with history rather than prehistory: it treats cultures as
wholes rather than collections of parts which can be detached to be placed
in evolutionary sequences. Taine is not an exception to this in dealing with
literature since for him it was an index of the rest, the expression of an
underlying psychology. In Taine and Bagehot it attempts to explain the
latter in terms of the new, partly Lamarckian-inspired physiology of
hereditary, conditioned reflexes which Mill, in Book VI of *The System
of Logic*, did not have but in a sense could be said to have needed. All he
had at that point was the old, associationist psychology, which still did
for Tylor all he wanted a psychology to do: explain erroneous beliefs.

In turning, finally, to Germany, we are turning to an altogether different
tradition, though one we have already touched on in reference to Renan,
who was influenced by it. Its central characteristics are two: first, not merely
an emphasis on regarding cultures as distinct wholes but an emphatic
assertion of the unique individuality of each, characteristically combined
with a metaphysical view of the culture of each people as embodying an
underlying, specific force, spirit or Idea, incarnated in the particular *Volk*
and its language, customs, myths and poetry. It was, in other words, the
Romantic conception of cultures derived, most obviously, from Herder and
the late eighteenth century, but also including as perhaps its most influential figure of the earlier nineteenth century the folklorist and student of
Germanic customary law Jakob Grimm (1785–1863). The second central
characteristic of the German tradition was its conception of myth, derived
ultimately from Giambattista Vico and rediscovered in the Romantic
period. Myth was not simply invention or falsehood, it was an alternative
and deeper way of seeing life than that which science could offer; a
concrete, poetic way natural to early man, which had been lost rather than

overcome. It and science represented the difference between poetry and prose, not between falsehood and truth; myths unified a sense of life in a way that could be expressed in no other fashion. A people without a unifying myth was culturally crippled and fragmented; this was the conception of myth which Wagner carried into the 1850s and beyond and which Nietzsche, drawing from him, articulated in his first work *The Birth of Tragedy* in 1872.

We cannot pursue this particular theme now, but it formed part of a long-lasting German tradition in the understanding of the relation between a people and its culture. Born in Romanticism, it was easiest to express in Vitalist and Idealist terms – Herder (1744–1803), for example, spoke of the informing spirit embodied in a people and expressed in its culture as *Kraft*, best translated here as 'vital force'. The survival of that tradition into the materialist decades from the 1850s to the 1880s, the comparative, empirical, 'scientific' study of peoples, their cultures and their psychology, expressed in various names as *Völkerkunde* and *Völkerpsychologie*, is, one is inclined to say, a remarkable case of adaptation of a native intellectual tradition to the demands of comparative anthropological science. German work remained visibly distinct from that of Taine or the British anthropologists.

Before considering this, there is a further element of German distinctiveness, this time in philosophy, which also needs to be considered and which forms a sharp contrast to the use of a concept of social evolution derived from biology or to Taine's insistence that his own method of explanation was simply a particular form of those employed in the natural sciences. This is the contrast of *Geisteswissenschaften*, the sciences of mind or culture, the human sciences, and *Naturwissenschaften*, the sciences of nature, with the assertion that the methods of the two are legitimately and necessarily radically different. Again there is a long philosophical tradition relevant here, in which Kant was a key figure, but the philosopher who chiefly formulated and justified the distinction in the 1880s and beyond was Wilhelm Dilthey (1833–1911). The concept of cultures as integral and unique had its epistemological counterpart in the notion that they were intelligible not through classification and explanations modelled on the natural sciences but existentially, from within, through lived experience, *Erlebnis*. This, Dilthey pointed out, is where the individual's social and cultural knowledge begins. The lesson for the philosophy of the sciences is that while we do not of course have an inward and sympathetic understanding of the feelings, impulses and intentions of atoms, so that our knowledge of them is necessarily external and purely inductive, we can understand the human world, as Vico had said, because we are human beings. The *geistige Welt*, the world of objective mind in Idealist terminology, is accessible to our minds because they are, as it were, made of the same stuff. More simply, we understand a culture because we inhabit it; the form of understanding analysed in Dilthey's philosophy is not the total comprehension of the world of objective mind – all history, all culture – spoken of in Hegel's metaphysics, it is understanding of particular human situations. To experience these is necessarily also to interpret them.

This kind of understanding may be deliberately cultivated, and applied to history; it was particularly Dilthey's aim to give a philosophical account of the possibility of historical knowledge. History was for him the prime case of *Geisteswissenschaft*. The natural sciences established general laws, the human sciences sought the meaning – hermeneutic understanding – of unique human situations. We shall have to consider the importance of this conception – which existed, of course, before Dilthey's particular philosophical formulation – in German historiography generally in the next chapter. The greatest German achievement of the nineteenth century in cultural history, it can be strongly argued, was the Swiss Jacob Burckhardt's *The Civilization of the Renaissance in Italy* (1860). It came earlier than Dilthey's work; the latter knew Burckhardt and deplored his lack of methodological self-awareness. But Dilthey's own achievement was not to initiate but to give a sophisticated philosophical account and defence of the notion of the independence of the human sciences, a task made pressing by some of the imperialistic claims for the applicability of the natural sciences of the kind we have seen in Spencer and in Taine. Actually, in so far as it exercised a direct influence on historical writing in Germany as *Geistesgeschichte*, the history of mind or spirit, it was perhaps more detrimental than liberating, though the same cannot be said of Max Weber's kindred conception of the importance of *Verstehen*, inner understanding, in the social sciences. In historiography the marks of *Geistesgeschichte* seem too often to have been over-use of the concept of intuition and, in conjunction with the assumption, like Taine's, that in the great man all the vital currents of the age intersect, a crop of dubious biographies of supermen – Bismarck, the Emperor Frederick the Second – rather than particular painstaking studies like Burckhardt's, of local episodes in cultural history.

But we have now to turn back to the science or sciences – for they were diverse – of culture and collective psychologies which form, in a sense, the German counterpart to British anthropology, but with marked differences.

The background to these studies in Germany, as Woodruff D. Smith makes clear (*Politics and the Science of Culture in Germany 1840–1920*), was the failure of German liberation in 1848 and the evidence of the social divisions which had largely contributed to it; either the lower classes had not rallied to the revolution at all or they had proved more radical than liberals found acceptable. One inference drawn was the need to understand the cultural foundations of politics and to transcend a psychology focused, in liberal fashion, on the individual. The mentalities and culture of peoples could not be ignored; political behaviour was group behaviour and a simple undifferentiated concept of 'the people' was inadequate to explain it. There were class mentalities, urban and rural, as well as national and regional ones, all of which needed to be understood for the roots of the different collective mentalities to be uncovered. Ethnography, *Völkerkunde*, and *Volk*-psychology became fashionable disciplines in the 1850s, one of the moving spirits being Rudolf Virchow, whom we have already encountered as microbiologist and, later, Reichstag politician. Others were Adolf Bastian (1826–1905), the Romantic conservative Wilhelm Riehl (1823–97), who began publishing his *Natural History of Peoples* in 1851, and Theodor Waitz (1821–64) in his *Anthropologie der Naturvölker* (1859) – the last term has no exact equivalent in English, though 'savages' came nearest; it must be understood in contrast to its counterpart, *Kulturvölker*, peoples with a cultural history and development. Waitz's notion of cultural change was of its diffusion, rather than development along parallel lines of evolution; diffusionism was to be, in the long run, the characteristic assumption of German anthropology, though it did not avoid notions of 'higher' and 'lower' cultures. Compared with British anthropology there was also an emphasis on different kinds of environment and diverse historical experiences. The most famous of German cultural psychologists was Wilhelm Wundt (1832–1920), an experimental psychologist who had been assistant to Helmholtz. Wundt came close to a conception of group minds, like the English social psychologist William McDougall (1871–1938) later, in line with the Hegelian tradition in German thought and the romantic conception of a culture as an active psychic force: language, myth and customs provided evidence for the state of the *Volk*-soul in each period.

From the 1880s onwards, broadly speaking, anthropology and the science of culture in Germany became shaped not, as earlier, by a sense of the intellectual weakness of an individualistic liberalism, but more by the powerful interest and excitement generated in Germany by the concept of colonization, focused initially on the creation of a German empire in East Africa. Similarly, in Britain it was sometimes said that an imperial power needed the understanding of 'primitive' peoples provided by anthropology. In Germany the chief academic contributor to the enthusiasm for colonization from an anthropological perspective was Friedrich Ratzel (1844–1904); there were also, of course, economists propounding the notion of an economic sphere of influence and protectionism as an answer to the economic difficulties created by German industrial expansion. Ratzel was interested in imperial expansion not in terms of trade but as settlement, the appropriation of new lands to support a surplus agricultural population. He was a Darwinian who, beginning as a radical liberal, had moved, like others after 1870, into the camp of the National Liberals, as an admirer of Bismarck, and became interested in colonial expansion. Methodologically Ratzel was a cultural diffusionist with a strong interest in the migration of peoples; he had himself travelled in the American West. Migrant peoples were colonizers and the crucial academic and practical question was to account for their success or failure. Ratzel's answers were cultural, not racial (it was a time in Britain of much talk of the natural, i.e. racial, talent of the 'Anglo-Saxons' for colonization). According to Ratzel it was the cultural characteristics, the cultural durability and adaptability, that migrants took with them, that ensured their success.

Migration, in his view, was not an option but a necessity for a people. A keen Darwinian, he rebuked Darwin for having, in his theory, paid too little attention to migration as a factor in the evolutionary success of species. He became the sponsor of the fashionable and in the long run highly ominous conception of the *Lebensraum* (living space) of a people. This became in due course focused in Germany not on the unpromising conditions for European settlers in East Africa but on Central and Eastern Europe. *Lebensraum* was defined as the geographical area necessary to support a species at its current population level. Population growth requires geographical expansion; evolutionary success is determined by the ability to adapt to the requirements of permanent migration. The alternative to such success is decline and extinction. Ratzel presented his concept in 1901, in a *Festschrift* for the organicist sociologist Albert Schäffle, initially in a biological context. Human beings, however, competed not as species, or races, but as bearers of a particular culture. Ratzel regarded a sturdy, pioneer individualism as a major advantage in colonization, as he had seen it in the American West, but this too was a cultural trait; it was therefore, in a sense, cultures which competed. In the

concept of *Lebensraum* Darwinism and the German tradition of *Volkskunde*
came together.

By the end of the century it had become more or less axiomatic that,
being unique, cultures confronted each other as adversaries. It had not
always been so. For Herder, in the eighteenth century, each cultural voice
added an element, so to speak, to the choir of Humanity. Moreover the
relation between a people and its land was a mystical bond, crucial to its
identity. In Herder, for a people to be annexationist would have been a
kind of self-contradiction. Following him, nationalists in all countries
before 1848 looked forward only to a peaceful future in a Europe in which
a nation, its territory and its state were coterminous. The naïveté of this
later became apparent: intellectually speaking, Darwin was added, as it
were, to Herder; a people, according to Ratzel, must expand or die. Which
brings us to Social Darwinism.

## 2.4 Social Darwinism, Eugenics and Race

'Social Darwinism' is a term of art, used by historians rather than by its
proponents. It has in recent years caused a degree of semantic confusion
which seems quite unnecessary. Essentially the semantic issue is simple:
the phrase needs, chiefly, to be distinguished from the wider term used at
the time, Social Evolution, which could be at least as much Lamarckian or
Spencerian as Darwinian. The term 'adaptative', too, when encountered
on its own, is probably primarily Lamarckian. 'Social Darwinism' therefore, which, being a retrospective term we can use as we choose, provided
we do not muddy the waters further, seems most conveniently reserved
for ideas which in a social context seem to try to mirror the concept which
is Darwin's most specific contribution to the theory of evolution, namely
natural selection. In the process of transposition, of course, such ideas
experienced various deformations, and Darwin was not necessarily always
the immediate source; Spencer, who coined the more tendentious phrase
'the survival of the fittest', often looks like the intermediary, and he had in
fact been exploring an idea very much like it from the early 1850s onwards.
But Spencer's phrase, along with 'the struggle for existence (or life)', 'the
war of nature', 'the threat of extinction', 'the strongest prevail' and others
similar, are pointers to a body of ideas, not necessarily congruous, which it
is convenient to refer to as 'Social Darwinism'.

Of course in the frequent attempts – growing in frequency it seems at
the end of the century – to apply the concept of struggle with the authority

of science, either as a bracing warning or more generally as the supposedly necessary and perhaps sufficient condition of progress, or both, many ambiguities remained. Indeed, the ambiguities were responsible for the widespread popularity of the practice and the invariably inconclusive polemics it generated. For there were two crucial and almost unnoticed weaknesses in all attempted social applications of Darwin's concept. When invoked as an explanation of historical change or 'social evolution', it yields only a platitude; when invoked polemically, as a prescription for survival of a particular group or the continuation of progress, it merely produced arguments as contestable as the positions they were called on to support. In biology, where the relevant situations can be precisely specified in terms of reproduction, variation, adaptation, survival, breeding, and where the theories it replaced were mainly creationist or teleological, Darwinism was revolutionary, even though its capacity for prediction remained practically nil; there was always an unspecifiable number of possible ecological niches which a given variation might cause to be filled, and variation itself was random. In social life, creationist and even teleological arguments were in any case less common; social explanation was more sophisticated than explanations in biology until the nineteenth century, and the fact of change was uncontested. The relevant factors, however, reproduction and the rest, were for the most part only employable as metaphors and debatable ones at that. In social life, accordingly, the theory of environmental selection amounted only to the claim that innovations prospered when circumstances were propitious. No methodological revolution followed.

Much more popular and frequently urged by what the French called the *struggleforlifeur* were allegedly Darwinian prescriptions for ensuring that the supposedly inexorable conditions for future progress or for success in the struggle were met. Darwinian principles were invoked to defend social hierarchy or to attack it (depending on whether it was thought of as 'natural' or 'unnatural'); to condemn state intervention and welfare or to demand them; to justify extreme individualism or to denounce it. They were called on in social, economic, international, racial, imperialist and colonial contexts (where indigenous peoples were sometimes said to 'disappear' by evolutionary law with the advance of the white man). Extreme laissez-faire theorists, statists, nationalists, utilitarians, racialists, anti-humanitarians, even utopian believers in a future of universal peace and cooperation, found something apparently Darwinian ready to hand. The forms of invocation varied from interjection into a political or after-dinner speech to voluminous accounts of human history in the evolutionist mode and diagnoses of the contemporary crisis, in which the stake was national survival, progress, or civilization as the author knew it. Each country produced its treatises and warnings. In Britain, discounting Spencer, there were C. H. Pearson's *National Life and Character* (1893) and the immensely popular *Social Evolution* (1894) by Benjamin Kidd (1858–1916), who also managed to turn the article on Sociology for which he was responsible in the 1902 edition of the *Encyclopaedia Britannica* (reprinted in the 1911 edition) into a Social Darwinist manifesto. The leading French Social Darwinist was Georges Vacher de Lapouge (1854–1935), author of *Social Selection* (1896), who wanted among other things to replace 'Liberty, Equality, Fraternity' with 'Determinism, Inequality, Selection'; his popularity in France was limited. The most obvious German counterpart, though it would have been a close-run thing among the competitors, was Otto Ammon (1842–1916), author of *The Social Order and its Natural Foundations* (1895). These names, of course, are representative, not exhaustive.

The reason for the universal applicability (or non-applicability; it was the same thing) of 'Darwinian' principles in social life is very simple. What Social Darwinists chiefly argued about, without consciously putting it in those terms, which would have given the game away, was which form of competition was desirable and ensured progress or, if one adapted to it successfully, survival, and which types of competition should be suppressed; to have recognized them all as potentially operative, as a Darwinian would do in biology, would have removed the point. No respectable Social Darwinist endorsed successful private criminality, though the occasional young nihilist may have spoken in that way; laissez-faire theorists expected law and order at home and tended to deplore international competition as promoting state activity, and imperialism as both militarist and protectionist, as Spencer did. Nationalists tended to favour state intervention in the interests of a healthy and united people, and for the sake of, to use the phrase popular in Britain in the early 1900s, 'national efficiency'. Enthusiastic colonialists did not always applaud political Empires, sometimes deploring their multiracial character. One could go on multiplying examples. Self-evidently Darwinism cannot adjudicate between such competing claims; the form such arguments took was first to decide whom one wished to be the victors or survivors, and then to endorse or condemn forms of competition depending on whether they seemed likely to ensure the desired result. They could assume this form because there is no clear answer, in human society, to the question 'between what' does the struggle take place? – human beings have many roles and can be grouped in a number of different ways – any more than biology afforded any answer to the question what are the desirable or legitimate forms of competition? The human ability to control competition, though in a sense a weapon to use against opponents in a struggle for dominance, is one which has little counterpart in nature, and the use of moral preference to justify such control is, it hardly needs saying, unique to human beings.

Though intellectually inconclusive and resting on a mistaken analogy, the use of Social Darwinist rhetorics in the late nineteenth and early twentieth centuries was not, so far as one can judge, negligible in its consequences, in the sense that for those who used them or took them seriously they tended always, as one might say, to raise the stakes: to create a sense of permanent crisis and to make vast issues of progress or retrogression, of national, cultural or racial triumph, survival or extinction appear to depend on policy alternatives. Crimes against the law of life and death were always, in this rhetoric, punished with extreme, inexorable and irreversible severity. It would, of course, be wrong to attribute the sense of crisis only to the rhetoric which expressed it and to purely intellectual causes. Middle-class fears mounted with the advent of democracy over much of Europe after 1870 and still more with the growth of socialist mass political parties. The international situation was inevitably tenser with the advent of two new players, Italy and Germany (the latter of immense and growing power) and because of the unappeasable French desire for the recovery of Alsace and Lorraine and deep anxiety over the relative decline of French power and a negative rate of population renewal. Germany naturally exulted in her power and sought to secure it in perpetuity before the optimal moment passed. Economic competition intensified as the effects of the rapid growth in German and American industrial power were felt on world trade. Protectionist economic doctrines flourished, especially in Germany, at the expense of the earlier free trade liberal economic orthodoxy. Partly in consequence, imperialist annexationist designs intensified, on a dwindling stock of desirable, annexable territory globally; imperialism was also sometimes seen as a palliative for rising class tensions at home.

All this is true and Social Darwinist rhetoric fitted it smoothly, but the rhetoric itself militated always against moderation, compromise and cool heads. It is hard not to feel that someone with the nervous system of Kaiser Wilhelm II should ideally never be allowed anywhere near a phrase like 'the struggle for existence'. Great-power status, imperialist expansion, the control of crime or disease, were spoken of not just as desirable but as matters of national life or death. Class and racial tensions too were projected onto the scale of world history, of continuing social evolution, as though the fate of nations or humanity, with alternatives of utopia or the extremity of grovelling degeneracy, of world domination or ultimate extinction or enslavement, hung poised in a balance between a bit more or a bit less social inequality or welfare or state regulation, another battleship or thousand square miles of jungle or desert. Moderation of expectations of victory or disaster was not a lesson likely to be learned in the reading rooms of Vienna haunted by the young Hitler, or in any other European capital, in the years before 1914. It was typical of the period's addiction to immoderate rhetoric that socialist parties adapted in practice to parliamentary life but retained the idiom of revolution.

The note of social panic was not absent from the sciences of culture generally, and their practitioners. Pitt Rivers saw his collection of weapons in their evolutionary series as itself a kind of weapon, precisely in the cause of moderating expectations: 'The law that "Nature makes no jumps" can be taught by the history of mechanical contrivances, in such a way as at least to make men cautious how they listen to scatterbrained revolutionary suggestions.' Evolution was counter-revolutionary. Frazer in 'The Scope of Social Anthropology' (1908), his Liverpool inaugural lecture, after, significantly, quoting Renan on civilization as the work of a small élite, identified for his audience the 'astonishing, nay alarming, truth that a mass, if not the majority of people in every civilized society is still living in a state of intellectual savagery'. Taine, who devoted much of the latter part of his life to writing on the French Revolution in his *The Origins of Contemporary France* (1875–95), with an emphasis on mass irrationality and savagery that made him a precursor of the 'crowd psychology' of the end of the century, would have agreed heartily. We have noted, too, the influence of liberal disillusionment and anxiety on the development of *Völkerpsychologie*. In the case of the Eugenics movement, in a number of countries, which we have now to consider, with its focus on human breeding and 'degeneration', social panic was the very soil from which it grew.

'Degeneration' is at first sight a surprising concept to emerge from an evolutionist and Darwinian context. Darwin had, after all, declared that it would be fatal to the theory of natural selection if it could be proved that any mutation harmful to the organism concerned had ever been perpetuated by hereditary transmission. Spencer, however, considering evolution not just as adaptative transmutation but, by definition, as increasing complexity, thought that retrogression might have been just as common, though almost all his attention was devoted to evolution. In 1880, with fears of degeneration gaining currency, the Professor of Zoology at Cambridge, Ray Lankester, took up the issue in a short essay provocatively entitled 'Degeneration. A Study in Darwinism'. Taking the concept of evolution as increase in complexity he argued that it could be diminished as well as increased by natural selection; it all depended on the environment. 'Degeneration may be defined as a gradual change of the structure, in which the organism becomes adapted to *less* varied and *less* complex conditions of life' (emphasis original). This could occur with cases of adaptation by parasitism, immobility or minute size. After contemplating for a while a very small life-form which might be said to have degenerated, Lankester drew an ominous lesson for 'the white races of Europe'.

Degeneration was a possibility his contemporaries were very willing to contemplate if not passively to tolerate. The chief scientific backing, however, came not directly from biology but from evolutionary psychology, where it was sometimes also spoken of as regression and occurred initially at least not as actual organic degeneration, though that might follow, but as a disease of function in individuals, and for 'the race' as the more rapid breeding of the already less evolved section of the population. It had become axiomatic in evolutionary psychology that reflex and instinct were formed before the higher centres of rational, deliberative, self-critical consciousness, which grew out of them. It was therefore surely natural that human beings' grip on their latest evolved faculties should be the most precarious, and some might scarcely have acquired them at all. Under stress, or the pressure of imitation, regression would be all too easy. Unconscious memories, whose existence was taken for granted (what else were reflex actions due to?) were a mass of sensitivities created by past experiences which could easily be reactivated, with the reflexes evoked by them, at any time, without conscious volition. The result would be a literal regression. As the psychologist and asylum director Henry Maudsley (1835–1916) wrote (*Body and Mind*, 1873), 'In the deepest and most secret recesses of mind there is nothing [at the moment] hidden from the individual self or from others which may not be thus at some time accidentally repeated.' Volition, Maudsley went on, is 'a physiological function of the supreme centres', which can be 'enfeebled by disease, decaying with decay of structure'. In cases of idiocy there sometimes appear or reappear remarkable animal traits and instincts. Brains themselves form a hierarchy, from men down through women and savages and perhaps hereditary criminals, to apes. Habitual criminals were moral imbeciles, 'a morbid or degenerate variety of mankind'. Maudsley's later work, *Body and Will* (1883), contained a

section on degeneration and emphatically asserted that disuse of a function eventually ends in the decay of the organ. Maudsley's Lamarckianism
is very evident throughout, as, explicitly, in a declaration like 'the acquired
infirmity of one generation will . . . become the natural deficiency of a
succeeding generation'.

Contemporary psychology was not, in general, likely to inspire
confidence in the power of the will. Taine described the mind, in *On
Intelligence*, in terms of a perpetual jostling for pre-eminence (he made the
Darwinian analogy) of past and present images, all capable of evoking
action. The compound they made was an inherently unstable one, except
where one especially powerful image held permanent sway. Sane lives, with
realistic assessment of situations, which Taine thought extremely rare, are
thus lived precariously between the alternatives of instability and obsession.
Taine's friend Théodule Ribot (1839–1916), the doyen of French psychology in the later years of the century, made a similar point in his *The Psychology
of Attention* (1890 ). Attention, which is a focusing of energy, required the
nicest of balancing acts to avoid atrophy and consequent apathy or delirium
on the one hand, as an uncontrolled state of associational flux, and on the
other the hypertrophy of obsession. In his *Maladies of the Will* (1884), Ribot
postulated a permanent exchange of energy between reflex and will; as
one increased the other diminished.

It has been suggested by Robert Nye, in his very useful study *Crime,
Madness and Politics in Modern France: The Medical Concept of National Decline*
(Princeton, 1984), that the gloomy character of French psychology in this
period is partly explained by the fact that – to a greater extent than Germany, where experimental psychology had a firm base in the universities –
its context was so largely pathological: those restrained as insane were by
far the easiest human beings to observe and to whom to apply tests; the
same considerations apply to Maudsley's work. There were also the famous
demonstrations of hypnotism by J. M. Charcot (1825–93) as part of the
treatment of hysteria at the Salpêtrière hospital in Paris, which immense
numbers of notable figures, including Taine and the young Freud, attended.
These demonstrated the power of suggestion and the apparent ease with
which it could override rational consciousness and will. Alongside the
pathological turn given to psychology there was also the omnipresent awareness of 'the masses', the term which significantly largely replaced the old,
resonant term 'the people' towards the end of the century. The masses were
often thought of, along with women with their predilection for hysteria,
as the less evolved part of the population and the most prone to regression.

The most prominent and systematic application of evolutionary psychology to this contemporary anxiety was made by Gustave le Bon (1841–1931), the pioneer of crowd psychology, in his best-selling *The Crowd* (1895). Le Bon was an élitist Social Darwinist, an extreme anti-Christian and anti-humanitarian liberal individualist. In *The Crowd* we see a somewhat fatalistic hostility to democracy and socialism combined with a 'scientific' interest in irrational behaviour. Le Bon uses 'crowd' in an extended sense: all assemblies, for example parliaments, are crowds. The crowd creates conditions, by imitation and contagion – which is sometimes spoken of as something literal and physical, like an electromagnetic field – in which the higher functions of consciousness, critical deliberation and the conscious exercise of will (which are essentially individual) are suspended and human beings regress to the level of reflex responsiveness. The predominance of crowds in modern society – democracy in fact – is therefore itself a kind of institutionalized regression. 'The substitution of the unconscious action of crowds for the conscious activity of individuals is one of the principal characteristics of the present age.' Crowd actions are 'far more under the influence of the spinal cord than the brain' and so, in the crowd, 'a man descends several rungs in the ladder of civilization'. Crowds respond to slogans, which synthesize diverse unconscious aspirations, and to images, not to concepts and arguments. Crowds are above all suggestible and are dealt with by their leaders as hypnotic subjects are by the hypnotist, but with the difference that the leaders themselves are drawn from the highly susceptible: 'They are recruited from the ranks of those morbidly nervous, excitable, half-deranged persons who are bordering on madness.' Le Bon's book gives an account of what Weber was famously to call 'charisma' and in Le Bon is called prestige. There is also a suggestion that scientific awareness of the character of crowds could provide the basis for their conscious, one could say cynical, manipulation by a leader; one must either be dominated by crowds or consciously control them with the aid of a scientific understanding of their nature.

The idea of science as the means to conscious control of mass society by a rational élite, acting to arrest an otherwise irresistible tendency to regression or degeneration, is also the central idea of Eugenics. The pioneer was Darwin's son-in-law, Francis Galton (1822–1911), who gave it its name, and an interest in Eugenics was the only form of Social Darwinism apparently licensed by Darwin himself. In a sense Eugenics, like much Social Darwinism, was Darwinism stood on its head: one decided whom one wanted to breed and to rear offspring and then tried to arrange the environment accordingly. It was akin to what Darwin in *The Origin* had called 'artificial selection'. The 'Darwinist' justification for this was that in human societies natural selection was in any case largely suspended; the society itself, its rules and conditions, form the most important part of the controlling environment – Lapouge's 'Social Selection'. But inadvertent social selection may run counter to what nature would have selected if given a free hand – not to mention what the society, or its influential members, wished to see as its future. Social selection, if not consciously controlled, might, by the preservation of the less 'fit' and their offspring, ensure not evolution but degeneration of the breeding 'stock'. 'Degeneration' became a word of power, menace and extensive currency in the late nineteenth and early twentieth centuries. The breeding of the less fit, degenerates, must be prevented. These were the insane, alcoholics, sufferers from hereditary diseases such as syphilis and tuberculosis, vagrants, criminals (criminality was often assumed to be heritable, an idea associated particularly with the Italian criminologist Cesare Lombroso (1835–1909)), the irresponsible, and what the English Charity Organization Society called the 'undeserving poor'. All these must be prevented if at all possible from passing on their hereditary attributes into the national – the context was invariably national, if only because only national governments could act – human stock, the race, as it was often loosely called, of the future.

Apart from the non-interventionist Eugenics of the withdrawal of the state from the support of the indigent there were also 'negative' and 'positive' versions of Eugenic intervention; the former concentrated on such issues as sterilization, segregation and obligatory medical tests before marriage. Socialists and nationalists, however, sometimes also supported bounties for healthy couples to produce offspring and state-provided maternal care. The last appealed to some feminists, along with birth control, like the leading German feminist Helene Stöcker (1869–1943). There were, as will be apparent from this list, plenty of opportunities for dissension among eugenists. If eugenists were sometimes social as well as biological élitists there was also an egalitarian eugenist argument against 'artificial' class barriers to the natural operation of sexual selection: an argument with obvious appeal to sexually confident members of the lower classes and a surprising alliance between Eugenics and popular romance.

It was universally agreed that the problems of degeneracy addressed by Eugenics flourished, above all, in the great cities. It was among the impoverished, semi-criminalized or criminal populations, the 'dangerous classes' and among vagrants that hereditary disease and moral degeneracy were chiefly to be found, rather than, say, in the inbreeding of isolated rural communities. Peasants, in this rhetoric, were apt to be sturdy, though not – in the novels of Emile Zola (1840–1902), for example – invariably. But emphasis and objects of greatest concern were apt also to vary from country to country, partly for demographic reasons. In Britain eugenic concern was a matter first of class. There was a time lag, in the latter part of the century, between reduction in average family size in the middle and working classes respectively. The less able, thrifty and responsible seemed to be outbreeding their intellectual and moral betters; the survival of the fittest, if not treated as an ironic tautology, seemed in danger of becoming a falsehood. London, too, with its swarming yet partly invisible masses of the unhealthy, ill-fed poor, became something of an obsession; invisible in the sense of partly inaccessible to the controlling hand of respectability, of clergy, doctors, school attendance officers, policemen. There was also a growingly felt unease over declining global and imperial power even when this seemed at its zenith; rivalry with Germany was the context for a good many pronouncements in the slang of Social Darwinism. In the early 1900s anxiety had been accentuated by the poor physical quality of the volunteers presenting themselves at recruiting stations during the Boer War, and a Parliamentary Committee on Physical Deterioration was set up which reported in 1904. The most obvious remedies were dietary and environmental, but the Lamarckian idea of environmentally induced *hereditary* defects had by no means died out.

Still less was it dead in France, where the concept of 'degeneration', in a context provided by France's declining birth rate and manifestly growing military and demographic inferiority to Germany, set up perhaps its most powerful tremors. There was a Lamarckian style of eugenist concern as well as a Darwinian one, which is not to imply that the two were clearly distinguished. In a context set mainly by Lamarckianism, denunciations of bad environmental conditions, essentially those of the great city, were not in competition with hereditarian explanations of enfeeblement or brutishness; seen as degeneration the two went together. As Nye points out, it was accepted that, once badly begun, the degenerative sequence could be expected, in Lamarckian terms, to proceed ever downwards; adaptation to bad conditions made people worse; the malign adaptations would be inherited and their bearers could be expected to make or find an even worse social environment for themselves and their offspring, and so on down the scale of degeneration to its end in the asylum or on the guillotine. This is the underlying thread in Zola's sequence of novels dealing with that late nineteenth-century counterpart to the House of Atreus, the family Rougon-Maquart, over whose members hereditary generation cast its dreadful shadow. The commitment to Naturalism in literature, of which Zola was the leading figure, was in a sense a fictional counterpart to Taine's determinism, though Zola himself pointed to the example of Claude Bernard's treatise on the experimental method in science, speaking of his own novel *Thérèse Raquin* (1867) as an experiment with two psycho-physical temperaments brought into conjunction, leading to its inevitable outcome.

Bleak though the assumptions of Lamarckian degenerationism were, there was, at least, in the importance accorded to the environment, a gleam of hope. Lamarckians were not entirely condemned, as Darwinians were unless means could be taken to control breeding, to fatalism. Improved environmental conditions should work favourable (heritable) effects, so there was a role for social amelioration as well as for eugenic controls over the breeding of the unfit. Eugenists were actually more likely to be social-ists of some sort, as a significant number were in Britain, than laissez-faire individualists bent on allowing the negative breeding controls of unrelieved economic competition, as well as a possible eugenic intervention enforced by law, to do their benign rough work. Eugenics spanned the political spectrum.

It did so in Germany too, but here the attack on Lamarckian environ-mentalism by the biologist August Weismann (1843–1913), whose theory of the germ-plasm as the basis of heredity, presented in 1892, was incom-patible with the heritability of acquired characters, had important effects, in promoting a shift from social meliorism to selective breeding alone as the only weapon against degeneration. In Germany, too, though the usual range and focusing of eugenic concerns were present, an ominous conjunction occurred. Racial theories flourished everywhere in the later nineteenth century, and anti-Semitism, in particular, became unprecedentedly virulent and widespread, and also, in France and Germany, politicized, from the 1880s onwards. In France it was an aspect mainly of exacerbated nationalism and a form of anti-capitalist rhetoric. In Germany, though it was these things too, it was also a response to large-scale Jewish immigra-tion from Central and Eastern Europe towards the end of the century, as a consequence of government-tolerated pogroms in the Russian empire. In Germany pre-existing eugenic ideas became, in the 1900s, entangled with pre-existing racial ones and notions of 'race purity'. The concept of germ-origin of disease, current since the 1870s, as another product of microbiology, also contributed, in a crop of military metaphors: the germ 'attacked' or 'invaded' the cells. The application of such metaphors to another kind of assumed invasiveness, that of alien 'blood' through inter-breeding, made a natural bridge between the concepts of hygiene and racial purity. It can hardly seem to be other than a portent that the Racial Hygiene Society was founded in Berlin in 1905, though the phrase expressed all kinds of eugenic concern, not just that with racial interbreeding.

There remained the question of what was to be kept pure, the question of racial classification. Historically, of course, this is to put the question the wrong way round; it was only the existence of a cherished idea of race that made the notion of invasion or adulteration of concern. We need to answer it, however, and in order to put the most immediately relevant concept of race into perspective we need to consider its origins. One origin is indeed in taxonomy, in the impulse to classification with which we began this chap-ter, developed chiefly by comparative anatomists from the later eighteenth century onwards. From the beginning, mental and moral characters had been, more impressionistically but apparently as confidently, attached to the anatomical classifications, especially craniological ones, on which the 'scientific' treatment of race differences chiefly relied. This united the ma-terialist intellectual climate of late eighteenth-century France, in particular, and the cultural bias of the medical men who mainly constructed the tax-onomies. 'Racial Science', therefore, was also from the beginning a science of culture; some held the only one. Related to this was the irresistible disposition to arrange human varieties as a hierarchy, with 'white', or what the physical anthropologist J. F. Blumenbach (1752–1840) had somewhat fancifully called 'Caucasian' (he owned a fine skull from the Caucasus in his collection) at the top, and negroes or sometimes Bushmen or Hottentots at the bottom.

It was becoming orthodoxy in the first half of the nineteenth century among physical anthropologists and through them to the wider intellectual community, that the Enlightenment (and Christian) assertion of human equality was mere dogma. Hostility to the consequences of the French Revolution, and the metaphysics of Natural Law which had produced the French Declaration of the Rights of Man as its manifesto, helped to make this in many circles a congenial notion. By the latter part of the century it had become something of a commonplace, and a mark of intellectual realism in the face of doctrinaire theorists, to assert that the theoretical foundations of democracy were refuted by science. Environmental explanations of human difference were in retreat too, and taxonomies focused less on such apparently superficial characters as pigmentation and skin texture, which might conceivably be the effects of environment, and more on anatomical criteria of classification. The great anatomist Cuvier, significantly an anti-evolutionist, dismissed the possibility of environments altering structure, though that, of course, was exactly what Lamarckians believed. The inability to explain anatomical differences among human groups or races, in the absence of a generally acceptable theory of evolution, had given rise by the mid-century to a view that races had separate origins and were in effect separate species; under the name 'polygenism' this then had some claims to be scientific orthodoxy, though of course Biblically unorthodox. The acceptance of evolution in the wake of Darwin's *Origin* removed the need to resort to polygenist explanations; even anatomy, given time, was malleable. But the influence of Darwinism was hardly egalitarian. If different species could evolve from a common origin, then a common origin did not entail that races had not evolved, as it were, into quasi-species, different evolutionary lines with now innate, distinct characters, physical and mental. The hierarchical classification could become, as in so many other cases, a conjectural evolutionary one, and inferiority a consequence either of degeneration or retarded evolutionary development. There was discussion of racial interbreeding as hybridism. It was clear that the offspring of such unions were not necessarily sterile, as in the case of true hybrids, but might they not be enfeebled, and sterile within a few generations? If so, that way would lie the ultimate horror of extinction.

Anatomical classification was the hallmark of physical anthropology; it flourished in France, Germany and Britain. Classifications of races in the early nineteenth century ranged from two to sixteen. Craniology took pride of place, but facial angles were measured, forearm to upper arm ratios calculated, and other wonders, as criteria of classification. Often in such taxonomies Europeans appeared undifferentiated, simply as 'the white race', and in extra-European contexts this was largely how they continued to figure, as European nations annexed or colonized much of the globe. Whether the classifications altered attitudes much, or merely reflected them, is open to doubt, though polygenist arguments were invoked in pro-slavery polemics in the antebellum United States, while Social Darwinist arguments were sometimes invoked to justify expropriation of indigenous peoples. The belief in the ineradicability of racial characters and the decay of confidence in directly environmentalist explanations tended to dampen expectations of rapid 'improvement' among subject peoples, a consideration relevant to missionary activity; even the long-term environmentalist explanation implicit in Evolution remained just that: long term.

Opportunities for physical anthropologists in Europe were naturally more restricted, but a number were undeterred. It has been claimed that in the three decades from 1860 twenty million Europeans (many, of course, made captive by compulsory schooling and military service) were subjected to anthropological measurement. The main theory was that of Andreas Retzius (1796–1860), who, as a way of tracing the migrations and origins of Europe's inhabitants, put forward the conception of two main types, dolichocephalic (long-headed) and brachycephalic (round-headed). The former were supposedly the descendants of invaders from the north, and the two types were identified as respectively Nordic and Mediterranean (also Alpine and even, sometimes, Asiatic). The types also supposedly correlated with complexion and hair colour: Nordics should be fair-haired and complexioned and blue-eyed. The German Social Darwinist, eugenist and racialist Otto Ammon was a keen supporter of the long-headed Nordics thesis.

In fact the results of the measuring were inconclusive, both for the claimed correlations and for national distribution: ethnic purity, by these criteria, seemed not to be characteristic of European nations. The whole thing would presumably have remained an anthropologists' game and to others a passing nuisance, had there not also been a powerful and long-standing myth of European origins, based on the idea of invasion from the north, to which the Nordic cranium might bring the support of scientific physical anthropology, and also a myth of Teutonic superiority easily reconceived in 'Nordic' ethnic terms.

Eighteenth-century antiquaries, around the time the physical taxono-mies began to be devised, but inhabiting a different intellectual world, had interested themselves, sometimes under the influence of hurt national pride and with polemical intent, in trying to establish the relations of modern European peoples to those spoken of by ancient geographers and ethnographers like Strabo and Tacitus: Celts, Goths, Scythians, Sarmatians. Celts and Goths or Teutons became the main players and honourable or despicable characteristics were freely attributed to them. The Teutonic myth derived largely from the *Germania* of Tacitus and from its role in English and French constitutionalism in the eighteenth century, where Saxons and Franks respectively, as Germanic peoples, presumably carried with them in their migrations the German institutions described by Tacitus, notably a love of independence and the absence of hereditary monarchy. The myth of 'Saxon freedom' was a persisting one in English politics in all classes, though by the late nineteenth century it derived its contemporary significance mostly from the notion that the English, as the 'Anglo-Saxon race' had a special talent, which was easily converted into a mission, for colonization. The notion that French society had been divided for more than a thousand years into a noble class of Germanic, Frankish invaders and plebeian Gauls was current throughout the eighteenth and nineteenth centuries, and was important to 'the father of racist ideology' Arthur de Gobineau.

Along with reference to classical texts, philology had been the tool, erratically used, of eighteenth-century antiquaries. The systematic study of linguistic relationships was only put on a firm footing at the end of the eighteenth century with the discovery of the relation of Sanskrit to all the main European languages. This not only founded the science of comparative philology – yet another classificatory-developmental schema – but gave rise in the early nineteenth century to the notion of a racial parent for the European peoples, an *Ur-Volk*, the Aryans, who had supposedly migrated from northern India to conquer and people the European continent in prehistoric times. The Aryans were christened by Friedrich Schlegel (1772–1829) in 1819. If the Germans were pioneers of the Aryan myth, the category had become established across European scholarship by the mid-century; Renan and Maine, in different contexts, were notable Aryanists. The Aryans were particularly welcome to those, and this included both the German Romantics and Renan, who wished to detach European ethnic and cultural origins from the Judaeo-Christian tradition and the authority of the Bible. The Hebrews eventually, with Renan playing a part, became spiritual antitypes; the Jews were materialistic and legalistic, the Aryans essentially spiritual and creative, Renan's 'children of light'; again one is reminded of the old theory of the elements, earth, air and fire particularly.

Virtually all Europeans were, if linguistic affinities could be transposed into ethnic ones, Aryans; but some, it became widely understood, as a result of promiscuous interbreeding, were less Aryan than others. The multiracial Roman empire came to be regarded as a particular source of mongrelization. The Nordic or Teutonic peoples, however, had largely held themselves aloof from this degeneracy. The Germans, as well as being the progenitors of constitutional freedom, were the purest of the European races, though it was usually understood that 'German' was to be given a wide significance, including English, Scandinavians and even sometimes Celts. Gobineau's work was a product not only of the Aryan theory but of the myths of German superiority in its French aristocratic, Frankish form. The context for Gobineau's fatalistic pessimism, expressed in his *On the Inequality of the Human Races* (1853–5), was above all class, and the identification of the French nobility as ethnically German. The Germans alone, as the purest of the Aryan stock, retained some virtue, but with the decline and elimination of the French aristocracy, all that remained was the mongrelized plebeians and universal levelling. Race was always the determining element in the creation of a civilization. Interbreeding was fatal to it, and in a wholly mongrelized Europe no worthwhile civilization could survive. Gobineau, a monarchist and self-appointed aristocrat (he assumed the title of 'Count'), was, it seems, yet another European intellectual for whom 1848 was a turning point, turning him, in fact, towards the idea of race in the context of social levelling. It was his achievement, if that is the correct word, to clothe hatred of democracy and pseudo-aristocratic nostalgia with a universal theory of racial degeneration.

Gobineau's work initially fell flat. His nostalgia for aristocracy and his pro-Germanism were hardly recipes for popularity in the France of the mid-century. His work became much more popular after a second edition in the 1880s. French democracy was in disrepute under the Third Republic; there were fears of socialism, and admiration of things German had become a form of national self-abasement. Predictably, Gobineau became popular in Germany; a Gobineau Society was founded there in 1894. The most obvious successor to Gobineau's racial interpretation of human history, with its denunciations of interbreeding, was Houston Stewart Chamberlain's *Foundations of the Nineteenth Century* (1899). Chamberlain (1855–1927) was an Englishman who had become Wagner's son-in-law and settled in Germany. We shall have to return to his ideas in Chapter 6; here it is enough to say that in his work the Jew emerges, as he does not in Gobineau, as the rival protagonist to the Teuton in the world-historical drama which, according to Chamberlain, was now unfolding.

Gobineau's work was in a sense mis-titled. There was nothing particularly novel about the notion of human inequality, though it was an obvious way of thumbing one's nose at French republicanism. What was original in Gobineau, apart from the extremity of his pessimism, was the establishment of racial purity and racial interbreeding as the key to all civilization and human history. It was the successor, in a sense, to the eighteenth-century identification of 'luxury' as the cause of the decline of states and civilizations. Gobineau's essay preceded Darwin's *Origin*, in which of course there is no such conception, yet by the end of the century it had joined it as one of the sources from which the notion of the race or nation as primarily a breeding population derived. Race had become identified, particularly in Germany, together with other concerns touched on in this chapter – regressive popular irrationality, the degenerating populations of great cities, national survival, the supplanting of religion and the dynamics of social progress – as one of the pressing issues which the tumid contemporary notion of the competence of science was expected to address.

# CHAPTER 3

## *Community and Modernity*

### *3.1 The Market and Modernity*

In the present state of Europe, a man of ten thousand a year can spend his whole revenue, and he generally does so, without directly maintaining twenty people or being able to command more than ten footmen not worth the commanding. Indirectly, perhaps, he maintains as great or even a greater number of people than he could have done by the ancient method of expense . . . Though he contributes, therefore, to the maintenance of them all, they are more or less independent of him, because generally they can all be maintained without him. (*The Wealth of Nations* (1776), Bk III, ch. iv)

In these succinct words Adam Smith summarized the consequence of what a later generation would learn, chiefly from Marx, to call the decline of feudalism and the rise of capitalism, which Smith called 'commerce and manufactures'. Smith's account describes the unintended emancipation of the individual from bondage to a lord. The means by which the rich consumer now contributes to the maintenance of many men, while the manufacturer or artisan and the merchant, in some measure dependent on his custom, nonetheless retain their full personal independence of him, is the mutual dependence of all of them on the impersonal institution of the market. It is the market which brings together the rich man's money, through his wants and purchases, and their work through the goods they produce or purvey, without their ever needing to be acquainted or even aware of each other's individual existence, much less their being in a relation of paternalist authority and servile or semi-servile dependence. The social consequence of the change – of the market in fact – is a society of free citizens, bound together only by what Thomas Carlyle was 60 years later to call 'the cash nexus' and Marx, at the same time, was to describe as a mode of life which, emancipated from the relations of personal domination in a feudal society, had become an impersonal mechanism, beyond control by any human will; the relations of capital and labour constituted a new form of bondage in which all, including the capitalist, were helplessly entrapped and of which all the other aspects of society were merely reflections.

The only way, according to Marx in his early writings in the 1840s – some not to be published until a century later – in which collective human will could assert itself over the relations of economic and social life was through the overthrow of the whole system by the one class, the proletariat, which having nothing but its labour to sell, not for profit but for mere subsistence, had no stake in it. In doing so the proletariat would act as the emancipator not only of itself but of all humanity, again asserting the control of human will over the arrangements of human society, whose members, under the domination of production for the market, and through it for profit and capital-accumulation, had become utterly estranged from each other. For one thing that Marx and Smith agreed on was that feudalism, a system of personal as well as tenurial dependence on a lord, had been replaced by something in its nature entirely impersonal, the market. Labour, no longer the hereditary property of the lord, as in serfdom, became a commodity to be bought and sold like any other; the landowner, in Smith's account, had voluntarily degraded himself from a warlord to a customer and rentier. To Smith the overall consequence was emancipation of the individual. To Marx and to Carlyle, wage slavery was worse than serfdom because wholly insecure and unmitigated by any personal human relationship.

These two perspectives set the terms of much social and political debate, and in some cases historical inquiry, in the second half of the nineteenth century, though not necessarily directly from those sources. In Marx's case the moral critique of capitalism in his early writings remained largely unknown to his contemporaries, for whom 'Marxism' became constituted above all by the predominantly economic critique he formulated in *Capital* (1867–94). One turn the debates constantly took was an historical one. When and how and with what consequences had the impersonal social and economic relations characteristic of modernity emerged, and the individual been emancipated, for better or worse, from the constraints and supports of the community in which he had once been so tightly held? We have already considered two answers to this, in the guise of Social Evolution, in Spencer and Durkheim. Another aspect of the historical perspective was the partial historicization of economics, or to use its earlier name, Political Economy. Smith's account of the market had been firmly placed in an historical, and indeed moral, context. In the ensuing generations Political Economy, particularly through David Ricardo in his *Principles of Political Economy* (1817), had become an ahistorical science of the 'laws' governing the ratios between the shares allocated to wages, profit and rent, under varying conditions, in a market economy, given a limited supply of land, with different levels of productivity for a given investment. How the system had come about was irrelevant. For Marx what mattered was that it seemed to have become one outside the control of human will. Capital, the product of past labour accumulated as profit, dominated the human beings who, for wages or future profits, under the pressure of competition, must work according to the economic laws which produced further capital accumulation; the system worked not for human beings, even capitalists who must also obey its laws, but to perpetuate itself. Its alleged inability to do so indefinitely because, essentially, of the crises of underconsumption caused by the tendency (in the model) of wages to diminish to subsistence level, was the message Marx preached in *Capital*.

Marx both accepted and did not accept the claim that the laws of Political Economy were inexorable. Within the system indeed they were; in fact he can be criticized for taking the economists' model of how a capitalist economy worked, including the tendency of wages to the level of subsistence, altogether too literally, to the detriment of his own predictions about it. But in another sense he did not: capitalism was not the way economic laws as such worked; it was only the way a particular kind of economy worked. There was an economic and social past before capitalism and there would be a communist future beyond it, brought about by the self-destructive nature of capitalism in which subsistence wages for prospective purchasers would necessarily produce crises of overproduction, and sealed by political revolution. The fundamental laws were not those of bourgeois Political Economy, but the historical laws which accounted both for the emergence and the supersession of capitalism, the materialist revision of the historical dialectic which Marx had taken from Hegel. Acceptance of this historical law, along with the refusal, on which Marx always insisted, to accept even a temporary bargain with the 'bourgeois State', became the hallmark of Marxist orthodoxy among Socialists and Communists, as in the newly legalized Marxist Social Democratic Party in Germany from 1890.

Marx's contemporary reputation was as an international revolutionary, as which he struggled with what he saw as shallow compromisers, notably

Ferdinand Lasalle (1825–1874), and childish anarchists (Bakunin) for control of the international working-class movement, and secondly as an historical economist or even economic historian. The turn towards history was one of the two main ways Economics, as Political Economy came to be called, developed in the nineteenth century, the other being yet further development, known as 'marginalism', in the direction of refined, and now mathematical, modelling of the working of the market economy. The conflict between the two in Germany was known as the *Methodenstreit*, the conflict of methods. The academic economists who, on the other hand, relativized economics in historical terms, were not, like Marx, revolutionaries, but they did, chiefly in Germany, notably broaden the scope of their subject. Economists in the mould of Wilhelm Roscher (1817–94) and Gustav Schmoller (1838–1917), sometimes identified as *Kathedersozialisten* (socialists of the professional chair), regarded issues of poverty and welfare and of the relation of economic policy to national power as centrally within their academic concerns.

For Marx the capitalist economy was the central feature of modern life because the materialist conception of history ordained that how procuring the means of subsistence was organized was always the primary causal agency in any society, everything else being derivative. Hence the state, in a capitalist society, was not an independent institution but a mere organ of the capitalist mode of production and the class relationships established by it. Marx's dogmatic claim, based on a materialist metaphysics, to knowledge of the invariable causal priority of the mode and organization of production over all the aspects of social life, such as government, laws, ideas, religion and culture – what he called the superstructure – was not, of course, acceptable to anyone but his socialist followers, though Durkheim, as we have seen, can be said to have made a rather similar claim, without the metaphysics, for the causal priority of adaptation and the economic division of labour, though he came to insist on this less in his later career. In so far as the elements of a society were thought of as systematically related, with a single predominant causal agency uniting them, the latter was most usually, as in Comte, J. S. Mill and Taine, identified as the governing idea of an intellectual consensus. When it came to specifying the central attributes of modernity, in contrast to traditional societies, tribal or feudal, a variety of answers was offered, and the theoretical question of invariable causal priority was often sensibly ignored. It was widely perceived that criteria of modernity – they would generally rather have spoken of 'progress' – included free labour and alienable private property, but also the impersonality or impartiality of the modern State, and the concept of equal citizenship (though not necessarily equality of political rights); the conscious, rational, controlled pursuit of given ends by appropriate means, whether as individual economic rationality or in the making of legal contracts, and legislation by the sovereign state contrasted with the binding force of custom and a multitude of overlapping jurisdictions. Finally there was what we now speak of as secularization, the removal of religious monopolies, civil disabilities and religious sanctions and censorship, enforced by law; in all countries secularization made up a large part of the content of liberal political programmes.

## 3.2 Community: The Mark, the Mir and the Guild

These alternative or combined specifications of modernity, of progress and its consequences, also often involved a refocusing of historical attention, from Smith's and Marx's primary interest in the transition from feudalism, which is also the focus of the Saint-Simonian, Comtean and Spencerian contrast of two social types as respectively Military and Industrial, to the emergence out of tribalism which engaged the attention, again of Spencer, but also of Bagehot and Durkheim as we saw in the last chapter. Indeed, to Henry Maine, one of the newer school in this respect, feudalism was actually a progressive step towards individualism because it involved the separating out of a concept of property which marked at least a half-way stage between co-ownership by a group of kin and the modern concept of free, disposable, individually-owned real property.

There were several reasons for this shift of historical attention backwards from feudalism to the kin-group or the village of co-proprietors. The concept of social evolution tended to drive attention back to the supposedly most primitive nuclear units. The waning political power of the aristocracies, especially in France, and the focusing instead on the issue of private versus collective property prompted by the rise of socialism, particularly in association with notions of land nationalization fashionable towards the end of the century, was another consideration. So too, though less obviously, was the development, above all in Germany, of the historical study of law, including ancient customary law. The development of a systematic discipline of historical jurisprudence is an under-acknowledged prerequisite of much historically-oriented nineteenth-century social thought; it underlies, for example, a good deal of Durkheim's *Division of Labour*. It encouraged confidence that the emergence of private property and the rational legal device of contract could be traced, from their remotest origins, in the gradual relaxation of the power of custom and status in the extended family of the kin-group.

In speaking of the relevance given to such inquiries by the importance assumed by socialism in the last quarter of the century, however, there is a need not to anticipate. The development of historical jurisprudence in Germany, and the focus on customary law, derived initially, in the first half of the century, from a Romantic and nationalistic interest in all the ancient manifestations of the collective life of the *Volk*. The seminal figure of Jakob Grimm, for example, was a Germanic folklorist and legal antiquary; the two, for him, were part of the same enterprise. There was, indeed, a considerable potential for political cross purposes as, later in the century, an initial Romantic conservatism touched hands with newer socialistic enthusiasms, over the head, so to speak, of the triumphalist liberal individualism of the mid-century represented, above all, by Maine. For him the emergence of disposable real property, and of the independent individual from ascribed status within the kin-group, represented the key to the difference between progress and stagnation: 'the movement of the progressive societies has hitherto been a movement from Status to Contract' and, in another epigram, 'the unit of an ancient society was the Family, of a modern society the individual'. Initially concerned with the early history of Roman law, in his later work, still drawing on German legal historians, he turned to the evidence, chiefly in ancient Teutonic society, for the group of agricultural co-proprietors known as the *Mark* community.

Maine was understandably irritated to find himself sometimes misunderstood as arguing that, because property was originally communal, modern property rights rested on a usurpation, or that because individual property rights were not natural in the sense of original, but were an historical product, they might also be superseded as 'society' reassumed its rights. He was arguing nothing of the kind, but others, including, rather remarkably, J. S. Mill, did. The socialist and historical economist Emile de Laveleye spoke frankly of the aim 'to establish historically the natural right of property as proclaimed by philosophers, as well as to show that ownership has assumed very various forms' (*On Property and its Primitive Forms*, 1878) and another radical academic, Charles Letourneau (1831–1902), wrote that 'In Western Europe the agricultural communities have been slowly destroyed by a series of usurpations and encroachments of the strong against the weak' (*Property: Its Origin and Development*, 1889).

The Teutonic *Mark* community, which some constitutional historians tried also to identify in Anglo-Saxon England, was admittedly archaic, whatever lessons it might hold. There was, however, a part of Europe – Russia – where the issue of village co-proprietorship and self-government was still a contemporary one, though it needed in the 1840s a Prussian nobleman, Baron von Haxthausen, with his intellectual roots in the romantic conception of the *Volk*, to draw academic and political attention to it. The modern Russian counterpart, apparently, to the Teutonic *Mark* was the *mir*, the peasant village commune. It became one of the two rival but in this respect parallel strands of Russian social thought in the middle years of the century. One was the Populist version of socialism developed by Alexander Herzen after 1848, according to which, taking its base as the existing peasant commune, Russia might find an independent way to a socialist future, missing out what Marxists called the 'bourgeois' stage and evolving directly from serfdom to socialism. Bakunin was another who rested hopes on the Russian peasant communities, though he also liked to dwell on their insurrectionary potential. The idea of a Russian short-cut to socialism or communism (the two were often used interchangeably though socialism became associated with parliamentary democracy towards the end of the century in Germany), was to be revived among the Bolsheviks of the early twentieth century, in this case notably without the enthusiasm for the peasantry. The other strand of Russian social thought to which the *mir* was crucial was that of the Slavophiles, opponents of the Westernization and liberalization of Russia. The Slavophiles were educated and articulate members of the gentry class whose conservatism was of that nineteenth-century nostalgic kind which made it a form of radicalism: Romantic, religious and, in the West, neo-feudal. In England it became aptly termed Tory Radicalism. Marx and Engels diagnosed this type of contemporary social criticism, in *The Communist Manifesto*, as 'Feudal Socialism'. The Slavophiles made, from the outside, as it were, the kinds of criticism of modernity, represented for them by the West, that were quite common in the 1830s and 1840s in particular. They were too radically hostile to everything that had occurred in Russia since the reign of Peter the Great a century and a half earlier to be in any ordinary sense conservative; hostile, in particular, to Peter's creation, the state bureaucracy on the German model, which they regarded as alien and utterly foreign to the Russian spirit, as well as hostile to contemporary Western liberalism and constitutionalism as individualistic, atomizing and shallowly rationalistic.

The natural and spontaneous cooperation represented in the *mir* was for them authentically and traditionally Russian, though nowadays its antiquity has been denied by scholars and its origins attributed to a device

of government for control and tax-gathering. Their other central principles
were Tsarism and Orthodox Christianity, both being set against legalistic
Western notions of constitutionalism and the intellectualized theology of
the Catholic Church. Both stood, instead, for consensus and harmony, *Sobornost*.
Their notion of Tsarism was essentially a patriarchal one, not to be confused with the Western notion of state sovereignty or to be conceived as having
any close connection with the government of, for example, Tsar Nicholas I.
Exalting the notion of an ideal autocrat is a well-known form of political
criticism in autocracies. Their commitment to the principle of unfettered
autocracy has to be set in the context of their denunciation of the tsarist
bureaucracy. Without the bureaucracy the Tsar's role could hardly have been
in practice much more than symbolic. If the Slavophiles exalted a patriarchal kind of autocracy they often came close to a communalist version of
anarchism. They were against the Western concept of decision by vote, for
example, because the will of the minority was overridden and disregarded;
consensus must be allowed to emerge. The two great Russian novelists
whose works bear marks of Slavophile doctrine, Dostoevsky and Tolstoy,
both exemplify a distinctive concept of Christianity recognizably more
Orthodox than Catholic or Protestant, but it is in Tolstoy that the anarchist
strand is drawn out and the idea of peasant wisdom and harmony with
nature and with other men is explicitly extolled. Turgenev, the Westernizer,
in *Smoke* mocked the Slavophiles' cult of peasant wisdom as adoration of
the symbol of dirt and ignorance, the Russian peasant's sheepskin jacket.

There was, of course, in the West no surviving traditional village commune to be given the kind of topical and even prophetic significance attributed
to the *mir*. Feudalism and then its extinction, the latter only completed in
Central Europe in 1848, had done their work too thoroughly. The *Mark*
community, in whose original significance and ubiquity in the ancient
Teutonic world, or even the ancient Aryan world as a whole, many scholarly
reputations were invested, had left at best only scattered and insignificant
vestiges in rural local customs. The communal ownership of land was none
the less a strongly felt contemporary issue and ideas of a socialistic character tended to fasten on the question of land ownership to an extent which
later generations would find puzzling. Conservatism, on the other hand,
often saw in the peasant and the independent artisan household the nucleus
of a more traditional and healthier society than that represented by a rural
proletariat and the drift to the cities. Such nostalgic preferences tended
to blur conventional lines of distinction between left and right, since the
common enemy was the liberal conception of the free market and its

manifest consequences. Thus the ideas of Pierre Joseph Proudhon (1809–65), who seems to have been the first ever to embrace the label 'anarchist' (earlier 'anarchy' was only a term of abuse) and whose prescription for modern society was something like a loose confederation of independent, patriarchal peasant and artisan households, had much more in common with those of the Catholic Frédéric le Play (1806–82), whom in some ways it is easiest to describe as conservative, though he was not wholly so, than either had with any classic liberal.

Another, this time unequivocally conservative because explicitly hierarchical, spokesman of this kind was the German student and idealizer of popular rural life, Wilhelm Riehl. He was another of those whom 1848 turned towards detailed social investigation as an antidote to the thin abstractions of liberal political thought. In a whole series of works in the 1850s and 1860s, of which one was characteristically entitled *Land und Leute*, 'land and people', Riehl portrayed and advocated an idealized version of traditional German society with a distinctly medieval flavour, which, repudiating a purely economic model or horizontal class stratification, focused instead on the social groups, the traditional *Stände* or 'estates', of German society: nobility, peasantry and *Bürgertum* – the German term for 'bourgeoisie', with its stronger resonance of civic pride and status is really indispensable here – including in its lower reaches the artisan class.

Riehl hated the great cosmopolitan city, and his writings hold a significant idealization of not only the traditional noble and peasant values, distinct but both indispensable, but of those also of the medieval city of merchants and citizens, still much nearer as a form of contemporary reality in Germany than, say, in Britain: modest in size, limited in outlook and aspirations, where commercial and artisan classes found the centre and focus of their lives in the city and its locality. Each *Stand* had its own values; economic life ministered to self-sufficiency and self-respect rather than profit-maximization. Thomas Mann, who came himself from an old merchant family in such a city, Lübeck, drew such a *Bürger* family in his novel *Buddenbrooks* (1901). In Mann's *The Magic Mountain* (1924) Hans Castorp's grandfather, in a city like Lübeck, is a rich merchant in good standing in his local community, but he is far from the image of the dynamic, grasping, risk-taking capitalist. He is a traditionalist whose sense of well-being and self-respect are derived from his secure position, his status and the respect it brings to him and to the family name in his own city; he is averse to risk and innovation and his satisfactions come from consumption rather than acquisition.

The sociological approach to capitalism and to economic life generally, with each *Stand* considered as the bearer of a distinctive ethos and body of values, became and remained an academic tradition in Germany, though not necessarily in the context of Riehl's kind of conservatism. It is reflected for example in the work of Werner Sombart and Max Weber in the early twentieth century. Weber famously treated the rise of modern capitalism, as the break with the traditional, inward-looking capitalism of medieval times, in terms of the values of sixteenth-century Calvinism, ascetic and unimpeded in the rational calculation of the application of means to ends (*The Protestant Ethic and the Spirit of Capitalism*, 1904–5). Sombart's *Der Bourgeois* (1913) inverts Riehl's conservative kind of evaluation; the dealer, the *Händler*, is narrow-minded and mean-souled compared with the true capitalist, the ruthless, enterprising, risk-taking capitalist-as-hero, the equivalent of the sixteenth-century buccaneer, an incarnation of the will to power. Neither Sombart's position nor Weber's has any connection with utilitarianism; they represent, rather, attempts to construct a distinctive and heroic ethic out of precisely the attributes of the capitalist most often singled out for humanitarian and communalist types of criticism. In both cases, however, the emphasis falls on the capitalist as a social and ethical type, not on the economic merits of the system he operates and helped to create, the free market.

But this is to anticipate. The two lines of thought we have been following so far in the critique of individualism, private ownership and the free market in which labour is a commodity, have focused on the notions respectively of a primitive co-proprietorship of the kin-group or the village commune and an idealized version of a stable society of orders, each with its own values and sources of satisfaction, embodied not only in the peasantry but in the limited, local, undynamic capitalism of the *Bürgertum* and the artisan guilds of the traditional city. These were brought together under a single concept, the *Gemeinschaft*, the community, and contrasted with individualistic and rationalistic modernity in all its forms, under the title of *Gesellschaft*, in the sociological classic by Ferdinand Tönnies (*Gemeinschaft und Gesellschaft*, 1887). To speak of the latter as modernity, however, is to take up an obvious implication rather than what Tönnies (1855–1936) says. He always tried, not very successfully, to retain a stance of academic objectivity in presenting his two types, and also resisted the obvious temptation to speak of them as an historical sequence, as Durkheim (who reviewed Tönnies' book) was later to do with his somewhat similar pair of categories in *The Division of Labour*. To have done so would have been too fatalistic for Tönnies, who could never altogether abandon the hope of a revival of the values of the community. Translation of Tönnies' title presents some not altogether soluble problems. *Gemeinschaft* goes easily into English as community, but its antithesis is more problematic. The standard translation as 'association' implies too much spontaneity and is really too wide. *Gesellschaft* is, of course, the German for business corporation and as a paradigm case it will do, but Tönnies intends it more widely; it includes for him, for example, the modern state. The utilitarianism, calculation, efficiency, and the limitation of sociability to an inessential byproduct suggested by 'business', however, are not misplaced. Since Tönnies' terms have established themselves to some extent in their original form in sociological writing it is easiest, as in some other cases, to leave them in the original language. Tönnies' polarity rests, as he makes plain enough, on a number of antitheses which go back as far as that between Romanticism and Enlightenment: at the epistemological level, for example, between felt, sensory knowledge as lived experience and knowledge through abstract conceptualization, deduction and induction. Tönnies' conception of *Gesellschaft* owed a good deal to the contractarian political philosophy of Hobbes in the seventeenth century; Tönnies was himself a considerable Hobbes scholar, to whom his modern successors still owe a debt for his archival work. The other major source for *Gesellschaft* is clearly Marx's critique of capitalist society, though in the latter the state is a mere creature of capitalism. Tönnies' own political inclinations were towards Marxist Social Democracy, but what gives his book, perhaps despite himself, its air of pessimism and fatalism is that it incorporates Marx's social critique but not his remedy; there is no mention of the revolutionary proletariat as the instrument of redemption. Tönnies was also unable to make up his mind whether socialism was the remedy for the dominance of *Gesellschaft* in the modern world or a manifestation of it. The key concepts for the explication of *Gesellschaft* were egoism, competition, acquisition and instrumental rationality; nothing is valued for its own sake but only as a means to exchange and further acquisition. Egoistic human beings choose to relate to each other only through the rational, calculating, artificial and terminable device of contract. There is also a somewhat Rousseauist, ironic passage on the function of politeness as what Tönnies nicely calls 'formless contracts', exchanges of compliment and tacit agreements to mutual forbearance.

It is clearly not accidental that Tönnies came from a rural small town on the west coast of Schleswig, an area in which vestiges of co-proprietorship and local self-government were more than usually apparent. His, one feels, is a classic case of the small-town boy in the big city (Berlin) who makes the resulting culture-shock into the material of his creative life. In a significant phrase he spoke of the great city as 'a society of strangers'. The same phrase could summarize his conception of *Gesellschaft*. The academic sources for *Gemeinschaft* were numerous, and Tönnies was generous and explicit with acknowledgements. Carlyle was one inspiration; Laveleye's book on primitive property was particularly important and so was one which we shall shortly have to consider in more detail, Otto von Gierke's work on the medieval German guilds. In bringing these together Tönnies unites, under the category of community, both the ancient village commune and the town life of the Middle Ages. He specifies, in fact, three successive modes of community: kinship, embodied in the household and the wider kin-group; locality, by which he means essentially the village; and fellowship (Gierke's term was *Genossenschaft*), epitomized in the medieval 'brotherhood' of the craft guild. All these communal forms of life are characterized by lived, unselfconscious social experience, cherished for its own sake and regulated by custom and fellow-feeling; such experience absorbs the individual's whole existence. The community stands for use and enjoyment of things, not exchange and acquisition; everyday life is suffused by religious feeling in all its aspects, social and material, so that much love and attention is devoted to their beautification. In eloquent passages which to an English ear recall William Morris, though there is no acknowledgement (which in Tönnies' case probably does mean what it does not say, though he read English easily), it is emphasized that under such conditions the craft work of the artisan is properly thought of as art.

Tönnies spoke of the medieval guild as 'the last and highest expression of which the idea of *Gemeinschaft* is capable'. Guilds were something of a cult in the later years of the nineteenth century, as anyone who has seen the last act of Wagner's *The Mastersingers* (1867) will have been reminded. Ruskin was another who felt the powerful attraction of a semi-religious fellowship, at once for mutual support and welfare, for sociability and for the regulation of craft standards and production, in contrast to the modern world of detested work, exploitation and competition, and the pursuit of production and profit for their own sakes, misdescribed, in his view, as wealth since it had nothing to do with well-being. He attempted to re-create the idea in the Guild of St George, which he founded and endowed. The chief academic source for knowledge of the medieval guild for the later nineteenth century was the widely influential work, to which Tönnies among others was indebted, by Otto von Gierke (1841–1921), *Das deutsche Genossenschaftsrecht* (The German Law of Association) (1868–81), a portion of which was translated into English in 1900 as *Political Theories of the Middle Age*, with a seminal introduction by F. W. Maitland (1850–1906), historian of the Middle Ages. Guilds and fellowships in various forms had, like co-proprietorship, a long history in Europe going back to the drinking clubs and *collegia* of Greek and Roman times. Characteristically they had some of the attributes of cults, with oaths and rituals of initiation and obligations of secrecy, mutual aid and communal feasting, and in the case of craft guilds, which appeared at the beginning of the high Middle Ages, with regulation of the quality and quantity of work. Some of their characteristics were taken over later by free-masonry in the eighteenth century and trades unions in the nineteenth; there were also some similarities to the secret societies, the nationalistic revolutionary 'Brotherhoods', which appeared in Europe in the post-Napoleonic period. Craft guilds themselves underwent a long erosion of their monopolies; the free market and the Rousseauist concept of the state were alike hostile to them. In France the Revolution destroyed them, as conspiracies against the general good and foci of corporate loyalty in rivalry with the nation. In Germany they lasted longer, but came under heavy pressure from economic liberalism in the mid-nineteenth century. Trades unions and workers' political organizations, and the national pressure groups representing various interests, often protectionist, in a sense stepped into the void they had left.

The virtual disappearance of the craft guilds by the later nineteenth century naturally made it easier to idealize them. For Gierke, though he was not the first to say it, the guild was the middle term between the household and the state, and it possessed the attributes of full, collective legal personality. In it, for him, were resolved the antinomies of the individual and the state, freedom and order. He also saw it as a distinctively German institution, expressing the special German gift for fellowship, for freedom combined with self-regulation. He recognized that in economic terms the guilds had lately become selfishly monopolistic, but he hailed the rise of new forms of association, labour unions, banking and producers' cooperatives, vocational and religious groups. He saw the power of cooperation as something to set against that of capital, but later, as he became more nationalistic, he became wary of trades unions.

Durkheim was another who, at the end of the century, saw in the guilds a model for future social development. He recognized that the modern collective consciousness, embodied in the state, enjoining respect for equal individual rights, was somewhat abstract and sociologically thin, lacking the emotional warmth and constant reinforcement in the dense texture of social life found earlier. The natural modern social unit, corresponding to the community earlier constituted by locality, was now, in a society characterized by a high degree of the division of labour, the occupational or professional group, which needed to form the new basis of association. It would provide the satisfaction and security of fellowship, mitigate the harshness of competition between practitioners of the same trade and nurture and enforce the professional ethic appropriate to each vocation. Durkheim recognized the typical malaise of modern society as that of the too free-floating individual, rootless and unattached, lacking a sense of direction because the surrounding social norms held him too loosely: the condition he identified in his monograph *Suicide* (1897) as 'anomie'. Durkheim differed radically from Tönnies in regarding the malaise of modernity, which also included class conflict, as transitional and therefore temporary, the marks of imperfect adaptation to the new state of affairs. It is the prophesied role of the professional associations in socializing the individual which constitutes the most obvious support to his continued evolutionist optimism.

In some respects Gierke, to whom both Tönnies and Durkheim were clearly indebted, was closer to the latter than the former; he too was not pessimistic, nor, unlike some of those who followed him in France and Britain, did he advance the idea of the real personality of groups in hostile rivalry with that of the state. For him state and *Genossenschaft* were complementary; European history was seen in a dialectical pattern, in which the group, in the Middle Ages, had been dominant; then, in the early modern and eighteenth-century Age of Absolutism, the state. The modern age would be one of synthesis. Gierke became a strong German nationalist, happy to recognize the nation as the larger community, as Tönnies, except for a period of enthusiasm, shared by many, during the Great War, was not. It was not surprising that Gierke became one of the academic leaders of propaganda for the German cause during the War.

In Britain and France in the 1900s the tension between the claims of the sovereign state and those for the real personality of groups was frequently seen as less easily resolved than by Gierke. Maitland, who as a Cambridge empiricist used the Idealist vocabulary of collective real wills with a suggestion of inverted commas, none the less clearly enjoyed using it, in its application to subordinate groups, to tease the proponents, for the first time now common in Britain, of the Idealist conception of the state as the embodied real or higher will, the best self, of its citizens. If, he argued, one could use the concept of real will or real collective personality applied to the state then other collective entities could claim the same privilege, and he spoke sceptically of the concept of state sovereignty as one that became more problematic and less useful in a world in which corporate life was constantly appearing in new forms, all claiming their legal right to existence as a matter of obvious right, not of concession. In what came to be called, in the early twentieth century, the political theory of Pluralism, in Britain and France it became commonplace that the rights of associations were, in some sense admittedly never fully clear, subtracted from the sovereignty of the legally omnipotent state. This was especially true of the French Anarcho-Syndicalist version of Pluralism, drawing on the anti-state tradition of Proudhon, and was fostered to some extent by the English Guild Socialism of G. D. H. Cole (1889–1959). The young Harold Laski (1893–1950) wrote typically when he wrote in the *Harvard Law Review* in 1917, 'Ours is a time of deep question about the state. Theories of corporate personality have challenged in decisive fashion its proud claim to preeminence . . . the groups it has claimed to control seem, often enough, to lead a life no less full and splendid than its own.'

While theories of an original European co-proprietorship in land undermined the assumption of the 'naturalness' of private property and hence gave comfort to socialists and especially to advocates of land nationalization, so theories of the real personality of groups were congenial to supporters of trades unions, especially at a time when, in England, there was still some judicial disposition to treat them as no more legal than the sum of their individual members. But trades unions were not the only associations to which such notions applied. Churches too qualified, as expounded by Maitland's pupil J. N. Figgis (1866–1919) in his *Churches in the Modern State* (1913). It was part of the appeal of Pluralism that by its inclusiveness, endorsing joint stock companies as well as anarchist *syndicats*, it spanned the political spectrum. In France, if there were anarchist pluralists there was also the influential work of the reformist jurist and advocate of decentralization, Léon Duguit (1859–1928), who attempted, in some respects like Durkheim, to provide a sociological rather than a metaphysical grounding for the concept of a higher law, above the legislative sovereignty of the state, from which rights were derivable. He was attracted too, like other pluralists (this too was glanced at in Durkheim), to the idea of a reconstruction of representative democracy along lines of functional, occupational rather than territorial representation.

Pluralism could sometimes seem a primarily philosophical or legal idea, either invoking the metaphysics of group personality in rivalry with a metaphysical concept of the state as the real will of its citizens, or else making the case for ease of incorporation and full corporate rights for bodies like trades unions. But the foundation of Pluralism usually turns out to be sociological and moral, an assertion of the psychological value of what Burke called 'the little platoon', the bodies smaller and more intimate than the state, to which individuals feel themselves to belong, and of the multiplicity of roles, richer in content than citizenship, they can derive from them. In practice, however, Pluralism always encountered a dilemma: if the sovereignty of the state remained, the various lesser bodies were ultimately legally at its mercy, to recognize or not, to control or to dissolve (as the French government dissolved the Catholic religious orders). That way might lead ultimately to the corporate state of Fascist Italy, in which the corporate bodies, integrated into the state, became merely its instruments. Alternatively Pluralism was drawn, as in one version in France, in an anarchist direction, in which case all the usual unresolved questions associated with Anarchism would arise; the potential conflicts between associations were without a mediator, and individuals, for example minors, whose membership might not be altogether voluntary, would lack a protector for their individual rights. Commonsense realism, therefore, would always, as before, tend to point towards the state and how its activities and responsibilities might be defined and shaped.

## 3.3 The Ethical State

In Germany, in particular, the tradition of state regulation and intervention was a powerful one, going back to the days of eighteenth-century Enlightened Absolutism and what was called 'cameralism' and in practice reinforced rather than weakened by the nationalist sentiments evoked in the struggle against Napoleon. It is true that nationalism superseded the notion of virtue in the subject as, above all, passive obedience, and threatened the dynastic principle, but in this politicized form, notably in the writings of J. G. Fichte (1762–1814), it exalted the powers of the state. The state was, or should be, the embodiment of the national will. It was not merely, as in classic liberalism, a device for providing individuals with security and adjudicating conflicts. Economic liberalism in the mid-century – which the Germans came to call, for obvious reasons,

*Manchestertum* – dented rather than cracked the heritage of paternalism and economic nationalism. Even in the heyday of laissez-faire in Europe the prophet of the protectionist mood which took hold towards the end of the century was a German, Friedrich List, in his *Natural System of Political Economy* (1841). Max Weber later spoke, as often, in the line of a powerful German intellectual tradition when he proclaimed with his inaugural lecture as Professor of Economics at Freiburg in 1895 that 'The Science of National Economic Policy is a Political Science'. In cases of conflict between orthodox economic theory and the national interest it was the latter which must prevail. We have already noted that in Germany the *Kathedersozialisten* in chairs of economics thought of poverty and intensifying class conflict as pathologies calling for scientific assessment and the application of policy, not just as inevitable consequences of market laws. Protestant churches interested themselves, in the new Reich, as in England in the same period, in 'the social question', i.e. poverty, and in Germany moved into an alliance with economic and social science in the *Verein für Sozialwissenschaft* or social science union, in which the young Weber became involved. However, he became impatient with its humanitarian moralizing, just as, though a keen nationalist, he found the overheated nationalism of some of the academic historians he knew, notably Heinrich von Treitschke (1834–96), rhetorical and unprofessional.

The German Marxists' great Social Democratic Party with its four million members by the end of the century, though it participated in elections, as its mentor Friedrich Engels advocated, and won a significant number of seats in the Reichstag, held itself otherwise aloof, waiting in theory for the moment when the representatives of the alienated proletariat, the international working class, would assume at once all the powers of the state in order to liquidate the remains of capitalism and create the classless society. In practice the German Socialist Party became something like another, though large and well organized, voluntary association, with its own ethos and culture of popular education, with reading rooms, publications, lectures, not necessarily on directly political subjects. Marx had called on the revolutionary working class to organize and educate itself for its historic role, without perceiving that the more organized and educated it became, the less like the utterly alienated proletariat with nothing to lose but its chains, and therefore the less revolutionary, it also became. The same applied to trades unions, which he also endorsed and which, once legalized, were able to bargain for higher wages and better working conditions. The intellectual foundations of German Social Democracy, formulated first by Engels, who died in 1895, and by its leaders Karl Kautsky (1854–1938) and August Bebel (1840–1913), were supplied chiefly by Marxist economic determinism. Capitalism, as spelt out in *Capital*, would destroy itself through its own internal contradictions, in successive and ever more intense crises of overproduction and bankruptcies; what was required of the working class was that it should be organized and conscious of its historic role and hence ready to assume the power that would fall into its lap when the moment should arrive. Revolutionary purity, meanwhile, required as complete an aloofness as possible from the institutions of bourgeois society, especially the state. Realism consisted in waiting for the laws of economics and history to work themselves out, in a kind of fatalism ironically reminiscent of the fatalism of those who proclaimed the inescapability of the laws of the market, and in a sense parasitic on it.

Inevitably there were others, though a minority, whose sense of 'realism' was more – even in a socialist context – realistic. Ferdinand Lassalle, Marx's old opponent, had urged socialists to make use of the state without waiting for revolution. Bismarck had taken the hint and adopted 'social insurance' as an anti-revolutionary measure. The leading 'revisionist' of Marxist orthodoxy in the last part of the century was Edouard Bernstein (1850–1932). Bernstein spent much time in London and was influenced by the Fabians and the example of British parliamentarianism. Philosophically, he was a child of the revival, in the last three decades of the century, in Germany and to some extent in France and Britain, of the influence of Kant. In earlier chapters we have come across the effects of neo-Kantianism in other contexts, helping to undermine over-simple notions of objectivity in both natural science and history, focusing attention on the perspective of the theorist or observer, who was also an agent. It had, of course, also its moral dimension; here it ran counter to any kind of fatalistic determinism, whether of the market or the Marxist laws of history, and also eroded any estimate of ends in utilitarian terms, as the maximization of happiness; instead it fostered a notion of social life as a field for the exercise of the disinterested, rational moral will, in whose perspective all human beings were ends in themselves and their own rational autonomy as moral beings the highest good they could attain.

Kantianism helped to emancipate Bernstein from claims that Marxist determinism was objective science, and he came to take a pragmatic and moral view of socialist doctrine: it was a guide to practice rather than an incontrovertible deterministic system. Pragmatism translated into a gradualist view of the transition to socialism. Contemporary evidence, in any case, seemed to be falsifying the grounds of Marx's predictions, particularly, perhaps, in England, which Bernstein knew well and which Marx had always expected to be the first country to lead the way in proletarian revolution as it had done in industrial capitalism. A series of Limited Liability Acts in the 1850s had made capital investment less individualistic and precarious. Trades unions became influential, first in the skilled trades, the 'aristocracy of labour', from the 1860s onwards. Far from becoming, as the Marxist model required, an increasingly homogenized pool of desperate, unskilled labour, the working class was increasingly differentiated and hierarchical with the emergence of new technologies and more complex business organizations. Marx had derived his picture not only from the Ricardian assumption of wages tending to the level of subsistence, but from Engels' observation of the cotton trade in Manchester in the 1840s, when old crafts like handloom weaving were succumbing to the competition of unskilled factory labour and new skilled occupations were not very apparent. By the 1890s it seemed that the polarization of the class system between a mass of unskilled labour on subsistence wages and a handful of monopolistic capitalist owners, on which Marxist predictions depended, had not occurred. If socialism was not the destined, automatically guaranteed outcome of history it was a moral ideal or nothing. Bernstein's 'Revisionism' became one of the many heresies identified by orthodox Marxism as defined by Engels and Kautsky.

In France, though there was a violent and conspiratorial Communist tradition dating from the later days of the first Revolution, much of the revolutionary impulse tended, following Proudhon rather than Marx, to be anarchist and syndicalist, though there was a Marxist parliamentary party at the end of the century. The reformist alternative was most obviously focused, in the same period, by a concept of 'solidarity' propounded by Léon Bourgeois (*On Solidarity*, 1896). Laissez-faire egoism of an unabashed, Social Darwinist kind did exist, but it was very much a minority position. Durkheim and Duguit were both touched by Solidarism. Its central theme, paralleled by the 'New Liberalism' in Britain in the same period, was the reconciliation of liberalism with government action for the removal of obvious social evils. Here too, in both countries, neo-Kantianism was one influence: people were ends, not means. The utilitarian tradition in English liberalism had never found favour in France; from the time of the Revolution economic thinking had tended to incorporate ideas of virtuous citizenship. Influential too in France was the Saint-Simonian tradition, combining enthusiastic endorsement of entrepreneurship and technocracy with a quasi-religious humanitarianism and a belief in class cooperation rather than conflict among the *industriels* – the industrious – in productive activity.

The reformist rival to Solidarism, distinctly Saint-Simonian and more oriented towards capitalist paternalism and cooperation in the workplace rather than state intervention, was the concept of 'social economy', *économie sociale*, which also had harmony between classes as its object. The founder of the *Société d'économie sociale* (1856) was Le Play, who had been touched in his youth by Saint-Simonianism and also influenced later by the concept of the village commune. A sociologist, with a huge appetite for facts, he also had a particular interest in the family. Solidarism and social economy and *mutualité*, the promotion of mutual aid societies such as popular savings banks, were all very obviously thought of as antidotes to class warfare and as efforts towards class reconciliation and harmony, but in their common opposition to egoistic individualism and unrestricted capitalism they are also another form of the aspiration to community.

In Britain the struggle for the soul of liberalism, or alternatively to replace it, was necessarily ideologically sterner, for it was in Britain that utilitarianism and Ricardian Political Economy, buttressed by moral and Nonconformist endorsements of the self-made independent character, had bitten deepest, even if they had never dominated so comprehensively as simplified models of the age of laissez-faire suggest. In other countries Britain was seen as the home of philistine utilitarianism and ruthless egoistic individualism, though in another image it was sometimes admired and envied for its political stability and the self-confidence of its governing class; both Taine and the nationalist German historian Treitschke surprisingly often cite Macaulay approvingly. In various aspects, economic liberalism, particularly Free Trade and freedom of contract, did cast a long shadow. The repeal of the Corn Laws in 1846 was definitive. Even at the end of the century, when Britain was under strong pressure from foreign competition in both industry and agriculture, and when the case was being made for Imperial preference, Protectionism, as advocated by Joseph Chamberlain, foundered on the rock of Free Trade principles and the political unacceptability of raising the price of the people's food. Gladstone's legislative interventions attempting to solve what had become in effect a land war in Ireland were bitterly opposed by some liberals because they breached the sacred principle of freedom of contract. Liberals of the 1850s and 1860s like Maine and his fellow lawyer Alfred Dicey (1835–1922) became conservative Cassandras in the 1860s and, finding a refuge from

Gladstone's populism and Irish Home Rule in Liberal Unionism, became almost indistinguishable from Conservatives.

For these reasons it is worth attending in some detail to the (mainly liberal) philosophical alternative to utilitarianism in Britain which, drawing on Kant and Hegel, became dominant from the 1880s to the 1900s, even though the connection between it and – highly tentative – measures of state intervention may be rather tenuous. The intellectual bases of the main power house – nowadays it would be called a think-tank – of British socialism at the end of the century, the Fabian Society, were rather different: conceptions of 'science' and efficiency, a revised anti-individualist evolutionism and utilitarianism, and the economic critique of capitalism and especially of the 'unearned' and socially generated surplus reaped for landlords in the form of rent.

A revised utilitarianism, developed out of the later J. S. Mill, was also one of the strands in the thought of one of the leading intellectual New Liberals, L. T. Hobhouse (1864–1929), along with a rewriting of Spencer's concept of Social Evolution. These were not, however, the only ones. Hobhouse's tract *Liberalism* (1911) has many traces of Mill but also, very evidently, some perhaps equally important of the inspiration of the English revival of philosophical Idealism, in the writings and teachings of T. H. Green (1836–82). Green's philosophy was more Kantian than Hegelian and remained individualistic in orientation, though it was a Kantian, not a utilitarian, kind of individualism. At the centre of Green's politics and ethics is the concept of the higher or real self, the self which, transcending casual and transient desires, seeks its full and consistent realization in willing the common good. It is easy to see how theoretically this could justify social intervention by the state, if the higher wills are thought of as expressed in it, but Green is very wary of any institutionalized form of the higher self which might relieve the individual of the continuous obligation to moral strenuousness, and his view of legitimate action by the state is correspondingly limited. Ostensibly a more radical departure from English political tradition, in its apparently full-blooded endorsement of an Hegelian concept of the state as the community's higher will, is *The Philosophical Theory of the State* (1899) by Bernard Bosanquet (1848–1923). Bosanquet is linked, moreover, to our earlier discussions by possessing a fuller and more concrete conception than Green's of the community whose higher will the state embodies. To appreciate Bosanquet's Hegelianism, however, it is first necessary briefly to consider the distinctive features of Hegel's idea of the state. It lies, of course, well outside the period which concerns us, dating from the 1820s, but in Britain it was new and even in Germany, as we shall see shortly, its influence was by no means exhausted.

It was a peculiarity of Hegel's concept of the state that it attempted to combine the claims of universal reason with those of what it is convenient here to call community. That is to say the concrete interests and attachments of the family and the corporate institutions of civil society are not, as in the Rousseauean version of the General Will, annulled, but comprehended and carried to the higher plane of the general good of all, represented by the state, which is therefore the embodiment of the ethical will of the community. Hegel's conception therefore – to step outside the Hegelian vocabulary – offered itself as the synthesis of modernity and community, of the universal, rational will to the highest good, as in Kant's ethics, with the concrete, historical community cherished by the Romantics and also, it may be added, with what Hegel calls 'the system of needs': the world of production and private property. Compared with the dynastic autocracy, Hegel's state has the impartiality and rationality characteristic of modernity: bureaucratic in its procedures (though it is also a constitutional monarchy), not swayed, that is, by respect of persons or private interests – the claim Marx came to deny. But the actual interests, sentiments and affiliations below the level of the state's impartial will are not of no moral account. They are how human beings are socialized, inducted into and incorporated in collective ways of life with their own more particular but still valid moral claims and disciplines. Only when these conflict with the general good must they give way to the higher will of the state. The individual therefore has a number of roles and allegiances, each valid in its own way, but only through the state does he rise to the highest level of moral self-consciousness and rationality, willing the good not for the sake of any lesser interest but because he is enabled to recognize it as such.

The Hegelian state was therefore neither the liberal, contractarian state, a power external to the individual but brought into existence by consent in order to secure the individual's most basic rights and interests from the encroachments of others, nor was it the Rousseauean General Will, which indeed supposedly represents the individual's higher, ethical self but which requires the elimination of all subordinate group wills, all corporate life distinct from itself. In British neo-Idealism it was Bosanquet who seized most fully and explicitly on the capacity of the Hegelian conception to reconcile the universal and the particular, the claims of the individual's higher self willing the general good and the concrete, various, spontaneous life of the community. Even Green had appreciated the need for what he called a 'prior morality' (i.e. an actual, non-Idealist one) as a stepping-stone to recognition of his exalted notion of the common good. There had to be, that is, what he called 'that impalpable congeries of the hopes and fears of a people bound together by common interests and sympathy' to create an actual community for the higher ethical will, as it were, to set to work on. It was a somewhat grudgingly admitted prior condition for the practice of the full, selfless rigours of the Kantian higher self, inspired by a will to self-perfection consisting in willing the common good for its own sake. The common good, for Green, however, could not be left defined in its mundane form. Just as there was a higher, ethical self, so there must be a higher ethical common good for it to will, namely the universalization of self-perfection, so that in willing the common good one willed that all one's fellow citizens might also be activated by the same selflessness. The highest good turned out to be identical with the universalization of willing the highest good. It is not surprising that Green's concept of the common good has been criticized as circular and hence vacuous. It has, arguably, left the mundane common good too far behind. Altruism of Green's kind is a hot potato which can be passed on but which no one consumes.

Bosanquet is much more generous and less condescending to the actual ways of life in a society, which he sees as beneficently, creatively various. His most basic idea seems to be not the Kantian one of the selfless ethical will but the one we associate with J. S. Mill and Wilhelm von Humboldt, which we shall have to consider in the next chapter, the concept of the fullest possible realization of human potentialities in each individual. This Bosanquet rather confusingly identifies with the Idealists 'best self', the self which is to be realized rather than the fluctuating, limited, divided actual self. The self is constructed out of thought and language, which are common possessions; the different dispositions of one individual at different times may vary as widely as they do from the dispositions of others. It is this which chiefly separates Bosanquet from Mill's notion of 'many-sidedness'. For in Bosanquet it seems that it is not really the individual's self-realization which is the supreme end, though it is a necessary part of it, but rather another idea, which also goes back to a Romantic rather than Kantian Idealist sources in the eighteenth century: the idea, chiefly attributed to Herder though it seems very unlikely that that mattered to Bosanquet, of humanity as a whole as the sum of all realizable human potentialities; this is embodied by each individual, Bosanquet says, only in fragmentary form. It is the function of the state, in its impartiality, to hold

up before the individual and to remind him of all the other human possibilities he himself does not embody, though others do, and to which he aspires
as his best, which in Bosanquet means his fullest, self. This is perhaps little
more than an extrapolation of Mill's principle that the realization of his
potentialities by each individual must be compatible with the rights of
others. The state, for Bosanquet, enforces and therefore in a sense embodies and comprehends, the compatibility of the multitude of realizable
selves.

But any actual state embodies these only partially because human communal life is unforeseeably, spontaneously creative. It is not for the state
to initiate but to ratify and as it were stabilize and hold up to consciousness
the benign innovations occurring at the lower levels, and thereby to embody
the higher – it would be easier to say 'wider' but Bosanquet is addicted to
Idealist terminology – potentialities to which the individual self may
aspire. Where Green's (Kantian) higher self is realized through a drastic
renunciation of the lower one, Bosanquet's, in the fashion of the German
concept of *Bildung* (self-education) enunciated by Humboldt and at least
partially advocated by Mill, is realized by an expansion of the consciousness of human possibilities and the attempts to live them. The materials
for such individual elevation of view, however, are already present in the
richness of social experience. Where Green's Idealist heaven is bare of all
furniture but self-perfecting Kantian moral wills willing their own and
each other's perfection, Bosanquet's is crowded with various human
possibilities, which it is the business of the state to bring into harmony
and so to comprehend without self-contradiction.

### 3.4 Nation and State in Germany

Hegel's philosophy lost its dominant position in Germany in the 1850s. In
the second half of the century, materialism, Schopenhauer and Kant all
loomed larger. In so far as the Hegelian legacy survived it did so mainly as a
concept of the state and in conjunction with the idea of the nation. The idea
of the nation-state, that is, was forged out of the tradition of Fichte and
Hegel, and was recognized to have been so. It was not accidental that two
of the most intellectually elevated anti-German polemics written during
the Great War, Hobhouse's book *The Metaphysical Theory of the State*
(1918) and Durkheim's ironically titled pamphlet *Germany Above All*
(1916), were essentially attacks on the Hegelian concept of the state,

though Durkheim's main immediate target was Treitschke (while Hobhouse's was Bosanquet). German nationalism, for them, was Hegelian. In considering, therefore, the reconcilability of the Hegelian state with some concept of community we have to be prepared to recognize the latter, most importantly, as, in Benedict Anderson's phrase, the 'imagined community' of the nation. It seems in many ways, in the nineteenth century, a natural connection to make; and so it seemed in what we may call the Fichtean-Hegelian tradition, yet it was not in its origins in Germany nor in the new Reich an unproblematic one.

Initially, in fact, the polarity represented by the two terms was a wide and even antagonistic one. In the late eighteenth century the impersonal, impartial, regulatory activity of the state had been brought to a high pitch of organization and refinement in some of the German states, notably Prussia. On the other hand, the Romantic concept of the *Volk* represented something violently antithetical to it, and was often intended to be so, compared with the more politicized concept, in Britain and France, of 'the people' or in the latter case also 'the nation'. The *Volk* was presented as the antithesis of the universal, rationalistic principles of Enlightened autocracy; the latter was alien and external to the unique ethos and customs of the *Volk* whose affairs it regulated. It was not for nothing that even in the 1880s, as we have seen, Tönnies included the state in the conceptual antithesis of the *Gemeinschaft*, itself a concept with close affinities with that of the *Volk*. In French republicanism the concept of the state was that it expressed the will of the nation, however problematic this might be in practice. Correspondingly, in France the concept of the nation was in its origin political; the nation was made such not by ethnicity and certainly not, as in the German volkish concept of nationality, by a common heritage of language, custom and myth. In France in 1789 these were either divisive rather than unifying or attached to the repudiated heritage of the monarchy. The nation was made, rather, politically, by the collective will to *be* a nation. Myth, language and a national republican culture might follow, and the French revolutionaries, and liberal republicans in the nineteenth century, worked hard to make them do so. In Germany, however, the cultural existence of the nation, as the *Volk*, was recognized long before the existence of, or even the desire for, the nation-state. It was in the Napoleonic period and after that the aspiration to a political form of nationality became expressed either in its more conservative form, as the wish to see the existing German states invested with the attributes, the popular sense of identification, the patriotic enthusiasm, of nationality – the *national* state; or, more radically, as the demand for a single pan-German nation-state. In one of these ways, perhaps, through the sense of nationality, the split between *Volk* and *Staat* might be healed and even the apparently self-contradictory notion of a *Volksstaat* be realized.

Before this could become plausible, however, a change had to be undergone not only by the concept of the *Volk*, politicized as the nation, but also in the concept of the state, which had to undergo a parallel transformation in the opposite direction: to become infused, partly under the influence of the French example, with nationhood. The chief theoretical agents of this fusion, with a corresponding moral and cultural exaltation of the state as the expression of a unique cultural individuality, the nation, were Fichte and after him Hegel, and, later, political historians, notably Leopold von Ranke and Heinrich von Treitschke, representing respectively what we have called the conservative and the pan-German versions of the national state. From Hegel derived the idea of the state as the embodiment of the highest ethical life human beings could attain. But each state was a self-sufficient ethical being; no higher law mediated its relations with other states. For Hegel morality was always merely abstract unless embodied in institutions; a law binding states would only be embodied in what Treitschke was to call 'the arid uniformity of universal empire', from which in the form of Napoleon the German states had just fought to emancipate themselves. It was, moreover, another key Hegelian principle that self-recognition, self-consciousness, presupposed the existence of another, the not-self. In this case the individual's moral identification with his state required that there be other states alien to him, and that the state could require from him, for its own survival, the highest sacrifice of all, that of his life. Anything less, according to Hegel, would make the state a mere utilitarian device, as in contractarian theory; the individual would lack the means of full moral self-realization, the transcendence of self through identification with the higher ethical life of the state. At the end of *The Philosophy of Right* (1821), Hegel makes the case for the national state (not the pan-German nation-state; Hegel is a German conservative writing in the 1820s). A pre-existing common sentiment of nationality is, as it were, the soil in which the ethical life of the state is best rooted. The sentiment of nationality makes a collection of individuals a people, though it requires a state to embody its consciousness of being one and to express this in the form of political will.

It was the fusion of the conception of the state as the highest ethical being with the Romantic idea of a people or nation as a unique cultural individuality, with its own value, incommensurable with any other, which shaped the assumptions of the German political historiography as practised by Ranke and his successors. It provided, as it were, the historian's protagonists. Ranke's influence derived to a significant extent from his reputation as a pioneer of new, sometimes spoken of as 'scientific', methods of research. It was as such, for example, that his reputation was propagated in England by Lord Acton (1834–1902), who had received his education as an historian in Germany. There is in fact a good deal of mystification in this. Ranke was certainly not the first to consult archives or to appraise the evidence of documents in terms of the access to events or the motives in distorting them of their authors. What does seem to be true is that it was primarily in Ranke's seminar that such practices became as it were 'professionalized', systematically propagated as the badge of professional ethics and respectability in the historian's *métier*. Acton himself gave the game away when he admitted that the importance of Ranke's method lay above all in applying it exhaustively, examining critically all the relevant archives, not just dipping into them. That was true, but hardly a Copernican revolution. It helps, of course, if like Ranke one can live to be 90. In Acton's own case it proved a recipe for self-sterilization as an historian.

Over-insistence on Ranke's 'scientific' method and objectivity has tended to obscure the importance of the metaphysics which underlay his historical narratives. History deals with individualities each of which is a manifestation of an underlying dynamic principle or Idea; for Ranke they were ideas as it were in the mind of God. But they were not, as in Hegel, arranged as a teleological sequence nor were they comprehensible abstractly and as a totality. They could be discerned only fleetingly, in particular historical configurations, which, being unique, can be grasped only in their dense, concrete complexity. Their inner meanings, moreover – this was good Hegelianism – are not manifested to the agents, even the greatest, implicated in them. As in Hegel's concept of 'the cunning of reason', which is akin to Adam Smith's 'unintended consequences', statesmen like Richelieu or Frederick the Great promoted the fulfilment of the particular historical Idea, the realization of the modern state in the world, while consciously pursuing only the interests of their own states. Critics said that this was retrospectively to sanctify wicked acts by justifying them on the scale of world history or more crudely by the view that might is right; Hegel could be indicted for the aphorism '*Weltgeschichte ist Weltgericht*' – world history is the world's tribunal. But there was sometimes something peculiarly elusive about the German historians' judgements. The sensed presence of a form of Idealist metaphysic projected into detailed, highly concrete narratives of the practice of *Realpolitik* seemed to cast a glow of high, retrospective significance over the latter. *Realpolitik*, incidentally, was a term coined in 1853 to express the need to turn away from the ideas and speculative arguments dear to the German liberal mind, in order to bring about national unification by harnessing real social and political forces. It came to have a general, Machiavellian significance.

The fusion of the traditions of Herder and the *Volk* on the one hand, and Hegel and the state on the other, could be heady and morally equivocal stuff. The state as the highest ethical idea, the embodiment of its citizens' highest selves, and the nation as a unique and uniquely valuable cultural identity or individuality, made a potentially intoxicating mixture, becoming, in due course, still more so by the application to it of a fashionable Social Darwinist rhetoric of struggle, survival and extinction.

### 3.5 Nationalism and the Critique of Modernity: Myth and Charisma

Nationalism had, of course, social as well as international implications. In both Germany and France after 1870 it could be critical and radical; in the latter it came close to destabilizing the parliamentary republican regime. In Germany the achievement, in the new Reich, of something like the nation-state, though with Austria excluded, was necessarily disillusioning to many of the hopes of national cultural and moral regeneration invested in it. The period of struggle for unification came, on the contrary, to seem like an heroic age, contrasted with a mundane and materialistic contemporary reality. To those, in particular, who cherished a nostalgic, Romantic, volkish conception of the nation, the accelerated pace of modernization, as industrialization, class division and administrative rationalization, was dismaying. Political unification was manifestly not matched by spiritual unity. Social divisions and tensions even intensified; one symptom of this was a greatly heightened anti-Semitism, in which peasants, artisans, pettybourgeoisie, Catholics and Protestants could for once find a common cause. Nationalists of a radically nostalgic, volkish kind found that a nation-state still possessed the attributes of the state: impersonal, apart from the somewhat disconcerting figure-head of Kaiser Wilhelm II, rationalistic, bureaucratic, it seemed still the antithesis of the spontaneous, unifying, vitalizing cultural and spiritual life of the *Volk*, to which the official class, the money-making capitalists and the proletarian urban masses all seemed equally indifferent. The concept of a *Volksstaat* seemed merely an oxymoron. One consequence was a search for an essentially religious revival of Germanic myth and ancient German values. The Wagner circle at Bayreuth was one centre for such aspirations, which we shall have to consider in Chapter 6.

Wagner, to the disgust of his former disciple Nietzsche, embraced his honoured position in the Reich. Others were more intractable. Perhaps the most striking instance of this antagonism, apart from Tönnies, was the Romantic nationalist and volkish critic of modern culture and Bismarckian Germany, Paul de Lagarde (1827–91). Lagarde's preoccupation too was an essentially religious one which we shall have to consider later (see below, pp. 213–14ff); God revealed himself in the unfolding history of the nations. One feature of the radical nationalism of the nineteenth century, stemming originally from Herder, was the concept of national mission. Each 'world historical' people, to use Hegel's phrase, was charged with its unique mission to humanity. It was an idea eagerly taken up by Mazzini, and by the Slavophiles; it became widely assumed that the fact that the Russian people had not yet spoken its word to humanity only afforded reason for thinking it must be about to do so, an idea also encouraged by Herzen. The idea of mission could foster a kind of nationalist radicalism because the mission, whatever it was in the particular case – democracy and rights of man, the values of community, spirituality, *Kultur* – was a trust and a responsibility, a duty to be worthy of and to fulfil. It was in that respect rather like – and was compared by Lagarde to – the relation of the ancient Hebrews to monotheism. The possession of a mission made each people, in a sense, a chosen one, which could be held to confer on it the right to do anything, overriding all other rights, the mission might require. It also meant, however, that much was required of its bearers. To Lagarde the Bismarckian Reich, in the midst of apparent success, was failing; the German nation needed not just improvement but a radical spiritual rebirth to make itself what it really, inherently, was, and to fulfil its calling and destiny.

Essentially what was called for was a rebirth of the spiritual qualities of the *Volk*; a lived rather than a conceptual relation to the world (Lagarde was a bitter critic of the over-intellectual and mechanical character of German education) and an organic, hierarchical ordering of society. To fulfil its mission the nation must be united, repudiating individualism, rationalism, materialism, democracy and life in great cities. It must also colonize Central and Eastern Europe. It was also virtually inevitable that Lagarde should be violently anti-Semitic, though it seems on cultural rather than on ethnic grounds: Jews were cosmopolitan, and Lagarde seems to have believed like a good many others in an international Jewish conspiracy to dominate the world. Lagarde embraced the idea of a German *Sonderweg*, a unique development of the national life radically different from the standard path to modernity represented – far too imperfectly, according to Max Weber – by the Bismarckian Reich. Lagarde yearned, and in this at least Weber was later to concur, for a leader; not a despot but a kind of tribal leader at one with the people.

Some of the values of Lagarde's kind of volkishness passed later into the Youth Movement in Germany in the 1900s, with its hiking and communion with nature and cultivation of comradeship, and also into the various patriotic unions like the Pan German League (1890), which are a marked feature of the period. Such extra-parliamentary associations, usually of a hyper-patriotic kind, were most obviously apparently single-issue pressure groups but more importantly represented ways of mobilizing and shaping opinion in the still relatively untried world of mass democracy, in conscious rivalry with the Socialist Party. The Youth Movement and the *Vereine* (unions or leagues) focused ways in which radical volkish ideas became active in large-scale associations and on the fringes of national politics.

Exactly the same kind of development, again often in conscious rivalry with socialism, of extra-parliamentary 'leagues' of various sorts, but mostly nationalistic in complexion, is evident also in France in the same period, the most prominent being the *Ligue des patriotes* (1882). There was also a *Ligue anti-sémitique* (1888), which startles now by its frankness. In terms of issues and rallying cries, the German concerns with eastwards expansion and agricultural protection, with colonization and building a navy, had their counterparts in French concern over national decline, military and demographic, and above all with the recovery of the lost provinces of Alsace and Lorraine, annexed by Germany after the war of 1870; the last was an obsession with Paul Déroulède (1846–1914), founder of the *Ligue des patriotes*. In both countries such associations represented in some ways a more vigorous and more ideologically vehement kind of politics than their parliaments. In France, politics in the Third Republic, thanks to an unstable party system, became a sequence of fragile coalitions with the same faces reappearing in different roles and combinations, in a parliamentary game widely regarded as inward-looking, self-seeking and corrupt. In Germany the Reichstag was outwardly impressive, like the parties which formed it, but actually limited in its powers both by the Federal Constitution, which gave an undue preponderance to Prussia, and the fact that ministers were chosen by and responsible to the Kaiser, not to it. The leagues, with their single issues, their organization, and their frequently hyper-nationalistic and anti-Semitic character, by contrast touched raw nerves of public anxiety, hope and paranoia. In Britain, too, such pressure groups came into existence – as in Germany there was a Navy League – and there was much trumpeted patriotism, particularly in connection with the idea of Empire, but the greater rootedness and maturity of parliamentary traditions and political parties made them generally more marginal.

The leading intellectuals in French radical nationalism were Charles Maurras (1868–1952), the founder and leader of the *Action française*, and the novelist, journalist and deputy Maurice Barrès (1862–1923). Maurras, though himself an unbeliever, came to represent the Catholic, monarchist and traditionalist right. Barrès is a more complex and interesting figure. He began as a self-proclaimed egoist and aesthete, in the long tradition of French intellectual contempt for the ordinary, the banal and the bourgeois. He also adopted a stance of conscious hostility to decadence. He combined a cult of the will with an aggressive fastidiousness and refused all commitment as a vulgar self-betrayal, explaining this view of life in his novel *The Cult of the Self* (*Le Culte du moi*) (1888–91). It was expressed in terms of a drastically binary and adversarial view of the relation of the self to the not-self, the latter being identified as 'the others', 'the barbarians'. Discovering the tedium of a pure, uncommitted narcissism, the cult of will in an ideological vacuum, Barrès underwent a kind of conversion. In one sense it was a revolution: the detached intellectual, cherishing his autonomy, became an active, committed controversialist and rabble-rousing populist politician. In another sense, however, he merely rewrote the initial antithesis in collective terms, becoming a violent nationalist and anti-Semite. The self was a collective self; it was the people with which one was identified, both by heredity and choice. 'The others' were other nations, with which relations were necessarily those of antagonism and struggle, and also certain unassimilable elements within the nation: cosmopolitan humanitarians and international socialists and the Jews.

Barrès' notion of national identity and the individual's relation to it, and his deterministic assertion of the innate unassimilability of the Jews, both require explanation in terms of his concept of heredity, which has been explored with exemplary lucidity by his most recent commentator, Zeev Sternhell. Barrès's conception was, like so many others in France and elsewhere, Lamarckian. Definitions of nationality in France, as we have already seen, had for obvious reasons to be political and historical rather than ethnic: France was an entity made by her kings; her ethnic, cultural and even linguistic composition was, at the time of the first Revolution, highly various. It was natural to assume, and the assumption persisted, that French patriotism must be constructed politically. *Peuple* and *nation* were not translatable as *Volk*. Renan spoke famously of the nation as made, metaphorically speaking, by 'a daily plebiscite'.

Barrès, however – with the aid of the Lamarckian concept of heredity which also, of course, and importantly here, contained an environmental element, and which he seems to have owed to the Social Darwinist (there is no contradiction) neurologist Jules Soury (1842–1915) – managed to reformulate the concept of tradition, the accumulated life-experiences and historic memories of the French people, in hereditarian terms. The experiences, the traditions, were inherited literally in a biological as well as in a cultural sense, as a form of unconscious collective memory, inherited in the nervous system which had absorbed them. Past lives, lived on the soil of France, were present still in the descendants of those who for generations had lived there. To be French was to have one's unconscious mind determined both (since the two were intertwined) by a particular physical and cultural environment and by a particular heredity: by *La Terre et les morts*, the soil and the ancestors. A similar German phrase, *Blut und Boden*, blood and soil, was later coined by the Nazi Walther Darré. Barrès was an irrationalist of his period, who not only accepted but embraced the domination of the unconscious, which for him meant the inherited, collective unconscious, over the conscious mind. Lacking the inherited unconscious impulses and attachments of a Frenchman, a Jew could never, even if he wished, become one (though Barrès came to modify this view during the Great War).

He had begun his active political career as a supporter of General Boulanger, the would-be dictator whose movement collapsed in 1889. Barrès seems always to have looked to the advent of a national leader who should establish a direct rapport with the people, presumably ratified by plebiscite, over the heads of the squabbling, self-interested parliamentarians. He also adopted a common version of anti-Semitism which allowed a populist critique of capitalism distinct from that of the international socialism he detested: the Jews represented the cosmopolitan finance capitalism which could function as a scapegoat for honest, patriotic French employers. It seems to have been the Dreyfus case in the mid-1890s which turned him definitively to the far right. While not underestimating the element of raw anti-Semitic prejudice of those who, like Barrès, opposed the revision of Dreyfus's conviction for spying, it is also important not to underestimate the national anxieties aroused, on behalf of the unity and the international and military position of France, by the prospective discrediting of the army. The army, always apt to look like the element of unity and stability in a frothy democracy, was at the heart of traditional France, the true France, virtually the only tradition all could readily, in principle, embrace, as well as the shield of national security. Barrès, unlike Maurras, never accepted monarchy as the only authentic line of French tradition, insisting on retaining the revolutionary tradition also, despite his dislike of its humanitarian and parliamentarian heritage. The inherited French collective unconscious should in principle have told Maurras and himself who was right, but apparently it did not.

We have already noticed the resemblance between the extra-parliamentary and patriotic leagues which mushroomed in France and Germany in the 1890s and 1900s. France produced no equivalent to the nature-worshipping camaraderie of the German Youth Movement, though a cult of youth generally was a feature of this period. What France did have was a proliferation of sporting clubs and an untraditional cult of athletics, borrowed from England – just as in England there were advocates of universal military service on the French and German pattern. Not all of this was necessarily patriotic; there was an international element too, which bore fruit in the revival of the Olympic Games by the Baron de Coubertin (1863–1937), though in France there were also rifle clubs. Athleticism represented one antidote to a perceived national decadence, an aspect of which was the over-intellectualized, hothouse character of French education – a similar criticism to the one Lagarde had levelled at the German educational system. It was also a theme Taine had picked up in England in the 1860s. Games, as almost any Englishman would have testified, were healthy and built character and team spirit. The anxieties focused by the idea of decadence, closely allied to but not quite identical with the idea of degeneration we considered in the last chapter (we shall need to look at this distinction again), and the intensity of the search for revitalizing antidotes, which could include a dedicated, patriotic élan, are again something not to be underestimated. Barrès was vitally concerned with the overcoming of national decadence. So, though he put it not in a national but an international, socialist context, and would one suspects have had no patience at all with the flannelled good manners of athleticism, was another major French theorist of the period, Georges Sorel (1847–1922).

Sorel is in some respects a Barrès of the left (or vice versa), though he was a more fertile thinker and was internationally influential. To speak of him, however, as 'of the left' is to beg important questions – as it is also, of course, to speak of Barrès and the right. It was certainly, however, as a man of the left that Sorel wrote his best-known work, *Reflections on Violence* (1908). Sorel's career is at least superficially more inconsistent than Barrès', in that it has been described as running the political gamut from Marxism through Anarcho-Syndicalism to Fascism (though no one has ever accused either of being a liberal). In fact if one looks at the deeper moral concerns of which overt politics were always, for Sorel, a provisional expression, he is remarkably consistent: his central concern was always with moral regeneration, for which there might be various political vehicles. There must be found a heroic alternative, sometimes earthy and manual, sometimes revolutionary, usually proletarian, to rationalistic academic pedantry, humanitarianism and parliamentarianism, all identified as forms of decadence.

Revolution, which he deals with in *Reflections*, in the form of the revolutionary General Strike, or perhaps more the myth of revolution, was important to Sorel not for anything specific it might achieve (to speculate on which was a form of pedantry) but for the moral rebirth, the revival of collective, fanatical zeal, beyond any rational intention, which bringing it about might kindle; he compared the revolutionary spirit sometimes to the fanaticism of the early Christians, sometimes to that of the armies of the French republic in the 1790s. Cherishing heroic values, usually in what he thought of as their rugged, peasant or proletarian forms, Sorel contemplated the contemporary world with the distaste of a moral aesthete: it was dead, grey, spiritless, tame, rotted with humanitarianism and pedantry; set to verse we might be hearing Swinburne. In some passages Sorel seems to suggest that the world might be regenerated if capitalism, now deplorably humane, were to resume its old ruthlessness. Like Sombart, he wants capitalists to be their true, dynamic, enterprising, ruthless selves. Revival required struggle and a vitalizing myth: the myth, for example – and it really is only for example – of the General Strike. Sorel fastened on this because the revolutionary syndicats, the anarchist unions, seemed to him the most combustible available material; later he became disillusioned and lost interest in them.

The myth is not a theory or a prediction but a call to action: questions of truth or falsehood are irrelevant. In expounding this concept Sorel draws explicitly on the authority of what he calls 'the new school' of scientific theorists, for the concept of theories not as pictures to be thought of as true or false but as instruments, to be judged by their results; he also draws on the pragmatism of William James. He could have found some warrant in the early writings of Karl Marx, notably the 'Theses on Feuerbach' (1844), had they been extant. Given a knowledge of Marx's whole *oeuvre*, which he did not have, Sorel seems in some respects a better Marxist than those who defined Marxist orthodoxy in his day, the historical-determinist leaders of the Marxist political parties, whom he not unreasonably regarded as ineffectual pedants. The latter, much-loathed category for him also clearly included the French positivist tradition, with its notion of the vocation of savants to lay down social norms. To Sorel, rule by professors was the most abject of all forms of tyranny.

Another point of contact between Sorel and Marx is their view of labour as the way man above all affirms himself, and Sorel's enthusiasm for what Marx called 'real, sensuous activity'. For Sorel free human labour is a form of struggle, a moral affirmation of the worker, just as intellectual work properly understood, as for example in scientific experiment, is also practical and sensuous; it is perhaps not irrelevant that he had been an engineer. The split between the intellectual and the practical, both ideologically and in the form of social classes, was particularly abhorrent to him, and some of his other writings deal with the origins of this fatal separation. The two chief early influences on Sorel were those of Renan and Proudhon, especially Proudhon's exaltation of the patriarchal independence of the peasant and artisan. In two works in 1889, one on the Bible, the other on Socrates, Sorel traced the same historical pattern; the early Hebrews and the early Greeks were warrior-farmer patriarchs, whose imaginative and intellectual lives were embodied in myths. Socrates and the Christian Church replaced myth with dialectics and intellectualized theory and created intellectual oligarchies of philosopher priests, separating intellectual from physical work. It is inevitable to make comparison with Nietzsche, especially with his account of the role of Socrates in relation to Greek myth in *The Birth of Tragedy* (1872) and his association of him with Christianity as the twin agencies behind modern decadence; there are of course other similarities. Commentary on Sorel, however, tends to play down the notion of Nietzschean influence, as it does in the parallel case of Barrès, relying on dates of French translations and references. Whether the track of ideas can be quite so precisely traced is open to question, but is not one for addressing here.

Highly consistent with Sorel's view of modern political life, probing it more narrowly but more deeply, is the classic work on democracy by Robert Michels, *Political Parties* (1911). Michels (1876–1936), a German with a French mother, and long resident in Italy, was a true cosmopolitan, and his book purports to be a general study of modern political parties, which it is to some extent, but it is most obviously a study of the German Socialist Party, of which he was a disillusioned member. It presents a picture of an entirely inward-looking institution, engaged not in its ostensible business of preparing for revolution – however that is done – but in perpetuating its existence, recruiting, organizing, creating careers for party officials, in almost every respect imitating the state which it purported to exist to overthrow. It was, in fact, above all a bureaucracy: routinized, tame, orderly, essentially uncreative. It must have given a shock to any reader initially inclined to idealize the still new political phenomenon of mass democracy, but of course Michels' picture was all the more disconcerting because the party so obviously at its centre was a revolutionary socialist one. It was more or less commonplace by now that French political parties were self-serving and inward-looking, more concerned with the constant reshuffling of the ministerial pack, while ordinary deputies secured their positions by procuring favours for their localities, than concerned with their ostensible objectives. But the German Socialist Party had preserved its revolutionary purity and integrity, declaring against all deals or compromises – though these were not in fact noticeably on offer. Yet it too, it seemed, by becoming a bureaucracy, had become assimilated to the entropic nature of modern life, to a world seen by some commentators – and we should, of course, have to include Barrès and Sorel as well as Michels – as tamed and routinized to a pathological extent, devoid of energy, leadership and any possibility of creative action. The yearning for leadership, in fact, led both Sorel and Michels to take an interest in early Fascism.

Among those who saw the contemporary scene in this way we also have certainly to include Max Weber (1864–1920), with whom Michels enjoyed close personal relations, though Weber's interests were, of course, far wider. He, too, embraced a heroic ethic which we shall shortly have to consider. He, too, saw life in terms of struggle, and repudiated all hedonism, utilitarianism and humanitarianism as beneath human dignity. 'There is no peace', he assured his Freiburg audience in 1895, echoing Jeremiah. For Weber values were chosen, not given, and their chief embodiments in the contemporary world were for him the individual's dedication to a vocation and the unique cultural values of a particular nationality. As a matter of will and commitment, not blood or tradition, he was a strong German nationalist, but one who despised both volkish sentimentality and anti-Semitism as policy, and the pompous but to him shallow façade of the

1. Proclamation of the French Republic (anon.), 1848.

2. (*right*) *George Sand*.
Engraving after Delacroix.
Bibliothèque Nationale, Paris.

3. Italian Conspirators.

4. (*above*) Proclamation of the
Roman Republic, February 1849.

5. Ernest Meissonier, *The
Barricade*, 1849. Musée du
Louvre, Paris.

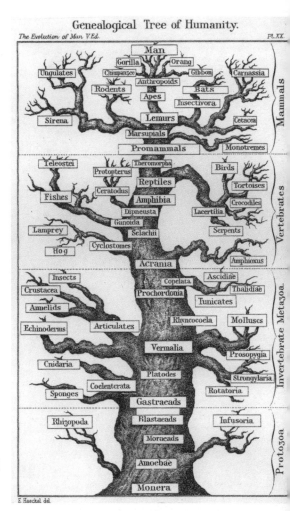

The Evolution of Man V.Ed.

Pl.XX.

**Man**

Gorilla · Orang

Ungulates · Chimpanzee · Anthropoids · Gibbon · Carnassia

Rodents · Apes · Bats

Anthropoids · Insectivora

Sirena · Lemurs · Cetacea

Marsupials

Promammals · Monotremes

*Mammals*

Teleostei · Theromorpha · Birds

Protopterus · Reptiles · Tortoises

Ceratodus · Crocodiles

Fishes · Amphibia

Dipneusta · Lacertilia

Ganoida

Lamprey · Selachii · Serpents

Cyclostomes

Hog

Acrania · Amphioxus

*Vertebrates*

Insects · Copelata · Ascidiae

Crustacea · Prochordonia · Thalidiae

Amelids · Tunicates

Articulates · Rhyncocoela · Molluscs

Echinoderms

Vermalia · Prosopygia

Cnidaria

Platodes · Strongylaria

Coelenterata · Rotatoria

Sponges

Gastraeads

*Invertebrate Metazoa*

Rhizopoda · Blastaeads · Infusoria

Moraeads

Amoebae

Monera

*Protozoa*

E. Haeckel del.

6. (*right*) From Ernest Haeckel, *The Evolution of Man* (1910).

7. Cathedral of Science: the Natural History Museum, South Kensington, London, 1880.

8. (*left*) Central Hall of the Natural
History Museum, South Kensington,
London, 1887.

9. Temple of Learning: the Reading Room
of the Bibliothèque Nationale, Paris, 1862.

10a and b. The Snarl: illustrations from Charles Darwin, *The Expressions and the Emotions in Man and Animals* (1872).

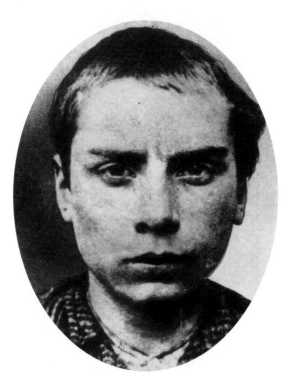

11a and b. Criminal Man according to Cesare
Lombroso (1911).

12. Félicien Rops, *Mors Syphilitica*, *c*. 1892.

13. A Russian Village: Fedor Vassilyev, *The Village Street*, 1868. State Tretyakov Gallery, Moscow.

14. The Degradation of Captain Dreyfus.

15. Ludwig Meidner, *Revolution*, *c*. 1913. Nationalgalerie, Berlin.

16. (*above*) Gabriel Ferrier,
*Salammbô*, *c*. 1881.

17. Portrait of an Aesthete:
Giovanni Boldoni, *Count
Robert de Montesquiou*, 1897.
Musée d'Orsay, Paris.

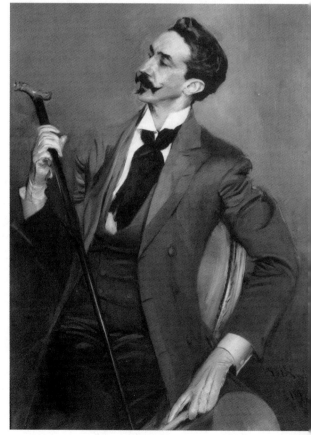

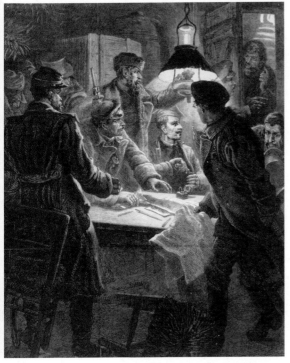

18. (*above*) Assassination of Tsar Alexander II. From the *Illustrated London News*, 1 March 1881.

19. Nihilists. From the *Illustrated London News*, 20 November 1880.

20. (*above*) William Holman Hunt, *The Shadow of Death*, 1869–73. City Art Gallery, Manchester.

21. *Siegfried*, Bayreuth, 1876.

22. The Brotherhood, *Parsifal*, Bayreuth, 1930.

23. The New Man: Ludwig Fahrenkrog, *The Holy Hour*, *c.* 1912.

24. (*right*) Gustav Klimt, *Jurisprudence*, 1903–7. Galerie Welz, Salzburg.

25. Umberto Boccioni, *The Street Enters the House*, 1911. Niedersächsische Landesgalerie, Hanover.

26. (*above*) Oskar
Kokoshka, *Pietà*. Poster
for *Murderer, Hope of
Women*, 1909.

27. Wassily Kandinsky,
*The Blue Rider*. Cover of
the *Almanach der Blaue
Reiter*, 1911.

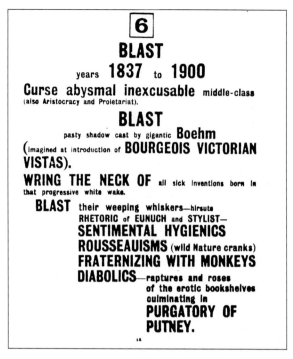

**6**

# BLAST

years **1837** to **1900**

Curse abysmal inexcusable middle-class
(also Aristocracy and Proletariat).

## BLAST

pasty shadow cast by gigantic Boehm
(imagined at introduction of BOURGEOIS VICTORIAN
VISTAS).

WRING THE NECK OF all sick inventions born in
that progressive white wake.

BLAST their weeping whiskers—hirsute
RHETORIC of EUNUCH and STYLIST—
SENTIMENTAL HYGIENICS
ROUSSEAUISMS (wild Nature cranks)
FRATERNIZING WITH MONKEYS
DIABOLICS—raptures and roses
of the erotic bookshelves
culminating in
PURGATORY OF
PUTNEY.

28. *Blast*. Page from the first issue, 1914.

29. Modernism in Architecture: the Steiner House, Vienna, designed by Adolf Loos, 1910.

*Kaiserreich*. The German *Sonderweg*, the compromise between an advanced industrial capitalism and a sham parliamentary life overshadowed by the archaisms of monarchy and aristocracy, was a weakness. The German *Burger* was tame and sycophantic, not enterprising and ruthless. Germans, he complained, lacked 'the Great Power instinct'. They preferred comfort to the heroic calling; Weber, like Sorel, drew unfavourable comparisons with the fanaticism of the French Jacobins. His classic study *The Protestant Ethic and the Spirit of Capitalism* (1904–5) is plausibly now regarded as an allegory for the German bourgeoisie, which exhibited none of the ascetic dedication, iron self-discipline and unrestrained pursuit of profit in full conviction of its righteousness that Weber clearly admires in the Calvinists of the sixteenth century. Germany needed such a dynamic bourgeoisie, just as it needed a fully functioning democracy, to modernize itself and compete in the modern world.

Above all it needed leadership. Weber's conception of leadership is expressed in his late lecture 'Politics as a Vocation' (1919) and in his conception of charisma. The charismatic leader owes his position not to inheritance or office but to the devoted adherence of followers drawn to him by the mysterious aura of authority, entirely personal to himself, which emanates from him. Owing nothing to the normal criteria by which authority is achieved and conceded, he necessarily comes from outside the system, whatever that may be, and his advent is entirely unpredictable. The prime cases are obviously the founders of religions, though Weber also entertained hope of a, in a sense parliamentary, form of leadership in which the leader is given mastery of his own party and of the state machine by a direct mandate from the electorate.

The notion of the charismatic leader who comes, unpredictably, from outside, is given its appeal by the overwhelmingly bleak picture Weber draws, in his classic account of bureaucracy, of all the institutions of the modern world. Bureaucracy is the supreme embodiment of end-means rationality, which Weber calls 'formal rationality' as distinct from value rationality, which is rationality in the service of a chosen moral end. Bureaucracy as such embodies no value, just as it is entirely impersonal. It has developed – a touch of Darwinism – because it is a supremely efficient instrument in any hands. It is a machine which can be turned in principle in any direction, though it has a powerful though blind internal momentum. It is also omnipresent in the modern world. There may be no public form of escape from it, because all forms of organization, the business corporation, the Church, the army, the state irrespective of its political complexion, political parties, including revolutionary ones – all are bureaucracies. It is indispensable to quote:

> A lifeless machine is the materialization of mind ... Also a materialization of mind is that living machine which bureaucratic organization represents, with its trained, specialized labour, its delineation of areas of competence, its regulations and its hierarchically stratified relations of obedience. In union with the dead machine, it is labouring to produce the cage of that bondage of the future to which one day powerless men will be forced to submit like the fellahin of ancient Egypt.[1]

In Weber's account of bureaucracy we may seem to have come full circle, from the impersonal mechanism of the market to Weber's living machine, but the latter seems to cover the whole terrain of modern life. It has affinities, obviously, with Marx's account of capitalism, but the revolutionary proletariat is nowhere in sight. In that respect it is Tönnies' *Gesellschaft* but emptied even of individualism. Tönnies' rational acquisitors are engaged in a Hobbesian game, the individual's ruthless search for competitive advantage; his is an account more compatible with the buccaneering kind of enterprise capitalism extolled by Sombart than with the corporate capitalism of the early twentieth century. In Weber's account all is corporate but nothing is communal. Community is as absent as the embodied higher ethical will of the Idealists. It is a world of purely formal rationality, routinized and made impersonal to the point where it merely seeks the continuity of the institution itself, in a moral and emotional void. Nothing is done for its own sake, yet nor is it done for any wider purpose; all is simultaneously purposive and purposeless. Impersonality, rationality and helplessness meet as the characterization of modernity in all its forms: state, politics, economy, *métier*. It was of course an ideal type, not a description, but Weber chose to give it the character of prophecy. The way out if there is one, the lightning-strike of the advent of the charismatic leader, since it arises not only outside the system of rationalization but outside rationality itself, unarguable in its nature, unpredictable in its occurrence, is necessarily a desperate one.

---

[1] Quoted from Arthur Mitzman, *The Iron Cage: an historical interpretation of Max Weber* (New Brunswick, 1985), p. 4n.

# CHAPTER 4

## *The Elusive Self*

### *4.1 The Burden of Freedom*

It is a useful platitude that the moral core of nineteenth-century liberalism was the absolute claim of individual autonomy, limited only by the equivalent claims of others. This implied, among other things, freedom from unexamined convention as well as from almost all restrictions on freedom of thought and speech. To fail to rise to the level of the individual requirements of such autonomy was to be less than fully human; to fail to respect it in others was to be a tyrant; to have its discovery and exercise clouded by traditional mystification was to be a candidate for emancipation. The identification and expression of the rights and duties that all this implied could vary widely, not only because circumstances differed but because of the variety of available idioms, deriving from a diversity of cultural roots: Romantic, Idealist, Protestant Nonconformist, egoistic or humanitarian. If the heritage claimed by nineteenth-century liberals included John Locke, Voltaire and the American founding fathers, it included also Luther, Kant, Schiller and Wilhelm von Humboldt.

The perceived obstacles and threats to individual autonomy could be even more various, requiring different idioms of opposition to them. They might be legal or insidious: tyrants and church establishment; age-old customs and taboos, or bourgeois timidity and conformity, and even the clichés of the unthinkingly 'progressive'. They might include the deadening effects of bureaucratic or professional routines or cultural banality, the pressure of democratic public opinion or, by the end of the century, the irrationality, volatile or conservative, of the crowd. The details of a liberal agenda therefore also varied, subtly from author to author, less subtly from country to country and decade to decade, particularly as domination seemed to pass from kings and priests to mass electorates and newspapers. In so varying, the requirement of personal autonomy could stretch to breaking-point what we are inclined loosely to think of as liberalism, shifting towards antinomian kinds of individualism ranging from a defensive, cloistral aestheticism to an aggressive revolutionary nihilism or anarchism.

All these, however, postulated the sovereignty, whose domain could be a matter of dispute, of an autonomous self, which naturally implies either its existence or attempts in various ways to create it. To put the alternatives starkly, passively to accept the conventions by which one was surrounded and one's apparently assigned role in life was to be less than fully an individual, while to repudiate them was to assume the burden of finding or imposing meaning for one's actions in the social and ideological void created by one's freedom.

The psychological penalty of failure in the latter – failure, that is, to translate the idea of freedom from a political rhetoric to an inner autonomy – could be high. Such failures had been a topic of literary investigation, in particular, from the post-Napoleonic period onwards, and were to remain a vital preoccupation. Some of the most striking explorations of the emancipated yet elusive self were Russian, for in backward Russia an emerging, Westernized intelligentsia naturally felt most acutely its own rootlessness, a condition for which Turgenev popularized the term 'Superfluous Man' (*Diary of a Superfluous Man*, 1850). The victim of this condition was prey to a perpetual and tormenting self-consciousness, precluding action or commitment, dissipating his life in words and self-examination, paralysed by a chronic failure of will. This was diagnosed not only in terms of the external conditions of Russian life in particular, but also as a baffled, never-ending search for the true, inner self, from whose indubitable impulses, or principles, free, self-directed action would flow, all else being hypocrisy and mere conformity to convention.

From its first flowering in Pushkin's *Eugene Onegin* (1831) and Lermontov's ironically entitled *A Hero of Our Time* (1839) to the great novels of Turgenev, Tolstoy and Dostoevsky in the second half of the century, the sense of aimlessness and weakness of will became a major theme in Russian literature, with the self as a tormenting question mark, together with various attempts to break the circle of self-consciousness through crime, Romantic love, religious or revolutionary commitment or participation in the unreflective, natural life of the peasantry. Turgenev's Rudin, in the novel of that name (1856), Dostoevsky's Raskolnikov in *Crime and Punishment* (1866) and Stavrogin in *The Devils* (1872), Tolstoy's Pierre in *War and Peace* (1869) and Levin in *Anna Karenina* (1877) either drew on their author's own experience or presented figures their contemporaries could recognize.

*Rudin* has plausibly been supposed to be based on the character of Bakunin, with whom Turgenev had shared lodgings in Berlin in the early 1840s.

The most intense, disturbing and direct exploration of the pathology of self-consciousness is the unnamed fictional author of the monologue Dostoevsky published in 1864, 'Notes from Underground'. He is, he tells us – we are never sure anything he tells us is true and he taunts the reader with this – a surly and disobliging petty official who has taken advantage of a small legacy to resign prematurely and lives, apparently, as a semi-recluse. He seems initially merely spiteful and cantankerous, distinguished only by his candour; he broods endlessly on petty slights in everyday life and fantasizes about avenging them, but the monologue begins at once to set about undermining this sense of a character who can be known as such. Has he not, he asks, been merely playing at malice and revenge, to which he feels no genuine inclination, wearing a mask of spite in order to be noticed and to have a character of some kind, a resting place from his endless self-examination? Sometimes, he tells us, he has even been benevolent, but his benevolence is as causeless and assumed as his malice: 'The fact is that I have never succeeded in being anything at all.' Behind the mask there is only a succession of other possible masks, including the literary persona he has assumed in order to address the reader.

The only thought he seems unequivocally to endorse is that there is no valid ground for anything one does or apparently is. The freedom we insist on to do as we will also cancels any reason for doing anything in particular. The man who arrogates to himself a character from which his actions may be deduced is essentially stupid because he persuades himself that he has valid grounds for his actions when he has not. Rational self-interest, even, provides no ground, because we can defy the requirements of our apparent interest and even take pleasure in doing so, in defying calculation and rationality. One prefers one's own will to anything else but the preference is a torment because there are no grounds in oneself for exercising it in any particular direction; there is only self-hatred – or is it just the appearance of self-hatred, another role the self assumes just in order to have one?

Dostoevsky's fictionalized monologue has been hailed as a founding text of what later became called existentialism. Certainly it announces persisting themes: the arbitrary assumption of a character just in order to have an identity of some kind – Dostoevsky's example was being a judge of claret – was an idea later exploited by Jean-Paul Sartre. The rejection of self-interest and the costs of freedom prefigure Dostoevsky's own later treatment of these ideas through the parable of the Grand Inquisitor, setting up an antithesis between happiness and freedom, in *The Brothers Karamazov* (1880). We should, however, almost certainly read 'Notes from Underground' differently if Dostoevsky had completed the intended second part, which would have placed it in an overtly Christian context; the world of the 'Underground Man' is a world without God and is therefore hell. Human freedom without God is a raw will grounded in nothing, a bottomless abyss of self-consciousness. There was a disposition in Russia to present the malaise of consciousness as a distinctively Russian one, while Slavophiles diagnosed it, not unpersuasively, as a disease imported from the West. Certainly Russian conditions for the educated, reared on exalted Western and Romantic notions of freedom in which Schiller and Byron were key figures, given a technical vocabulary and personal responsibilities apparently nothing less than cosmic in the metaphysics of Fichte and Schelling, were particularly unpromising. It seemed often impossible to find a field, mundane and limited and offering opportunities for the exercise of responsibility and a measure of freedom in practical activity; in Russia public life required intolerable compromises with a barbaric and tyrannical social and political order offensive to all imported notions of Western liberalism. Self-education, the inner emancipation represented by the absorption of Western culture, in a small circle of friends centred on the university or on the production of a journal, or perhaps conducted almost alone in the tedium of a country estate among one's serfs, seemed the only alternative to a timid, self-seeking conformity in the bureaucracy. Since speech as well as action were suspect and could easily be treated as criminal, imprisonment or exile, enforced or chosen, were always possibilities.

But it is clear that Russian conditions only intensified a malaise which produced symptoms among educated young men across Europe, particularly from the 1820s to the 1850s, but more obviously in France and England than in Germany; in France in the 1830s it was identified as the *maladie du siècle*, the sickness of the age, found, in various forms, in the novels of Benjamin Constant (1767–1930), Stendhal (1783–1842) and de Musset (1810–57) in particular, while Byron was a major influence across Europe. The conditions we can invoke – they were sometimes invoked at the time – to explain it were literary and historical, spiritual and practical. The Romantic and Revolutionary and Napoleonic heritage sometimes fostered aspirations 'beyond the fitting medium of desire', as Byron had written, hailing Napoleon as an *alter ego*, with inevitable contrasts between the heroic immediate past and the stifling present. It was true that the attempted reimposition after 1815 of the European *ancien régime* tended to attach political and religious conditions to spheres of activity outside the purely commercial.

In the Prologue (above, pp. 17–19) we noted that in England, though political life was more open, especially after 1832, the Anglican Church retained its grip on higher education and there were practically no academic careers open independent of clerical ones. To resign from one's Fellowship or parish on religious grounds therefore tended to block the most obvious avenues to useful and responsible activity, while to live for long with the question 'what do I really believe?' was a formidable incitement to introspection. One spokesman of the generation of the 1840s and 1850s, James Anthony Froude, whom we considered in the Prologue, who followed this path and described it in his novel, *The Nemesis of Faith* (1849), virtually created there an English 'superfluous man': 'nature has brought beings into existence who have no business here'. Pressed into a clerical career for which he feels no vocation and which he finds intolerable without conviction, Froude's protagonist seems to exhaust his resources of will and character in resigning it and thereafter drifts with no sense of direction. Froude and some of his contemporaries saw him, and his author, not as a unique but as a representative case. Such men 'want the strength to carve out their own independent road, and the beaten roads offend their sensibility'. Similar notes were struck by his Oxford contemporaries Arthur Hugh Clough and Matthew Arnold.

Clough exposed not only the melancholy of lost faith but also the sense of disengagement and therefore, supposedly, irresolution, which he dealt with at length in his flippant contribution to the literature of 1848–9, the epistolary poem 'Amours de voyage' (1849), which we considered briefly in the Prologue (above, p. 22). Clough's anti-hero considers joining the cause of Italian freedom and finds his commitment insufficiently felt and therefore inauthentic. One can contrast but also align this with Turgenev's Rudin, who says 'I am ready to surrender myself completely, greedily, utterly – and yet I can't. I will end by sacrificing myself for some nonsense in which I won't even believe', and who dies on a barricade in Paris in June 1848, perhaps in fulfilment of his prediction. Clough's protagonist makes the opposite choice, defending it with an ironic, almost parodic reference to a more individualistic, self-centred kind of liberalism ('Still, individual culture is also something'). Liberalism in the public mode could also be a kind of fanaticism and in all fanaticism there is perhaps something willed and therefore artificial and evasive. Perhaps, he says, the moment will call up the appropriate action. But

> What I cannot feel now, am I to suppose that I shall feel?
> Am I not free to wait for the ripe and indubious instinct?
> Am I forbidden to wait for the clear and lawful perception?
> . . .
> I do not like being moved; for the will is excited; and action
> Is a most dangerous thing; I tremble for something factitious,
> Some malpractice of the heart and illegitimate process;
> We are so prone to these things, with our terrible notions of duty.[1]

Nietzsche's remark in *Twilight of the Idols* (1889) is apt here: 'In England, in response to every little emancipation from theology one has to reassert one's position in a fear-inspiring manner as a moral fanatic.' Clough here refused to comply and it seems that his ironies were not well taken by contemporaries. Where the modern reader is likely to see an independent tough-mindedness, Victorians seem to have read more literally, and Clough became for them, partly under his friend Arnold's sponsorship, a paradigm case of vacillation; he was not really 'a man of character'.

### 4.2 'Character'

This term among the mid-Victorians was, as Stefan Collini has shown, pervasive and crucial in pointing to a complex of approved and desired qualities. For a definitive statement it is natural to turn to the doyen of Victorian intellectual liberalism, John Stuart Mill. To begin with 'character' and 'Victorian', however, is to anchor him a little prematurely in a British context. It would be better to begin a little further back. Mill was a Francophile who constantly rebuked his compatriots for their insularity and prided himself on including in his thought all the major strands of intellectual modernity in Europe. He drew the line, it is true, at Idealist metaphysics, always remaining firmly within the English empiricist epistemological tradition which he derived from his father, James Mill. Apart from that, however, and the abiding but subsequently adulterated utilitarianism he had imbibed from the same source, he learnt, as he

---

[1] Arthur Hugh Clough, 'Amours de voyage', IV, XI, in *Clough: Selected Poetry*, ed. J.P. Phelan (London, 1995), p. 112.

acknowledged, much from French and German writers: the Saint-Simonians, Comte, Tocqueville, Goethe, Wilhelm von Humboldt. Coleridge and Carlyle were certainly important to him, but their roles, for Mill's generation, were very much those of impresarios in England of German ideas.

The central event of Mill's life, the breakdown he experienced as a young man, with an at least partial break with his inherited English utilitarianism, can easily be set, as is done partly by Mill himself in his *Autobiography* (1873), in a European context. Romanticism and the new social, moral and historical ideas of the continent figure largely in his account of his recovery. It is possible, however, also to offer a European context of another sort for the breakdown itself, which Mill treats mainly as peculiar to himself and his upbringing. He recognized that aspects of Romanticism, though not under that name, played a part in his emotional revival, but also noted obliquely that the breakdown itself was a kind of recapitulation of its characteristic malaise. Pointing to the different effects on him of Wordsworth's and Byron's poetry, he remarks that he could draw healing from the former but not from the latter, because Byron's state of mind 'was too like my own'. Mill too, perhaps, though we do not usually think of him thus, should be counted among those Europeans who, encountering 'Childe Harold', as Matthew Arnold said, 'made his woes their own' – or found that they already were.

The chief symptom of Mill's breakdown as he describes it was apathy, that paralysis of will and desire with which we are already familiar and which we may well call a loss of the sense of self. Brought up to think of all merely inherited beliefs as prejudice, he was also programmed by his father to be the next leader, intellectual and political, of the English Utilitarians, the Philosophic Radicals. He was deeply hurt by the gibe that he was a 'manufactured man'. It was, he came to feel, that artificially constructed self, not his own creation but his father's, which had collapsed, and he became drawn to Romantic notions of spontaneity of feeling, mainly through Wordsworth, and to the idea of free self-development, in constant negotiation with the variety of experience, represented initially chiefly by Goethe and which he borrowed later from Goethe's friend Humboldt for the epigraph, and much of Chapter 3, of *On Liberty* (1859). Though he claims that it is compatible with an enlarged definition of utilitarianism – a claim which is still debated – Mill places individuality, individual self-development, and the necessity for variety of circumstances, at the centre of the progressive liberalism formulated in *On Liberty*.

In Mill's argument – he has versions of it from the 1830s onwards –

individuality, the unique, autonomous and manly energetic self, is threatened above all by the pressure to conform to what Tocqueville taught him to see as democratic public opinion and as characteristic of the modern world. His early breakdown seems to have left him always haunted by a fear of the loss of will and animating energy, but in his maturity the fear is projected onto the prospects for Western society as a whole and is seen in terms not of dramatic collapse but of a gradual, insidious process of entropy, produced by the power of conformity, and the stifling of all richly energetic individualities and the flattening of the variety of circumstances and experiences by which they are nourished. The only hope, it seems, lies in what one might call the liberal-as-hero, the strong man rising above the surroundings constituted by a multitude of narrow minds and timid souls, to the fearless exercise of independent reason and the equally fearless creation of his own – to use the classic Victorian term – character.

Mill acknowledges no Nonconformist cultural roots, as in justice he should have done, for this conception, though Herbert Spencer did. Instead, he makes his picture a distinctly continental one by opposing what he provocatively calls 'pagan self-assertion' to 'Calvinist self-denial', and drawing his characterization of the former from German eighteenth-century neo-Hellenism in the (recently published and translated) essay of Humboldt. The alternative to the inspiriting example of ripe and vigorous individualities, of the liberal-as-hero, is presented by Mill in stark terms: not just, as one might suppose, a mundane rubbing-along with received ideas, but homogenization – 'Chinese Stationariness', the failure of the springs of cultural energy and social progress, the stagnation to which modern life tends. Democratic society is the thief of character, compressing the autonomous self into a mild, tepid, socialized compound, without originality or vitality. Strenuous self-assertion, within the limits imposed by the equal rights of others to non-interference, seems alone to offer hope.

It is perhaps useful at this point to take a sideways glance for a moment at a work published the year after *On Liberty*, in which, quite unconsciously, of course, Mill's call for vigorous individualities (though not always with respect for the rights of others) seems to receive an historical echo, a demonstration that individualism had been once neither narrow nor philistine, and an evocation of the undemocratic predecessor of public opinion, fame. The individuals to whom we are introduced in Jacob Burckhardt's *Civilization of the Renaissance in Italy* (1860) are, according to him, precursors of modernity, yet they are far from the drab form modernity was frequently felt, not least by Burckhardt, to be assuming. Pagan – or more accurately neo-pagan – self-assertion is rampant; the consonances between Burckhardt and Mill are of course constituted by the heritage of German Hellenism and widely shared fears about democracy. In the Middle Ages, Burckhardt told his readers, men knew themselves only as members of social categories; the Renaissance saw the vigorous birth of modern individual self-consciousness. Burckhardt's individuals – scholars, artists, *condottieri*, despots – inhabit a precarious world of opportunity and danger, of immense achievement and equally immense reversals of fortune (like, one feels inclined to say, early nineteenth-century capitalism, but much more various and colourful). Denied the legitimation of birth in a fixed social order, they rely only on their own qualities of nerve, will, talent and accomplishment to survive and to impose themselves (as Machiavelli enjoined) on circumstances. They are fiercely emulative, often amoral, proud, passionate, avid above all for pre-eminence and fame. The self-consciousness of Renaissance man is presented as a source not of hesitation and anguish but of vitality and self-delight. Written for a world often disposed to see itself as a grey, uniform, entropic one, Burckhardt's Renaissance Italy is a society whose unleashed energies can only with difficulty be controlled and often are not. It is easy to be reminded of Tacitus in the *Germania*, writing of fierce, hardy, independent Germans for a tamed and decadent Roman aristocracy, as well as of the fact that a younger colleague of Burckhardt's at Basel was to be Friedrich Nietzsche.

But to return to Mill: if we take a wider, prospective view of Mill's celebration of energy of character and variety of experience we can see it as threatened, in the longer term, not only by the enfolding embrace of democratic manners and opinion but from within, by the pulling apart of its two components. Mill's always somewhat aristocratic endorsement of vigorous self-assertion, that is, needs only a half-turn to the right to prefigure the post-Nietzschean search for a heroic ethic in – or against – modernity which became fashionable at the turn of the century. On the other hand, in Mill's celebration of variety of experience, as the vital nourishment of individuality, there is an adumbration of the aesthete's creed, which began to be widely disseminated a decade or two later by authors remote indeed from Mill's own sensibility and sense of propriety, and whose writings cut the link Mill had supposed to exist between assimilation of experience and the creation of an actively vigorous character. Retrospective reading is, of course, always unfair, yet read in the light of these two cultural developments of the later nineteenth century, which we shall have to consider in the next chapter, some of the pronouncements of Mill's *On Liberty* cannot help assuming an ironic character.

Finally, and to resume an earlier discussion, to lay the stress that Mill did on emancipation from prejudice and custom and conventional opinion in the creation of an autonomous self was necessarily to lay a heavy burden on the individual to discover an alternative, to find in the emancipated self more than a space, an absence to be supplied – how? One answer might have been 'by pure reason', but Mill was too much a utilitarian to make reason a substitute for motive; desire must make an entrance at some point. But Mill had learnt by his upbringing that desire, or at least what might pass as desire, can be constructed. His answer to the obviously looming threat of determinism was to invoke the concept of 'character' as a cause. One's will was free if one's actions proceeded from one's character – and one's character, it might be added, must be made, as a process, by oneself and not by the will of another. Quite what it was for a character to be made by an as yet unmade self was arguably left unclear, but it has to be remembered that Mill, with his early experience of having been, far more obviously than most human beings, as it were programmed, seems always to dread less the void of a contentless self revealed by freedom than the substitution for the self of something alien to it, masquerading as the self: the opinions of others. He found in fighting against this a vocation, entirely consistent with historic liberalism, which for him solved the problem, though philosophically it could be seen as an evasion.

Ironically the role Mill assumed in later life was very close to the one his father had chosen for him and so relentlessly trained him for. It is as though Mill had first to demonstrate his freedom to repudiate it, by a collapse into apathy, before he could take it up again as his own. In returning, after his crisis, to making an intellectual career of the pursuit of scientific truth and its diffusion as political persuasion, Mill returned to the ground where liberalism was least problematic, leaving the abyss of self-consciousness to take care of itself. There was still work for the classic liberal agenda in Britain up to the time of his death in 1873. In some contexts traditional demands like freedom of speech and conscience, and equality of opportunity irrespective of status, could still function unequivocally and forcefully. One such cause, to which Mill made a contribution (*The Subjection of Women*, 1869), was that of women's emancipation, though as became habitual with him he tried to give all the credit to his wife.

'The Woman Question' as it was sometimes called, was, like the earlier opposition to slavery, perfect ground for the exercise of basic liberal principles, even though many in other respects good liberals failed the tests it set. It was, that is to say, concerned with the extension to another class of rational creatures of freedoms already appearing in any liberal agenda as belonging to men as equal and rational beings. Disputes tended to focus on the matter of fact: female rationality. Because the issue was essentially a simple one, and raised so starkly the fundamental question of equal human freedom, it was sometimes able to assume, in the literature of the middle and later years of the century, the dramatic, heroic, uncompromising character which political liberalism itself could seldom now inspire, recalling the dramatic moments of an earlier, more innocent age in the politics of the rights of man: the rhetoric of the American Revolution or Schiller's *Don Carlos* (later to provide the basis for Verdi's opera), or the prisoners' chorus in Beethoven's *Fidelio*.

Memorable examples of the dramatic assertion of female will and freedom included Jane Eyre's 'Mr Rochester, I will *not* be yours' (*Jane Eyre*, 1847); the slamming door which electrified London theatre audiences in 1889 as Nora Helmer walks out on her appalling husband at the end of Ibsen's *A Doll's House* (1879); the pistol shot at the end of his *Hedda Gabler* (1890); and the comic as well as touching episode in Bernard Shaw's *Pygmalion* (1912) when Eliza Doolittle throws his slippers at her mentor. An unusually positive ending, for Ibsen, to his play *The Lady from the Sea* (1888) occurs because the husband gives over to his wife the free choice of whether or not to leave him for the mysterious seaman who has a folk-loric kind of psychological hold over her. The choice she makes could easily seem one for comfort and security over adventure, but it is not. It is, rather, an option for reality over fantasy, and an act of self-emancipation because the freedom to act breaks the spell. There are, on the other hand, images of imprisonment in marriage akin on a domestic scale to the powerful depictions of prisons during the *ancien régime*. Dorothea Brooke and Gwendolen Harleth in George Eliot's *Middlemarch* (1872) and *Daniel Deronda* (1876); Isabel Archer in Henry James's *Portrait of a Lady* (1881); and Ibsen's *Hedda Gabler*.

To see later nineteenth-century feminism as unproblematic liberalism is perhaps to throw some light on the attitudes of some of its male supporters, particularly Ibsen (1828–1906) and Shaw (1856–1950). Not, of course, that there is anything unproblematic about Ibsen's own concept of the free self; it is too complex and too embedded in the texts of his plays and poetry to be plausibly summarizable. In the early dramatic poem *Peer*

*Gynt* (1867) it is the central question posed by the work, but Peer, who tries to be an untrammelled free spirit, true only to himself, lives only in a chameleon-like succession of roles: his freedom is merely picaresque. Ibsen, however, also uses women to explore questions of will and self; convention weighed so heavily on women that it seemed self-evident that they could achieve personal freedom only in defiance, while marriage could plausibly figure as the residual form of slavery. 'Liberty,' Ibsen noted, 'consists in giving the individual the right to liberate himself, each according to his or her needs.' Shaw, in his long essay on Ibsen ('The Quintessence of Ibsenism', 1891), presents woman's emancipation, in a fashion he claims as Ibsenite, as a war to the death with the Victorian shibboleth of 'duty', which she must repudiate in order to begin to live: 'unless Woman repudiates her womanliness, her duty to her husband, to her children, to society, to the law, and to everyone but herself, she cannot emancipate herself'. Her significance for Shaw, that is, seems to derive from the extremity, the comprehensiveness, of her unfreedom. As in Marx's version of the proletariat, the agent of general emancipation must come from the most enslaved. 'Woman', because of the extent of her alienation from her vital self, must, to be emancipated, become the enemy not of this or that injustice but of the whole fabric of conventional morality; it is hard for the reader to repress the idea of a stalking horse.

Women themselves, naturally enough, often saw matters differently and elected to be high-minded liberals demanding inclusion in the freedoms liberalism had won, rather than to be Ibsenite or Nietzschean revolutionaries against 'morality'. Jane Eyre, admittedly in an earlier period, had found her ultimate self in 'the still small voice' of conscience, which, in her case had voted against passion and for established moral law. Feminist movements in the later nineteenth century flourished most in parts of Europe traditionally Protestant; even in France Protestant backgrounds seem to be over-represented. A liberal-Protestant, sometimes Kantian, kind of high-mindedness was one form it could assume. Jane had listened to the Protestant's final court of appeal, conscience. For later, more fashionable thinkers, the obligations on women, as rational creatures, of a Kantian kind of moral freedom in submission to the higher, rational, impartial self, could bear no less heavily than on men. One French feminist wrote in a socialist journal in 1900, 'The decisive revolution is the inner revolution; the freest . . . is the one who belongs most to herself, and this freedom is ultimately measured by the degree of autonomy of the "ego". The worst tyrants are those we maintain or allow to live within ourselves; our bad instincts, our mindless passions, our unreasonable temptations, and all our atavistic vices.' Jane Eyre had been there before her: 'I need not sell my soul to buy bliss. I have an inward treasure from within me, which can keep me alive if all extraneous delights should be withheld, or offered only at a price I cannot afford to give.'

Ibsen and Shaw need not have disagreed, but the emphasis is not theirs and all the more reassuring to a middle-class readership for it. What is at stake here is clearly a good deal less than a Nietzschean revaluation of all values. The designated revolutionary agent does not always accept the role assigned to it, often preferring to claim its rights within something like the status quo; the proletariat can prefer embourgeoisement to revolution. Feminists in the late eighteenth century had demanded the 'rights of women'. So long as such rights were denied to women there would be life in the old arguments, as well as a refurbishment of the concept of equal rationality in an age when its only philosophically fashionable form had become Kantian Idealism. It was natural that some feminists should add to the Enlightenment argument for equal rights a philosophical version of older Protestant notions of self-mastery and self-denial.

But there was also a more subversive version of female emancipation derived not from Protestant individualism or Enlightenment rationalism but from Romanticism. In this version, of which in the mid-century George Sand had been the supreme exemplar, passion and sexuality were central; the rights claimed were those of the heart rather than the mind, and the claims were compatible with notions of a distinctively feminine nature. To adopt this was necessarily to be a kind of revolutionary, since convention as well as law stood so implacably and comprehensively in the way. Not surprisingly, therefore, such ideas were found most richly represented in the years of utopian optimism, the 1830s and 1840s, among the Fourierists and Saint-Simonians and those influenced by them, like Herzen, who had to accept the consequences of his wife's taking them literally. In the grimmer and more gradualist mood of the second half of the century, rationalism and the focus on legal rights, the extension of the normal liberal agenda, tended to prevail, but the Romantic, antinomian strand re-emerged around the end of the century. Particularly in Britain and Germany, like-minded souls, men and women, sought each other in small, utopian-minded sects, fellowships of the new life (the group of precisely that name became a feeder to the Fabian Society) in which sexual equality and female sexuality were upheld, often alongside other regenerating enthusiasms such as vegetarianism, teetotalism, eugenics and wearing wool next to the skin. A Nietzschean idiom of self-affirmation was more appropriate here, and by the later 1890s in German it was becoming available: the Social Democrat Lily Braun wrote of 'The will to power, the highest possible development of the personality as the goal of the individual, the superior human being as the goal of humanity.' Mill would not have disagreed, provided the latter recognized his or her obligation to act as an example and inspiration to others, and would certainly have acknowledged women, under the proper circumstances, as likely candidates.

## 4.3 The Flux of Experience

While women were engaged in reclaiming their essential selves, and were even in a sense helped by the extreme obviousness of the barriers to their doing so, some of their male contemporaries seem to have been equally busy losing theirs or even denying that they had ever existed. The prevalence of the Kantian Idealist notion of a true or higher self, transcending the flux of mere unstable stimuli and impulses, can give a partly false impression. The nearer we approach to the end of the century the more fashionable seems a denial, on psychological or epistemological grounds, of the existence of an enduring ego through the indeterminate, irreversible flux of sensory experience and images, which was all that the phenomena of consciousness seemed to present to introspection. By the end of the century the notion of 'character' was beginning to look like a form of naïveté, discordant with the tendencies of advanced thought. Bernard Shaw mocked it in its typically English form in *Man and Superman* (1903): 'your pious English habit of regarding the world as a moral gymnasium built expressly to strengthen your character in, occasionally leads you to think about your own confounded principles when you should be thinking of other people's necessities'. This was a sharp socialistic jab at Green's kind of highly moralized liberalism.

But the Idealist's conception too was typically a social one, and it was common to hold that the idea of the isolated self was unintelligible. We saw earlier (Chapter 4) Bosanquet affirming that similar states of consciousness to our own, occurring in others, need be thought of as no more distinct from ours (indeed perhaps less) than different states of consciousness at other times in ourselves. Bosanquet was there drawing on the other seminal figure in English Idealism, alongside Green, F. H. Bradley

(1846–1924), in, for example, his *Ethical Studies* (1876). The higher true self was an *extended* self, and could only become so by comprehending more of the possibilities revealed to it in human society. Bradley wrote tersely: 'the difficulty is; being limited, and so not a whole, how to extend myself so as to become a whole? The answer is, to be a member of a whole.' In Bradley's metaphysics, to be limited was to be fragmented and self-contradictory, since only some logical possibilities were realized while others were excluded, whereas truth was a totality, the sum of all possible relations. In his metaphysical treatise *Appearance and Reality* (1893) therefore, Bradley later adopted an extreme version of a very un-English paradox, the unreality of the individual.

This was the consequence of pushing to the limit the intellectual thrust of the metaphysics of Objective Idealism as it had been formulated in Germany early in the century. On the continent it was, rather, contemporary psychology and epistemology which exercised their disintegrating effect on the concept of the self. When Le Bon wrote in *The Crowd* that 'it is only in novels that individuals are found to traverse their whole lives with an unvarying character', drawing attention to radical discontinuities in consciousness, he was speaking self-consciously from the weight of sophistication provided by modern scientific psychology. It is, in fact, to France or rather to Paris, where such valedictions have since become commonplace, and to Austria, that we have chiefly to turn to read the contemporary obituaries of the stable ego. Earlier (Chapter 2) we considered the pathological bent of French psychology in this period, and its tendency to deploy this even in consideration of the 'normal'; hence its interest in dreams, hallucinations, dual or multiple personality as a disorder, and the dramatic supplanting of individual will, rationality and character achievable through hypnotism.

Le Bon, in fact, must be counted as a disciple of Taine in psychology. In this line of thought, as we have seen already, consciousness was a field where ideas and images, past (memory) and present (sensation), constantly contended in an endless flux for domination (Taine uses the Darwinian analogy), for monopoly of attention, which none ever achieves totally or finally, so that all the others still remain subliminally present, ready to be called up by some new stress or stimulus; resurgence of the suppressed remained an ever-present possibility. Moreover, once the provoking sensation had passed there was little to distinguish the image to which it had given rise from illusions, hallucinations. Equilibrium consisted in walking the thinnest of lines between a complete surrender to the flux, apathy, and on the other hand monomania, possession by one image to the exclusion of all others. Paradoxically, 'stability' of character was most clearly exhibited in the insanity of monomania.

Another, even more radical version of the questioning of the stable self was to be found in the epistemology of the Austrian physicist Ernst Mach, which we considered briefly in Chapter 1. Mach, seeking the elimination of all metaphysical entities, refused to recognize any other form of existence than experienced sensation, while identifying the latter as an irreversible flux which could be given an appearance of stability only in the artifice of language, by conceptual fictions postulating things and laws. Nowhere, however, were there materials for the construction of a concept of the self except as a sequence of sensations, as David Hume had maintained a century and a half before. Selves, like things, were fictions. It seems, following Mach, to have become something of a café cliché in Vienna around the turn of the century to speak of the concept of the self as irretrievable (*Der Selbst ist unrettbar*). The closest analogy in France in the period, though it is one with important variations, was the highly influential philosophy of Henri Bergson (1859–1941), who also invoked the phenomenology of consciousness to establish the notion of an unrepeatable flow of diffuse experience in which all sharp boundaries of the individual self appear to be submerged.

The literary exploration of Mach's dissolution of the self was conducted notably by his disciple Robert Musil (1880–1942), who also wrote a book on Mach's philosophy, in his post-war novel *The Man Without Qualities* (1930–42). Less clear-cut but tempting is the claim for an analogous connection between Bergson and a leading conception of Marcel Proust's *Remembrance of Things Past* (*A la Recherche du temps perdu*) (1913–27). It may be dangerous to stress particular influences, but a good deal in Proust's novel, and particularly in its treatment of the idea of personal identity, invites placing in the general context of French psychology, including Taine as its doyen. In Proust's novel, 'character' is notoriously unstable through time, while the narrator displays an interest, like Taine, in the liminal states where the conscious mind relaxes its grasp, as between sleeping and waking. He stresses how one's earlier selves and later ones become strangers to each other, the deepest emotions of the earlier becoming later difficult or impossible to recall when no longer felt. Other people exhibit marked inconsistencies of behaviour, and shed and assume apparently incompatible characters with disconcerting (and, some readers have felt, implausible) unpredictability. Consistency, while it lasts, is most obviously, as in Taine, an overmastering possession by a single fixed idea, the Proustian obsession of jealousy. The narrator, in love with Albertine, recapitulates the obsessive behaviour of his prototype in jealousy, Charles Swann, in his love for Odette.

The slipperiness of experience, sensory, emotional and social, and hence the difficulty in finding an anchor for it in an enduring sense of self and of meaning in one's life, famously represented the challenge that the narrator (and, we presume, the author) takes up in the decision, recorded at the end of the book, to make a work of art from his own past. He is inspired by the sense that transcendence of the flux of time is represented for him by half-buried memories of particular moments, fleeting experiences which have remained subliminally present and of abiding though elusive significance for him, mysteriously connecting past and present, but recoverable only by a heroic, sustained endeavour, embodied in a work of art, the novel itself.

It may be that Proust (1871–1922) derived the notion of such an endeavour of memory at least partly from Bergson, but behind the diagnosis of the discontinuities it is intended to heal seems to lie a generation of French psychological assumptions. This is nowhere more suggestive than in its opposite, in the treatment of the concept of continuity. Proust's novel is in fact highly sensitive to the fact of endurance, the sense of the past in the present, not just fleetingly but as an unbroken continuity still visible or audible. This is, of course, a theme much exploited in the literature of the later nineteenth and early twentieth centuries: the English reader thinks first of George Eliot (1819–80), Thomas Hardy (1840–1928) and Rudyard Kipling (1865–1936) (in the 'Puck' stories and poems). Proust's narrator is acutely responsive to the traces through which the individual becomes aware not only of his own, highly discontinuous past, but of the wider past represented by class or nation, embodied in names, physiognomies, topographies and language. Again, therefore, it is tempting to invoke Taine, and the categories of 'race', 'milieu' and 'moment'. Two of the chief carriers in the novel of the continuities and common characteristics to which these categories refer are the servant Françoise, epitome of the traditions and character-traits of the French peasantry, and the Duchesse de Guermantes, partly in her ancient name but more in the pure yet curiously rustic French she speaks, at once provincial and aristocratic, in which she maintains an unconscious link with an older France, with the *ancien régime* which, superficially, she and her circle play at maintaining.

At the individual level both characters can be disconcerting –

Proustian, one might say. The Duchess confounds the idealized picture
the narrator originally constructs of her from her name and title; even
Françoise, the devoted servant, shocks him by the way she speaks of him
among others of her class, when she thinks him out of earshot. Stability,
continuity, are found at the level not of the individual but at those of
race, milieu and moment (Proust, of course, does not quote the words), whose
reality writers of this period tend to assume, or to speak of, with a literalness and confidence which we now are apt to find startling or naïve. Proust
stresses that the individual bearers of such continuities are unconscious
of them, though they may pride themselves on others more superficial.
Indeed, in the psychology of the later nineteenth century there is a marked
contrast between the precariousness and elusiveness freely attributed
to the conscious mind and the endurance – the fixed, confidently identified
attributes – of what was called 'the Unconscious' or 'the unconscious mind'.

## 4.4 The Unconscious

It needs to be stressed that there are some contrasts here with the ways
subsequent generations have learnt from Sigmund Freud (1856–1939) to
employ the concept of the Unconscious. Handling the notion of consciousness gingerly, with a strong sense of its incoherence and slipperiness,
writers of the late nineteenth century often spoke of the attributes of the
Unconscious with the same untroubled literalness with which evolutionists, which they also were, spoke of vestigial organs, which for them, though
not wholly functionless, the Unconscious resembled. It is true that they
stressed, as Freudians have been apt to do, the fragility of the mind's
conscious control, while in the Unconscious, latent but still potentially
overwhelming, lay the mass of instincts which might at any time resume
their sway over the individual. 'The conscious life of the mind is of small
importance compared with its unconscious life', Le Bon wrote, while
Maurice Barrès spoke of 'Consciousness, what a small thing on the surface
of ourselves.' It was because the Unconscious, as reflexes conditioned
into instinct, or something akin to instinct, and for the most part
inherited, represented the enduring and hence in a sense stable part of
the self that, under stress or in mental illness, it came again to the fore.

But this is, of course, in some respects significantly different from
the concept Freud was developing in the 1890s and 1900s in the context
of psychoanalysis, which from being initially the possession of a sect

(the first International Psycho-Analytical congress was held in 1908) became, in the years after the First World War, pervasive in the general culture. The previously standard notion of the Unconscious, in so far as it incorporated the concept of instinct, had something in common with the Freudian concept of the 'Id', and it touched conscious (not necessarily individual) life through the notion that it stored images derived from experience which could sometimes act as triggers. Its chief differences from the concept deployed by Freud arose from the extent of its Lamarckianism: it was heritable, largely collective, and only in part derived from the experiences of the individual. Freud's conception was far more individualized in content, though it had a common strategy which Freud tried to describe. Freud's Unconscious was also more dynamic, and in its own distinctive fashion articulate. It was the trickster within, cunning, active and flexible in the games it plays with the conscious mind and the analyst if there is one, advancing its enigmatic confessions and then retreating, when pressed, into further obscurities, always disclosing yet not disclosing what it can bear neither to leave alone nor to reveal. It has its own language, derived partly from the old psychological concept of the association of ideas, but symbolically ingenious in a manner similar to Frazer's savages (see Chapter 2), in their practice of contagious and sympathetic magic. Freud later read Frazer with interest and close attention and derived something from him for his essays in conjectural prehistory, notably *Totem and Taboo* (1913). It was also, notoriously, a punster. Freud worked out the symbolic language of his Unconscious in the first of his major writings, *The Interpretation of Dreams* (1900).

Though in Freud all significant buried memories seem to be charged with the same (sexual) energy and to have similar traumatic origins, the Freudian Unconscious is above all an individuality; that is why, according to Freud, it must be hunted in pairs, analyst and analysand, in their interaction. It is individual because its repressed traumas are individual, however common its experiences – so common that the myths of mankind, according to Freud, attempt to articulate them. The language of the Unconscious is therefore both general and particular; some of its symbolism derives from universally perceptible resemblances (though some confidently announced Freudian equivalences, like that between going upstairs and sexual intercourse, may not command the immediate assent of the unconverted), while other parts may draw on associations unique to the individual. But above all, for the purpose of the contrast we are considering, the Freudian unconscious *speaks*.

Highly individual creation though it was, Freudian psychoanalysis had, as Freud acknowledged, its own specific antecedents, most notably Charcot (again) and the treatment of hysterical traumas (i.e., those with no obvious physiological cause) by hypnosis rather than attempted physical remedies. If such traumatic conditions were not physiological then they must presumably be psychological in origin. Freud also acknowledged philosophers and novelists as pioneers in the realm of the Unconscious: Schopenhauer, Nietzsche, Dostoevsky. But though it is certainly of interest that the concept of an unconscious mind was already widely diffused, the contrasts between Freud and other contemporary explorers of the Unconscious – Spencer, Taine, Hartmann – are really more obvious than the resemblances.

For the most part, in the evolutionist psychology of the later nineteenth century the Unconscious was more collective than individual; individuality was a late (and for some fragile) flower of evolution. The Unconscious was produced, not by repression of instinct in human society, but rather by its partial supersession in the human species by the conscious mind as the chief tool of adaptation to the environment, so that the Unconscious was now to an extent latent, rather than overtly active all the time as in animals. Its content was made up not of unique traumatic events in the life of the individual but by continually repeated experiences, in the individual and the species, leading to the creation of reflex responses to the familiar stimuli. The latter, interiorized probably in the nerve cells, were inherited, so the Unconscious was the heritage of the race – roughly any human groups breeding together in a given environment. Le Bon said, echoing Taine, that the unconscious substratum 'consists of the immutable common characteristics handed down from generation to generation, which constitute the genius of a race'. It still manifested itself therefore, but in the individual a return to the dominance of the Unconscious was a literal evolutionary as well as individual regression. But this Unconscious was certainly no trickster; its power lay in its ability to recall and draw on the experience of a hundred ancestors. As such the concept could arouse enthusiasm, especially among nationalists, as well as apprehension. It could even, in such circles, for which Barrès is the leading spokesman, become a focus for piety and self-assurance, as in a sense it does for Proust's narrator in the form of Françoise. It could function as an explanation for widely shared feelings and behaviour; 'race-instinct' was an accepted explanatory category. But it was not ingenious, not sophisticated, as the Freudian Unconscious was, and that was largely the source of its appeal. If the conduct of the Freudian Unconscious destabilized the conscious self, there was at least one sense in which the *collective*, nineteenth-century Unconscious stabilized it. It had strong affinities with the Romantic cult of the people or *Volk* or peasantry, and it also represented a fashionably biologized version of the concept of tradition.

The fullest and most original idea of the Unconscious, apart from Freud's, current in the early 1900s was that of the immensely influential French philosopher Henri Bergson, whose ideas have been seen as apparently playing a part in the gestation of Proust's novel. We may begin a consideration of Bergson by recalling the concluding part of Chapter 1, above: the flow of existence, and the fictional character of concepts, seen essentially as tools in the struggle for life. For Bergson the rational, analytic intellect was itself a specialized tool, evolved to serve the practical needs of the individual, and from this derived its limitation in any, necessarily disinterested, attempt to grasp existence more holistically.

Merely as reason, conceptualizing existence in order to control it and adopting causal explanations by reference to stable laws of nature, intellect postulates a closed world of endless repetitions. To quote from what became Bergson's best-known work, *Creative Evolution* (1907): 'It is of the essence of reason to shut us up in the circle of the given.' Then Bergson gives a turn, strenuous and one could say moral, to the kind of thought we encountered earlier, particularly in the work of Ernst Mach. In concrete existence there are no repetitions; existence is a ceaseless, unrepeatable flux and hence concepts are merely useful fictions. But, as Mach put it, 'If the ego is not a monad isolated from the world but a part of it, in the midst of a cosmic stream from which it has emerged and into which it is ready to dissolve back again, then we shall no longer be inclined to regard the world as an unknowable something.'[2] But to know it, one might add, one must be, as it were, *inside* the flow.

Bergson puts this thought, or something like it, to strenuous purposes of self-affirmation and self-transcendence. To grasp existence in its concreteness, as pure, unrepeatable duration, the intellect must turn on itself, as philosophy, to transcend the limitation it has imposed on itself for specialized and practical purposes. One of Bergson's key polarities, in fact, is disinterested, philosophical reason set against the practical, self-interested use of reason and the scientific thought which grows from it. Intellect, in

[2] Quoted in Theodore M. Porter, 'The Death of the Object: *Fin de Siécle* Philosophy of Physics', in *Modernist Impulses in the Human Sciences 1870–1930*, ed. Dorothy Ross (Baltimore, 1994), p. 141.

postulating repetition and working with concepts, has estranged itself from the ever-changing uniqueness of existence itself. Only in the rediscovery of itself in another form, as intuition, can intellect relocate itself in flowing, concrete existence, and have direct, unmediated knowledge of it.

Only thus, moreover, through the disinterested exercise of intuition, divorced from practical intention, which is necessarily limiting, into the inner nature of existence, can we discover our freedom. The superficial, ordinary, social self is guided by adjustment and repetition: we might now say role-playing. But when we act with our whole self, which is a summation and concentration of all our past experiences, our slumbering, unused memories, we are free. There is a firm gesture here in Bergson to the concept of the individual Unconscious, as a repository in which nothing is lost, though it may elude the conscious mind. It is not surprising that the conception of Proust's *Recovering Lost Time* (to use one of the possible translations of *A la Recherche du temps perdu*), has been seen as an example of it.

Bergson's identification of the self with its whole past is the reverse of the determinism it might at first seem to be. It is not that our past determines how we shall act. Rather, it requires a concentrated act of will to, as it were, gather and focus our whole self in order to act freely and creatively, in contrast to the repetitive, perfunctory acts of our fragmented practical, self-interested self. It is like the Idealists' concept of the true, higher, integral self, but built now out of the fashionable materials of the flow of existence and the Unconscious mind. Bergson turns it into a kind of call to action, as a form of self-expression which, since we do not normally attain to it, is also a call to the transcendence of our ordinary, socially defined self by 'a plunge into pure duration'. Hence, 'the more that we succeed in making ourselves conscious of our progress in pure duration, the more we feel the different parts of our whole personality concentrate itself [sic] in . . . a sharp edge, pressed against the future and cutting into it unceasingly.' It is in this that life and action are free.

In this the concentrated action of the individual is parallel to the creativity of existence itself in evolution. For Bergson the latter is not teleological any more than it is causally determined; it is open-ended and self-driven. The cosmic impulse, the *élan vital*, running as a current through all life (like Schopenhauer's and Hartmann's 'Will') – in which, through cellular reproduction, are linked past, present and future as a continuum – is an impulse to transcend itself, to novelty. We understand its creativity, according to Bergson, because 'we experience it in ourselves when we act freely'. The conceptualizing intellect always looks backwards, but in free creative action the self is whole and will and intellect are one. As in traditional Idealism, that is to say, though now expressed in evolutionist language, intellect must transcend its limitations, its narrow egoism, to grasp existence as a whole, and when it does so it discovers that the meaning of existence is freedom. It has done so, however, not by conceptually mastering and stabilizing it, by recognizing the real as rational, but by projecting itself into the flow as intuition and will. In the flux of existence we discover meaning and a task.

# CHAPTER 5

## *Constructing the Self*

### *5.1 Work of Art and Microcosm*

We have been led well into the early twentieth century in considering Bergson at the end of the last chapter, pursuing the theme of existence as flux, and the gathering together of all the individual's resources of energy and unconscious memory to fling himself into it in freedom, not drowning but creating. To consider other conceptions of self-making as a task requires initially a journey backwards, at least to the 1860s and 1870s, before arriving again on the shoreline of the twentieth century.

There were two contrary ways, which nevertheless became entangled, in which the question of personal identity and autonomy tended to be put: the problem of experience and the problem of action. Attempted, lived answers to them occupy much of the exploratory moral history of the period and attempting to trace it in these terms will form the subject of this chapter.

Again it is appropriate to begin in France. There are reasons for this, which were touched on in the Prologue. In Germany, at least until the establishment of the Empire in 1871, nationalism and a covert revolutionary politics, often sublimated in the pursuit of science with a materialist bent, absorbed attention. In France the revolutions of 1848–9 had represented a more radical loss of political innocence; workers and bourgeoisie had come to open warfare in circumstances in which it might be hard to identify with either, and in 1851 the Second Empire, established by a *coup d'état*, had been ratified by a plebiscite, periodically renewed; liberalism and mass suffrage could seem incompatible. In Germany, though liberalism tended in the ensuing years to assume a harsher, more self-consciously 'realistic' nationalist character, the main critique of modernity still tended to assume its old, Romantic, volkish form. In Britain, 'intellectuals' – the word has to be used with hesitation precisely because of what has now to be said about them – continued to manage to find morals largely unproblematic in a post-Christian world. Leslie Stephen, after resigning his Cambridge college fellowship on religious grounds, bluffly summed up: 'I now believe in nothing, to put it shortly; but I do not the less believe in morality, etc., etc. I mean to live and die like a gentleman if possible.' He did. No wonder Nietzsche irritatedly declared – he was chiefly referring to George Eliot for whom the sacredness of duty was unquestionable – that 'For the Englishman morality is not yet a problem' (*Twilight of the Idols*). One wonders what he would have made of 'etc.' Lack of exploratory zest in life was what Mill accused his compatriots of in *On Liberty*, though one has to wonder, again, how he would have reacted to some of the pioneering efforts, later, of the 'decadents' of the *fin de siècle* to extend the boundaries of experience by the exercise of a perverse imagination and their endorsement of what they were fond of calling 'sin'. Mill, asked to share some responsibility, would no doubt have felt that he had lifted the lid of Pandora's box. The liberalism which licenses all which does not harm others is a capacious one but Mill's sense of what it might contain was surely limited, in a fashion perhaps characteristically English and mid-Victorian, by a certain primness of imagination; he did explicitly allow a proper disapproval of 'lowness' of taste. For all his castigation of English narrow-mindedness, he clearly relied on his countrymen in general to behave like – well, gentlemen. Yet another speculation: how much of his Francophilia could have survived exposure to the supper conversation, as described in the Goncourt brothers' journal, at Magny's restaurant in Paris when the intellectual and literary élite of the Second Empire was gathered there?

To turn to France is to become immediately aware of something certainly akin to Mill's sense of the threat of a stultifying democratic public opinion (partly derived, admittedly, from a Frenchman, Tocqueville) but with its own accent and emphasis and a vehemence for which hatred seems the only word. The antagonism of French writers to what was thought of as the ominous, flattening effect of 'American manners', goes back beyond Tocqueville's book, to the 1820s; it is expressed by Balzac and by Stendhal, who dedicated his works to 'the happy few'. Closer to home the enemy was the *bourgeois*: fatuously, complacently, ignorantly, conventionally enlightened and progressive. Flaubert with loving hatred compiled an anthology of such *idées reçues* in his posthumously published *Bouvard et Pecuchet* (1881). The corresponding German (and later English) term, as we have seen, was 'Philistine', originally a student term of derision for the citizenry, the worthy but blinkered *Bürgertum*.

Contempt for bourgeois taste and opinion was only part of the story. There was a perhaps justified sense that what was seen as a pervading banality was an attribute of modern life as such, and a sense, very evident from the middle of the century in Flaubert and Baudelaire, that modern culture was itself stale and used up. Even the words one was forced to use, the writer's materials, were made into clichés by having been in too many mouths; and even the bizarre experiences, exotic or perverse, through which one might seek escape from the pervading banality of life, were perhaps in the end worn, tedious and disillusioning. As Baudelaire put it in a poem in his collection *Flowers of Evil* (*Les Fleurs du mal*) (1857): plunge into the abyss, heaven or hell no matter which, to find something that will be new. Freedom itself, though they continued to require it – Flaubert and Baudelaire were both prosecuted for obscenity during the Second Empire – seemed to call for some extraordinary imaginative effort or creative artifice if it were not to issue only in dull hedonism and drab humanitarianism. The noisily prophetic, self-dramatizing style of French high Romanticism, of Chateaubriand and Victor Hugo, had come to seem fustian, the striking of noble or pathetic attitudes. Though there were parallels elsewhere – Swinburne (1837–1909) and the Pre-Raphaelites in England, for example – it is hard to match in the English – or German-speaking worlds the intensity of disillusionment and disgust with the tedium of contemporary life expressed by French writers in the 1850s and 1860s.

From the hatred of the predictable routines and commonplace opinions of ordinary bourgeois life a vocation had to be found, a self constructed. The self created out of such antagonism would have necessarily to be eccentric, eremitic or aggressive, or all three, beyond anything in which the liberal man of character or the populist revolutionary would be likely to engage. This was notably the case with the narcissistic creation for which Baudelaire found the formula (though he did not create him; the prototype was Beau Brummel and the earlier literary source Balzac), which he followed himself: the Dandy. The Baudelairean figure of the Dandy, on which he wrote a classic essay, was the outcome not of the cultivation of the past and the exotic which so often provided solace for disgust with modern life – the Pre-Raphaelites again, and in a different way Flaubert provide examples – but of a search for the possibility of a kind of heroism, an aristocracy self-created out of fastidiousness and *hauteur*, in the modern world.

Baudelaire's celebration, in other essays, of the life of the modern city, especially in its aspects of pleasure-seeking and self-display, and their

anti-types and collaborators, crime and prostitution, reads like a prefigur-
ation of the later celebrations of it by the Impressionists. The Dandy, for
Baudelaire, represented the last possibility of distinction in an egalitarian,
democratic society; his cold narcissism had, Baudelaire claimed, an almost
religious kind of dedication and self-discipline. The Dandy is, or it would
be better to say is one version of, the self as work of art, where art means,
emphatically, artifice. He is not purely self-regarding, however. His
emotional self-isolation requires the crowd to set it off, and he knows and
is acutely aware of the impression he makes; he enjoys the pleasure, as
Baudelaire puts it, of astonishing others while being himself never aston-
ished. He is the *flâneur*, the stroller, the detached observer amidst the
carnival of the modern city. Not exactly homeless, but never domestic, he
is something like the Romantic Wanderer-figure, made urban, cool, self-
sufficient and modern. He is at the heart of modern society, and unmistakably
its product, yet wholly insulated from any demands it might make on
him. His sympathies, aesthetic not sentimental, are engaged only by fellow
outsiders, the outcasts, the prostitute and the criminal ('The Dandy', *The
Painter of Modern Life*, 1863).

Flaubert offers a variant on the themes of detachment, self-discipline
and observation; not as self-presentation, the self as work of art, but as a
significant mutation of the concept of the artist. In Flaubert's case it involved
a disciplined repudiation of the Romantic clichés of prophetic inspiration
and self-expression. The vocation of the artist required, on the contrary, a
form of self-suppression; it was the devoted practice of a craft from which
the self was rigorously excluded except in the austere, fastidious selectivity
by which the work of art was made; it was the dedication not of the prophet
but of the anchorite. Just as Flaubert sometimes spoke as though he hated
having to use a pre-existing language, turned to cliché by common use,
which could be redeemed for art only by the most severe selection and
precision, so he said he wished he could create art out of nothing, a novel
without a subject, since the subject was irrelevant. A work of art could
be made, in *Madame Bovary* (1856), of a woman's attempt to live a life
constructed out of second-hand, second-rate Romantic images of herself,
in the banal setting of marriage to a boring provincial doctor. The artist's
self was focused with maximum concentration and intensity only on its
task; Flaubert spoke of being only an eye, an observer.

Yet there was another, contradictory – one can call it late Romantic –
side to Flaubert's creative imagination, which was also influential on the
next generation, which was profuse, exotic, grotesque and self-indulgent,

straining against the limits of human experience and particularly the experiences available in mid-nineteenth century France. This is the side represented in other novels, *Salammbô* (1862) the lurid, sado-masochistic story of a Carthaginian princess, and *The Temptation of Saint Anthony* (1874), which rewrote the history of early Christianity and paganism in fantasies of blood and sex, and seems to owe something to Renan's scholarly studies of ancient religions.

To try to generalize a little more, what we have here is a tension, sometimes expressed as in Flaubert as an oscillation, between the creation, by discipline, controlled artifice and fastidious rejection, of something in its way perfect, a self or a work, and on the other hand a notion of omnivorous observation and assimilation, testing the limits of experience and living vicariously a multitude of other lives; Flaubert famously said 'Madame Bovary is myself.' In the latter is implicit the idea of the artist, or perhaps merely the aesthete, as microcosm or compendium, with a Faustian greed for experience of all kinds, aided by bizarre imaginings and sometimes doings, recreating in himself through the use of literature and history, all the experiences of mankind.

In the two antithetical or balancing requirements of selectivity and assimilation, we have a version of an old polarity in aesthetics, going back, chiefly in Germany, to the late eighteenth century, between formal perfection and the immediacy and intensity of emotional or sensuous experience. In the mid-nineteenth century it is found classically in Nietzsche's *The Birth of Tragedy* (1872) in the balancing requirements of the Apollonian and the Dionysian aspects of Greek tragedy – where the former stands for the formal element in a work of art, epitomized in the humanized yet aesthetically perfect individuals of the Olympic pantheon; and the latter, embodied in the dithyrambic chanting of the chorus, is derived from the orgiastic rites of an original nature cult, in which all individuality is submerged in the immediate, sensual and terrifying, collective experience. The special quality of Greek tragedy, Nietzsche argued, depended on the balance between the two elements, serenity and terror; the former enabled the Greeks to face the latter. Aesthetic form, the Apollonian, is associated with poise, with individuality, with consciousness. The Dionysian calls up the raw, chaotic impulses of nature, something like the blindly striving universal Will of Schopenhauer from which the only redemption lies in aesthetic contemplation. But the precursors which suggest themselves for Nietzsche's conception also lie further back, in the eighteenth-century aesthetic ideas whose proponents are Winckelmann, Lessing and Schiller, from which derive the notion of greatness in a work of art as depending not only on the perfection, the nobility and serenity, of its form, but also on the energy, emotion, even in some cases terror, on which it is imposed and to which it gives coherence and, by an artistic *tour de force*, beauty. The supreme exponents of this were, it was held, the Greeks.

The notion of a necessary creative tension between poise and individuality on the one hand and the extent and intensity of experience on the other was applied in this aesthetic not only to works of art but, expressed through the conception of *Bildung*, to self-development. The ideal self was a synthesis, poised but not inhibited, enriched but not overwhelmed by diversity and intensity of experience. This was the conception Mill appropriated from Humboldt and made more strenuous and less aesthetically serene in *On Liberty*. Mill's 'forced' individuality, invigorated by its testing of a diversity of experience, is braced for action. Mill paid lip-service to the notion of such a character as an end in itself, but he clearly wanted it to be up and doing. Others, increasingly, promoted another version: the 'beautiful soul', to translate Schiller's phrase, was its own justification, and the notion of action, from Arnold's idea of culture expounded in *Culture and Anarchy* to Walter Pater's *The Renaissance* (1873) and *Marius the Epicurean* (1885), gently effaced itself.

The tension between poise, individuality and selectivity on the one hand, and receptivity to experience, often vicarious in its pre-digested form of art on the other, remained, however. It could be resolved – or sometimes not – only in the individual case. Frigidity threatened in the case of the former, personal disaster, submergence of identity through over-enthusiastic exploration of the exotic or the perverse, in the latter. Insanity, addiction or the police were not wholly remote possibilities. Arnold opted firmly for selectivity; the cultured self was made through exposure to 'the best that has been thought and said', all three key words, 'best', 'thought' and 'said' were reassuring. Arnold made the poise represented by culture as much a collective as an individual matter; culture was tradition, centrality, the opposite of and remedy for (*pace* Mill) eccentricity. The worst said about it was that it was some-what over-fastidious and effete. The Dionysian seems far away from this kind of Hellenism, but twenty years earlier, in the guise of a 'youth beloved of Pan' in Circe's palace, Arnold had expressed the burden of the artist condemned to live many lives and vicariously to experience many intensities:

> They see the Centaurs
> On Pelion: – then they feel,
> They too, the maddening wine
> Swell their large veins to bursting: in wild pain
> They feel the biting spears
> ... such a price
> The Gods exact for song:
> To become what we sing[1]

Arnold's poem reviews a number of possible historic, cultural moments for the poet to re-experience, but the most famous poetic evocation of such an inventory of possibilities (though in prose) was the meditation or fantasy Walter Pater (1839–94) wove around Leonardo's 'Mona Lisa' in *The Renaissance*. Familiar though it is, extended quotation is unavoidable.

> All the thoughts and experience of the world have etched and moulded there ... the animalism of Greece, the lust of Rome, the mysticism of the middle age with its spiritual ambition and imaginative loves, the return of the Pagan world, the sins of the Borgias. She is older than the rocks among which she sits; like the vampire, she has been dead many times, and learned the secrets of the grave; and has been a diver in deep seas, and keeps their fallen day about her, and trafficked for strange webs with Eastern merchants; and as Leda was the mother of Helen of Troy, and, as Saint Anne, the mother of Mary ... The fancy of a perpetual life, sweeping together ten thousand experiences, is an old one; and modern philosophy has conceived the idea of humanity as wrought upon by, and summing up in itself, all modes of thought and life.[2]

The totality of human culture is, so to say, a museum of stored experience, continuously available through art for vicarious exploration and re-creation. Through the access the aesthetic sensibility has to it, the self too can become a microcosm, attained through contemplation. Though the idea of the mind as microcosm is not new, in its elaborate, eclectic historicism Pater's idea, as he acknowledges, could hardly have been formulated before the nineteenth century. 'Modern philosophy' here is surely the

---

[1] Matthew Arnold, *The Strayed Reveller*, in *Poems of Matthew Arnold*, ed. K. Allott (London, 1965), pp. 223–37.

[2] Walter Pater, 'Leonardo da Vinci', *The Renaissance: Studies in Art and Literature* (London, 1964), pp. 122–3.

Hegelianism becoming fashionable in Pater's Oxford. Pater's prose-poem inevitably attracted parodies, including a good one in Evelyn Waugh's *Decline and Fall* (1928), where the new Mona Lisa is Captain Grimes, but even better, and closer to the source, was Max Beerbohm's. Announcing his retirement, at the age of 24, in his first book elegaically entitled *The Works of Max Beerbohm* (1896), Beerbohm wrote that he would seclude himself in the suburbs, where

> I shall look forth from my window . . . and, in my remoteness, appreci-ate the distant pageant of the world. Humanity will range itself in the columns of my morning paper. No pulse of life will escape me. The strife of politics, the intriguing of courts, the wreck of great vessels, wars, dra-mas, earthquakes, national griefs or joys; the strange sequels to divorces, even, and the mysterious suicides of land-agents in Ipswich – in all such phenomena I shall steep my exhaurient mind . . . I shall soar from ter-races of stone upon dragons with shining wings and make war upon Olympus . . . Among books that charm and give wings to the mind will my days be spent . . . Nor will I try to give anything in return . . . Only art with a capital H gives any consolation to her henchmen. And I, who crave no knighthood, will write no more.[3]

Here Beerbohm beautifully catches the connection in aestheticism between comprehensiveness and passivity; to act, to achieve, is to limit oneself and even the creation of a work of art seems a sweaty vulgarization. The theme of literature and history as liberation from the limitations of the individual life is, again, an old one, but the nineteenth century, more than ever before, had made possible, as Beerbohm saw, a kind of Faust-as-consumer, given, on condition only of abstinence from any inclination to action, a kind of omnipotence; not through anything so inconvenient as a diabolic pact, but through the century's own cultural omniscience combined with a rentier's income. Possessed of these, the *fin de siècle* aes-thete possessed all times, all cultures and, vicariously, all sensations, through salerooms and curio shops and *de luxe* editions, through imperial plunder and the commerce of the world, through hothouses, brothels, great public libraries, art galleries and museums, and even, for the mildly adventurous, travel and Baedekers. For survival amid the eclectic whirl of vicarious, and occasionally even actual, experience, the understandable need was for a principle or habit of discrimination, which, in the absence

[3] Max Beerbohm, 'Diminuendo', *Works and More* (London, 1930), pp. 122–3.

of a stable, socially constituted ethic and aesthetic, like eighteenth-century neo-classicism, was necessarily personal, an individual taste and fastidiousness.

Pater's novel *Marius the Epicurean* is full not only of accounts of 'a perpetual, inextinguishable thirst after experience' as a philosophy of life, and a 'consummate amenity' in its reception, so as to 'fill up the measure of [the] present with vivid sensations', but also of the constant employment of adjectives expressing discrimination: 'select', 'choice', 'scrupulous', 'nice'. Omnivorousness and fastidiousness are the two poles between which Marius (theoretically – we are not told much about his actual experiences) lives: 'The thirst for every kind of experience, encouraged by a philosophy which taught that nothing was intrinsically great or small, good or evil, had ever been at strife in him with a hieratic refinement . . .' Marius is a kind of priest of aestheticism, religiously attentive to the possibility of the exquisite moment, but also a critic, appraising and grading life as it passes by him – or him by.

Some 'decadent' young men in the 1880s were more robust and less earnest, playing with cultural eclecticism as a kind of game. George Moore described in his *Confessions of a Young Man* (1888) how he and a friend furnished his apartment in Paris:

> The drawing-room was in cardinal red hung from the middle of the ceiling and looped up to give the appearance of a tent; a faun, in terracotta, laughed in the red gloom, and there were Turkish couches and lamps. In another room you faced an altar, a Buddhist temple, a statue of Apollo and a bust of Shelley . . . in picturesque corners there were censers, great church candlesticks, and palms . . . I bought a Persian cat, and a python that made a monthly meal of guinea-pigs.[4]

This was eclecticism as an expression of high spirits, as self-parody and provocation. But the exotic actually endured could be formidable. Earlier Romanticism, in its explorations of the exotic and bizarre, of opium and hashish, had sometimes dwelt on images of delirium in which, as in Nietzsche's account of the Dionysiac frenzy, individuality and will are surrendered.

In the later nineteenth century, one kind of symbolic self-condemned victim was the poet as damned soul: Baudelaire, Paul Verlaine (1844–96), Arthur Rimbaud (1854–91) – Satanist, alcoholic, drugged. Another,

[4] George Moore, *Confessions of a Young Man* (London, 1961), pp. 60–1.

however, the victim not just of conventional poetic vices but of cultural eclecticism carried beyond a game was the European (this covered Rimbaud too) 'gone native'. Such casualties, most often English, seem to increase or at least draw more attention towards the end of the century, as part of the seamy side of European expansion and perhaps, too, as the hold of its agents on Christian pieties brought from home weakened. Such a victim was literally a lost soul, self-exiled from his own kind and forfeiting his European identity, but unable to find another except as a derelict, consoled by opium or drink, quarrelsomeness or self-abasement. In English folklore he seems often to have been educated at Balliol College, Oxford – to emphasize the height from which he has fallen.

But the most profound and enigmatic case study is Conrad's Kurtz in *Heart of Darkness* (1899), who at times in the story seems to stand for the whole of exploitative, humanitarian, Christian, progressive Europe. Kurtz succumbs to isolation and his alien environment. Having made himself a sanguinary god-king, he dies exclaiming 'the horror, the horror', presumably speaking of what he has found within himself. Clues to what this may be are liberally planted: the wilderness 'had whispered to him things about himself which he did not know . . . irresistibly fascinating. It echoed loudly within him because he was hollow at the core.' What things? The narrator finds an echo in his own obscure response to the throbbing drums from the river bank, a clue to what Kurtz had found. Beyond that the story does not take us: to a naked Freudian Id, divested of all the controls of ego and super-ego; to a Schopenhauerian blind cosmic Will; or to a submergence of individuality in the cult of some African Dionysus. All seem possible. Kurtz's case is several things. One is a literal regression, degeneration: 'The mind of man is capable of anything – because everything is in it, all the past as well as all the future.' The civilized man can slide up and down the scale of savagery and civilization because he contains it all within himself, as microcosm, through atavistic race-memory. But encouragement is also given to a more relativist, less 'progressive' interpretation: Kurtz points to an existential emptiness which the embrace of culture, composed of necessary illusion, normally conceals, and which man cannot bear to encounter directly. The unbearable confrontation is the nemesis of cultural transplantation.

The only rival 'truth' with which it can be faced down is said to be 'your own capacity for faithfulness', and that most notably exemplified is faithfulness to a calling, in this case chiefly seamanship, and even its technicalities: ultimate, objective certainties in a world of lost bearings and confused principles. One finds something like this in Kipling's stories too, but also a more optimistic version of inhabiting and mastering the alien, of unity in multiplicity, in the idea he popularized of the Englishman as cultural chameleon, able to pass as various kinds of native but still with the ethics of the club in his veins and an undimmed loyalty to the Raj. In his novel *Kim* (1901), however, Kipling does not blink at the psychological costs of divided loyalties. It is not wholly a game because Kim, the British boy brought up as a native, is far more inwardly Indian than the disguised British agents who recruit him. In life T. E. Lawrence (1885–1935) recorded something similar of his role in the Arab Revolt during the Great War. A British officer living as an Arab among Arabs, he became dedicated to the Arab cause in which he had initially enlisted for the experience and as a kind of personal test of will; he felt, he says, towards the end of his time in Arabia, as though he were going mad (*The Seven Pillars of Wisdom*, 1926).

But the most famous casualty of the cult of experience, the aesthete as martyr, was of course Oscar Wilde. Wilde seemed initially well protected by high spirits. He was proof against parody, which he seemed to invite. When a life is avowedly constructed as artifice, what is the point in denouncing it as a pose? Charged with posing he treated the accusation as a dullard's slowly dawning comprehension. It is clearly a mistake to treat him as a typical aesthete of the period, though he became by self-advertisement the best known, and also became, like Byron, as famous in France as in Britain and perhaps more highly regarded. He was too extrovert, good-humoured, sociable and exuberant to be at all typical. He was not even particularly fastidious; unfortunately for him not fastidious enough. It was a tragic irony that on the one occasion he reacted to the charge of posing it ruined him; the card from Lord Queensberry on which Wilde based his libel action read: 'To Oscar Wilde posing sodomite.' Wilde (who may have misread it) was induced to treat this as an accusation of homosexuality, which it was and which was true. But had he been content as usual to treat the line between pose and actuality as inexplicable he might have been safe. His fatal and fundamental mistake was to take real life both too seriously and not seriously enough. Unlike some aesthetes, who seem to have been content mainly or exclusively with their fantasies, he required (as a normal man, one is inclined to say) its pleasures but was too buoyant and genial, until it was too late, to take the measure of its formidability and cruelty.

## 5.2 'Decadence' and 'Life'

It is a further irony that in Wilde's chief work on aesthetics, the dialogue entitled 'The Critic as Artist' (published in *Intentions*, 1891), life, art and criticism form a hierarchy in which life is constantly trumped by art and – here is the originality – art by criticism. The originality leads to an almost Platonic loftiness and unworldliness, though the prose is often deepest purple. The doctrine preached by the instructor in the dialogue is an amalgam of Plato and Hegel with an Idealist version of the Lamarckian concept of evolution. There is also at the outset a, presumably somewhat ironic, antinomian echo of Mill's liberalism expressed in the Swinburnean language of the *fin de siècle*: a justification of 'Sin' as 'an essential element in progress' and the alternative to stagnation: 'By its curiosity sin increases the experience of the race. Through its intensified assertion of individualism it saves us from monotony of type.'

Wilde answers, though not quite explicitly, the charge levelled against the age (and most particularly its aesthetes as an aspect of the general charge of decadence), that it is creatively exhausted, a critical, 'Alexandrian' age, capable only of commentary on what has been created in the past. Wilde rebuts this not by defending modern art and literature from it but by admitting it and turning the admission into an affirmation. The archetypal modern figure is, indeed, not the artist but the critic; it is in him that 'the culture of the century will see itself realized'. But this is no matter for regret, since Wilde's argument (just as in an earlier dialogue, 'The Decay of Lying', it exalts art over life) here exalts criticism over art in a Hegelian fashion as a higher, more expanded level of self-consciousness. The practice of art necessarily implies concentration, limitation. The critic seeks self-expression only through the sensitive (Wilde likes the word 'impassioned') contemplation and interpretation of the art of all styles and periods, and, in constantly seeing in it new facets, is a kind of creator. The critic, that is, stands to art as the artist stands to life, using it as a starting point for a new creation, making self-conscious what had before been merely instinctual and experienced.

A good deal of Wilde's argument is Platonic in flavour: contemplation is superior to action; all actual instances of beauty are necessarily fragmentary, needing to be seen and placed as such at a higher level of contemplation. The critic is the philosopher in a new guise, the human embodiment of that higher, contemplative consciousness, made so by the total, historical perspective he is able to command. What is comprehended, however, is not just thought but the intensity of emotion embodied in works of art of all periods and styles. The critic is a microcosm 'to whom no form of thought is alien, no emotional impulse obscure'. He enjoys the serenity of the Platonic philosopher while living, through art, a multiplicity of lives; he sounds rather like the child of Faust and Helen of Troy imagined by Goethe. The reference to an Idealist version of evolutionary biology, however, becomes even more explicit than Platonism, invoking 'the scientific principle of Heredity' as 'the collective life of the race'. Heredity, which in the world of action circumscribes and limits, in the world of thought and assimilated experience justifies the view of the most developed mind as a microcosm. It is imagination that 'enables us to live these countless lives', and imagination is 'concentrated race-experience'. So we move on to yet another parody of Pater, this time, presumably, in unequivocal homage, licensed, rather remarkably, by the evolutionary concept of a collective unconscious mind: 'And so, it is not our own life that we live, but the lives of the dead, and the soul that dwells within us is no single spiritual entity . . . It is something that has dwelt in fearful places, and in ancient sepulchres has made its abode. It is rich with many maladies, and has memories of curious sins . . .', and so on. The critic is both universal and self-centred, omnivorous and secure: 'Calm and self-centred, and complete, the aesthetic critic contemplates life . . . He at least is safe. He has discovered how to live.'

He is also, however, something like the point or purpose of life itself. Evolution – this was a common conception of the time, glossing contemporary biology with a metaphysics that went back to Schelling and Hegel – is the ascent of nature into mind and self-consciousness. In Wilde's argument the critic–aesthete is the highest point of that process, because, reflecting, he reflects on all human experience. The man of action is merely the realization of nature's inarticulate energy; it is only through criticism that 'Humanity can become conscious of the point at which it has arrived', so that 'The critical Spirit and the World Spirit are one'. The meaning of Pater's oblique reference to 'modern philosophy' is now explicit if not perhaps altogether modern.

Later nineteenth-century aestheticism was characteristically a hypertrophy, for which Wilde here gives an exalted justification, of one side of human nature, the receptive and discriminating, at the expense of the self as agent and social being. Statements of an opposing kind, like the rigorous moral Kantianism expressed in the idea of an apparently selfless higher self, or socialist or solidarist enthusiasm for being a cog in the social machine or putting one's shoulder to the wheel of social progress (which Durkheim, specifically rejecting the dilettantism of 'many-sidedness', speaks of as the modern form of self-fulfilment) were more likely perhaps to provoke an extreme individualism than to soften it. The exaltation of the self as agent and the search for the possibility of an heroic ethic in modern life were often expressed in an antagonism both to 'decadence' and to 'humanitarianism', as we have already seen in the cases of, for example, Sorel and Barrès. This stance became common towards the end of the century, and we shall have to consider it in the conclusion of this chapter.

First, however, we need to look generally at the concept of 'decadence' and its critique. In association with this there is a potential confusion which cannot be wholly resolved, since it arose from a real conceptual overlap which contemporaries often did not bother to notice. The conceptual sibling, sometimes no more than a semantic *alter ego*, of decadence was a concept we have already considered in Chapter 2, 'degeneration'. It is possible and not wholly misleading to attempt to be strict in making a distinction. 'Decadence' was usually thought of as a condition of the highly educated, and was associated with the arts. 'Degeneration' was applied in those contexts also, sometimes to offer much the same diagnosis. But the reverse did not altogether hold. 'Degenerates' were seen typically in the form of a deliberate perversity in the upper classes but in the lower they were often thought of as endemic. Degeneration, moreover, suggests regression, decadence exhaustion As a concept the former derived at least ostensibly from biopsychology; the latter chiefly from the history of culture, with particular reference to declining Rome. Neither in use nor theory, however, was the distinction clear-cut. The concept of decadence, for example, relied explicitly or implicitly on an organic analogy with youth, maturity and senescence. Morbidity and madness were frequently invoked in the discourse of decadence, especially as fostered by the conditions of modern life in great cities, to which, in its glitter and distractions, its incessantly changing tumult of impressions and its moral isolation was ascribed a chronic over-excitation of the nerves. The life of the city, which the Impressionists celebrated, with its gas-lights and its uncoordinated movement and din, could be both exhilarating and overwhelming. For the young, working-class apprentice aesthete in Henry James's *The Princess Casamassima* (1886), gazing into the shop window of London life, 'nothing in life had such an interest or such a price for him as his impressions and reflexions. They came from everything he touched, they made him vibrate, kept him thrilled and throbbing, for most of his waking consciousness . . .

everything struck him, penetrated, stirred; he had in a word more views of life, as he might have called it, than he knew what to do with.'

By the censorious, appetite was seen to grow morbidly by what it fed on. The morbid individual 'exhausts all the devices of ingenuity in order to enhance and multiply desires and to vary the modes of their gratification' (Henry Maudsley, *Body and Will*, 1883). Decadence of this kind, and literal degeneration were, according to Maudsley, actually biologically related. It was a (Spencerian-sounding) law of life that an organism can become too complex to retain its equilibrium in the face of its environment, while 'the more complex the organism the greater the number and variety of its diseases'. With exhaustion of the higher centres of consciousness as a result of over-excitation, the lower would resume their sway, but degeneration, according to Maudsley, was never simple regression to an earlier state, which in its own terms was biologically sound though 'lower', but to a morbid version of it, for example in sexual perversion. The inference drawn is that 'great cities, which are the centres of the best intellectual light, become naturally the centres of the greatest vices'. It is not surprising that Maudsley saw degenerative tendencies in modern art. The most famous work of the period which took this view, Max Nordau's widely selling polemic, *Degeneration* (1895), which saw the central characteristics of the age as perversity and the paralysis of the ability to act, diagnosed tobacco, alcohol and life in large cities as predisposing causes; modern art was pathological.

Another diagnostician of decadence, under that name and, so to speak, from the inside, was Taine's and James's protégé, the novelist Paul Bourget, in his *Essais de psychologie contemporaine* (1883). For Bourget (1852–1935) too, decadence was a pathological state of the nerves and a contemporary European cultural condition, whose literary prototypes were Baudelaire and Flaubert in France, Schopenhauer in Germany, and the exponents of Nihilism in Russia. But Bourget saw a connection between the pathology of decadence and high artistic achievement, which opened the way to re-garding the decadent artist as a sacrificial figure, expressing the modern condition and exploiting his psychological wounds for the purposes of art. 'Decadence' became one of the many terms which, applied sorrowfully or pejoratively, came to be adopted as a badge; a journal entitled *Le Décadent* was established in 1886.

The line between the embodiment and the critique of decadence could be a fine one. J. K. Huysmans' *A Rebours* (1884) (the title is untranslatable, but 'Other Way Round' will do) is not usually, and certainly was not, read as a critique. On the contrary, it was hailed as 'the breviary of the decadence', and was supposedly the 'poisonous' book which helped to undermine the moral sense of Wilde's Dorian Gray (*The Picture of Dorian Gray*, 1890). Yet it is not impossible to read it as a kind of critique, while seeing it as advocacy means ignoring a number of evident incongruities. In fact neither category will quite do. Certainly Huysmans' novel embraces the conception of decadence as a morbid perversity. Its protagonist, the aristocrat des Esseintes, is thin-blooded, neurasthenic, product of an exhausted hereditary line. Huysmans had been a disciple of Zola, and the master-notion of Zola's 'Rougon-Maquart' series of novels, of a cumulative hereditary degeneration, is signalled from the outset. Made master of his circumstances by a sufficient income, des Esseintes is the victim of a tortured fastidiousness which makes nature and everyday urban life equally repellent to him. After an initial period of calculated eccentricities, he withdraws into an almost hermit-like existence, in which all his experiences, all his sensations, are to be carefully controlled. Like Wilde's aesthete as critic later, he will 'settle beforehand what [his] experiences are going to be'.

Huysmans' novel is essentially made up of des Esseintes' series of attempts to provide himself, through art and décor and imagination, with a completely controlled sequence of various experiences matching his various moods. There is an evident enjoyment of this in Huysmans' writing, amounting to a kind of complicity, yet the episodes are also often clearly intentionally comic; the suggestion of a rich child with a lavishly furnished toy-box is irresistible, as when des Esseintes tries to recreate indoors the experience of being at sea. In another, consistently with his view of the superiority of art to nature, he creates the essence of flowers and the open air with scent bottles, including 'a few drops of the perfume "new-mown hay"'. Des Esseintes is a pioneer of what is now called 'virtual reality' and makes it a substitute for everything else. Eventually his worn-out constitution and unnatural way of life take their toll. One symptom is an inability to take food in the normal way, and having to be fed by enema (a vivid justification of the title), for which the doctor provides a prescription which des Esseintes treats as a menu, working out for himself 'recipes of a perverse epicureanism' and 'even planning meatless dinners for Fridays'.

That much of the novel is funny or pathetic seems to have escaped its decadent admirers; it raises inevitably the question of the distance Huysmans puts between himself and his creation. He had learnt his craft in the naturalist school of Zola and one possible way to read his novel would be as a kind of quasi-scientific case study of a contemporary type, 'the Decadent', very much as practised by the naturalists. There is too much sympathy and even apparent identification in the writing for this to be a complete account, though it cannot be dismissed altogether. The sufferings and ultimate desolation of the protagonist's life of isolation and artifice, and his final prayer to God to take pity on his unbelief (Huysmans himself became a Catholic), make possible another interpretation, in which he is a pilgrim and martyr, testing the limits of the spiritual condition of modernity in a *reductio ad absurdum*. None of these possibilities alone seems entirely persuasive or entirely redundant. If the book can be read as a kind of critique it is of an intensely inward and concrete kind.

For the most broadly generalized and yet still intimately involved critique of contemporary cultural and psychological decadence, and the most vigorous confrontation of it with challenging, seminal and problematic conceptions of 'life', 'action' and 'will', we have to turn to Friedrich Nietzsche (1844–1900). The concept of decadence in Nietzsche's work as a whole is an overarching one, stretching far beyond the immediately contemporary: Socratic dialectic, Platonic and Christian other worldliness, Christian asceticism and guilt, are all identified as agents of the cultural sickness of European civilization. We shall have to consider other aspects of this later. Nietzsche is, of course, a protean and inexhaustible writer; any more adequate consideration of him than can be offered here would have to include, and probably begin by, a discussion of how to read him, or rather his various works. The discussion here, so far as it goes, is not intended to provide a thumbnail sketch – that is what encyclopaedias are for – but to bring consideration of him to bear, as relevant, on the issues which have emerged so far, and others later.

In the present discussion we have to consider most directly the argument of his essay on the use of the past ('On the Advantage and Disadvantage of History for Life', 1874), where the preoccupation with the assimilated past and its connection with passivity and abstention from action, which we have been considering through the image of the self as microcosm, is identified by Nietzsche as a radical historicization of thought and experience. He finds this fundamental to contemporary German culture and education; it is the antithesis and enemy of what here he consistently calls 'life': creativity, energy, originality and action. Historical over-awareness, the sense of living always retrospectively, paralysing the will to live, is in this essay the particular form which the burden of self-consciousness, to which Nietzsche's writings constantly revert, assumes. It is for him specifically the malaise of contemporary Germany, with its historically oriented education and what he calls its 'consuming historical fever'. The past, which the strong nature can assimilate and use, selecting from it what is inspiring and vitalizing, crushes the weaker. The past is not for appreciation nor study nor assimilation for its own sake, but for the use of life, as inspiration to action.

Nietzsche speaks here of the use of the past, and of the false cult of impartiality, of objectivity, towards it, but the application of his argument to the examples we have been considering is constant and apt. Like the self-appointed decadents and their critics he draws the analogy with Rome. As the ancient Roman failed to preserve his identity 'in the influx of the foreign and degenerated in the cosmopolitan carnival of gods, customs and arts, so it must go with modern man who continuously has the feast of a world exhibition prepared for him by his historical artists; he has become a spectator merely enjoying himself'. Again Nietzsche writes ironically:

> the historical virtuoso of the present time . . . has developed in himself such a delicate and sensitive sensibility that nothing human remains alien to him; the most diverse ages and persons immediately reverberate in familiar sounds on his lyre; he has become a reverberating passivity.[5]

But all is etiolated and second-hand; not the original passions and experiences but only their shadows. Nietzsche, of course, already knows well in its Hegelian form Wilde's kind of argument for comprehensiveness of consciousness as the highest form of human self-realization and the culmination of man's history: 'the race is at its height for only now does it know itself and has become revealed to itself'. Nietzsche's retort was 'Your knowledge does not complete nature but only kills your own.' Modern man needs above all the ability to forget, to limit his knowledge for the sake of action and 'an ever-heightened sense of life'. The agent of this 'hygiene of life' is to be German Youth, on which Nietzsche calls in conclusion, to save German culture from its sterilizing academicism. Nietzsche is always least convincing when he turns from his appallingly searching examinations of individual weakness and self-delusion – grounded, as he freely admits, in self-knowledge – to propose social

---

[5] Friedrich Nietzsche, *On the Advantage and Disadvantage of History for Life*, trans. Peter Preuss (Indianapolis, 1980) pp. 33–4.

remedies and recipes for redemption. Even so the mawkishness of the conclusion is something of a shock. The implausible myth, encouraged by his sister's treatment of his literary remains, that Nietzsche was a prospective supporter of Nazism (like the equally implausible one during the Great War, on the Allies' side, that he was an apologist of German militarism), has now few or no advocates, so it may be safe to admit his encouragement, with that of his disciple Julius Langbehn (1851–1907), of what became in the 1900s the German Youth cult. Also on the charge sheet, on the basis of this essay, is encouragement of that gruesome genre, to which contributions were made in the same period, the 'inspiring' biography of the great man, in which the requirement of uplift in the reader takes a long precedence over that of respect for the past in the author.

Nietzsche, of course, only pointed in the general direction of these things, just as, at the end of *The Birth of Tragedy*, he found the promise of redemption in Wagnerian music-drama, to his later acute discomfort. It is more important to recognize the considerable similarities in Nietzsche's writings, considered more widely, with some of the features of the cults of the self we considered earlier. For Nietzsche too the self has to be made not, certainly, merely through assimilation, but through action; but nevertheless in a remarkable isolation. The imposition of will on the flux of experience, random impulse and the urge to comforting self-approbation, by what Nietzsche calls 'self-overcoming', is a self-regarding, self-referential spiritual exercise, not a social experience, and its obstacles are within. The attribution of meaning to life is essentially an individual, not a social task. Nietzsche's fastidiousness, too, when (fortunately rarely) he contemplates 'the herd' is scarcely exceeded by des Esseintes, who also provides an ironical echo to Nietzsche's conception of life as 'experiment'. Even the latter's frequent invocation, radically alien to the shuddering aesthete, of 'action', is at best half-misleading. He is not really concerned with the consequences of action, with what it brings about, which alone makes it a completed action, but with the quality of life, of the acting self, which the action expresses and which is the real object of moral, and one could equally say aesthetic, appraisal.

Nietzsche has something like Flaubert's aristocratic disgust with the used and repeated, the stale, second-hand, 'democratic' character of language and concepts. Incidentally, Flaubert a quarter of a century earlier, in a letter written on his trip to Egypt, foreshadowed Nietzsche's critique of historicism: 'Poor wretches that we are, we have I think, considerable taste because we are profoundly historical; we admit everything and adopt the point of view of whatever we are judging. But have we as much inner strength as we have understanding of others? Is fierce originality compatible with so much breadth of mind?' Originality requires a kind of ferocity; to avoid the already used we have constantly to rethink and re-forge life.

From a thought akin to this derives Nietzsche's scorn for the scientist's and savant's cult of objectivity. In depersonalizing knowledge, science and scholarship are self-condemned to construct a view of the world in common, through a cooperative intellectual endeavour and a conceptual currency which means the same whoever is handling it. For Nietzsche 'Good is no longer good if it has been in my neighbours' mouth' (*Twilight of the Idols*). 'Good', being lived, is necessarily individual, even idiosyncratic, and is falsified by the interpersonal character of language. More obviously, however, what makes the scientific vocation objectionable to him, the dedication to the pursuit of an objective truth as a way of life – which he criticizes in, for example, *The Genealogy of Morals* (1887) – is its moral complacency and its self-immolating character. The scientist or savant (we may think of Taine) treats his choice of vocation as though it were self-evident, rather than a choice among others of how to live, and instead of using truth and enquiry in the service of life makes a fetish of them, sacrifices his life, himself, to them.

The condemnation rests on a distinction which is a fine and sometimes itself not a self-evident one, but it is important. It is a fine one because Nietzsche's notion of self-overcoming is always in danger of edging over into a kind of asceticism. For Nietzsche the distinction was a fundamental one. The self-discipline and constant self-testing which concentrated and intensified life as their expression were at the opposite pole from the self-denial and repression which (for us premonitions of Freud are inescapable), diverting the will to power inwards against the self, breed as in Christianity, self-hatred, guilt, rancour towards the healthy, fulfilled and superior, and, as a general attitude towards life, a Schopenhauerian pessimism.

Language can easily accommodate such nuances as plausible antitheses. In practice distinguishing between self-discipline and repression, self-testing and self-torture, sublimation and self-denial, may not always be easy. Dedication embodied in a vocation provides an instance. Presumably, for a Nietzschean, everything must depend on questions of self-consciousness and perhaps degree: monomania, fanaticism, lack of self-knowledge on the one side, irony on the other – irony, that is, which recognizes with Nietzsche that we live and even intensify life by necessary illusions. To escape the solemnity with oneself which Nietzsche denounced as 'seriousness', irony is the crucial weapon, yet it is easy enough to think of it as debilitating. That is why it is a test of the vitality which can live with it and overcome its effects without stifling the self-knowledge it offers.

The question of vocation is important to have raised because it is there, in the next generation in Germany, coming to maturity in the 1880s, in time to catch the flood-tide of Nietzsche's influence, that one finds some of the most impressive apparent examples of a transmuted Nietzscheanism (there are plenty of unimpressive ones). In a world characterized by the flux of consciousness and bare of any metaphysical guarantee of moral meaning, the idea of vocation offered an obvious way of testing, forging, stabilizing the self in a social context, through chosen, regulated, disciplined activity, and self-chosen acceptance of its obligations. In it might even lie, in modern society, the possibility of a lived heroic ethic.

### 5.3 The Calling and the Deed

Despite, or perhaps because of, the power exercised since the eighteenth century by the concept of the division of labour, the idea of specialization, even in Adam Smith (though with the notable exception of Durkheim), was often deprecated over the same period. 'Many-sidedness', particularly in the myth of the free Athenian citizen, was extolled. *Bildung*, free self-development on the one hand, and specialization, the narrowing of the self to a trade on the other, were moral and educational rivals, and the latter for long continued to bear its Athenian stigma of servility. The former was often seen as supremely exemplified in Goethe, yet it was Goethe's novel *Wilhelm Meister* (1796), which began the rehabilitation of the latter as the injunction to do in life what lay nearest to one's hand. Thence it noisily re-emerged for the nineteenth century in the articulation, by *Wilhelm Meister*'s translator into English, Thomas Carlyle, of a conception of Duty, which, unlike the Kantian universal, adjusted itself to any given amount of specificity and social differentiation. Here, in Carlyle, we have strong echoes of the old, Calvinistic notion of the calling and of God as almighty taskmaster. We have already seen some late cultural offshoots of this, without the intrusion of God, in Conrad's and Kipling's sense of sacredness or salvation in the demands of the job in hand and even its technicalities.

In twentieth-century sociology the classic foundation of the conception of vocation or calling (the German word *Beruf* covers both) as the ethical shape of a life is Max Weber's *The Protestant Ethic and the Spirit of Capitalism*, together with his two late lectures on 'Science [the German, *Wissenschaft*, also includes scholarship] as a Vocation' (1919) and 'Politics as a Vocation' (1919). Durkheim's Preface to the second edition of *The Division of Labour* (1902), which treated professional ethics as the most precisely focused form assumed by modern ethical life, points in the same general direction. It was a natural development in a social stratum whose sense of identity, though partly constituted by a liberal education, was buttressed by professional status. Except for the aristocrat or rentier, *Bildung* and *Beruf* would both be necessary to self-esteem, but the emphasis could naturally vary. The origins of the sanctification of the latter, the calling, were, as Weber noted, Christian and Protestant.

The German term for the self shaped, not as in *Bildung*, through its opportunities, but through the acceptance of its responsibilities, was *Persönlichkeit*, the English translation of which is much nearer 'character' than 'personality'. Its roots lay in the version of German protestantism known as Pietism and in the 'higher self', to which we have therefore, by this route, returned. The achievement and maintenance of such a self was readily seen as threatened by the distinctive conditions of the modern world; the loss of faith in life's meaning, the perceived relativity of values recognized in historicism, the restlessness of attention fostered by a multiplicity of distractions. To these the 'decadent' succumbed and from them he attempted to shape a life of withdrawal and artifice. Weber, however, like Nietzsche, but less abstractly, sought the making of the self through action, and, possessed of a powerful sociological imagination, had a strong sense of the need for a social field for the endeavour towards self-realization, and for a form of self-regulation – an overcoming of the indeterminate state of flux, which he seems to have seen with a sense of vertiginous horror – through consistent, responsible, dedicated action.

The paradigmatic historical case – selected and inspiring, as Nietzsche might have said – was the seventeenth-century Calvinist entrepreneur, whose self-discipline, asceticism, rationality in pursuit of ends and disregard for all customary limitations on the pursuit of profit, had provided the psychological and economic energy which had created modern capitalism. That energy was derived, according to Weber, from the Calvinist conception of the calling. Every man was directly responsible to God, and only to God for his actions. Dedication to the calling, in this case economic, was a form of service, and success in it an indication of being one of the elect. It required asceticism in private life, watchfulness at every moment, and re-investment rather than consumption. In its dedication and asceticism it was an individualist, lay and Protestant version of the religious vocation. Weber saw the disciplined and regulated monastic life as a precursor of modern forms of rationalized activity, but where the monk's vocation was turned inwards, that of the Calvinist entrepreneur was conducted in the world.

In Mill's *On Liberty*, that strenuous Victorianized apologia for *Bildung* as the – perhaps somewhat surprising – motor of continued progress, Calvinism figures as the antithesis: repression, the narrowing of human possibilities, till the only approved form of energy is that devoted to business. Weber responded to the narrowing and repression as to a form of heroism, a dynamism that changed the world. The problem was to discern the possibility of such energy and moral heroism in a demythologized modern world. Without the almighty taskmaster the modern conception of vocation must do without the external sanctions, becoming an end in itself, the only responsibility being that which acceptance of it imposed. Not only is there for Weber no transcendental sanction but – and here the stance became, probably not accidentally, Nietzschean – there is therefore no possibility of rational, ethical mediation between the requirements of different choices of commitment: we can each, as Weber puts it, serve only one god. Politics, science, art and religion, considered as vocations, are each jealously exclusive in their demands on their votaries. Thus the view of politics, for example, endorsed in 'Politics as a Vocation' can fairly be described, as with a good many of Weber's generation in Germany, as Machiavellian; effective political action imposes its own requirements, which must be observed by those who choose it and which cannot be reduced to those of private ethics. Not that the political vocation is equated with the individual lust for power; that is simply another form of self-indulgence, and what Weber seeks in the concept of the calling is the self-discipline through which the self is realized and made effective; the political agent must seek and choose what to achieve and must subsequently choose and act in the fullest awareness of the consequences of what he does. The only political ethic is an ethic of responsibility and this is it. For what is to be chosen there can be no rules or prescriptions; that is a matter of free choice and commitment. In Weber's case his fundamental commitment was to the idea of the nation, and specifically to the interests of Germany as a Great Power. In that too he was a child of his time.

Another of the gods one might serve, and in serving choose a vocation, Weber recognized, was art: here as in religion, there were no outward responsibilities or admissible care for consequences; one was responsible only to one's own vision. Flaubert's ascetic dedication would presumably have won his approval. In Wilhelmine Germany, though the vocation of the artist, as also in contemporary France, attracted much attention, its most elaborate fictional exploration is found in the writings of Thomas Mann (1875–1955), touched (like Weber and perhaps more obviously) by the legacy of Nietzsche, in addition to the influences of Wagner and Schopenhauer. Mann attends directly to the question of artistic vocation in a number of his works, particularly *Death in Venice* (1912), *Tristan* (1902), *Tonio Kröger* (1903) and, much later, *Dr Faustus* (1947). In them the languor and passivity of the aesthete and the threatened loss of will and identity tend to assume a distinctly Schopenhauerian form, as the relaxation of the will to live; the dialectic of life and death is often central, and while the former is presented sometimes in its crassness and crudity, the latter acquires overtones not only of seductiveness but of fastidiousness and distinction, and the tension between the two gives the writing much of its imaginative energy. It also inevitably colours the treatment of the theme of the vocation of the artist.

The imaginative remaking of the world in the form of art, the imposition (with echoes of Schiller and Nietzsche) of form on the chaotic flux of experience and desire, seems sometimes presented as the highest form that life, as the will to power, can assume. But the practice of art is dangerous to the self, for much the reasons the critics of decadence had detected and exaggerated: it requires the imaginative exploration of and even identification with the emotionally chaotic and the instinctual, what Mann calls 'the abyss'. As a way of life the artistic vocation can be a pretext for a mere Bohemian loucheness and self-indulgence. Mann invites his readers to see in the self-dedication of the true artist an analogy with the sober, responsible ethics of the Protestant, North German, merchant stock from which he sprang. But the artistic vocation is dangerous because dedication and discipline are not enough; in excess, or alone, they mean aridity and self-repetition.

The artist must live between the rival dangers of chaos and sterility; this is the dilemma which informs both *Death in Venice* and *Dr Faustus*. Again we have to remember a century and a half of German speculation on the work of art as a synthesis of spirit and matter, form and passion, with Nietzsche's *Birth of Tragedy* as Mann's immediate precursor, and remember, too, its implications for the aesthetics of human personality, as a synthesis of poise and passion, serenity and experience. Apollo and Dionysus both required their due. In *Death in Venice* Mann dramatized this in terms of an oscillation rather than a synthesis, a surrender of will ending in the protagonist's death, stripped of dignity, facing the sea like a parodic Tristan achieving his own *Liebestod* (love-death). The artistic vocation has claimed its victim, but before he dies Mann allows him, spurred on by his passion, a last, brief creative renewal, in which he writes an essay which is, we are told, a perfect fusion of passion and intellect, 'a thought that thrilled with emotion, an emotion as precise and concentrated as thought'. There is arguably a kind of self-pity here, a concept, fostered by Bourget and others, of the artist's life as a kind of sacrifice to art of emotional balance and dignity. The concept of vocation, as Nietzsche saw, was always prone to run to self-immolation. The paradox to which Mann draws attention, however, is that the vocational ethic, through which will and identity are affirmed, may seem in the case of art to have the surrender or at least suspension of that identity as one of its requirements.

The artistic vocation also, of course, requires talent, though this is a requirement easily forgotten. Anyone, however, given the will to the deed, can sacrifice his life – or kill. The latter is, as Dostoevsky's Raskolnikov in *Crime and Punishment* convinced himself, the simplest form of 'action', the creation, once and for all and at a stroke, of an identity, as a murderer. A crime is like a vow or initiation, since through it one becomes what one has done, but without the need, unlike commitment to a vocation, for a continuing act of will to sustain it. In that sense it is a character paid for in one transaction, and only acts incurring guilt can buy it. Reputations can be earned for generosity or courage, but consciousness knows that it is only as good or as brave as its current state. One can say, as Raskolnikov does, that one accepts one's guilt; it would be meaningless as well as fatuous to say that one accepted one's generosity or courage.

The interest in crime or homicide as the paradigm case of free action, or the source of an identity, seems to have been a particularly, though not exclusively, Russian one. In violence convention was defied and, ideally, consciousness and action were merged. Russian literature in the nineteenth century explored these notions and their psychological inadequacy. One kind of case, which includes Raskolnikov, was what we might call the Napoleon in a bed-sitting room, the superman beyond ordinary standards of morality; Raskolnikov's prototype was Hermann in Pushkin's macabre story *The Queen of Spades* (1833), who even tried to look like Napoleon. Tolstoy's *War and Peace* begins with a discussion of Napoleon and crime. Crime could be thought of as the supreme assertion of will and so, projected onto the scale of world history, could Revolution; for Bakunin, at least, the two concepts were closely allied. It is perhaps unclear whether we should think of Revolution as a deed, the ultimate defiance of the world as it exists, or as a vocation, since a life could be dedicated to it, as Bakunin's was. Bakunin's most recent biographer, Aileen Kelly, sees in his idea of Revolution essentially a subjective quest for personal wholeness, for a reconciliation of reflective consciousness with the external world through will and action, with the ostensible object, a federalistic, communitarian Europe, as incidental. Bakunin wished, that is, simultaneously to submerge his personal identity in the world-historical process as Revolution, and also to impose himself on it and dominate it.

Bakunin had, since the 1840s, theoretically endorsed all acts of destruction as revolutionary. From 1869 he began to fall under the sway of the young terrorist and conspirator Sergei Nechaev (1847–82), with whom (the proportion is not clear) he composed the classic statement of revolutionary terror as a vocation, 'The Revolutionary Catechism', with its denial of the world and its theatrical renunciation, in the manner of religious vows, of individual personality: 'The revolutionary is a lost man; he has no interests of his own, no cause of his own, no feelings, no habits, no belongings: he does not even have a name . . . not just in words but in deed he has broken every tie with the civil order . . . and with the ethics of this world.'

Both Bakunin and Nechaev were in their ways confidence artists. Nechaev was an actual crook and murderer (of a fellow revolutionary student; Dostoevsky took the episode for the plot of *The Devils*). But the Russian terrorist cells were real, if politically ineffectual, and while they expressed themselves only in isolated acts of violence, the preparation for these, conspiracy, could be a way of life and a form of dedication. Between 1881 and 1911 their bag of victims included three ministers, a prime minister, a brace of generals, a grand duke and a tsar. There were also many abortive efforts. But terrorism and assassination were not confined to Russia. Around the turn of the century its victims included a King of Italy, an Empress of Austria, a Spanish Prime Minister and Presidents of France and the United States. It was common to speak of such acts as 'anarchist' and the assassins themselves sometimes claimed the label, though the connection with any political object was often tenuous; apologists coined the term 'the propaganda of the deed'. In France anarchism was chic; among subscribers to the anarchist journal *La Révolte* were the writers Alphonse Daudet, Anatole France, Stéphane Mallarmé, Oscar Wilde and the painter Camille Pissarro.

In the early 1890s in France there were random bombings in public places, in which a political point was indiscernible (though one exploded in the Chamber of Deputies). They could perhaps be thought of in the same light as Sorel's idea of the General Strike, in the sense that the outcome was irrelevant, the moral or anti-moral character of the act itself everything. The perpetrators were caught and, after execution, regarded in some intellectual circles as martyrs. They seem in each case to have acted entirely alone, from hatred of affluence or, perhaps more, out of deepest obscurity, to make a mark, to offer a violent, unequivocal demonstration of their existence. Dostoevsky's 'Underground Man' would have understood, and his creator in *The Devils* offered the profoundest understanding of the terrorist mentality in literature. These terrorist acts were a kind of *reductio ad absurdum* of the concepts of individual freedom and will, shrunk to an isolated, randomly directed, essentially inconsequential act of destruction. But not always inconsequential: a similar act, the product of conspiracy and nationalism rather than individual self-assertion, led directly to world war.

# CHAPTER 6

## *Immanence, Revelation and Transcendence*

### *6.1 Incarnation*

The idea of incarnation, of God-as-man, has been, understandably, ever since the early Christian Councils of the Church which defined it, a precarious equipoise. There is, that is to say, a perennial temptation to pull it in one direction or the other: towards, on the one hand, liberating the *logos* from the flesh, postulating a Christ who was pure spirit, or, on the other, emphasizing his humanity to the point where he becomes special only as an inspired teacher and his divine sonship merely a symbol of God's relation to all mankind. The two most famous, or notorious, presentations of the figure of Christ to the nineteenth century, David Friedrich Strauss's *Life of Jesus* (1835), whose after-effects were still being powerfully felt when our period opens, and Ernest Renan's *Life of Jesus* (1863), exemplify these opposing tendencies.

Strauss's work, which prised loose so much wavering orthodox faith in the middle years of the century, etherialized the figure of Christ to the point of making his existence as a man irrelevant. It was as a mythic personification, the imaginative projection of Jewish messianism in the first century AD, that Jesus could be released from the flesh, as it were, and treated in Hegelian fashion, as a moment in the development of Mind, a mythically embodied pure concept whose philosophical, ethical meaning, the self-revelation through the consciousness of humanity of the immanent World Spirit, those instructed could easily disentangle from its local and mythological guise. The critic, Strauss wrote, 'sees in history only the presentation of the idea of the oneness of man and God'. Christianity is, none the less, for Strauss at that point, 'the sublimest of all religions', the highest conception reached by the human consciousness in the mythological mode, which, properly understood, was 'identical with the deepest possible [Hegelian] truth'.

Strauss himself went on to lower things. As we saw in Chapter 1 (above, p. 48), in his last work, written just before his death, entitled *The Old Belief and the New* (1872), he emphatically cut the last strings even to a mythologized and Hegelianized form of Christianity, in which he claimed that no modern person really any longer believed; he embraced 'the Universe' as revealed by science, in which he purported to find an all-pervasive spirit of love. Strauss's later belief remained, of course, a common one on which we have already touched (p. 52 above). To those, however, whose capacity for devotion remained focused on the figure of Jesus, it did so less on the personified Hegelian Idea, though this could be incorporated, as on the historical figure of Jesus in his humanity and therefore as a real historical person. With a basic confidence in the gospel sources, apart from their witness to the miraculous, and some imagination, Jesus could be presented and emotionally responded to as though he were the hero of a novel, whose inner thoughts and feelings could be guessed at and sympathized with. Such an imaginatively reconstructed Jesus, human but knowable as an individual, could continue to provide inspiration and a focus for piety. Even a Christianity divested of the miraculous could remain unique in its significance for mankind, as in Strauss's *Life*, but with the emphasis transferred from the mythically expressed leap of consciousness in the Hebrew *Volk* to the unique spiritual genius of the real historical person whom it had represented and in some measure, by mythologizing it, distorted. It is the latter version that we find presented in Renan's *Life of Jesus*.

For Strauss it was an interpretative axiom that miracles do not occur; they are the product of mythically excited imagination. The reports of miracles are therefore manifestations not of events, now in any case irrecoverable, but of the minds through which reports of them have passed. This was an axiom for Renan too, but for Strauss the historicity of the life of Jesus was both irrecoverable and in any case irrelevant, since 'Christ' was essentially a collective mythic creation of the early Christians; for Renan the historical, which for him meant purely human, Jesus remained crucial, a focus, even in his humanity, for poetic moral and devotional sentiment and adoration. Renan accepts the gospel outlines of the life of Jesus, purged of the miraculous, and applies to it an imaginative – some said sentimental – sensibility to create an intimately knowable, profoundly loveable character. His Jesus is a young man of extraordinary charm, gentleness and grace; sometimes Renan's vocabulary for this is painfully winsome. He is also, however, the supreme religious genius of mankind, 'the highest summit of human greatness', preaching a religion of love, purity of heart and human brotherhood, an ecumenical humanism invested with poetry and sublimity. Renan seems to waver between regarding him as a visionary who conveys a kind of revelation and as a moral teacher whose maxims are not new in content but are made, by his example and presentation of them, unprecedentedly poignant and attractive.

Renan's Jesus, though purely human, is a figure for all ages, at once historically located and transcendent. The specific location is originally part of the charm; Renan had recently visited, and been much taken by, the Galilee district, which in his account becomes the setting for an idyll. Jesus' early ministry is a 'delightful pastoral', evoked with topographical minuteness and idealized local colour. But the location in time, the fanaticism and superstitions of the age (which to Strauss were the point), to which Jesus himself proved not wholly impervious, make the outcome of the story a tragedy. It becomes the story of a religious genius and teacher trapped in his role by the expectations of his followers as well as the malevolence of his enemies, the priestly establishment he challenges. The sweetly sublime teacher becomes the Messiah. The legendary features of his life were a kind of 'spontaneous conspiracy', in which Jesus himself was half-reluctantly, half-credulously, complicit: 'the adoration of his disciples overwhelmed him and carried him away'. His miracles were 'a violence done him by his age'. In Jerusalem the enchanting teacher of Galilee is enmeshed in the religious politics of the age, and is almost corrupted by them; his tone becomes harsher as well as gloomier. It is his heroic death which restores sublimity to the story and guarantees immortality to the teaching.

Renan, a former seminarian, had passed in the 1840s through the same crisis, at once intellectual, spiritual and vocational, as the Oxford 'spoiled priests', Clough and J. A. Froude, and with the same kind of outcome: the refusal to take full clerical orders and a subsequent lay career, accompanied by a certain sense of martyrdom for truth and an abiding religious wistfulness. Renan dedicated himself to monumental scholarship in the field of early Christianity and its Judaic roots, on which he became an acknowledged authority; the *Life of Jesus* was the first volume of a history of Christian origins. With the scholarship, and the rejection of miracle, there went a continuing disposition to exalt and poeticize the religious consciousness and its manifestations; Renan has been aptly called a romantic positivist. Though he appears not to have been deeply versed in Hegel, his underlying concept of religion in human history seems to have been that familiar one drawn from German Idealist metaphysics, from Schelling and Hegel, earlier in the century, which also informed Strauss's work: human consciousness gradually worked itself into a full awareness of universal moral and spiritual truth, though of course the Idealist way of putting it would be that the immanent idea worked its way to full self-consciousness through human history.

In Renan the content of religious truth, in what sounds like an echo of Saint-Simonianism, is emphatically humanistic, a message of human brotherhood. Requiring a personal focus for devotion he fastened it upon an historically knowable, human Jesus. But Jesus was pre-eminent rather than unique. The developing human consciousness was articulated through individuals at particular moments, which could be described as revelatory; of these Jesus was the supreme individual, the birth of Christianity the supreme moment. Jesus remained special as Christianity in Strauss's *Life of Jesus* remained special, but in both cases in degree not in kind. In that sense both views were immanentist rather than transcendental: God was in history, in mankind, and was progressively and successively revealed. This was the nearest Jesus and historic Christianity could be brought to uniqueness of status without resort to the miraculous.

For miracle remained, of course, in a sense the crux, above all the virgin birth and the Resurrection. It was not only the incompatibility of the miraculous with the faith increasingly placed in the invariable laws of nature that was involved here. More specific, in what we may call the Straussian tradition, was the claim to historical understanding of the real genesis of the miraculous. As Matthew Arnold put it, the human mind was turning away from miracles because 'it sees, as its experience widens, how they arise' (*Literature and Dogma*, 1873). The solvent here was not directly science but critical (often called 'scientific') historical and textual scholarship. Scholars who had become accustomed to disentangling and explaining the legendary elements in ancient classical texts such as Herodotus, Livy and Plutarch, in which the miraculous made frequent appearances without, of course, claiming the belief of Christians, could hardly refrain indefinitely from applying the same interpretative methods to the Christian scriptures.

An English novel which enjoyed a *succès de scandale* in the 1880s, being critically reviewed by Mr Gladstone among others, was *Robert Elsmere* (1888), by Arnold's niece Mary Ward (Mrs Humphry Ward). It effectively dramatized the predicament of a young clergyman, drawn initially to secular historical research with no thought but that of pleasant mental exercise. Looking into the early medieval history of France he finds himself drawn inevitably into consideration of the reliability of testimony and the ways of assessing it. He finds then, with horror, that he cannot read the gospels in the same trustful manner as before: 'his trained historical sense, the keen instrument he had sharpened so laboriously on indifferent material now ploughed its agonizing way, bit by bit, into the most intimate recesses of thought and faith'. He finds emerging from the gospels 'the image of a purely human Christ'.

Finding this incompatible with his role as a clergyman, though he recognizes that others did not, he resigns his living but continues to believe 'in God and a spiritual order', resisting contemporary forms of immanentism, it seems, and remaining a theistic transcendentalist. Renan, however, is a strongly felt and obliquely acknowledged presence in Ward's novel (as he surely is in Arnold's *Literature and Dogma*, with its definition of religion as 'morality touched by emotion'), and Elsmere sees his new task, which is to find a religion suitable to the age, as being 'to reconceive the Christ'. Seeking to combat 'this Atheism of the great democracies' and to recreate a 'company of the faithful', he preaches a religion of human brotherhood among the working men of South London; he founds a 'New Brotherhood', for whose implausibly rapid expansion the author vouches, as she does for the irresistible youthful charm which seems to make Elsmere a type of Renan's Jesus. Elsmere's brotherhood would in fact have taken its place among a number of humanist associations and cults in London in the period, including no less than two (more and less ritualistic) versions of the Comtist Religion of Humanity and the earnestly secular Ethical Society.

Elsmere's movement, however, is strikingly Jesus-centred. As in Renan's *Life*, Jesus as a focus of religious emotion has outlasted, for Elsmere, his miraculously attested divinity. The argument for this which he supplies to his working-class congregation is not negligible, but he seems a little blithely indifferent to the implications of its contingency. The appeal is to heritage – even, in another idiom one might say, to folk mythology. Jesus is 'our precious and invaluable possession as a people' and 'that symbol of the Divine which, of necessity, means most to us'. It was in a sense the historical contingency of that argument which Strauss exposed in changing his mind about the supreme symbolic importance of Christianity he had proclaimed in his *Life of Jesus*. In *The Old Faith and the New*, nearly forty years later, Christianity has lost the special status in human history earlier claimed for it. The passage of time, for Strauss, has eroded it. It is simply no longer believed in by the educated world. Sentiment and symbolism, apparently, are not likely to be so capable of an indefinite flourishing independently of literal belief in a unique divine sonship as they had seemed in Renan and for Elsmere.

There were many others, of course, for whom in any case the transcendental status of Christ and Christian dogma could not be reduced to these immanentist terms. One admittedly simplified but useful way in which the history of much theology in the later nineteenth century can be read is as a struggle to restrain the strong contemporary current of thought towards immanentism and progressive revelation from turning into a full-blooded pantheism (as it seems to do in Strauss's last thoughts) and to retain a sense of the uniqueness of the Christian incarnation, even after the claims of literal verbal inspiration and inerrancy in the Bible had been abandoned and scriptural authority over Cosmology and natural history surrendered to the scientists.

The latter surrender, which could be given the character of an emancipation of the Christian gospel from historical inessentials, was being vigorously signalled in England by the more 'advanced' Anglican clergy in the 1870s and 1880s. Arthur Stanley's (1815–81) funeral sermon in 1875 for the great geologist Sir Charles Lyell, whose name was indelibly associated with the notion of the empire of natural causality and with an age for the earth computed in many millions of years, hailed Lyell's (and Darwin's) views as 'a grander prelude to [man's] appearance on this globe, than that which makes him coeval with the beasts that perish'. Stanley spoke enthusiastically of 'the high reconciliation of religion and science' and confidently of the needlessness of 'theological panics' in the face of advancing scientific discovery. Frederick Temple (1821–1902), who had been one of the contributors to the scandalous *Essays and Reviews* (1860), two of whose clerical authors had been tried for heresy, and who later became Archbishop of Canterbury, used his Bampton lectures of 1884 to make peace with evolution, while naturally fastening on science's lacunae: the creation of life and the analysis of human consciousness and free will. It was visibly a relief to have done with rocks, plants and animals; a relief too, for Christians, that science could not as yet explain everything.

But the historicity of Jesus and the unique sense to be attached to his incarnation were intractable. It seemed to some that faith in these could be more securely grounded by moving from debated textual niceties to a personal and moral inner response to the figure of Jesus and by accepting more wholeheartedly the implications of the concept of an incarnation at a particular historical moment. The former postulated a reciprocated love, the latter an acceptance that what might be termed Jesus' 'secular knowledge' would be that of his age; he need not be required to be infallible in such matters but allowed to share the beliefs of his time as he shared its everyday life. Both tendencies can be seen in pictorial representations of Jesus popular in the nineteenth century, which, like those of the eighteenth century, eschewed vivid depiction of his physical sufferings. Jesus as the loving saviour (one could if one preferred read 'helper') of mankind is epitomized in perhaps the most acclaimed icon of the mid-century, the statue by the Danish sculptor Bertel Thorwaldsen, completed in 1827, a picture of which George Eliot kept over her desk to provide inspiration and consolation while she was translating Feuerbach's humanist *Essence of Christianity*. Thorwaldsen's figure was idealized in the classical manner, which remained common. Another idiom of idealization, that of the German Nazarene school, emphasized a youthful, soft, lyrical gentleness which seems entirely consonant with Renan's later, verbal portrait, as both are with Walter Pater's adjectives for the Christ-figure worshipped by the early Christian community he places in *Marius the Epicurean*. Their Christ is very Renanian: 'serene, blithe and debonair', not the crucified but a hellenistic Good Shepherd from pastoral. Pater, wishing to imply some future new revelation for the nineteenth century still to come, hints at the serial character of such revelations: the figure of Christ 'seemed to have absorbed, like some rich texture in his garment, all that was deep-felt and impassioned in the experiences of the past'. The Christ-figure might be the Good Shepherd, but he was also, it seems, Pater's own version of the Mona Lisa (see above p. 176).

In a pictorial context heavily biased towards sentimentalization as well as idealization, the somewhat brutal realism and deliberately mundane circumstances of Millais's *Christ in the House of his Parents* (1850) naturally evoked fierce denunciation; the figures are indeed somewhat gratuitously uncomely. The same kind of realism is found in Holman Hunt's *Jesus Washing Peter's Feet* (1852) and *The Shadow of Death* (1873). It was all consistent with the more earthy kind of humanism and Christian Socialism of the period. The Christian Socialist Thomas Hughes wrote a book called *The Manliness of Christ* (1879). Other examples were those by the German painters Eduard von Gebhardt (*The Last Supper*, 1870) and Karl von Uhde (*Christ in a Peasant Family*, 1885). Another form of 'localization' was an orientalizing of the Christian story to which Renan's *Life* contributed, though Holman Hunt's *The Finding of the Saviour in the Temple* (1856) was an earlier example. Like Renan, Hunt regarded travel in Palestine as essential.

Social concern was to be another significant theme in Protestant Christianity in both England and Germany in the second half of the century. In England a contrast has often been drawn between *Lux Mundi*, the collection of essays which constituted a kind of manifesto of liberal Anglicanism published in 1887, and *Essays and Reviews* nearly thirty years earlier. *Lux Mundi* shocked some, but there was no attempt at persecution. More significantly, where *Essays and Reviews* was largely defensive, concerned to save essential Christianity from the damaging attacks of the secular intellect by jettisoning Biblical literalism, the later essays were more affirmative, both of personal faith and of an outward-looking social concern. One of the chief influences, both theological and social, on the *Lux Mundi* group was F. D. Maurice (1805–72), who had earlier helped to inspire the Christian Socialists of the 1850s and to found the London Working Men's College. Another was the combination of Idealist philosophy and civic responsibility sponsored by T. H. Green which we considered in Chapter 3. Though he died in 1882, Green remained the dominant intellectual influence in Oxford, the milieu from which the essays largely derived. Green, though a vigorous philosophical immanentist, for whom Christianity was 'the expression of a common spirit, which is gathering all things in one', was recognized by Christians as a naturally pious soul as well as a philosophical defender of the spiritual against materialism and positivism. In fiction as 'Mr Grey' he was a model and inspiration for Elsmere.

The focus of *Lux Mundi*, as its subtitle indicated, was on the spiritual and ethical meaning of the Incarnation; it has, in modern times, been contrasted with the more punitive character of the Evangelically oriented Christianity of the first half of the century in Britain, with its emphasis on sin, judgement and atonement, coupled sometimes with an inflexible view of human worldly suffering. In *Lux Mundi* faith was represented less in dogmatic terms than as an active response of the whole self to 'the living Christ', while the conception of Christ's 'kingdom', following Maurice, gave liberal Anglicanism a humanistic orientation towards social concern and action. Christianity postulates a transcendent divinity, but the essayists' bent was towards diminishing, under the sign of the Incarnation, the distance between the human and the divine, through the immanent presence of Christ in each human being.

Christian social action was a natural corollary; though not unprecedented, it became a general and growing feature of the period, in England as in Germany, from the 1880s onwards, as the godless populations of the great cities thrust themselves on attention as 'the social problem'. One manifestation, bringing together liberals and High Churchmen, was the Guild of St Matthew (1877), another the more broadly based Christian

Social Union (1889). Such movements had parallels in other countries, notably in France the Society for Social Economy (1856) inspired by the Catholic Frédéric Le Play, and the German Evangelical Social Congress later in the century.

In Germany the most influential theologian and scholar to shape ideas of faith and of the historical Jesus in the second half of the century was Albert Ritschl (1822–90). His influence in some respects has analogies to the strand in English theology represented by Maurice. Ritschl's starting-point was, understandably, repudiation of the Straussian conception of a mythological Christ as the vehicle of a profound philosophical idea. For Ritschl, theology must be decisively divorced from metaphysics. To philosophize away the historical Jesus and the uniqueness of the Christian revelation was abhorrent to him. In so far as he was indebted to philosophy it was to Kant, for his stress on free will and moral action rather than speculative reason as the access to spiritual reality. Christian faith was a response of the whole person to the historical person of Jesus, a response which incorporated an inescapable moral claim; faith in Christ was a kind of value judgement. Ethics was central for Ritschl but it was not a purely humanistic ethic; it was dependent on the self-revelation of Christ, whose mission was to found the kingdom of God, as a moral community united in Christ and in love. Christianity is essentially practical, the faith of a religious community, the Church. One of Ritschl's pupils was to be Ernst Troeltsch, whose reputation rests on his monumental study *The Social Teaching of the Christian Churches* (1912).

Ritschl's theology, compared with that of Strauss, re-established the historical Jesus, while his emphasis on faith as a personal revelation, a total response to a felt moral presence, shifted the emphasis from the contentious ground of dogma and miracle. The historical knowability of Jesus remained, of course, central. Strauss, in 1872, consistently with his earlier writings, proclaimed him unknowable. More disconcerting was a newer voice and another line of argument. For the Christ of faith needed to be not only historically knowable but, when known, the kind of historical figure on whom the (essentially humanist) religious sensibility of the nineteenth century could plausibly project its own religious ideal. Here, in the historical sense of the critic, which Renan had extolled and proclaimed essential, identifying it with a cultivated sense of the strangeness of the past, lay a new danger: not to the historical Jesus but to the Christ of nineteenth-century faith. Elsmere, exploring early medieval sources, had experienced a vertiginous sense of the gulf between his own age and theirs. Yet in trying

to cling to the historical Jesus it had seemed to him, and his creator Mary
Ward, and to Renan too, sufficient merely to excise the miraculous to liberate Jesus in all his unparalleled moral splendour for the continuing use of
the present. But what if the historical Jesus partook of that strangeness?
This was the disturbing thought of Albert Schweitzer (1875–1965) in his
*Quest of the Historical Jesus* (1906). If accepted, it undermined the whole
Ritschlian tradition. The more fully known the historical Jesus became, the
more firmly historically located he became in the messianic, eschatological
context of the first century. In doing so he became more alien, more difficult, or even impossible, to identify with the Christ of modern faith. The
nineteenth-century desire to know, in all the immediacy and specificity of
time and place, had become self-defeating; the desire to know, and the
desire to relate to, were in conflict. Schweitzer wrote that Jesus, when historically recovered, 'passes by our time and returns to his own'. Defenders
of the historical Jesus against Straussian mythologizing were presented
with a Jesus more historical than they had anticipated or wanted.

Ritschl's own guns, as it were, had been turned in the opposite direction,
against the tendency of Idealist metaphysics which it shared with the
more Romantic kind of materialism (see above p. 52), to postulate an
immanent tendency in nature to the development of consciousness and the
awareness of universal truth, whose successive stages could be thought of
as occurring in human history in a series of quasi-epiphanies or revelations,
as crucial moments of advance for the human spirit. For Ritschl, following
Kant, the latter was crucially distinct and different in kind from nature. This
is, of course, a traditional conflict, between, on the one hand, transcendentalism and the assumption of a war between spirit and matter, and on the
other a belief in the immanence of spirit in matter, in which if there was a
struggle it was a dialectical one, characteristically culminating in a complete
fusion, a material world totally comprehended by mind.

It is not a necessary consequence of transcendentalism that there should
be only one, unique, revelation of God to man. Once the paradox inherent
in any idea of divine incarnation has been overcome, there is no reason why
a deity should not have more than one avatar. It can, however, reasonably be
regarded as a definition of Christian faith that it takes the incarnation of
Christ to be the one unique and indispensable bridge between a transcendent divinity and fallen man. An immanentist belief, however, tends to see
such moments as serial and cumulative. But there were possible modulations between these apparently irreconcilable views, more and less distant
from the Christian tradition. Within nineteenth-century liberal Christianity,

for example, to postulate a gradual progress in moral and spiritual knowledge lifted the heavy burden placed on the unsuspecting authors of the
Old Testament by nineteenth-century expectations of what could be
regarded as exemplary. We have already seen, too, the intellectual and moral
authority enjoyed by the immanentist Green among the liberal Christian
essayists of *Lux Mundi*.

Conversely, a range of possible modulations of attitude towards traditional Christian faith can be found among those who had broken with it
to embrace a fashionable immanentist metaphysics, ranging from hostility
(treating Christianity as historical lumber to be cleared away), to a strong
residual piety. As we have seen, the latter could go so far as to regard the
Christian revelation as one among many but still in a sense unique, as the
latest, highest, unsurpassable manifestation of universal spiritual and
moral truth. But this, as we have also now seen, if a seductive option, as the
nearest one could get to a reconciliation of modern thought and Christian
tradition, was also precarious. A heritage of pious sentiment, unsupported
by dogma, might wither with the passage of time. Scholarship might
reveal a Jesus too alien to fulfil modernity's requirements. The notion of an
unsurpassable revelation 2,000 years ago, unless underpinned by Christian
dogma, jarred badly with ideas of progress. On the whole it was easier, and
in a sense more optimistic, to regard the series of revelations, in which that
of Jesus could be accorded an honoured place, as incomplete. Even Renan
at one point drew a parallel between the Christian revelation and the fashionable notion of national mission; each people had, supposedly, its unique,
its distinctive message, its cultural gift to mankind, as the Greeks had
contributed philosophy and democracy and the Romans law. To apply
this thought to Christianity was to make it – as Hegel had in fact done –
indispensable and one of a noble company, but not incomparable, either
before it or since.

Sometimes this thought, the concept of serial or cumulative revelation,
including Christianity, was turned to for comfort and hope. We have just
seen this in the case of Walter Pater. If Christianity could incorporate the
best of Hellenism, Pater broadly hints, might not some subsequent analogous synthesis occur between Christian tradition and modernity: a new
Renaissance (he often uses the word), a new living faith? Thomas Carlyle,
much earlier, had proclaimed the need for, and even seemed to prophesy
the imminence of, some new *Mythos*, as he put it, for the modern world,
since the whole of previous history exhibited a series of such. The World-
Spirit was a phoenix, destroying itself to be reborn. This was Carlyle at

his most Germanic and Idealist; he was apt to oscillate between a German Idealist language for the immanence of spirit in matter and history and a Scottish Calvinist transcendentalism invoking an imperious and implacable deity.

It is with the former that we are now concerned. Some new embodiment of spirit, it was often felt, some credible, liveable faith, was surely overdue in the selfish, faithless, materialistic nineteenth century. Historicist immanence, the notion of serial embodiments of spirit, serial revelations, though literally incompatible with a Biblical conception of apocalypse and a 'second coming' of the transcendent, nevertheless fostered a mood of tremulous or exuberant, quasi-apocalyptic expectation. Before 1848, as we saw earlier (above, pp. 12–13), the anticipated epiphany was sometimes located in 'the people', and identified with Revolution or, for Carlyle, 'Democracy'. Afterwards it tended to assume less directly political, more spiritual or cultural forms. Such expectations, as we have seen in Renan, Pater and Elsmere, could be tuned in the key of a traditional Christian sensibility. Very often they were not and Christianity could appear as an obstacle, or even the enemy of a world needing to lay a pale Jesus to rest and hail its Siegfried.

## 6.2 Myth and Revelation

One of the most striking invocations of imminent spiritual renewal, which its author subsequently repudiated, was the conclusion of Nietzsche's *The Birth of Tragedy*, conceived under the influence of Schopenhauer and Wagner and the stirring events of 1870: the Franco-Prussian war and the advent of a new, unified Germany. Earlier we considered Nietzsche's essay as an exercise in aesthetics, whose remoter sponsors are the aestheticians of the later eighteenth century, and particularly Lessing and Schiller. The conception of the Dionysiac, and of music as giving direct access, unmediated by any representation, to the striving cosmic will animating all life, is even more obviously derived from Schopenhauer, and is set by Nietzsche against the, to him superficial, notion of Greek serenity and cheerfulness. The latter emerged, epitomized in Socrates, when the deep, tragic sense of life was being lost. Early Christianity, rather remarkably, is at that point complimented by Nietzsche for despising such cheerfulness, though it entirely missed the sublimity of the earlier Greek conception embodied in Attic tragedy.

Nietzsche's essay is, among other things, one of the nineteenth century's, speculative accounts of secularization in human history; in that context it may be compared, for all the manifest differences, with Maine's *Ancient Law*, Fustel de Coulanges' *The Ancient City* and Durkheim's *The Division of Labour in Society*. Instead of being triumphalist, however, or even merely soberly appraising, in tracing the rise of a rationalist individualism, it is a story of decline and fall. Naturally the latter prompted ideas of possible redemption, which Nietzsche here propounds under the influence of the most immediate and obvious of his mentors, Wagner, through the latter's redemptive conception of the spiritual and social role of reborn ancient tragedy in the form of Wagnerian music-drama, the 'total artwork'. Through collective participation in it, the German people, and ultimately European culture, could be regenerated and something like a unifying, inspiring *Mythos* re-created. In the sublimity of Wagnerian music-drama, drawing on the ancient myths and legends of the *Volk*, and expressing, supremely, the profoundest intuition of the terror and exhilaration of existence, experienced through music, the malaise of modern culture could be transcended, though Wagner's and Nietzsche's accounts of the latter differed: for the former it was primarily materialism, social fragmentation and bondage to capitalism, for the latter superficial 'Socratic' rationalism, facile optimism and trivial hedonism.

Nietzsche at this point, however, concurred with Wagner in promoting an atavistic, even xenophobic version of the reborn Germanic spirit as the agent of renewal, struggling against the contamination of alien, and specifically Latin or French, triviality; it was this Germanic self-exaltation which the mature Nietzsche would come to see as vulgar, without at all abandoning the messianic impulse. He sought to discipline and refine the latter into a call for individual self-overcoming, repudiating his discipleship to Wagner and becoming his own Messiah, most overtly in *Thus Spake Zarathustra* (1883–5). But though Nietzsche came to reject a vulgar, nationalistic Teutonism, his denunciation of 'Alexandrian' cultural eclecticism in *The Birth of Tragedy* continued to inform his sense of what constituted modern decadence, the decadence of a culture

> Condemned to exhaust all possibilities and feed miserably on every culture under the sun . . . What does our great historical hunger signify, our clutching about us for countless other cultures, our consuming desire for knowledge if not the loss of myth, of a mythic home, the mythic womb?[1]

---

[1] Friedrich Nietzsche, *The Birth of Tragedy*, trans. R. Golffing (New York, 1956), p. 137.

Nietzsche would later reject the seduction of the womb and denounce Wagner himself as a symptom of decadence, seeing modern man as doomed to create his own myths and to live and act in an ironic tension with them, but in the reference to 'historical hunger' the diagnosis offered in *The Advantage and Disadvantage of History*, which we considered earlier (pp. 186–7), is already prefigured.

But enthusiasm for the content of Teutonic folklore and myth was, in the young Nietzsche, clearly second-hand Wagnerianism, and it was to be transitory. Though there were to remain elements from the Feuerbachian, emancipatory image of Wagner's Siegfried in Nietzsche's more mature thought, it was in part transcended and certainly made far more complex; his own intimate identification was with the mythic Dionysus and the prophet Zarathustra, as well as with his decadent anti-selves, as it were, Socrates and Christ. In Wagner, however, the German inheritance was an inextricable part of his inner self and it was bound up with his messianic vision. The latter kept at least partly alive in him the apocalyptic mood of the 1840s, though it became markedly less political and more purely 'spiritual', and he continued, of course, to draw on Germanic legend and mythology, popularized by the German Romantics earlier in the century.

It was the nationalist strain in his own form of Romanticism which drew him first to the medieval German poem, the *Nibelungenlied*. He had already drawn on German legend for his earlier operas, *Tannhäuser* and *Lohengrin*. He was heir to the enthusiasm of the German romantics for Teutonic mythology and folklore, embodied above all in the *German Mythology* of Jakob Grimm, which Wagner knew well. The Romantic theory of myth which Wagner inherited was that it was both the immediate, poetic, apprehension of truth in a form inaccessible to analytic reason, and that it was the collective creation of the people, the *Volk*. The revitalization of myth through art, above all the fusion of all the arts in musicdrama, would be a spiritual redemption of the modern world, sunk in money-worship and the frivolity of a view of opera which saw it merely as relaxation.

The idea of drama, and of a national theatre, has possessed a special place in German culture ever since the work and aspirations of Goethe and Schiller in Weimar in the late eighteenth century. In that context the claims which Wagner made for his music-drama as a kind of redemptive national ritual, an idea later at least partially embodied in his opera house at Bayreuth, become more understandable. The analogy of the place of drama in the life of the ancient Greek city state was an inspiration for Germans. The Greek drama, being the dramatic enactment with music and dance, of a shared myth, had supposedly the character of a collective religious performance, binding the citizens together as participants in a ritual rather than merely as spectators at a theatre. The notion of its revival, and the importance attached to it, could perhaps only have taken root in modern times in a country like Germany, lacking any political centre or focus for national life, whose allegiance was therefore given to and expressed through cultural symbols rather than national political institutions. The neo-Hellenic German notion of the functions of drama, which finds in Wagnerian music-drama its most ambitious embodiment, was in a sense an alternative to the failed Frankfurt Parliament set up in 1848 to produce a constitution for a federated Germany, though for Wagner music-drama reached levels of the national soul quite inaccessible to the mere conduct of political debate. This exalted, almost apocalyptic, sense of mission was to be a source of an ominous cultural anxiety in Germany after unification in 1871, when, inevitably, the actual political institutions of a unified modern industrial state, however great a source of national pride, could not satisfy the spiritual hunger for transcendence and regeneration.

These were distinctively German elements in Wagner's great project, which, deeply rooted in German cultural experience and tradition, set him somewhat apart from his contemporaries in the cosmopolitan decades of the 1840s and 1850s. The same was not true, however, of the distinctive, modern, revolutionary, anti-capitalist content which his revitalized German myth was initially at least to bear, in conscious rivalry with Christianity as well as in conscious opposition to the contemporary world of money, social hierarchy and established authority.

The later Wagner, for the mature Nietzsche, had sold out, becoming the complacent pet of the anti-Semitic German nationalists, an official 'great man'. In his last opera, *Parsifal*, he even seemed to have become reconciled to Christianity, in its form most hostile to life, in its cult of celibacy as the emblem of purity of heart. This was not wholly accurate; *Parsifal* is a complex work to which we shall have briefly to return later. Certainly Wagner was violently anti-Semitic, as he had been since the 1840s, and he enjoyed his success and filled complacently the role of great man of Germany. On the other hand, like others of a Romantic, volkish turn of mind, he was not really at ease with the materialistic new Reich, just as the would-be redeemer was perhaps not entirely placated by the role of cultural icon. The opera house he built at Bayreuth, with its annual festivals, was, after all, only a symbolic fulfilment of the earlier apocalyptic, democratic dream of the historic and revolutionary social role of music-drama. The same fate in a sense overtook it as it did William Morris's vision of cultural regeneration through rediscovery of joy in work; there are similarities between aspects of Wagner's thought and the English Arts and Crafts movement, expressed most notably in *The Mastersingers*. Morris and Company produced high-cost works of craftsmanship for well-off aesthetes, just as Bayreuth, for all its piously uncomfortable seating (another analogy with Morris) and devotional atmosphere, was necessarily an experience for an élite.

For the later Wagner the new Germany remained obstinately unregenerated, and privately his discontent with it seems to have been almost as great as Nietzsche's. In his last years one of his closest intellectual friendships was with Arthur de Gobineau, whose pessimistic conception of racial mingling as the explanation of contemporary, and inevitable, cultural degeneration we considered earlier (above, Chapter 2), though Gobineau's famous 1855 essay, recently translated into German, did not stress the anti-Semitic note. The Wagner circle, towards the end of the century, became an important though far from unique source not only of anti-Semitism but of volkish, racist messianism and mysticism. In it was perpetuated the tension we considered above in Chapter 3 between volkish ideas of community, anti-materialism and spiritual regeneration, and the more complacent, Hegelian tradition of statist nationalism now embodied in historians like Heinrich von Treitschke and in the figure of Bismarck. To speak in this way is to make schematic what was often more entangled, but, to appreciate the nationalist version of the messianic impulse, which persisted after unification, it is important not to draw too complacent a picture of nationalism in the new Reich, or to ignore the elements of unappeased social nostalgia and cultural atavism, the continued yearning for some, often vaguely conceived, deliverance from spiritual emptiness and the stresses or banality of modernity. Anti-Semitism was one symptom of this, but so, in some cases, was a sense of almost apocalyptic expectation, fearful or impatient and potentially paranoid. It was sometimes not clear whether the recreation of a pure, united *Volk*, the guardian or embodiment of German traditions and culture, would be a precondition or a consequence of the looked-for regeneration.

Wagner expressed the idea in almost acceptable form and with incomparable panache in *Mastersingers*. More persistent in him, however, is the theme of redemption, which informs his whole *oeuvre*, from his first great opera *The Flying Dutchman* (1843) to the last, *Parsifal*. As we saw in the Prologue, it is customary and surely justified to see a tension, and a progression, in Wagner between a conception of redemption which is optimistic, Feuerbachian and revolutionary, epitomized in Siegfried, the free, fearless hero, a stranger to self-consciousness and guilt, and a 'spiritual' conception of redemption through renunciation, articulated for Wagner by Schopenhauer and associated, from the mid-1850s, with an interest in Buddhism, and identified, in the *Ring* cycle, with Wotan and Brünnhilde, and perhaps still more in *Tristan and Isolde*. The theme of the redemptive function of art, and the idea of a Wagnerian mission to make the German people worthy of itself and able to discharge its cultural mission to the world, became key ideas of the Wagner circle at the end of the century. The notion of a new *Mythos*, adumbrated in Wagnerian music-drama and presaging a kind of successor to Christianity, was another. It could be thought of, depending on the degree of attachment to Christian traditions or to a full-blooded Teutonic atavism, either as a Germanic form of Christianity purged of its Jewish, or Pauline, elements, or as a revival of Teutonic paganism, the Norse pantheon and sun-worship. What was common was the assumption that revelation and redemption were not unique, once-and-for-all, as in Christian orthodoxy, but successive, and that a new one was at hand.

If the Wagner circle was one source of such ideas in Wilhelmine Germany it was by no means the only one. It would be beyond the scope of this book to try to trace in detail, as scholars like Fritz Stern and George Mosse have done, the development of volkish, religious, mystical ideas from the traditionalism and social nostalgia of the 1850s (see above, Chapter 3) to their more radical, apocalyptic, often violently anti-Semitic development, complicated in some cases by contact with Social Darwinist and eugenist ideas, around the turn of the century. We have to be selective. Apart from Wagner himself the publicist who perhaps best illustrates the long span of volkish-redemptive sentiment from the Romanticism of the first half of the century to nearly its end is the oriental and Biblical scholar – in some respects a German counterpart to Renan – and radical nationalist, Paul de Lagarde, whom we have already considered briefly as a critic of the new Reich (above, pp. 136–7).

Lagarde's influence reached its height immediately after his death, in the decades before the Great War. Partly through his disciple Julius Langbehn (1851–1907), he was a particular influence on the back-to-nature rambling and comradeship of the German Youth Movement of the early twentieth century. Lagarde, initially a child of the Romantic nationalism of the period before 1848, began a vigorous career as a journalist as well as scholar in the 1850s. In his eventual role of outspoken critic of the statist rationalism and the spiritual apathy and aridity of the Bismarckian Reich, he combined many of the themes we have been considering: the traditionalist hatred of large-scale industry and suspicion of the state; nostalgic agrarianism, endorsement of hierarchy and enthusiasm for handicrafts. But he was also an expansionist nationalist, advocate of a new German colonization of the Slav lands of the south and east in a huge, German *Mitteleuropa*, which he proclaimed as an aspect of the German mission. He was not a biological racist, but an anti-Semite of a kind not uncommon in France also, for whom the Jews represented capitalism and cosmopolitan modernity, and he believed in a Jewish conspiracy directed towards world domination.

In the present context, however, what makes Lagarde interesting is not so much these familiar features as the overtness of the religious foundation of his nationalism. He represents an extreme case of a theological immanentism. God was present in, and revealed himself through, each *Volksgeist*, and his manifestations were successive. One, but only one, had been through the early Hebrews, whom Lagarde admired as a *Volk* united by a religious consciousness. The idea of national missions, and of the fulfilment of each as a kind of epiphany, which Strauss had interpreted philosophically and Renan, as we have seen, touched on in his own *Life of Jesus*, was made by Lagarde the central feature and in a sense the justification of his nationalism. It is, incidentally, not surprising to find that he was a friend of Renan and equally unsurprising that he conducted a feud with Ritschl. For Lagarde the Christian gospel was the latest, and so far the fullest, self-revelation of God in history, but it was to be surpassed in its Germanic successor.

The concept of national mission, here given a specifically religious character, was propounded by Lagarde, as so often, in a mood not of complacency but of impatience and irritable self-criticism. The German nation was failing, through egoism, rationalism and materialism, to fulfil its true nature and mission; the epiphany was being retarded and the Germans must be recalled to their high destiny. *Mitteleuropa* was an aspect of this, but the spiritual dimension was the most important. As so often, again – as also in Wagner – the content remained misty; the *Volk* must create its *Mythos*, but Lagarde's guidelines clearly contained elements both of Christianity and of ancient Teutonic myth and ritual.

Further still from an atavistic Wotanism and still gesturing to Christian roots was the thought of perhaps the most influential spokesman for such ideas in the next generation, Wagner's English son-in-law Houston Stewart

Chamberlain (1855–1927). Lagarde, as a rival prophet, had held aloof from Wagner: among other disqualifications from close association, he hated Wagner's music. Chamberlain, however, who became the most influential voice of the Wagner circle after the latter's death, approved of Lagarde, and his ideas seem to bear the impress of Lagarde as much as, or perhaps more than, that of Wagner himself. Chamberlain's chief work, *Foundations of the Nineteenth Century* (1899), gives no role to music-drama. What is stressed is the prospect of a new era dominated by Aryan spirituality, of which the Germanic branch of the race is now the only possible bearer, and of which Christianity was perhaps an adumbration; Jesus, according to Chamberlain, was not a Jew. On the other hand Lagarde's traditionalism, his agrarian and hierarchical predilections, make no figure in Chamberlain's book, which is concerned above all with race, and in that respect is the most obvious successor to Gobineau's, as an account of world history in which race, racial purity and racial mixture, are the key explanatory elements.

But Chamberlain, unlike Gobineau, is not a fatalistic pessimist. Fulfilment of the Germanic peoples' spiritual mission depends on the preservation of their racial purity, which is their most immediate responsibility. The Jews, who are presented as formidable, not contemptible, are the great historical antitype of the Aryan, the only other pure race (though they are also spoken of as the product of racial mixture; consistency was not Chamberlain's strong point). The Latins, on the other hand, are merely hopelessly mongrelized Aryans, the product of the 'chaos' of racial intermixture in the Roman empire, and are hence in thrall to the international power of the Catholic Church, which, with the multinational Austrian empire, is the successor to Rome, the embodiment of the 'anti-national' principle. To some extent Chamberlain still seems to be reflecting the antagonisms of an earlier period, when Prussia and Austria vied for the leadership of the new Germany, as well as Bismarck's conflict with the Catholic Church over education, the *Kulturkampf*. Chamberlain's sympathies are markedly North German and Lutheran. He shared with Lagarde a sympathy with the Germans of the Austrian empire in their struggle with the Slav populations of the empire, which focused on the role of German as the official language.

The Habsburg empire was also, of course, a *bête noire* of contemporary English liberals, among whom it was a commonplace that only in a relatively homogeneous population was self-government possible. Nationalism had been a liberal creed of the first half of the century, and to those who identify racism automatically with the political right it may be disconcerting to see how far nineteenth-century racial ideas sometimes represent a transposition into racial terms of typical liberal themes; Gobineau's and Chamberlain's fear of racial mixture and homogenization echoes the characteristic liberal fear, as in Mill's *On Liberty*, of the disappearance of individuality in what we have learnt to call mass society. Gobineau, originally a royalist, was no liberal, but Chamberlain in another political incarnation, as it were, seems to have been an English liberal, a supporter of Gladstone. In his characterizations of the Aryan and Germanic virtues, as well as the opposite vices of Latins, there are often liberal as well as Kantian echoes; Kant along with Goethe and Shakespeare, was one of Chamberlain's heroes. Aryans were not only spiritual, in contrast to Jewish materialism, they were also spontaneous, free, self-determining individuals, in contrast to Hebrew legalism, the rigidities of Catholic theology and the despotism of Catholic church discipline. One important antitype for Chamberlain was Ignatius Loyola (incidentally a Basque and hence not an Aryan). The Germans – Chamberlain, like English Whigs, draws on Tacitus – exhibited a nice blend of individualism and loyalty, with, at their best, a capacity for submission to a self-imposed law of conduct, which sounds like, and probably is, a combination of the Whig cliché about the English reconciliation of liberty and order with the Kantian conception of moral freedom as voluntary submission to the rational moral law.

Chamberlain's racism, though all-pervasive, was not strongly biological in its characterizations. That, for him, would have been materialistic. He often treats race as self-evident or a matter of spiritual affinity or self-recognition, rather than resorting much to the contemporary ethnologist's tool-kit of cephalic indices and the like (see above, Chapter 2). He agrees, however, that one of its expressions is in physiognomy, and there are amusing 'demonstrations' that, from facial characteristics, we can identify such a well-known German as Luther as being undoubtedly German. The face is the outward expression of the soul. As often in racialist ideas, one is reminded of earlier, pre-modern ways of thinking. Chamberlain's references to 'noble' and 'debased' characteristics seem best interpreted, not as a nineteenth-century biological determinism, in the manner of the Social Darwinists, but as a version of the pre-scientific notion of 'correspondences' between moral qualities and physical ones; the face is an emblem of the soul as a lion is an emblem of courage. This may seem contradicted by the emphasis Chamberlain gives to breeding, but it is not. Nobility, after all, was traditionally a matter of genealogy as well as moral qualities, and a noble line could be contaminated by an infusion of base 'blood'; nineteenth-century racial ideas owe a good deal to the supposedly scientific or scholarly recasting of such ideas.

Breeding, or rather the absence of interbreeding, was crucial for Chamberlain, because the Germans (a category which stretched well beyond the German political nation), as the only more or less pure Aryan racial stock, are the last hope of an otherwise mongrelized and therefore cultureless mankind – the latter an echo of Gobineau. The maintenance of racial purity is therefore the necessary condition for the fulfilment of the renewal of Aryan spirituality, the Germans' cultural mission to humanity. Across its path stand the Jews, not only as the spiritual antitype of the Aryan but as the authors of a racial conspiracy to adulterate German blood. Chamberlain seems to take quite literally the idea that Jews consciously intend, by the procreation of hybrids by Jewish men with German women, while retaining strict endogamy for Jewish women, to become the only pure race and thereby to dominate the world. Their central characteristic is an implacable will. It becomes the duty of Germans to keep their blood pure. The stakes are enormously high. The Germans – this was a common thought – rescued the world once, in delivering it from the Roman autocracy and its attendant corruptions: 'but for the Teuton everlasting night might have settled on the world'. But the crisis, not only because of the threat of miscegenation but because of the possible inadequacy of the Germans to their new world-historical task, is in the present: 'it is because of the lack of a true religion that our whole Teutonic culture is sick unto death'. The fulfilled mission would bring a world of almost unimaginable splendour, a culture outdoing the glories of ancient Athens.

But what *exactly* was the mission, and what would be the content of the revelation? What, after all, could the average German, aware of his cosmic responsibilities but not himself a Goethe or a Kant, do to be worthy of his racial heritage and of his world-historical task? The only clear answer seemed to be to refuse to allow his daughter to consort with Jewish young men. Chamberlain's vagueness is understandable. It is no light matter, arguably overtaxing the resources of even the later Nietzsche, to delineate a new post-Christian spirituality that goes beyond a bland humanism with pious overtones, like Elsmere's. But such vagueness seems the perfect recipe for inducing an historical and cultural anxiety scarcely to be alleviated by honest Teutonic endeavour. The Germans' cultural responsibilities were screwed to their highest pitch, but how they were to be discharged remained enigmatic. It is perhaps not altogether surprising, as well as lamentable, that Jew-baiting, which Chamberlain did not directly encourage, may have seemed the easiest way of doing one's bit for the regeneration of European culture. The new *Mythos*, the spirit's new vesture, remained elusive. It is one thing to believe in the possibility of serial revelations, of successive epiphanies; another to make one happen to order. But if the race or *Volk* was inadequate to its role, it might be that it was impeded not only by its own inclination, instead, to a materialistic egoism, but by some hostile, alien power, which it was easiest to identify with the Jews.

The search for a new myth, or the refurbishment of old ones – Wotan or Dionysus – found its counterpart in more individual attempts at transcendence of the material and of everyday existence, and sometimes overlapped with them. These found expression in the formation of brotherhoods or fellowships – not only, of course, in Germany – for the shared promotion of various panaceas: vegetarianism; teetotalism; sexual liberation and equality; mystical contemplation; Dionysiac, eurythmic, barefoot-dancing; and so on; which the Germans spoke of, comprehensively, as *Lebensreform*, the reformation of life. These, as we saw earlier (Chapter 3), overlapped with pressure groups dedicated to shaping the course of evolution rather than passively enduring it, through 'scientific' interference in the form of Eugenics or racial hygiene. The turn of the century saw a plethora of such groups in various countries, ranging from the aggressively secular and humanist to the neo-pagan and the self-consciously spiritual or mystical, and, sometimes, the ritualistic. The apocalyptic mood seems to have been particularly intense in Germany, understandably, in the years after unification, with the inevitable disillusionments it in some cases brought. Even the phrase 'Second Reich' has an apocalyptic ring to it; Constantine, after all, had founded his new Rome as the centre of a new Christian empire. One product of the movements for *Lebensreform*, along with a good deal of anti-Semitism, was Zionism in one of its aspects, as a vision of the emergence from the ghetto and the transformation of the Jewish intellectual and trader into a pioneer desert farmer.

Eugenics, which we have already considered in another context (above, Chapter 2), was, as it were, the hereditary dimension of *Lebensreform*, sometimes incorporating an almost religious kind of self-purification and dedication in the interests of the race, accompanied by a new 'scientific' creed. The prime example is the religion of nature worship approached through science, propounded by the evolutionist Ernst Haeckel under the name of Monism. Haeckel founded the Monist League in 1905 and many contemporary strands came together in Monism: hostility to Christianity and propaganda for science and the scientific outlook, especially Darwinism; a traditional German Romantic cult of nature and the German landscape; an optimistic, teleological style of evolutionism; 'hygiene' and selective breeding; an insistence that the new cell theory in biology showed that subordination is the law of organic life: 'Each cell, though autonomous, is subordinated to the body as a whole.'

## 6.3 The Occult

There was nothing secretive about Haeckel's message. He was an immensely successful popularizer of science and proselytizer for his own views, as well as a scientist of genuine and eclectic achievement. The membership of the Monist League soon reached 6,000. But in other circles there was a flourishing of the concept of occult knowledge, possessed only by initiates, who therefore formed a kind of brotherhood or even 'Order' of adepts and elect spirits, with a spiritual leader or teacher and a mission to recover and pursue a vital, redemptive, hidden truth. The earlier enthusiasm for secret societies and brotherhoods in the 1830s and 1840s, of the kind Mazzini patronized, was political; half a century later, though not always without an exaltedly political dimension, it was predominantly mystical. Wagner struck a contemporary and prophetic note in *Parsifal*: the Knights of the Holy Grail form a closed order, secluded from the world; their function seems purely ritual, to renew life by performing their appointed rite under their undying priest-king, whose mysterious unhealed wound disables him from performing it until the advent of Parsifal as a type of redeemer. The folkloric roots of this seem very clear; we seem on the point of grasping Frazer's Golden Bough (see Chapter 2, above), with the spring renewal of life (Good Friday in *Parsifal*) associated with the sacrifice of the dying god-king, and with the Holy Lance reclaimed by Parsifal doing duty for the Golden Bough itself, *avant la lettre*. The Christian context seems by comparison almost superficial, and was perhaps, for once, reacted to superficially by Nietzsche.

The notion of an order or brotherhood focused on ritual derived not only from the Grail legend but also from Rosicrucianism, founded in the seventeenth century and experiencing a revival in the second half of the nineteenth, and from Freemasonry. Another contributor was the partly legendary history of the medieval order of the Templars, connected by name at least with the Temple of Solomon and condemned by the Church for the alleged possession of an heretical secret doctrine. The idea of secret knowledge derived, of course, from many sources: from Gnosticism and neo-Platonism in late antiquity, and from the Hebrew Kabbala and the magical writings of the supposed Hermes Trismegistus, all revived at the time of the Renaissance. Towards the end of the nineteenth century mystical cosmological doctrines were to receive a substantial infusion from Hinduism and Buddhism, a preoccupation sometimes covered by the notion of an ancient 'Aryan' wisdom. The idea of the latter became sufficiently important for the study of it to acquire a name, 'Ariosophy'.

The concept of a tradition of occult knowledge fed, and fed on, not only the self-esteem of the initiate but also a sense of cultural persecution or deprivation. Why, after all, had the now hidden knowledge been forced underground and only tenuously preserved, but by persecution, most probably Christian? In Germany and Austria in particular, such occultism could take a racial as well as assertively pagan turn. *Lebensreform* (a term so convenient it is tempting now not to confine its use to German-speaking lands) sometimes became entangled with or expressed notions of a tradition of occult pagan knowledge. The sense of persecution, of being immersed in an element that was both hostile and unclean, from which Eugenics drew strength and which also nourished French aestheticism, with its hatred of the *bourgeois*, was particularly prone to assume a racial form in Austria, a German enclave in an empire in which Magyars and Slavs were increasingly assertive and Jewish immigration from the east greatly increased towards the end of the century. Austrian-German nationalists had been cheated in 1871 of their hopes of a pan-German Reich; Germanic racialism was a natural response.

To trace the strains of racialist occultism, as has been done by Nicholas Goodrick-Clarke, is to explore areas of the bizarre usually beyond the scope of 'respectable' intellectual history, but, though it is important not to lose a sense of proportion about their prevalence, the time and place require it. There were also overlaps with prominent, more mainstream, Social Darwinist Monists like Otto Ammon and Ludwig Woltmann (1871–1907). The most influential mystagogue or mythologizer seems to have been Viennese from a Catholic family, Guido List (1848–1919), who later added the 'von' to his name (as Gobineau also ennobled himself; racialists were understandably touchy about their genealogies). List grew up with the common volkish enthusiasms to which were added the study of astrology and the Kabbala.

From these materials List constructed the legend, meant to be taken literally, of an ancient Aryan-German theocracy of priest-kings whose wisdom was preserved in symbolic form in German folklore, runes and ancient Teutonic rites. They were the priests of a now largely lost Teutonic nature-religion, centred on sun-worship and an immanent god-in-nature, with which the cult of Wotan was associated, and ruled an hierarchical tribal society based on breeding. List became a kind of volkish archaeologist and antiquary, identifying ancient sacred sites of sun-worship and Wotanism, and attributing secret symbolic meanings to, among other things, the heraldic devices of the medieval nobility. The Gnostic element in List's beliefs was constituted by the idea of an all-pervading spiritual force, of which all things were an emanation; this seems to have been not his own idea but borrowed from the fashionable Theosophy of Madame Helena Blavatsky, which we must consider shortly. List's ideas were a fusion of Theosophy and German folklore and mythology – hence 'Ariosophy' – to create the notion of a primal Teutonic and Wotanist natural and spiritual knowledge, which carried a component of racial eugenics.

The name given to the ancient German social order and doctrine presided over by the priesthood of Wotan was the *Armanenschaft*, a Germanization of a term in Tacitus's *Germania*. The priests seem in some respects to echo Plato's Guardians, not only in their knowledge of breeding but in the dissemination of two doctrines, one for the vulgar and an esoteric one for the élite, for whom there were grades of initiation. Memories of this doctrine were subsequently to be found in the usual components of an occultist tradition, Templars, Rosicrucians, Masons, the medieval craft-guilds, and in alchemy and astrology, as well as in German folklore. Vestiges of the ancient religion – one is reminded of W. B. Yeats, to whom we must also turn shortly – were to be found among such vagrants as tinkers, gypsies and minstrels. List was, predictably, in the German volkish manner, an admirer both of the peasantry and the guilds. Equally predictably, his view of the world was also touched by quasi-apocalyptic notions of renewal. The *Armanenschaft* had been destroyed by Christian persecution, which had identified its remnants with the agents of Satan. It must be restored in the form of a caste society in which Aryan masters rule over non-Aryan labourers. Within the ruling race there would be ten grades of hierarchy. List himself would be Grand Master.

Despite his addiction to summer solstice festivals, however, List seems to have been a publicist and pseudo-scholar rather than priest or thaumaturge, a more fertilely imaginative and literal-minded version of Lagarde or Chamberlain (and one is occasionally reminded of another

ex-Catholic, Auguste Comte), not a practising magus, though it appears
that he did make his symbolical and archaeological discoveries with the
aid of illuminating states of trance. He also successfully published
colourful novels set in the early Teutonic period, and made a name in
Pan-German and anti-Semitic circles as a journalist. He contributed a
millennial note to German propaganda during the Great War, about
which he was enthusiastic. In 1908 his admirers founded a List society
for propagating his ideas, which it seems to have done with some success.

In terms of the specificity of his message, and his non-appearance in
the ratings of European high culture, List stands at the opposite pole from
another noteworthy spiritual guide of the period, the highly regarded
poet and enigmatic messiah, Stefan George (1868–1933). George's world
touched, on the one side, the esoteric, ineffable mysteries of the French-
bred aesthetics of the Symbolist movement in poetry and drama, on the
other the more down-to-earth German world of Ariosophic occultism. As
a young man he had formed a member of the circle in Paris of the guru of
Symbolism, Stéphane Mallarmé (1842–98). In Germany he had been
briefly in touch with a pagan-gnostic circle called the Cosmics. There were
rumours that the circle of young men George formed around himself
indulged in ritual secret ceremonies and regalia; there were also whispers
of homosexuality. All that seems clearly establishable is that initiates took
an oath of allegiance to the Master, George, and that poetry was recited in
an atmosphere of high, hieratic, solemnity. Compared with a vulgar occultist
and publicist like List, George was a figure of Olympian, fastidious, aristocratic aloofness. Compared with the single-minded devotion to the religion
of art of the French Symbolists, however, he was almost a public figure,
gathering around himself the mantle of a portentous messianism.

It seems that he conceived of his circle of young male disciples as a
spiritual élite or aristocracy, being trained in self-perfection for some
unspecified form of leadership of the future Germany and even of Europe,
whose spiritual life and culture they would revitalize. Though the religion
of art and a Nietzschean kind of pursuit of self-overcoming were stressed
notes, there seems to have been also a whiff of occult-spiritual gnosis or
knowledge about the George cult, as well as a hint of a world-redemptive
role. One icon of the circle, for example, was the Emperor Frederick II, whose
medieval reputation included an association with paganism, alchemy and
astrology, as well as the notion of a world-redeemer. George was versed in
the prophetic writings of the medieval monk Joachim of Fiore. It was understood in the George circle that the master was a spiritual teacher from

whom any intimation was priceless, and intimation, rather than anything so vulgar as a doctrine, was what was on offer. George seems to have not only accepted but encouraged this view of himself and assumed without discomfort the role of the regenerator of German culture; as Nietzsche said of Wagner, self-directed irony was not one of his characteristics.

However, since George's chosen means of communication was to a small circle of initiates, and his more public utterance was in the form of a Symbolist poetry which, if it veered more towards allegory than that of his French counterparts, none the less remained esoteric, the content of the redemptive message remained obscure. Among the numerous rough beasts slouching to Bethlehem to be born, to borrow the imagery of Yeats' poem 'The Second Coming' (1939), George cuts an aloof, elegant and even reticent figure. He kept the Nazis at a distance when they wished to court him and his only discernible effect on German history was through his disciple Claus von Stauffenberg, who planted the bomb that exploded in Hitler's headquarters in 1944.

So far, discussion of one national culture at a time has led us up to the First World War and even beyond. To turn to France, therefore, involves a significant chronological retracing of steps. As we have seen, the closest French counterpart to George, Stéphane Mallarmé, the leading figure of the Symbolist movement in French literature in the 1880s and 1890s, was considerably older and may have been an influence on the young George. Aristocratic fastidiousness and esotericism they had in common, but the French writer – and this was a national characteristic at the time – devoted himself solely to the religion of art, with no public or messianic over-tones. In a country self-identified as in decline, French aesthetes had usually little interest in the historical future, except when perversely accepting the label 'decadent' or – as Edmond de Goncourt did, contemplating the Prussian Uhlans in Paris in 1870 – welcoming the advent of barbarism.

In the Symbolist aesthetic, the intense focusing on the thing taken as a symbol, the perception of its numinous aura, gave access to another, as it were parallel, invisible world of light and ecstasy which the poet, in particular, was privileged to glimpse. As the young André Gide (1869–1951) wrote, paradise was not far off but close at hand, beneath everyday experience. One had only, as it were, to pierce the material veil or turn the symbolic key. This is an aesthetic which comes close, obviously, to 'ordinary' occultism, or mysticism, devoid of any historically apocalyptic expectations. It is also not far from magic, the idea of manipulation of the phenomena of the visible world through access to its correspondences in the other, by the use of symbol, rite and incantation. There was, indeed, a ritual, incantatory quality about the reading of Symbolist poetry; the analytic, discursive intellect is placed in abeyance in favour of the rhythmic and evocative qualities of language.

The concept of a world beyond – *au-delà* – accessible by such means was common. Baudelaire, an important influence, concurring in a mystical tradition opened to him chiefly, it seems, from his study of the eighteenth-century mystic Emanuel Swedenborg (1688–1772), had believed in 'correspondences', real connections, not merely analogies, between the visible and invisible worlds. Such correspondences also existed between the experiences of the different senses: between, for example, sound and colour. This idea was taken up by Huysmans – as often with him, it is hard to distinguish between homage and parody – in his idea of des Esseintes' 'mouth-organ', a liqueur-dispenser. The concept of correspondences made symbolic motifs not merely psychologically evocative but vibrant with possibilities of esoteric meaning. The underlying search was for a restoration of meaning and mystery to a world apparently emptied of poetry and rendered banal by science. The parallel with occult ritual practices is obvious and close. Many artists of the period, including Huysmans, Mallarmé, Guillaume Apollinaire (1880–1918) and the novelist Leon Bloy (1846–1917) felt an affinity with or took a close interest in occultism. Huysmans, like Baudelaire before him, was fascinated by Satanism and the idea of the black mass.

Despite the fact that both were drawn to the occult, another striking difference between French aestheticism and German apocalyptic nationalism, apart from the ahistorical character of the former, is their respective attitudes to nature. In France, the Baudelairean rejection of the natural and cherishing of perversity as a kind of creativity and distinction, were strong, and were expressed particularly strongly by Huysmans. Imagination offered a superior alternative to nature, with the poet as perceiver or creator of alternative worlds. Despite the interest taken in heredity by literary Naturalists like Zola, it is hard to think of notions, in the France of the 1880s and 1890s, of spiritual aristocracy in connection with the concept of 'hygiene'.

It is true that this is subject to some qualification in both directions. There was, from the 1890s onwards, as we have seen (Chapter 3) a reaction in France against 'decadence' and the emergence of what might be called sporting-club nationalism. Conversely, there was a strand of pessimism, inspired by Schopenhauer (also highly influential in France), in German aestheticism: a cultivated death-wish and even a horror of mere nature (vividly expressed in Thomas Mann's *Tristan*, in a wonderfully appalled description of a baby as a kind of incarnation of the raw will to existence). Nor, of course, was the theme of perversity absent. Nietzsche made the point that it was right that Siegfried's birth, as the inauguration of a new era of human freedom, should arise from the breaking of a profoundly established rule, that against incest. Thomas Mann wrote a story of brother–sister incest with a strong Wagnerian reference. But in general the contrast will stand; the relation of harmony with or antagonism to nature as the mark of an élite – Nietzsche is even an example – tended to be different in the two countries. List's association of the occult tradition with a lost nature worship would perhaps have been less well received in France.

This is another way of saying that there the links apparent in Germany between the occult and the volkish are harder to find. The latter is a term not easy to apply in any case in France, though the cult of soil and ancestors in late nineteenth-century nationalism approaches it; Barrès (above, Chapter 3) had an interest in the deities of ancient Gaul analogous to German Wotanism. But the nearest to a connection between nationalism and mysticism in France was the mystically tinged, nationalistic Catholicism which was a presence in French literature in the years immediately before the Great War, in the work of Paul Claudel (1868–1955) and Charles Péguy (1873–1914), with its embracing, simultaneously, of the supernatural and of the virtues of the peasantry, united in the story of Joan of Arc. But this was hardly occultism.

Occultism proper, if we may so call it, as a fascination with magic and the idea of a tradition of occult knowledge, was, however, strong in France. Magi were not in short supply. The Abbé Constant, known as Eliphas Levi (1810–75), gave accounts of magic, its history and practice, in two works in 1856 and 1869 respectively. Joséphin Péladan (1858–1918), another deviant Catholic who called himself Sûr Merodack, founded in 1888 with Stanislas de Guaïta the Kabbalistic Order of the Rosy Cross, claiming to have revived the traditions of the Rosicrucians. Huysmans believed that the new Rosicrucians were Satanists. There was in fact a perceptible overlap between eccentric Catholicism and occultism in France; Huysmans himself became reconciled to the Church. Sometimes the cultivation of mystery and visions straddled a frankly irrationalist form of Catholicism and the murky world of the mystagogues.

Liberal Catholicism had been a strand in the French Church, if a relatively weak one, since the time of the democrat priest Félicité de Lammenais

(1782–1854) in the 1830s. Abortive attempts were made in the ensuing decades to make some accommodation with science and Biblical criticism. An initiative, the so-called *Ralliement*, was made under Pope Leo X in 1892 to reconcile the Church and the Republic. But French liberal Catholicism was highly fragile. Republicanism tended to be militantly anti-clerical, positivist or materialist, and provoked an intransigently reactionary Catholic response. Articulate French Catholicism in the early twentieth century tended to be populist, nationalistic, anti-Semitic and defiantly irrationalist, exalting the miraculous and ideas of atonement and vicarious suffering.

Catholicism, as in Austria, was, however inadvertently, one of the nurseries of French occultism. Péladan, who was also an erotic novelist, founded a new, allegedly Catholic order. There were fringe Catholic prophets, visionaries and millenarians. Notable was the Abbé Boullan, who proclaimed himself the successor of the millenarian heresiarch Eugène Vintras, who had enjoyed a personal vision of the Archangel Michael in 1839; Boullan (1824–93) called for a spiritual élite to hasten the end and to perform sacrificial rites to atone for the sins of the world and free man from matter – an echo of gnostic Catharism. He saw himself as a spiritual healer through sexual relations. He was, not surprisingly, unfrocked by the Church hierarchy (Huysmans thought he was murdered by black magic). In addition to proclaiming the imminent third reign of the Holy Ghost (in Joachim of Fiore's prophesies the era of the Holy Ghost followed those of God in the Old Testament, and Christ), presaging the return of Christ in glory, Boullan professed a 'secret doctrine' relating to the ascension of the soul from the material to the spiritual plane, in which sex notably played a part; it was, in fact, a redemptive rite. Here Gnosticism seems to touch hands with the self-consciously modern versions of *Lebensreform* which stressed the creative and therapeutic aspects of sexual liberation, like the sect formed at Ascona in Switzerland around the charismatic figure of Otto Gross, which drew the fascinated attention of Max Weber. But, in contrast, Boullan's version was darkly shadowed by Manichaeism, the antagonism of the spiritual and material worlds characteristic of Gnosticism.

The most cosmopolitan and internationally influential syncretic version of the tradition of occult spiritual knowledge in this period was the 'Theosophy' of Helena Blavatsky (1831–91), generally known as Madame Blavatsky, which came to contain a substantial component of ideas culled from the Hindu sacred writings and to stress reincarnation. Blavatsky was Russian by birth; the notion of Russian spirituality was something of a cliché in the later nineteenth century. The ideas of a Russian spiritual mission went back to the beginning of the century. In 1886 the Vicomte de Vogué published *The Russian Novel* in French, hailing Russian (essentially Dostoevskian) mystical profundity and intensity of faith focused on sin and humility. In Germany the volkish critic Mueller van den Bruck (1876–1925) sponsored an edition of Dostoevsky's works which also fascinated the young Hungarian critic and philosopher and future eminent Marxist, Georg Lukács, who interested Weber in Dostoevsky. For Weber, Dostoevsky and the pacifism and anarchist Christian socialism of Tolstoy, became the archetype of an all-or-nothing devotion to a religious ideal, reckless of consequences, which he could not accept but could not but respect. In the early twentieth century belief in superior Russian spirituality and the therapeutic powers of Russian holy men promoted the careers in the West of G. I. Gurdjieff (1865–1949) and P. D. Ouspensky (1878–1947), as thaumaturges and mystics with a distinguished following.

Her Russian name may have been no handicap, but Helena Blavatsky made nothing of her Russian background. Her immediate provenance was the United States and initially she might have seemed merely part of the great American tradition of fake mediums, though later she abandoned mediumship. There was a painful episode when she was exposed by the English Psychical Research Society for using fraudulent means to produce spirit manifestations. The Society was itself a characteristic institution of the period, with an impressive academic membership, centred on Trinity College, Cambridge, dedicated to the pursuit of evidence of an afterlife and paranormal powers of the mind, but also to assessing the evidence with the most exacting scientific rigour. Blavatsky, however, blossomed as an adept in the kind of imaginative scholarship characteristic of claims to occult knowledge. Her influence spread after the foundation of the first Theosophical Society in New York in 1875; there were many branches in other countries by the end of the 1880s. A further stage was marked by the publication of her book *Isis Unveiled* in 1877. *The Secret Doctrine* (1888) and *The Key to Theosophy* (1889) followed, by which time she had relocated the headquarters of Theosophy in Madras. She wrote in *Isis Unveiled* that it had been written as a contribution to 'the Titanic struggle that is now in progress between materialism and the spiritual aspirations of mankind'.

The secret doctrine was the essential core of the world's religions – hence 'Theosophy'. The great sacred writings, the Bible, the Kabbala, the Hindu Vedas, the book of Hermes Trismegistus, are all to be regarded as allegories, repositories of an esoteric meaning, which is essentially the universality and omnipotence of spirit. The Blavatskian doctrine is an extraordinary compendium of religious and occult tradition, all made compatible through imaginative allegorical interpretation, whose principles were allegedly taught to Madame by invisible Indian spirit instructors.

The largely new element which Blavatsky added to the Western occult tradition was a heavy dose of orientalism. There had been an interest, in Germany in particular, in Indian spiritual wisdom since early in the century, with Friedrich Schlegel as its chief impresario. Schopenhauer had been imbued with Buddhist ideas. In the mid-century the key figure was the French orientalist Eugene Burnouf (1801–52), the teacher both of Renan and of the German-born Oxford Professor of Sanskrit, Friedrich Max Müller (1823–1900). It was Burnouf's translation of Buddhist writings that Wagner read in 1855. Max Müller completed his edition of the Veda in 1873 and then set about editing a series of English translations, *Sacred Books of the East.* Max Müller himself, whose affiliations in England were of a liberal Anglican, Broad Church kind, was in some respects a typical German nature-worshipper in the Romantic mould. For him nature furnished intimations of the infinite. The great natural phenomena possessed a 'theogonic' quality. Man himself possessed a religious faculty alongside reason and perception, which responded to this. Max Müller held, and became famous for, the belief that the deities in various Aryan mythologies derived from a misunderstanding caused by personifying the names of the great natural forces, especially the sun. This did not for him devalue, but rather enhanced, their poetic quality. He retained, that is, the Romantic conception of myths as a form of poetic cognition, while attempting a 'scientific' account of their origins. They expressed real, if misunderstood, religious intuitions, and Max Müller wanted to use the word 'theosophy' but found to his annoyance that it had been irreversibly appropriated for Madame Blavatsky's 'Secret Doctrine'.

The content of the latter was complex not only in its sources but also in its exposition. The central concept is one which replaces the idea of creation by that of emanation from an eternal One, as a perpetual and all-pervasive cosmic energy, manifested as a complex hierarchy of spirit and matter. In the lower degrees spirit acquires an increasing mixture of concreteness, culminating, though it would be better to speak of reaching its nadir, in the material world. This hierarchy of being, reminiscent of neo-Platonism, provides as it were the niches for a graded multiplicity of powers. Between each grade of being there are echoes or correspondences, which can be used as rungs to spiritually higher modes of existence. The hierarchy, in fact, was also a cycle, or rather series of cycles, between the extremes of pure spirit and materiality, its phases marked by the signs of earth, water, air and aether. The present was, predictably, the lowest point of the cycle, with the spiritual force of human beings at its weakest. But for the individual reincarnation offered the chance of jumping stages, and the possibility of spiritual growth which could be enhanced by the acquisition of spiritual knowledge. Madame Blavatsky's task, and that of the Theosophical Society, was to aid in that process of enlightenment. The goal was essentially liberation from the limitations of earthly existence, the bondage of materiality. Salvation was not by faith or works but by knowledge and will, the latter being far more powerful than was generally appreciated.

There were various terms for the manifestations and assurances of the hovering presence of the spiritual – strictly speaking the more spiritual – world, inaccessible to natural perception but able to be focused by the concentrated spiritual energy of the instructed. One was 'ether' (or 'aether'), the invisible fluid bathing and connecting all matter. Another was 'the fourth dimension' (e.g. P. D. Ouspensky, *The Fourth Dimension*, 1910). Both of these were gestures of appropriation towards contemporary science in its new, more immaterialist mode: to physics and to the non-Euclidean geometries engaging the attention of mathematicians. The example of electricity often seems discernible behind invocations of an invisible spiritual energy. Other markers that one was in the presence of theosophical discourse were 'aura' and 'astral body' and 'astral light'. The last was the pervasive medium of which particular entities were congealed forms. The 'aura' which surrounds each human being is of two kinds, the mental and the emotional; these can become detached and free-floating, when they are 'thought-forms' of different colours, determined by their quality.

Helena Blavatsky died in 1891. Thereafter the leaders of the Theosophical movement were Annie Besant (1847–1933) and Charles Leadbeater (1847–1934). Theosophy became even more emphatically identified with the promotion in the West of ideas derived from the East, as well as the promotion of the Indian Jiddu Krishnamurti (1895–1986) as the new incarnation of the World-Teacher, a role he repudiated in 1929. It was all too much for the General Secretary of the German Theosophical Society, Rudolf Steiner (1861–1925), who, still strongly attached to a distinctively Christian form of mysticism, broke away in 1912 to found his own Anthroposophical Society.

But the impetus to more diffused forms of occultism was not exhausted. The notion of correspondences and symbols as points of entry to the bright and fascinatingly peopled and furnished spiritual world, free of the limitations of the body and of ordinary perception, continued to have an attraction for creative artists, of whom perhaps the most notable were the poet W. B. Yeats and the painter Vasili Kandinsky. In Yeats (1865–1939) we see what we have found to be rare in France though more common in Germany, a fusion of interests in the occult and in the volkish, or what, in an Anglo-Irish context, lacking the full resonances of the German term, it is best to speak of as Celtic folklore and mythology and the possibility of its use for a modern spiritual and national reawakening. Yeats' beliefs and activities on the one side bear comparison with those of Wagner, particularly the focus on drama as central to the idea of national identity and renewal. What Wagner found in Norse mythology and German legend, Yeats found in Celtic mythology and the traditions and folk-memories of the Irish peasantry.

In his autobiography Yeats described how, as he says, deprived of the religion of his childhood by Huxley and Tyndall, 'whom I detested', he made himself

> a new religion, almost an infallible Church, of poetic tradition . . . passed on from generation to generation by poets and painters, with some help from philosophers and theologians. I wished for a world where I could discover this tradition perpetually, and not in pictures and poems only, but in tiles around the chimney-piece and in the hangings that kept out the draught.[2]

The traditions preserved in the fairy-tales of the Sligo countryside became part of the furniture of Yeats' mind, as runes and folk motifs filled the more undisciplined mind of Guido von List. Congealed into symbolism, this way of thinking fostered a conception of symbols which emphasized their perennial character, their saturation with the deepest emotions and imaginings of mankind. It pointed, thus, not only to tradition but even to a kind of collective unconscious memory or World-Mind, of the kind later associated with Carl Gustav Jung, and forming a bridge to the idea of a tradition of occult knowledge.

In 1901 Yeats wrote a summary of his belief in the occult. It begins

---

[2] W. B. Yeats, *Autobiographies* (London, 1950), p. 116.

with the instability of the self, and the arbitrariness of the division between the self and others.

(1) That the borders of our minds are ever-shifting, and that many minds can flow into one another, as it were, and create or reveal a single mind, a single energy.

(2) That the borders of our memories are shifting, and that our memories are part of one great memory, the memory of Nature herself.

(3) That this great mind and great memory can be evoked by symbols.[3]

These beliefs Yeats refers to as having been 'handed down from early times and been the foundation of nearly all magical practices'. He is not, that is, proclaiming a symbolist literary credo but instructing the reader in the fundamentals leading to a belief in magic. Here symbols are not so much the foci of emotional energy, sanctified by poetic tradition; they are the esoteric emblems, usually geometrical though colours were also important, identified in occult magical traditions and perhaps devoid of imaginative or emotional resource outside them. Yeats' chief induction into the occult seems to have been initially through Theosophy; he joined the Theosophists' London Lodge in 1887. Soon afterwards he became an early member of the Order of the Golden Dawn, a neo-Rosicrucian group founded in London in 1889. It was highly organized and ritualistic, as the Theosophists were not, with rites of initiation and a hierarchy of grades of membership corresponding to the 10 emanatory spheres in the Kabbala, and devoted to the practice of what Yeats frankly calls magic. Another early member was Aleister Crowley, who refers unflatteringly to Yeats in his uncandid memoirs.

For Yeats the Order was a mystic community; collective meditation on the elemental symbols and the performance of rites were means to focus and intensify the psychic energies of the participants and produce what Yeats calls 'visions of truth' in the depths of the mind. But the symbols also had an energy of their own which could be employed by the adept. As he put it, 'symbols and formulae are powers'. Later, becoming disillusioned with the Order, he turned to the more private practice of mediumship, aided by the discovery that his wife apparently possessed powers as a medium,

[3] Quoted in Graham Hough, *The Mystery Religion of W. B. Yeats* (Brighton, 1984), p. 44.

evinced particularly in automatic writing. Fundamental theosophical notions, as, for example, in the reference to the *Anima Mundi*, the World-Soul, one of the greatest of the intermediate powers, in the famous poem 'The Second Coming', had established themselves as a permanent part of the furnishing of his mind and poetic imagination, partially displacing the Celtic mythological inspirations of his earlier period.

In the visual arts the painter who most explicitly acknowledged and exemplifies the influence of theosophical ideas in his visual symbolism is Vasili Kandinsky (1866–1944), who, like Yeats, was originally drawn to folkloric motifs. He expressed his theosophical ideas not only in painting but in a book, *On the Spiritual in Art* (1912). The key theosophical concept is that of 'vibration': words, colours, shapes and musical tones can evoke vibrations in the soul which thus gains access to the pervasive cosmic energy. Like the symbols with which Yeats tinkered in his Golden Dawn period, they did not have to be natural objects, and a connection has been suggested here with the origins of abstract art. The 'real' world lies beyond the phenomenal one, with symbols, as ever, as the keys to unlock the former, which is a realm of floating, shimmering colour and light. Following this line of thought, the representational in art could be seen as materialist, abstraction as spiritual.

To have spoken so much of hieratic orders and brotherhoods, dedicated to the recovery and pursuit of occult knowledge and in some cases to magical rituals, is to have spoken of a minority, even a specialized, kind of interest, even if we forbear from describing it as eccentric. It has been justified here not only because the notion of occult knowledge sometimes touched the imaginations of major artists, as well as producing myths of persecution and reflecting Manichaean views of the contemporary world, but because of its affinities, in its straining against the bondage of the materialistic and the banal, with wider intellectual currents of the period.

The antithesis of spirit and matter could sometimes be starkly posed, but some form of self-fulfilling immanence, or else a material-spiritual hierarchy of gradations, as in Theosophy, were more common. The desired breakthrough to a higher plane of individual consciousness, of spiritual progress, was identified in a variety of idioms, and in terms of various underlying spatial or temporal models, indicated by prepositions – 'above', 'behind', 'beneath', 'beyond' – often not clearly distinguishable but all pointing to a present and parallel yet only fleetingly perceptible other world.

The two assumptions we have been considering (historic, apocalyptic expectation and a co-present invisible world) were in a sense in competition as migration advertisements to the restless spirit, though not without possibilities of collaboration. There is an analogy with the rival and even incompatible strands in Christianity, the messianic and the sacramental. The former, predominantly Protestant, emphasizes the second coming of Christ, resurrection in the body and a general judgement, and the inauguration of a new world order; the latter, predominantly Catholic, stresses the regular administration of the sacraments, which annihilate the temporal distance between the believer and Christ, and the immediate posthumous judgement of each individual as, at the moment of death, he or she slides from this world to the paradisal or infernal other worlds which co-exist with it. Despite the alien, oriental trappings of Theosophy it is, as we have seen, possible to make out both these ways of thinking, divested of Christian dogma, persisting with considerable vigour (the first predominantly in Germany, the second more in France) in the late nineteenth and early twentieth centuries. What both express is a common impatience with the limitations of a mundane, de-mythologized human existence and a disenchanted world.

# Epilogue
## Avant-garde

We declare that the splendour of the world has been increased by a
new beauty: the beauty of speed. A racing car . . . is more beautiful
than the Winged Victory of Samothrace . . . Beauty now exists only
in struggle . . . We want to glorify war – the world's only hygiene –
militarism, patriotism, the destructive act of the anarchists, the beautiful ideas for which one dies, and contempt for women. We want to
destroy museums, libraries and academies of all kinds . . . We shall sing
the great crowds excited by work, pleasure or rioting, the multicoloured,
many-voiced tides of revolution in modern capitals. We shall sing the
nocturnal, vibrating incandescence of arsenals and shipyards, ablaze
with violent electric moons, the voracious stations devouring their
smoking serpents . . . We launch from Italy into the world this our
manifesto of overwhelming and incendiary violence, with which today
we found Futurism, because we want to liberate this land from the fetid
cancer of professors, archaeologists, guides and antiquarians. (Filippo
Marinetti, *The Futurist Manifesto*, 1909)

It is possible to deal with this famous proclamation as with any other piece
of intellectual history, uncovering (as an act of professorial revenge?) the
layers of its intellectual archaeology. There are, clearly, Social Darwinism
and Nietzsche (the necessity for struggle, the Nietzschean abhorrence of
the official guardians of historical memory); Bergson probably (dynamism,
*élan*); the anarchist tradition of Bakunin (violence, destruction, incendiar-
ism); Walt Whitman's celebration of the teeming crowds of workers of the
industrial world and their unleashed energies. The Manifesto was, of course,
designed to shock and still can, in its raw aggression and vaunting mascu-
linity, even if we are now accustomed to blasphemies against the heritage
of high culture. For despite the manifest intellectual influences it *was* new.

Of all the many avant-garde movements ('avant-garde' migrated from its earlier military and political contexts into the arts in France in the late nineteenth century) immediately before the First World War, Futurism was the most self-conscious and self-advertising, if shorter on artistic achievement than its rivals, and may therefore for the moment stand for all of them, not as exactly typical but as an extreme case. Apart from their genuine novelty what is still startling in these artistic movements is their extraordinary compression in time: a bare five to seven years in which to create modernity, between 1905–7 and 1912. These years span the exhibition by the *Fauves* ('wild beasts') including, notably, Matisse in Paris in 1905, and the formation in the same year of the group of young artists in Dresden known as the Bridge (*Die Brücke*); Picasso's *Demoiselles d'Avignon* (1907) and his and Georges Braque's move on to Cubism; Schoenberg's breakthrough to atonality in music in his Second String Quartet (1907–8) (which included settings of poems by Stefan George); the early paintings of Kandinsky (and his justification of abstraction in painting in *The Spiritual in Art*) and of Oskar Kokoschka (1886–1980) which may be said to culminate in the group of Expressionist painters in Berlin in 1912 under the name *The Blue Rider* (*Der Blaue Reiter*). The same period saw the first theatrical performances of Expressionist works: Frank Wedekind's seminal *Spring's Awakening* (*Frühlings Erwachen*) about adolescent sexuality, written in 1891 but not put on until 1906, in Berlin, in a heavily censored version; Kokoschka's macabre, enigmatic and disturbing *Murder, Hope of Women* was put on in Munich in 1908. These years also saw the first 'abstract' theatrical experiments, notably Kandinsky's *The Yellow Sound* (*Der Gelbe Klang*, 1909) which made its effects purely through sound, lights and movement, and Schoenberg's opera *The Fortunate Hand* (*Die Glückliche Hand*), which he described as embodying the renunciation of any conscious thought or plot. The Futurists too were to experiment with theatrical events created by lights, sounds and cries and depersonalized performers with toneless voices and expressionless faces.

Generalizing, it is possible to speak of a move towards abstraction, but it was at this point a tendency rather than a goal; it would be more accurate to speak of the abandonment of illusionistic realism and a widespread and deliberate disruption of its techniques of representation such as perspective, naturalistic acting and narrative, logical syntax and consistency of genre. We can also draw an analogy between the abandonment of the organizing disciplines of perspective and narrative and those of tonality and thematic development in music. Instead, there were spatial and verbal arrangements, juxtapositions of images and sounds and colour, whose 'logic' seemed allusive and associative rather than sequential or descriptive.

'Modern' is, of course, the most conveniently general label, and it (though not the much later 'Modernism') was freely used during the period as a kind of flag. It covers, however, many variants and even incompatibilities, as well as important analogies. The latter derive partly from what the modern was set against, the creeds of the previous generation, particularly Naturalism, Impressionism and Symbolism. (Futurism's declaration of war on Symbolism, 'Let's Murder the Moonlight', was apt, economical and funny.) To put the modern revolt in a wider context, relevant to this book, however, and to set it, as it deserves, against not only its immediate antecedents, to which, inevitably, it owed some debts, but also against the nineteenth century generally, and indeed many centuries of artistic, literary and musical tradition before that, we can begin by taking a cue from Futurism and speak of the antithesis of Modernism and Historicism.

The latter possesses its high generality partly because of an ambiguity which can be useful here. It contains first the notion of 'historicizing', meaning the adoption of cultural motifs, styles and modes of thought derived from the past, either as an aesthetic repertoire or, more seriously, as an attempt to bring about a desirable or necessary revival (the paradigm case is the Renaissance), revitalizing the jaded current aesthetic conventions. But it also contains what may be called 'historicism' in a more general and systematic sense, as the belief or assumption that history as a whole forms a meaningful sequence or, as we now tend to say, grand narrative, even a teleological one, to which the present is attached in an intelligible and reassuring continuity, as tradition, progress or consummation.

Modernism (to use the convenient, more recent term) was not always wholly able to shake off the latter assumption. Its genuine novelty is marked, however, by its wholesale refusal to present novelty in the guise of revival and therefore its renunciation of the comforts and inspiration of the past. The renunciation was not absolute – one can instance the inspiration some Expressionists derived from the harsh strength of sixteenth-century German woodcuts – but it was comprehensive enough and it was itself a novelty. In the century and a half before 1900, to go back no earlier, innovation in the arts and radical rejections of the dominant conventions had characteristically taken the form of revivals.

The late eighteenth century, particularly Germany, had found in ancient Greece, and particularly in Doric, a noble simplicity with which to counter the florid elaborations, coming to be seen as respectively pompous and frivolous, of Baroque and Rococo. The Romantics restored the cultural credit of the Middle Ages and by the 1830s Gothic was rehabilitated, as a serious – for its devotees *the* serious – architectural language. The Pre-Raphaelites, the prototypical aesthetic avant-garde (along with the rather earlier Nazarenes in Germany) found a cleansing purification in the Italian later Middle Ages, while the Arts and Crafts movement which derived from it clothed a modern-sounding functionalism in a medieval vesture. *Art Nouveau* (in German *Jugendstil*, the young style), to which it in turn gave impetus, though genuinely innovative in its sinuous lines derived from natural forms, did not deny itself access to the bazaar of historic styles and mythologies.

The same allusiveness is prominent in literary forms of late nineteenth-century aestheticism. The aesthete's search for the exquisite experience, which seemed to promise an immediate encounter with the world, in fact promoted the opposite: the mediation of such experiences through art, seen as a sequence of styles of perception and therefore thoroughly historicizing them. Naturalism, the apparent antithesis, invoked the historically condi-tioned consciousness in a different sense. A novelist like Zola was a master-chronicler of the age, a kind of contemporary social historian who willingly embraced the massive responsibilities this entailed. Philosophy, Biology and Psychology were characteristically presented in the historic mode. The nineteenth-century grand narratives of the emergence of mo-dernity, Hegel's presentation of the self-disclosure of the idea of the state and Herbert Spencer's celebration of its withering away, presented their versions of the present, as Marx did his of the future, as the predetermined culmination of the whole of the significant past. The result in all these cases was to the cold eye of Nietzsche, as we have seen (Chapter 5), a hypertrophy of the historical sense, a life lived at second hand, paralysed by awareness of its self-acknowledged place in an historical continuum.

From the 1870s, therefore, beginning with Nietzsche, we see the stirrings of a reaction and have looked at some of its manifestations in various sorts of voluntarism and a cult of the idea of action, hopeful or desperate. Among the more optimistic we may instance Bernstein (whom we considered in Chapter 3), insisting from the standpoint of Kantian morality that the present could be judged, not merely diagnosed, and that Socialism was therefore a remedy, not a prediction. Among the most extreme we found Sorel, willing to attack the present with any weapons, all regarded pragmatically, though he was not entirely immune to the tendency to idealize aspects of the past, particularly the warrior–farmer patriarchy of ancient Israel and Greece. In Bergson we saw an attempt to see the recuperation of our past not as sti-fling but as a means to wholeness and hence to the possibility of action and creativity, making the energized self a cutting edge to an indeterminate future. In the last chapter we saw occultists and Symbolists postulating an other, spiritual world, co-present in time with the mundane one, to which at least partial access might be gained through willed concentration and self-discipline. All these offered in various ways liberation from the burden of history, whether the latter was seen as an inexorable developmental logic whose outcome was the iron cage of modernity, or as an oppressive cultural museum in which all possible action or experience seemed anticipated, stored, documented and already lived. The contemporary term for the latter was decadence, and it was against such decadence that the rude and violent gestures of Futurism were largely directed.

It had been Nietzsche, above all, who had cast himself as the prophet of liberation, and in the 1900s, his influence, beginning in Germany in the later 1890s, was at its height all over Europe. If the new cultural climate, compared with the *fin de siècle*, seems significantly different, more aggressive, forward-looking and strident, with the condition of being modern seen not as a predicament, as earlier, but as a kind of opportunity, then the chief explanation is probably Nietzsche's influence, assuming we disregard the numerological influence of the turn of the century, which may have touched some minds as '*fin de siècle*' seems to have done.

Nietzsche's influence was so great and extensive not only because of the power, intellectual and rhetorical, of his writing – aphoristic, scornful, witty, intimate and, particularly in *Thus Spake Zarathustra*, at times exaltedly prophetic – but because his message of liberation operated at a number of different levels: cultural, epistemological, psychological and ethical (including sexual). Nietzsche's targets included the weight of inherited culture, the tyranny of concepts and the deification of reason, the self-deceptions and hypocrisies of Christian and bourgeois ethics, the sterility and the pretensions of the *savant*, the comfortable evasions of 'progressive' thought, the perversion of sexual energy into guilt and asceticism. Some of these we have already considered, but the critique of metaphysics, seen by Nietzsche as the emancipation of our sensuous experience from the mystification and reification of concepts, needs attention here. It was the revolt – not only Nietzschean, of course – against the standardization of perception by the fixed concepts imposed by intellect and convention that was to be central to much of the artistic and linguistic experimentation of the next generation. Behind this, even if it is not always immediately apparent, stands Nietzsche's pervasive legacy, though Mach (see Chapter 1) and Bergson were also important philosophical presences.

One of the most pertinent Nietzschean texts here is *The Twilight of the Idols*, in which Nietzsche looks at a philosophical question as old as Heraclitus, whom he cites and whom he predictably admired. Existence is fluid, concepts are static. Concepts therefore obscure, mystify and standardize experience, distancing us from it so that we come to see language as the superior order of reality, to which existence conforms. In the Platonic version with which Nietzsche is primarily concerned here (though the whole German Idealist metaphysical tradition is also implicated), the philosopher (Socrates), according to Nietzsche, teaches us to despise sensory experience, both epistemologically and morally.

Socrates and Plato made a divine despot of reason, tyrannizing over instinctual and sensory existence. Life, as endless flux, was denigrated; changelessness was made the test of the real, and the appearance of it was achieved by the fetishization of language. Concepts spuriously made definite and timeless what is actually experienced as fluid and ever-changing. It is this fetishization (we recall the comparable if sentimentally humanist enterprise of Feuerbach (see the Prologue), for whom 'man' at least was an essence) which Nietzsche in *Twilight* set out to overthrow; its subtitle is 'How to Philosophize with a Hammer'. The iconoclasm is conducted with exhilaration and wit, but also with an awareness of the terror of the void which it creates. The terror, indeed, is part of the exhilaration, as awareness of it becomes a test of courage. Awareness of the inability of concepts to fix and stabilize existence is also awareness of its meaninglessness and absence of value until we, by an act of will, give it meaning and value. It is pointless to ask what is the value of life; 'life itself evaluates through us when we establish values'.

To find the courage to face this awareness is an act of self-emancipation and it is twofold, because the Platonic philosopher's contempt for the bodily, the sensuous, was at once epistemological and moral. Hence emancipation from the tyranny of reified language is also the emancipation of the sensuous and instinctual from an otherworldly morality. Life celebrates its emancipation in art, in a passage which recalls the evocation of the Dionysiac in *The Birth of Tragedy* and also reads like a premonitory manifesto for much of the avant-garde art and poetry that was to follow more than a decade later. A precondition of art is what Nietzsche calls, in a passage which scarcely bothers to conceal its own quasi-orgasmic character, intoxication:

Intoxication must first have heightened the excitability of the entire machine: no art results before this happens. All kinds of intoxication, however different their origin, have the power to do this: above all the intoxication of sexual excitement, the oldest and most primitive form of intoxication. Likewise the intoxication which comes in the train of all great desires, all strong emotions; the intoxication of feasting, of contest, of the brave deed, of victory, of all extreme agitation; the intoxication of cruelty; intoxication in destruction; intoxication under certain meteorological influences, for example the intoxication of spring; or under the influence of narcotics; finally the intoxication of the will, the intoxication of an overloaded and distended will.[1]

There are, of course, profound Romantic roots for this. In its own time the closest parallels in art are perhaps with the hectic, visionary poetry, proto-modern in many respects, of Arthur Rimbaud. But Nietzsche's celebration of a Dionysian creativity derives its long-term importance not only from its own rhetorical power but from its context in the argued critique of the tyranny of language. There it is possible to see foreshadowed not only Expressionist auto-intoxication and terror but the more widespread Modernist attempts to escape from the constraints of logic, syntax and even, sometimes, from the obstinately denotational character of words, as well as the attempts to open out to passing experience in all its incoherence, through acceptance of the abrupt collision and juxtaposition of images and feelings which the dissolution of stabilizing concepts and the logical sequences between them permitted.

Modernism, therefore, was concerned, as a defining characteristic, not only with disrupting the serial character of logic and narrative but with challenging the techniques of representation, verbal and visual, by which the illusion of a world of stable characters and things, governed by inten-tion and causality, had been sustained. Life as experienced, and particularly in the typical modern experience of life in the city, with its moving crowds and traffic, was not like that. Its constantly shifting perspectives, seen, for example, from a tram or a train, its dazzling lights and screaming hoard-ings, its countless meaningless, momentary encounters and avoidances, its fleeting juxtapositions of signs and objects, human beings and machines constituted a new reality.

The Impressionists had made a beginning in representing it, but only by freezing it in particular perspectives and moments of time, and they were beginning too, particularly in Germany, to be subject to charges of superficiality. 'Expressionism' as a descriptive term seems to have appeared

[1] Friedrich Nietzsche, *Twilight of the Idols*, trans. R. J. Hollingdale (Harmondsworth, 1968), pp. 71–2.

just before 1914 as an antithesis to Impressionism. The Impressionists were allegedly materialistic and concerned only with the surface of things. One charge never levelled at German Expressionism was deficiency of soul. Amid the excitement engendered by the new aesthetic perception and its opportunities there was also sometimes a kind of puritanism. Illusionistic realism was not merely superficial but hypocritical, making things seem reassuringly what they were not, like the moral façades of bourgeois life and individual pretension exposed, naturalistically, in the previous generation by Ibsen and Zola. The stance of the new avant-garde was not generally political but it was certainly often adversarial and even, as we have seen, aggressive.

Its oppositional stance, expressed here through a kind of ferocious playfulness, is well caught by the opening manifesto – clearly owing something to the Futurists – of the journal *BLAST* founded in England in 1914 by Wyndham Lewis (1882–1957) and Ezra Pound (1885–1972) to act as the mouthpiece of the new movement christened by Pound 'Vorticism'. It reads

BLAST
years 1837 to 1900
Curse abysmal inexcusable middle class . . .
BLAST their weeping whiskers – hirsute
RHETORIC of EUNUCH and STYLIST–
SENTIMENTAL HYGENICS (etc).

The whiskered authority of the Victorian (1837 to 1901, actually) paterfamilias is clearly indicted, but the manifesto was more like aesthetes' infighting than social critique. 'Rhetoric of Eunuch and Stylist' sounds like an echo of the strident virility of the Futurists' blast against the velleities, the yearning, twilight half-tones and tentative magic of Symbolism.

This was fairly typical. At first sight there seems a good deal in common between the generation we are now considering and the revolutionary generation of the 1840s with which we began. The closest parallel we have seen to the first Futurist Manifesto is the famous article by Bakunin, quoted in the Prologue, in which, hailing the coming Revolution, he claimed that the passion for destruction is also a creative passion. Another analogy is the expression of hope in both periods through the cult of 'Youth', which was a watchword, laden with promise, though sometimes now also with pathos, of the 1890s and 1900s as it had been in the 1830s and 1840s. It occurs in significant compounds, particularly in Germany: the Youth Movement; and the *Jugendstil*. An avant-garde journal in Munich in 1896 bore the title

*Jugend*; the manifesto of the *Brücke* group of artists was a call for collaboration to 'Youth' everywhere. In Germany there were *Wandervögel* ('wandering
birds', i.e. hikers), in France for the first time sporting clubs, in Britain
Boys Brigades and Boy Scouts. Wilde's *Dorian Gray* was a hymn to Youth,
Wedekind's *Spring's Awakening*, Thomas Mann's *Tonio Kröger* and Robert
Musil's *Young Törless* were explorations of the vulnerability, sensitivity
and hazards of youth and the incomprehension of its elders.

But there were also instructive differences from the 1840s. Humanitarianism verging on sentimentality, so much a keynote of the earlier period,
was, if hardly extinct in the 1900s, considerably less intellectually chic than
will, aggression and struggle, 'the punch and the slap', as Marinetti put it
with the Futurists' inimitable indifference to bathos. We see this particularly in attitudes to sexuality. In both periods demands for sexual liberation,
particularly for women, were intellectually fashionable; after decades in
abeyance, it became an aspect of Feminism at the turn of the century.

But the literary and pictorial exploration of sex in the 1900s lay still
under the shadow of the perversity and misogyny of Decadence, as well
as of a sense, derived notably from Strindberg, of an antagonism between
the sexes as implacable as that between fathers and sons. Male sexuality,
to judge by its artistic manifestation, was streaked with sado-masochism,
anxiety and dread, just as the contemporary science of sex dwelt on
psychopathology, whose doyen, before Freud, was Richard Krafft-Ebing
(1840–1902), whose *Psychopathia Sexualis* was first published in 1886.
An extreme example of sado-masochism in literature was one of the
earliest Expressionist dramas, Kokoschka's heavily allegorical *Murder,
Hope of Women* referred to above. It was not quite thus in the days of
the Saint-Simonians and George Sand and the 'rehabilitation of the
flesh'. Even Gustav Klimt (1862–1918), who in his *Danae* (1907–8) depicted
perhaps the period's most appealingly sensuous representation of gratified
desire, peopled his murals, commissioned for the great hall of the
University of Vienna to symbolize Medicine and Jurisprudence (1901–7),
with some terrifying maenads in the manner of the *fin de siècle* (Philosophy,
in another panel, was let off more lightly just with some vaporous sky-
floating of a neo-Baroque kind and a murky sphinx). The subsequent
controversy has given Klimt a niche in the martyrology of the avant-garde,
but looking at the pictures it is possible to sympathize with the outraged
professoriate. This is perhaps another way of saying that an avant-garde
artist who accepts a public commission puts himself in a false position,
which Klimt seems to have done with a rather remarkable innocence.

If the avant-garde of the 1900s was largely apolitical and even introverted, it tended to elide the distinction between art and action in a quite different sense from the social propaganda of the Naturalists Ibsen and Zola. Its relevant idea here, carried only a little further, was the doctrine of later nineteenth-century aestheticism that, as Wilde put it, 'Art expresses nothing but itself', which entered powerfully into the aesthetics of early twentieth-century Modernism. The work of art was not an attempt to represent something other than itself, but something done. In painting, colour, for example, was not a means of imitation but a language of expression. Art was action just as the theatrical performances of Kandinsky, Schoenberg and, later, the Futurists, are better described as events rather than dramas.

So far, under the useful generalizations of Modernism and the avant-garde I have allowed terms like Expressionism and Vorticism to pass unanalysed. Obviously, nothing like a full account of the various movements and styles within Modernism can be given here, but it is clearly necessary at some point to be a little more discriminating. Comprehensiveness would be defeated not only by complexity and the idiosyncrasies of individual artists but also by the sheer number of movements. The new self-consciousness about technique and its revolutionary consequences produced unprecedented variety, an explosion of sectarianism within a general revolutionary consensus only equalled by sixteenth-century Protestantism. If the languages of representation and artistic expression were no longer agreed there might, in principle, be any number of them, and it could seem an obligation to discover and explore them. Apart from the most obvious movements, Cubism, Futurism, Expressionism and Vorticism (predominantly located in France, Italy, Germany and England respectively), there were Fauvism, Orphism, Unanimism, Purism, Suprematism and many others. 'Isms' are an indicator of the avant-garde. Another, in Germany and Austria, is the word 'Secession', beginning with the Munich Secession in 1892; eventually, fissiparous tendencies being what they were, we have the Secession from the Secession, the Berlin 'New Secession' in 1911. The word Secession, and its prominence in Germany and Austria, marked, by antagonism, the continuing court and ministerial patronage of, and hence control over, opportunities for artists to exhibit their work, as well as the naturally oppositional relationship between the avant-garde and what we may call the craft guild of established artists, the opposition Wagner dramatized and tried to provide with a resolution in *Mastersingers*. Court control, almost a court monopoly, still prevailed in the theatre in capitals like Berlin, Munich and Vienna, just as in Dresden in Wagner's day, when, as *Kapellmeister* he was a court employee in 1848 (see the Prologue). This is the significance of the theatrical groups calling themselves the Free Stage or Free People's Stage (*Freie Volksbühne*) in these cities in the 1900s.

In the avant-garde camaraderie these oppressive conditions encouraged, and in the necessity for collaboration in theatrical productions, there was a kind of counter-force to the fissiparous tendency that was a feature of early Modernism: the crossing over of interests from one art to another (Schoenberg's painting, for example) and collaboration in the production of something like the Wagnerian total art-work (*Gesamtkunstwerk*). The Wagnerian conception was one inheritance here but also relevant was the Baudelairean and Symbolist conception of synaesthesia: correspondences between the perceptions of the different senses, epitomized in the title of Kandinsky's theatrical production, *The Yellow Sound*. The supreme example for the period of something like the total art-work was the pre-war performances of the Russian Ballet under Sergei Diahgilev; the most obvious example is the 'Prélude à l'après-midi d'un faune', from a sonnet by Mallarmé, scored by Debussy, designed by Bakst and danced by Nijinsky. The mixture of genres characteristic of Modernism, as well as the Dionysiac, demotic and primitivist interests of its artists, resulted in the incorporation in pictures and in some cases in drama of elements from circus, carnival and cabaret, as well as from African and Pacific sculpture.

Not all 'isms' shared the self-consciousness of the Futurists or announced themselves with manifestos or professed to share a comprehensive ideology. Some, like German Expressionism, emerged gradually in various centres and the unifying label was applied retrospectively. Cubism in France developed essentially without histrionics, within a technique of painting taking its starting-point in Post-Impressionism, particularly the work of Paul Cézanne (1839–1906), though it later found an impresario in the poet Guillaume Apollinaire (1880–1918), while Schoenberg seems to have developed atonality half-reluctantly, by pursuing an inner logic of musical development. The various movements possessed different degrees of internal coherence, German Expressionism being perhaps the most protean. It was not so much a movement as a loose ensemble of shifting, overlapping, splitting and re-forming associations of artists, together with a number of poets, to whom the name was applied to indicate the presence of something like a common style and conception of art: a characteristic violence of colour and brush strokes laid across a surface with little or no illusion of depth; in poetry and drama a broken, stutteringly declamatory manner, with sharp, incongruous collisions of images, evoking the phantasmagoria of the freely associating consciousness – the latter, of course, characteristic of Modernism generally.

There is in Expressionism a general inclination to the grotesque and macabre which is part of the German tradition; some of its effects are anticipated in Romantics like Jean Paul Richter and E. T. A. Hoffmann. It is an art adapted to the expression of extreme states of the human condition; in drama it veers characteristically towards allegory, in painting to apocalyptic themes and religious imagery, most particularly to the life and sufferings of Christ. Faith and suffering were becoming fashionable themes in Germany in these years. A series of translations of Dostoevsky's novels began publication in 1907 and the writings of Søren Kierkegaard (1813–55) began to attract attention after more than half a century of neglect. Kokoschka and Kandinsky painted religious subjects and so, insistently, did Emil Nolde (1867–1956). The intellectual fathers of Expressionism include Nietzsche, Mach and Bergson; in poetry there is Rimbaud, who was translated into German in 1907; in painting there were again the Post-Impressionists, but in this case chiefly Paul Gauguin (1848–1903), and above all Vincent van Gogh (1853–90) and the Norwegian Edvard Munch (1863–1944).

In German Expressionism there is none of the urban flippancy sometimes apparent in Modernism in France, Italy and Austria. The city, though sometimes explored, tends to be a place of terror and alienation rather than a source of energy and exhilaration. Nature was used by the Expressionists not, of course, for imitation but as an inspiration and point of departure. In some of their pronouncements there are strong echoes of a traditional Romantic ambition to enter into the inner life of things, to touch its essential being. The painting was indeed something done or, if one prefers, 'said', not an imitation, but might it not also be a kind of reaching out to something beyond the artist's self. The German language already had a well-used and ample mystical and metaphysical vocabulary for this, which we have encountered earlier in Chapter 1: the painter Franz Marc (1880–1916), who was killed at Verdun, spoke of 'a pantheistic sympathy' and 'the rhythm that beats in all things'. Marc struggled with the contradictions but it took more than a new aesthetic, proclaiming that the work of art expresses nothing but itself, to stifle the national bent for a pantheist metaphysics, just as the latter had infused and overcome the scientific materialism of the 1850s and 1860s (Chapter 1, above).

It is not only in Germany, however, that we find echoes of a metaphysical or epistemological monism, for which one source may be Ernst Mach

(Chapter 1) and the philosophical and literary dissolution of the concept of the self (Chapter 4). It is present also in the Futurists, in their aspiration to 're-enter life', to abolish the distancing effect of mere representation and to grasp and contain not just optical images but the total experience. One Futurist recommendation, in pursuit of the abolition of what they called 'the literary I', was the eradication of pronouns and the use only of infinitives, producing a prose of pure occurrence in which subject and object would be confounded and tenses eliminated. Simultaneity was a central preoccupation of almost all Modernism. It was this that prompted the adoption of varying perspectives in Cubism within a single painting, and more generally substituted juxtaposition for narrative sequence, thereby making space rather than time the dominant dimension, and making painting rather than literature the dominant art. Instead of 'literary' paintings there were now, as it were, poems made of collages or images: 'Imagist' in the term coined by Ezra Pound, baptizing another 'ism'. Apollinaire and the Futurists also experimented with placing lines and phrases of poems in different spatial configurations on the page so that the poem was seen like a picture, not read serially.

It was the Futurists who made or at least advocated the most strenuous attempts to dissolve the boundaries between the self and the experienced world. Of course there was a difference from traditional Romantic pantheism. The Romantic sought or experienced unity with Nature, like Childe Harold in the Alps: 'Are not the mountains, waves, and skies, a part / Of me and of my soul, as I of them?' (Byron, *Childe Harold's Pilgrimage* iii, lxxv). The Futurist sought union with the modern city, with technological civilization and above all with the machine. Man, transcending himself, would become a machine. Marinetti wrote in 1912, 'we must prepare for the imminent and inevitable identification of men with motors'. There is a painting by the Futurist Umberto Boccioni (1882–1916), one of a number of urban panoramas by him, significantly entitled *The City Invades the House* (1911), which is exactly what it does, abolishing the distinction between inner and outer, private and public space. The new pantheism centred on the god-in-the-machine aspired, if we take its spokesmen literally, not merely to represent and celebrate but to fuse with the roar and dazzle of modern technological life. Marinetti spoke almost religiously of daubing oneself with industrial effluent and breathing in the exhalations of blast furnaces; devotional exercises are traditionally uncomfortable and even humiliating. Technology had long figured as the archetypal form of human alienation; the Futurists' solution was simple: complete the alienation and become whole again by identifying with it in Dionysian rapture. The modern world-soul was the dynamism, the rhythms, of the machine.

In attempting to extract a core of Modernist ideas from the variations in their expression and to pass at least some tentative judgement on their coherence one is tantalized by an insistent polarity. It is one which will naturally occur to anyone who looks at a Cubist picture alongside an Expressionist one, a Braque, say, compared with a Kokoschka. It is not, we can note at once, the distinction between representation and non-representation; virtually all Modernist painting before the First World War retained some hold on representation, though it was employed in different ways, rather than reaching pure abstraction, and none of it, by definition, aimed at pure illusion. It is more like the polarity pointed to by T. S. Eliot when, partisanly, he wrote in 'Tradition and the Individual Talent' (1919) that poetry 'is not the expression of personality, but an escape from personality'. There is a remote affinity here to the distinction between classic and Romantic but a more useful comparision is with the antithesis in aesthetics, traditional since the eighteenth century, which is represented by Nietszche in *The Birth of Tragedy* as the Apollonian and the Dionysiac (Chapter 5), standing respectively for aesthetic Form and for liberated elemental energy. Here, not to take on board too much historical and philosophical baggage, we might more unpretendingly speak of it as the polarity of cold and hot. There is also an allied but unfortunately not identical distinction, between an art of reduction and an art of plenitude (though individual artists, of course, may practise both).

In Cubism as it emerged after 1907 we seem to have an extreme example of the will to Form, not completely abstract but reductionist, analytic and austere in its sacrifice not only of painterly narrative and its attendant emotions but also, virtually, of colour. Expressionism, of course, characteristically used colour as a language of emotion; often of extreme emotion and of violent, starkly juxtaposed colour. Its swirling forms, echoing van Gogh, often suggest the action of a kind of creative hurricane. Kokoschka's poster for his play *Murder, Hope of Women* used colour and contortion (not the Cubist rearrangement) of the human figure with what one hopes is an unsurpassable violence: the male seems to have been not merely murdered but flayed. But enough has perhaps been said of Expressionism; we need to attend a little further to Form.

Again the master-concept is quite familiar: it is that of the work of art as end-in-itself, made so by its formal qualities, which is one aspect of nineteenth-century aestheticism from Flaubert onwards, just as, on the

other hand, the aspiration to plenitude, to contain modern life, can be seen
as a Whitmanesque, demotic modification of the nineteenth-century
aesthete's historicist desire to make himself a microcosm of the world's
cultural experience, with the examples usually aligned with a scrupulous
regard for chronology. (George Moore's eclectic bric-a-brac, which we
glanced at in Chapter 5, was more nearly premonitory of Modernism. But
to return to Form. Flaubert's wish to write a novel about nothing antici-
pates by half a century Apollinaire's declaration that the subject of a work
of art no longer matters. Such formalism, as Nietzsche saw, is locked in an
antithetical yet intelligible relation to the intensity of awareness of flux,
incoherence, chaos, just as Flaubert's austerity needed the psychological
relief of immersion into the overheated gorgeousness of his *Salammbô*.

Language and art had traditionally been thought of as mediations between subjective consciousness and the world. But if the mediations were
seen as delusive and their 'languages' as crumbled away, then the inner and
outer worlds must be either more violently and chaotically brought together
or else they must be seen as radically disjoined. This seems to be the key to
two major, contrasting kinds of Modernism; we may also call them exoteric
and esoteric. The first kind of response we have been considering was to
attempt to project consciousness outwards into the world-flux, treating
the boundaries between the self and the world as dissolved in a perceptual
monism, as in Mach's philosophy. Boccioni's picture cited above is a good
example. The other, however, pointed to a self-created world of pure form
and logical coherence which, as again in Mach's philosophy, was recognized
for what it was, namely artifice, and was redeemed by that awareness
from the bad faith of assuming it to represent the world. Such artifices, logic,
mathematics, scientific theories, are coherent and intelligible because as
human creations they can be constructed to conform to the internal rules
of their organization and hence be given a man-made objectivity. If coherence could not be found in the chaos of raw experience it could be embodied
in pure form. In the reinvigorated positivism which emerged after the war
as the 'Vienna Circle' (whose intellectual foundations were being laid in
the pre-war period) with its characteristic abhorrence of rhetoric, and its
insistence on precision, logic and mathematics were seen as structures
of non-referential tautologies.

It does not seem far-fetched – the young Ludwig Wittgenstein was
involved in both – to see this as in some respects an analogue for the emergence in Vienna from the late 1890s, and also in Germany, of the Modern
movement in architecture. Experience is incoherent and formless, but

some human creations – geometry, engineering and other forms of technology, and architecture, as well as the more abstract ones mentioned above – could be seen as an alternative, a contrast, to the messiness of human existence. So, just as one might attempt to render raw experience in an art of derangement, of incongruous juxtapositions and collisions of images, of fragmentary allusions and odd assimilations and transitions, akin to dream-logic, so one might on the other hand create an architecture of pure form by stripping away all historical allusion, all striving for impressiveness, status or nostalgia, and allowing the function of the building and its technological means and structural imperatives to speak for themselves.

Futurism, in particular, may initially seem to resist assimilation to the suggested polarization of Modernism, into Dionysiac immersion in experience on the one hand, escape into the objectivity of artifice on the other, though Expressionism, Cubism and architectural Modernism seem to fit it rather well. Rhetorically, clearly, Futurism lies at the omni-assimilative, superheated end of the spectrum, yet it took the machine as its aesthetic paradigm and preached a dehumanized future. But the latter is partly misleading. The machine it worshipped was not just a precision tool, an embodied function, but a total sensuous experience: hot, smelly, and above all fast. As Futurism sought to dehumanize human beings it simultaneously anthropomorphized or bestialized the machine; the 'famished roar' of motor cars, for example, as though cars made more noise when needing petrol. Futurism is recognizably a roughneck neo-Romanticism with mechanical toys, not a reductionist purism.

What we have been pointing to in the Modern movement in architecture is more like a psychological interpretation of its imperatives than the early history of the movement. Its historical antecedents, as Nicolaus Pevsner showed in a classic study (*Pioneers of the Modern Movement*, 1936; later editions were entitled *Pioneers of Modern Design: from William Morris to Gropius*), lay in ideas of Ruskin and the innovatory English Arts and Crafts Movement begun by William Morris, particularly their adherence to the idea of the fitness of form to function as a requirement of 'honesty' in design. The opening shots in the campaign for Modern architecture, notably the book of that title published in 1895 by the Viennese architect Otto Wagner (1841–1918), were, like Futurism, radically anti-historicist. The only possible point of departure for Modern architecture, Wagner argued, was modern life, which, being unprecedented, required a unique style of its own. Architectural principles must be fundamentally rethought and the first step must be to throw off all allegiance to the past.

Another Viennese figure, Adolf Loos (1870–1933), who had lived in Chicago, then probably the most architecturally innovative of the world's cities, and whose own designs were more original than Wagner's, went further. He proclaimed in his adherence to the master-concept of function, that the concept of style was pernicious and must be abandoned altogether; architecture was not 'art' and buildings must manifest their structural principles. There is sometimes in the advocacy of the new architecture a suggestion of the contemporary enthusiasm for *Lebensreform*, considered in earlier chapters, which looked to the creation of the 'new man' (and woman) through preferred forms of 'hygiene', and which also gave the world Jaeger (woollen) suits, nudism and versions of eugenics. Absence of ornamentation and structural honesty in building could also be seen as a form of hygiene; it was, according to Loos, a sign of 'spiritual strength'. Germany, too, played a part in the creation of architectural Modernism, notably in the work of Hermann Muthesius (1861–1927) and Peter Behrens (1868–1940). The German Crafts Association (*Deutscher Werkbund*), forerunner of the post-war *Bauhaus*, was founded in 1907 to foster collaboration and Modernist principles in building and design, and the Austrian *Werkbund* was established three years later.

It would be an oversimplification to take the functionalist rhetoric of the pioneers of architectural Modernism simply at face value, ignoring the psychological and cultural satisfactions offered at the time by the idea of a dehumanized architecture of pure structural form. (We cannot know what functions a house is to have until we have decided what functions human beings are to have.) There is a romanticization of technology and its 'requirements' (in this rhetoric technology sets the conditions, human beings conform to them, as in a technological version of determinist Marxism). The identification of the human subject with the means he employs is testified to by Pevsner in his history, which is also a celebration: 'The architect, to represent this century of ours, must be . . . cold to keep in command of mechanized production, cold to design for the satisfaction of anonymous clients'. Modern architecture, it seems, required a new (cold) man to create it as well as being designed for new (anonymous) men.

Pevsner's reference to representing 'this century of ours' is a reminder, too, that alongside the supposed functional imperative and the radical anti-historicism there was, in the other sense, a profoundly historicist mentality at work. The necessity for the Modern style was supposedly imposed by history, by the historical moment. In other fields modernity was seen in deliberately jumbled and intercut literary genres; authors experimented with multiple personae and a poem or a symphony (notably those of Gustav Mahler, 1860–1911) might contain discordant allusions and emotional registers; artists deployed incongruous techniques of representation in the same work. In architecture, however, it was decreed that there was to be one and only one Modern architectural style because that was what the age required. In his other classic work, *An Outline of European Architecture* (1943), Pevsner ruminated, in his conclusion to what is in a very proper sense a 'grand' narrative, whether Modernism was its final closure. It seems not; Post-modernism in architecture, unlike literature, seems genuinely a break with the immediate past. It can be said, however, that now that Soviet Communism has collapsed in Eastern Europe, the most visible, indeed tangible, residue of all the great nineteenth-century grand historical narratives of progress is Modern (not Post-modern) architecture; set, abidingly, in concrete.

The most obvious disruption of any such optimistic or utopian narrative of progress was, of course, the Great War, just as the Revolutions of 1848–9 had been at the beginning of our period. Initially the war was, as is well known, hailed almost universally with enthusiasm; sometimes as a new beginning, the long-awaited renewal of European civilization or, not only by the Futurists, as 'the world's only hygiene'. Few historians, writers, philosophers, artists stood, at the outset of war, aside from the general exalted partisanship, though some were already disillusioned (or dead) within months or even weeks. Initially there seemed to be spiritual elevation in it enough for all. Theorists and others of a volkish bent rejoiced in the sudden unanimity of national feeling and purpose, so elusive in peacetime: the coming together of peoples and rulers and of classes, the *union sacrée* in France, the *Burgfrieden* (literally 'Fortress-peace') in Germany; Britain seems to have coined no special term but the sentiment was the same. Nietzscheans welcomed struggle and the opportunity for the exercise of heroic will; Bergsonians exuded *élan*, not least, unfortunately, General Ferdinand Foch of the French Army High Command; Futurists, loving the machine, destruction and violence, repined that Italy was not in the war and campaigned – a training-ground for post-war Fascism – for intervention, which was achieved in 1915. German defenders of culture, notably Thomas Mann, announced that the war was one against Western materialism; Christians, and others, sought self-sacrifice and self-transcendence. Among those who after the war continued to exalt the warrior ethic were Marinetti, who was wounded and decorated, and the 'decadent' poet, wartime aviator and nationalist adventurer Gabriele D'Annunzio (1863–1938); both vied unsuccessfully with Mussolini for the leadership of Fascism.

An extreme avant-garde individualism and self-identification in terms of modernity and an atavistic nationalism seem at first sight to form an antithesis as stark as can be imagined. But this needs substantial qualification. In the yearning for Dionysiac energy, and in a willed annihilation of self which could seem no more than an enthusiastic acceptance of the typical Modernist dissolution of the stable ego, the antithesis becomes blurred. In the Futurist determination, in particular, to break down the barriers between the 'I' and the world and 'enter life' there was a bridge to identification with supposedly new forms of collective existence. It was like Maurice Barrès's self-surrender to a collective French identity which we saw in Chapter 3 except that Barrès's idea of the latter was located where a volkish thinker, by definition, must find it: above all in the peasantry and traditional rural life.

Just as the intellectual currents of the time flowed in 1914 towards the idea of war, so, though there were now strong counter-currents of disillusionment, horror and pacifism, they flowed in the post-war world in some cases to Bolshevism but also to Fascism or French and German ultranationalism. So long as the enemy was defined as bourgeois-liberal decadence and materialism and the values claimed were expressed in such abstractions as 'dynamism', 'life', 'renewal', 'youth' and, indeed, 'revolution', it was not difficult for members of the intellectual avant-garde to see in these movements a macrocosm of their own. Totalitarian regimes, though they continued to affect this Nietzschean-sounding rhetoric, once established embraced for obvious reasons the useful virtues of order, discipline and obedience. Fascism and Nazism readopted some traditional institutions and their values, such as the family (volkishness prevailing over Nietzscheanism), though they remained faithful to their love-affair with technology. Hence the Third Reich, like the Soviet Union, repudiated the artistic avant-garde as a symptom of decadence or, in the phrase the Nazis liked even better, following the Zionist writer Max Nordau, 'degeneration'.

One thing the war had been widely expected to produce was a new cultural epoch. Yet though, as a collective experience, it was far more shattering, more apocalyptic, than could have been imagined, it did not. The extraordinary years 1907–12 had done their work too thoroughly for that; had the war been delayed by a decade, cultural historians would now no doubt be happy to find in it an explanation for such a dramatic cultural transformation. One noteworthy avant-garde movement, Dada, the parent of Surrealism, emerged during the war in neutral Zurich. But essentially, with some modifications in its expressive languages, the post-war avant-garde was still recognizably the pre-war one. In a sense the latter is still ours. Experiment has become the norm; its different idioms are to pre-war Modernism what schools of art in the seventeenth, eighteenth and nineteenth centuries had been to the mimetic techniques established at the Renaissance: essentially variations. Post-modernism in literature, for all the critical volubility expended on it, looks more like a gloss on Modernism than its historical grave-digger. Modernism is our tradition.

# Select Bibliography

Primary sources have been cited in the text. This bibliography of secondary works is a selective one, determined chiefly by the extent of my own debts, which I am glad to be able to acknowledge here, and by what seemed most likely to be useful to the reader. Where a work is cited more than once I cite it first with full bibliographical details and have subsequently given only the author and short title, followed by an indication in parentheses under which chapter the fuller citation may be found. I have cited foreign works only in translation.

## Prologue

The classic essay from which I have borrowed part of the title is L. B. Namier, *1848: The Revolution of the Intellectuals* (Oxford, 1971). On the period generally E. J. Hobsbawm, *The Age of Revolution, 1789–1848* (London, 1977) is useful, as on the themes of the Prologue is J. H. Talmon, *Political Messianism: The Romantic Phase* (London, 1960). On Wagner see Ernest Newman's classic biography, *The Life of Richard Wagner* (4 vols, Cambridge, 1976); also Peter Burbidge and Richard Sutton (eds), *The Wagner Companion* (London, 1979), Ronald Taylor, *Richard Wagner: His Life, Art and Thought* (London, 1979) and Bryan Magee, *Aspects of Wagner* (rev. edn, Oxford, 1988). Aileen Kelly's impressive study of Bakunin, *Mikhail Bakunin* (New Haven and London, 1987), is a critical portrait of a complex character. See also Franco Venturi, *Roots of Revolution: A History of the Populist and Socialist Movements in Nineteenth-century Russia* (New York, 1966), on his role in the Russian terrorist and populist tradition, and James Joll, *The Anarchists* (London, 1964). The bibliography on Marx is, of course, immense; particularly relevant here is David McLellan's *Karl Marx: A Biography* (3rd edn, London, 1995). For introductions to Hegel's and Marx's thought, see J. Plamenatz, *Man and Society: Political and Social Thought from Machiavelli to Marx* (3 vols, London and New York, 1992) and Iain Hampsher-Monk, *A History of Modern Political Thought* (Oxford and Cambridge, Mass., 1992). Isaiah Berlin, *Karl Marx* (2nd edn, Oxford, 1948) is still a useful introduction. For an introduction to Feuerbach, see Eugene Kamenka, *The Philosophy of Ludwig Feuerbach* (London, 1970). On Herzen there is Martin Malia, *Alexander Herzen*

*and the Birth of Russian Socialism 1812–1855* (New York, 1971) and Edward
Acton, *Alexander Herzen and the Role of the Intellectual Revolutionary*
(Cambridge, 1979); Acton is critical of Malia's view that Herzen was already
disillusioned with the West and intellectually turning back towards Russia
even before the July Revolution. See also Isaiah Berlin, 'Herzen and his Memoirs', in his *Against the Current: Essays in the History of Ideas* (Oxford, 1981);
and his *Russian Thinkers* (London, 1978). E. H. Carr's *The Romantic Exiles:
A Nineteenth-century Portrait Gallery* (London, 1933) is still valuable and very
readable. For Turgenev see Leonard Schapiro, *Turgenev: His Life and Times*
(Oxford, 1978). On Germany see E. M. Butler, *The Saint-Simonian Religion in
Germany: A Study of the Young Germany Movement* (Cambridge, 1929) and for
other aspects of Saint-Simonian influence see Richard Pankhurst, *The Saint-
Simonians, Mill and Carlyle: A Preface to Modern Thought* (London, 1957). Edmund
Wilson, *To the Finland Station* (London, 1972) is still well worth reading on
these topics. The utopian temper is well discussed in Frank E. Manuel, *The
Prophets of Paris* (New York, 1962). See also Jack Hayward, *After the French
Revolution: Six Critics of Democracy and Nationalism* (London, 1991). For Mazzini
and Italy see H. Hearder, *Italy in the Age of the Risorgimento* (London, 1983),
Denis Mack Smith, *Mazzini* (New Haven and London, 1994) and E. E. Y. Hales,
*Mazzini and the Secret Societies: The Making of a Myth* (London, 1956). On
George Sand, see Curtis Cate, *George Sand: A Biography* (London, 1975) and
Patricia Thomson, *George Sand and the Victorians: Her Influence and Reputation
in Nineteenth-century England* (London, 1977). For reactions to the revolution
see particularly E. Kamenka and F. B. Smith (eds), *Intellectuals and Revolution:
Socialism and the Experience of 1848* (London, 1979). On Tocqueville generally,
see Larry Siedentop, *Tocqueville* (Oxford, 1994). For Flaubert and Baudelaire
I have drawn on Philip Spencer, *Flaubert: A Biography* (London, 1952), Victor
Brombert, *The Novels of Flaubert* (Princeton, 1966), and *The Hidden Reader:
Stendhal, Balzac, Hugo, Baudelaire, Flaubert* (Cambridge, Mass., 1988) and
F. W. J. Hennings, *Baudelaire the Damned* (London, 1982) and Lois Boe Hyslop,
*Baudelaire* (New Haven and London, 1980). On Gobineau see Michael Biddiss,
*Father of Racist Ideology: The Social and Political Thought of Count Gobineau*
(London, 1970). For 'Bohemianism' see César Grana, *Bohemian versus Bourgeois*
(New York, 1964). Stefan Collini, *Arnold* (Oxford, 1988) is an excellent introduc-
tion. On Clough see Katherine Chorley, *Arthur Hugh Clough: The Uncommitted
Mind* (Oxford, 1962). For Froude see Waldo Hilary Dunn, *James Anthony Froude:
A Biography* (2 vols, Oxford, 1961 and 1963), much of which is in fact
Froude's autobiography. There is a large bibliography on the Pre-Raphaelites
and on Ruskin. William Gaunt, *The Pre-Raphaelite Tragedy* (London, 1965)
and George P. Landow, *Ruskin* (Oxford, 1985) are useful introductions. For
Schopenhauer see Bryan Magee, *The Philosophy of Schopenhauer* (Oxford, 1983)
and D. W. Hamlyn, *Schopenhauer* (London, 1980).

## Chapter 1

Apart from the works on Russian intellectual life cited above (Prologue), see also, for the first section, Ronald Hingley, *Nihilists: Russian Radicals and Revolutionaries in the Age of Alexander II (1855–81)* (London, 1967). For section 2 of this chapter I am heavily indebted to Yehuda Elkoma, *The Discovery of the Conservation of Energy* (London, 1974) and Frederick Gregory, *Scientific Materialism in Nineteenth Century Germany* (Dordrecht, 1977) and am glad to have the opportunity of acknowledging my obligation to them. As a reference work for general biology I have used chiefly W. Coleman, *Biology in the Nineteenth Century* (Cambridge, 1977). I am also indebted to R. M. Young, *Mind, Brain and Adaptation in the Nineteenth-Century* (Oxford, 1970). Roger Smith, *The Fontana History of the Human Sciences* (London, 1997) is useful. The bibliography on Darwin and Darwinism is immense; I have concentrated on the reception of Darwinism. See particularly Michael Ruse, *The Darwinian Revolution* (Chicago and London, 1979), Thomas F. Glick (ed.), *The Comparative Reception of Darwinism* (Chicago, 1988) and Alfred Kelly, *The Descent of Darwin: The Popularization of Darwinism in Germany 1860–1914* (Chapel Hill, 1981). Daniel Gasman, *The Scientific Origins of National Socialism: Social Darwinism in Ernst Haeckel and the German Monist League* (London and New York, 1971) has a tendentious title and has been criticized for exaggerating the right-wing character of the Monist League, but is in a number of ways useful. Works on Herbert Spencer have tended to focus on his social and political thought. The most generally helpful is J. D. Y. Peel, *Herbert Spencer: The Evolution of a Sociologist* (London, 1971). For science, religion and materialism in England see Frank Miller Turner, *Between Science and Religion: The Reaction to Scientific Naturalism in Late Victorian England* (New Haven, 1974) and the same author's *Contesting Cultural Authority: Essays in Victorian Intellectual Life* (Cambridge, 1993). Susan Budd, *Varieties of Unbelief: Atheists and Agnostics in English Society 1850–1960* (London, 1997) is also useful. For France see Reno Virtanen, *Claud Bernard and his Place in the History of Ideas* (Lincoln, Neb., 1960), H. W. Wardman, *Ernest Renan: A Critical Biography* (London, 1974) and Leo Weinstein, *Hippolyte Taine* (New York, 1972). Unfortunately, Taine's *Vie et correspondance* (4 vols, Paris, 1902–7) has not been translated. On Naturalism in literature see Lilian R. Furst and P. N. Skrine, *Naturalism* (London, 1978) and Roland N. Stromberg, *Realism, Naturalism and Symbolism: Modes of Thought and Expression in Europe 1848–1914* (London, 1968). For conceptual changes in physics see Theodore M. Porter, 'The Death of the Object: Fin de siècle Philosophy of Physics', in Dorothy Ross (ed.), *Modernist Impulses in the Human Sciences 1870–1930* (Baltimore and London, 1994). Antonio Aliotta, *The Idealist Reaction against Science* (1912, English trans. London, 1914) and Karl Pearson, *The Grammar of Science* (1892, 3rd edn London, 1911), though falling within the period and therefore primary sources, are also useful as commentary on contemporary intellectual developments. For the English 'crisis of faith' and late Victorian cosmic gloom Walter Houghton, *The Victorian Frame of Mind* (New Haven, 1963) and Jerome Buckley, *The Triumph of Time: History, Progress and Decadence* (London, 1967) remain useful.

## Chapter 2

On comparative anatomy, the politics of museum curatorship and transformism in the tradition of *Naturphilosophie*, see Nicolaas A. Rupke, *Richard Owen: Victorian Naturalist* (New Haven and London, 1994). For evolutionism in archaeology see particularly M. W. Thompson, *General Pitt-Rivers: Evolution and Archaeology in the Nineteenth Century* (Bradford-on-Avon, Wilts., 1977). George Stocking's *Victorian Anthropology* (New York and London, 1987) is a magisterial study. Peel, *Herbert Spencer* (cited in Chapter 1) is relevant again here. For Durkheim see particularly Steven Lukes, *Emile Durkheim, His Life and Work: An Historical and Critical Study* (London, 1975), and for Frazer Robert Ackerman, *J. G. Frazer: His Life and Work* (Cambridge, 1987). See again Wardman, *Renan* and Weinstein, *Taine* (Chapter 1). The latter has a good account of Taine's theory of cultural determinism. For the origins of the German tradition of cultural studies see Isaiah Berlin, *Vico and Herder: Two Studies in the History of Ideas* (London, 1976), Georg Iggers, *The German Conception of History: The National Tradition of Historical Thought from Herder to the Present* (Middletown, Conn., 1968) and Andrew Lees, *Revolution and Reflection: Intellectual Change in Germany during the 1850s* (The Hague, 1974). On *Völkerpsychologie*, etc. I am particularly indebted to Woodruff D. Smith, *Politics and the Science of Culture in Germany 1840–1920* (Oxford, 1991). On Dilthey see H. Stuart Hughes, *Consciousness and Society: The Reorientation of European Social Thought 1890–1930* (London, 1959) and J. Owenby, *Dilthey and the Narrative of History* (Ithaca, NY and London, 1994). On Social Darwinism see particularly Mike Hawkins, *Social Darwinism in English and American Thought 1860–1945* (Cambridge, 1997), Linda L. Clark, *Social Darwinism in France* (Alabama, 1984), Greta Jones, *Social Darwinism and English Thought: The Interaction between Biological and Social Theory* (Brighton, 1980), M. Banton (ed.), *Darwinism and the Study of Society* (London, 1961), D. P. Crook, *Benjamin Kidd: Portrait of a Social Darwinist* (Cambridge, 1984) and by the same author *Darwinism, War and History: The Debate over the Biology of War from the Origin of Species to the First World War* (Cambridge, 1994). On ideas of degeneration and mass irrationality I have found particularly valuable Robert A. Nye, *Crime, Madness and Politics in Modern France: The Medical Concept of National Decline* (Princeton, 1974) and the same author's *The Origins of Crowd Psychology: Gustave le Bon and the Crisis of Mass Democracy in the Third Republic* (London, 1975). See also K. W. Swart, *The Sense of Decadence in Nineteenth-Century France* (The Hague, 1964), Daniel Pick, *Faces of Degeneration: A European Disorder 1848–1914* (Cambridge, 1989), J. E. Chamberlin and S. L. Gilman, *Degeneration: The Dark Side of Progress* (New York, 1985), Andrew Lees (ed.), *Cities Perceived: Urban Society in European and American Thought 1820–1940* (New York, 1985) and Susannah Barrows, *Distorting Mirrors: Visions of The Crowd in Late Nineteenth-century France* (New Haven, 1981). On Eugenics see Geoffrey Searle, *Eugenics and Politics in Britain, 1900–1914* (Leyden, 1976), Bernard Semmel, *Imperialism and Social Reform* (London, 1964) and Paul Weindling, *Health, Race and German Politics between*

*Unification and Nazism, 1870–1945* (Cambridge, 1989). Gasman, *Scientific Origins* (Chapter 1) and Clark, *Social Darwinism in France* (above) are also relevant here. For issues of Aryanism and race see particularly Biddiss, *Father of Racist Ideology* (Chapter 1), Leon Poliakov, *The Aryan Myth: A History of Racist and Nationalist Ideas in Europe* (trans. E. Howard, London, 1974), George Stocking, *Race, Culture and Evolution* (New York, 1968) and Geoffrey G. Field, *Evangelist of Race: The Germanic Vision of Houston Stewart Chamberlain* (New York, 1981).

## Chapter 3

A good general study of the social thought of the period can be found in Geoffrey Hawthorn, *Enlightenment and Despair: A History of Sociology* (Cambridge, 1976). A study with a particular emphasis on the concept of community is R. A. Nisbet, *The Sociological Tradition* (New York, 1962). For the earlier history of political economy see Donald Winch, *Riches and Poverty: The Intellectual History of Political Economy in Britain, 1750–1834* (Cambridge, 1996). On neo-medievalist social thought in England see Alice Chandler, *A Dream of Order: The Medieval Ideal in Nineteenth-century English Literature* (London, 1971). See again Plamenatz and Hampsher-Monk on Marx (Preface). For Maine see G. A. Feaver, *From Status to Contract: A Biography of Sir Henry Maine 1922–1888* (London, 1969) and Alan Diamond (ed.), *The Victorian Achievement of Sir Henry Maine: A Centennial Reappraisal* (Cambridge, 1991). On the *Mark* community and an historical economics see Stefan Collini, Donald Winch and John Burrow, *That Noble Science of Politics: A Study in Nineteenth-century Intellectual History* (Cambridge, 1983), Chs. 7 and 8. For the *mir* in Russian thought and Slavophilism see Richard Hare, *Pioneers of Russian Social Thought* (rev. edn, New York, 1964), Andrezej Walicki, *The Slavophile Controversy: The History of Conservative Utopia in Nineteenth-century Russian Thought* (Oxford, 1975) and Leonard Schapiro, *Rationalism and Nationalism in Nineteenth-century Russian Political Thought* (New Haven and London, 1967). On guilds see particularly Anthony Black, *Guilds and Guild Society in European Political Thought from the Twelfth Century to the Present* (London, 1984). For Pluralism see Rodney Barker, *Political Ideas in Modern Britain* (London, 1978) ch. 4. On Bernstein's Revisionism see Manfred B. Steger, *The Quest for Evolutionary Socialism: Edward Bernstein and Social Democracy* (Cambridge, 1997). For French social and political thought R. Soltau, *French Political Thought in the Nineteenth Century* (London, 1931) is still useful. See also Hayward, *After the French Revolution* (cited in Prologue), Sandford Elwitt, *The Third Republic Defended: Bourgeois Reform in France 1880–1914* (Baton Rouge and London, 1986), W. Logue, *From Philosophy to Sociology: The Evolution of French Liberalism 1870–1914* (Illinois, 1983), E. Wallwork, *Durkheim: Morality and Milieu* (Cambridge, Mass., 1972), Michael Z. Brooke, *Le Play, Engineer and Social Scientist: The Life and Work of Frédéric Le Play* (London, 1970) and generally, R. Gildea, *The Third Republic from 1870 to 1914* (London, 1988).

For English Idealist political ideas and the New Liberalism see Melvin Richter, *The Politics of Conscience: T. H. Green and his Age* (London, 1964), Sandra den Otter, *British Idealism and Social Explanation: A Study in Late-Victorian Thought* (Oxford, 1996), Peter Clarke, *Liberals and Social Democrats* (Cambridge, 1978), Stefan Collini, *Liberalism and Sociology: L. T. Hobhouse and Political Argument in England, 1880–1914* (Cambridge, 1979) and Michael Freeden, *The New Liberalism: An Ideology of Social Reform* (Oxford, 1986). Nationalism and the state in Germany are discussed in H. Stuart Hughes, *Consciousness and Society* (cited Chapter 2 above), ch. 6 (v). For the fortunes of German liberalism see James J. Sheehan, *German Liberalism in the Nineteenth Century* (Chicago, 1978). Friedrich Meinecke's classic *Cosmopolitanism and the National State* (1903, trans. Robert B. Kimber, Princeton, 1970) is a primary text but is also valuable as commentary if allowance is made for its perspective. On Treitschke see A. Dorpalen, *Heinrich von Treitschke* (New Haven, 1957). H. W. C. Davis, *The Political Thought of Heinrich von Treitschke* (Westport, Conn., 1973) is predictably hostile given the date of its first appearance (1915) but can be used as an introduction. On volkish ideology and nationalism see Robert W. Logue, *Paul de Lagarde 1827–1891: A Study of Radical Conservatism in Germany* (Cambridge, Mass., 1962), Fritz Stern, *The Politics of Cultural Despair: A Study in the Rise of Germanic Ideology* (California, 1963),. George L. Mosse, *The Crisis of German Ideology: Intellectual Origins of the Third Reich* (London, 1964). For its implications for politics in the Wilhelmine period see L. E. Jones and J. N. Retallack, *Between Reform, Reaction and Resistance: Studies in the History of German Conservatism 1789–1945* (Providence, RI and Oxford, 1993), David Blackbourn and Geoff Eley, *Reshaping the German Right: Radical Nationalism and Political Change after Bismarck* (New Haven, 1980).

On the French nationalism of the radical Right see M. Curtis, *Three against the Third Republic: Sorel, Barrès and Maurras* (Westport, Conn., 1976), C. S. Doty, *From Cultural Revolution to Counter-Revolution: The Politics of Maurice Barrès* (Athens, Ohio, 1976), Robert Tombs (ed.), *Nationhood and Nationalism in France: From Boulangism to the Great War* (London and New York, 1991) and Zeev Sternhell, *Neither Right nor Left: Fascist Ideology in France* (trans. D. Maisel, Princeton, 1986). It is a pity that Sternhell's valuable though controversial *Maurice Barrès et le nationalisme français* (Paris, 1972), to which I owe much, remains untranslated.

For Sorel see particularly I. Horowitz, *Radicalism and the Revolt against Reason: The Social Thought of Georges Sorel* (London, 1961), J. R. Jennings, *Georges Sorel: The Character and Development of his Thought* (London, 1985) and John Stanley, *The Sociology of Virtue: The Political and Social Theories of Georges Sorel* (Berkeley and London, 1981). Joll (cited Preface) and Stuart Hughes can also be used.

For Michels see Robert A. Nye, *The Anti-Democratic Sources of Elite Theory: Pareto, Mosca, Michels* (London, 1977). German Sociology in this period is now well served with commentary, while the works on Max Weber listed below are only a small selection from a now extensive bibliography. See Arthur

Mitzman, *The Iron Cage: An Historical Interpretation of Max Weber* (New York, 1970) and the same author's *Sociology and Estrangement: Three Sociologists of Imperial Germany* (the other two are Tönnies and Sombart) (New York, 1975). Particularly useful is Harry Liebersohn, *Fate and Utopia in German Sociology 1870–1925* (Cambridge, Mass., 1988). The central account of Weber from the point of view of the present chapter is Wolfgang Mommsen, *Max Weber and German Politics 1890–1920* (trans. M. J. Sternberg, Chicago and London, 1984). There are valuable essays in Wolfgang J. Mommsen and Jürgen Osterhammel (eds), *Max Weber and his Contemporaries* (London, 1987) and Scott Lash and Sam Whimster (eds), *Max Weber: Rationality and Modernity* (London, 1987). See also W. Struve, *Elites against Democracy: Leadership Ideals in Bourgeois Political Thought in Germany 1890–1933* (Princeton, 1973) and E. Kamenka and M. Krygier, *Bureaucracy: The Career of a Concept* (London, 1979).

## Chapter 4

For the opening section see again the bibliography on Russian intellectual life given for the Preface and Chapter 3 above. On the idea of character in England and the legacy of Mill see Stefan Collini, *Public Moralists: Political Thought and Intellectual Life in Britain 1850–1930* (Oxford, 1991). Good introductions to Mill are William Thomas, *Mill* (Oxford, 1985) and Alan Ryan, *The Philosophy of John Stuart Mill* (Basingstoke, 1998). See also Plamenatz (cited Preface), vol. II, ch. 5, on Bentham and Mill, and Hampsher-Monk (cited Preface), chs. 7 and 8. J. W. Burrow, *Whigs and Liberals: Continuity and Change in English Nineteenth-century Political Thought* (Oxford, 1988), ch. 4, develops more fully some of the points made in this chapter. On feminist ideas Ursula Vogel, 'Rationalism and Romanticism: Two Strategies for Women's Liberation', in Judith Evans *et al.* (eds), *Feminism and Political Theory* (London and Beverley Hills, California, 1986) is particularly helpful. See also Tjitsk Akkerman and Siepo Stuurman (eds), *Perspectives on Feminist Political Thought in European History* (London, 1998), especially chs. 8–10, and Jennifer Waelti-Walters and Steven C. Hause, *Feminism of the Belle Epoque* (Lincoln, Neb. and London, 1995).

Nye, *Crowd Psychology* (cited Chapter 2 above) and Weinstein on Taine (cited Chapter 1) are relevant again here. On ideas of the unconscious, H. F. Ellenberger *The Discovery of the Unconscious: The History and Evolution of Dynamic Psychiatry* (New York, 1979) is slight and is limited by its determination to make all lines converge on Freud. Though distrust of Freud's accounts of his work have grown in recent years, the best short account of the early development of his psychoanalytic ideas is still perhaps his own in *Five Lectures on Psycho-Analysis* (trans. J. Strachey, London, 1957). The best short introduction to Bergson is Lesek Kolakowski, *Bergson* (Oxford, 1985).

## Chapter 5

The bibliography on Flaubert and Baudelaire cited in the Preface is relevant again here. So are Pick, *Faces of Degeneration* and Swart, *Sense of Decadence* (cited Chapter 3 above). To these may be added Jean Pierrot, *The Decadent Imagination 1880–1900* (Chicago, 1981), R. Gilman, *Decadence: The Strange Life of an Epithet* (London, 1979), E. C. Hansen, *Disaffection and Decadence: A Crisis in French Intellectual Thought 1848–1898* (Washington, DC, 1982) and A. E. Carter, *The Idea of Decadence in French Literature 1830–1900* (Toronto, 1958). For England see David De Laura, *Hebrew and Hellene in Victorian England: Newman, Arnold, Pater* (Austin, Texas, 1969). Holbrook Jackson, *The Eighteen Nineties: A Review of Art and Ideas at the Close of the Nineteenth Century* (new edn, London, 1927) is written with the intimacy of recollection. Bibliography on Nietzsche is very extensive. Peter Stern, *Nietzsche* (London, 1978) and Walter Kaufmann, *Nietzsche: Philosopher, Psychologist, Antichrist* (Princeton, 4th edn, 1974) are good introductions. On Nietzsche's influence see Steven E. Aschheim, *The Nietzsche Legacy in Germany 1890–1990* (Berkeley, 1992). The German Youth Movement is discussed in connection with Paul Langbehn in Stern, *Cultural Despair* and Mosse, *Crisis of German Ideology* (both cited in Chapter 3 above). The bibliography on Max Weber in Chapter 3 is again relevant here. On *Personlichkeit* and vocation I have found particularly valuable Harvey Goldman, *Max Weber and Thomas Mann: Calling and the Shaping of the Self* (Berkeley and Los Angeles, 1988). For Russia see again Kelly, *Bakunin*, Venturi, *Roots* and Joll, *The Anarchists* (Prologue), to which may be added A. Yarmolinsky, *Road to Revolution: A Century of Russian Radicalism* (New York, 1959).

## Chapter 6

On representations of Christ I am particularly grateful to Dr Cordula Grewe for private information. See also Norman Vance, *The Sinews of the Spirit: The Ideal of Christian Manliness in Victorian Literature and Religious Thought* (Cambridge, 1985). I am again grateful to Frederick Gregory, this time for his valuable *Nature Lost? Natural Science and German Theological Traditions of the Nineteenth Century* (Cambridge, Mass., and London, 1992). Wardman's *Renan* (cited Chapter 1 above) is relevant here. I here also used Claude Welch, *Protestant Thought in the Nineteenth Century* (3 vols, New Haven and London, 1985), Ninian Smart et al., *Nineteenth Century Religious Thought in the West* (3 vols, Cambridge, 1985), B. M. G. Reardon, *From Coleridge to Gorve: A Century of Religious Thought in Britain* (London, 1971), Alec R. Vidler, *The Church in the Age of Revolution* (London, 1961) and the same author's *A Century of Social Catholicism 1820–1920* (London, 1974), and Daniel L. Pals, *The Victorian 'Lives' of Jesus* (San Antonio, Texas, 1982). On the contrast with the intellectual climate in Britain in the first half of the nineteenth century I am indebted to

Boyd Hilton, *The Age of Atonement: The Influence of Evangelicalism on Social and Economic Thought, 1785–1865* (Oxford, 1988). The Wagner bibliography given in the Prologue is relevant again here, as is the literature on volkishness (Lougee, Stern, Mosse), cited for Chapter 3. See also Field on Chamberlain (*Evangelist of Race*, cited Chapter 2). For occultism in Germany and Guido von List I am wholly dependent on Nicholas Goodrick-Clarke, *The Occult Roots of Nazism* (London and New York, 1992). For Stefan George see discussions in Liebersohn, *Fate and Utopia* (cited Chapter 3) and Roy Pascal, *From Naturalism to Expressionism* (London, 1973). For the Stauffenberg connection see Michael Baigent and Richard Leigh, *Secret Germany: Claus von Stauffenberg and the Mystical Crusade against Hitler* (London, 1991). For France see Pierrot, *The Decadent Imagination* (cited Chapter 5), A. G. Lehmann, *The Symbolist Aesthetic in France 1885–1895* (2nd edn, Oxford, 1968) and Stromberg (cited Chapter 1 above); D. G. Charlton, *Secular Religions in France 1815–1870* (Oxford, 1963) is useful, and I am indebted to Richard Griffiths, *The Reactionary Revolution: The Catholic Revival in French Literature 1870–1914* (London, 1966). Stuart Hughes (cited Chapter 2 above), deals with Péguy and French nationalist Catholicism in *Consciousness and Society*, ch. 9. For Yeats see particularly Graham Hough, *The Mystery Religion of W. B. Yeats* (Brighton, Sussex, 1984) and for Kandinsky see Maurice Tuchman et al., *The Spiritual in Art: Abstract Paintings 1890–1985* (New York, 1986).

## *Epilogue*

The two general works to which I am most indebted in this chapter are Christopher Butler, *Early Modernism: Literature, Music and Painting in Europe, 1900–1916* (Oxford, 1994) and Peter Nicholls, *Modernism: A Literary Guide* (Berkeley and Los Angeles, 1995). Nicos Stargos (ed.), *Concepts of Modern Art* (rev. edn, London, 1981) and Paul Griffiths, *Modern Music: A Concise History from Debussy to Boulez* (London, 1978) are useful introductions, and I have found the latter far more comprehensible than a musical illiterate has any right to expect. For Expressionism I have used chiefly Wolf-Dieter Dube, *The Expressionists* (trans. M. Wittall, London, 1972) and John Willett, *Expressionism* (London, 1970). Peter Gay, *Weimar Culture: The Outsider as Insider* (New York, 1968), though primarily concerned with the post-war period, is relevant and stimulating. On 'Youth' see chiefly now John Neubauer, *The Fin de Siècle Culture of Adolescence* (New Haven and London, 1992) and George Mosse, *The Crisis of German Ideology* (cited Chapter 3 above). Nikolaus Pevsner's *Pioneers of Modern Design from William Morris to Walter Gropius* (rev. edn, London, 1960) remains, as I said in the text, a classic. Roy Pascal, *From Naturalism to Expressionism* (London, 1973) is impressively comprehensive on this period in Germany. For the concept 'avant-garde' see Renato Poggioli, *The Theory of the Avant Garde* (Cambridge, Mass., 1968). For responses to the war I am indebted in particular to R. N. Stromberg, *Redemption by War: The Intellectuals and 1914* (Lawrence,

Kan., 1982) and Ariel Roshwald and Richard Stites (eds), *European Culture in the Great War, 1914–1918* (Cambridge, 1999). For responses to the city, apart from works cited above, see E. Timms and D. Kelly (eds), *Unreal City: Urban Experiences in Modern European Literature and Art* (New York, 1985). For European culture at the turn of the century generally see E. Timms and P. Collier (eds), *Visions and Blueprints: Avant Garde Culture and Radical Politics in Early Twentieth-century Europe* (Manchester, 1986) and for Germany G. Chapple and H. H. Schulte (eds), *The Turn of the Century: German Literature and Art 1890–1915* (Hamilton, Ont., 1978). For particular centres see Peter Paret, *The Berlin Secession: Modernism and its Enemies in Imperial Germany* (Cambridge, Mass., 1980); Gerhard Masur, *Imperial Berlin* (Newton Abbott, 1970); Carl Schorske, *Fin de Siècle Vienna: Politics and Culture* (Cambridge, 1961); R. Pynsent (ed.), *Decadence and Innovation: Austro-Hungarian Life and Art at the Turn of the Century* (London, 1989) and W. M. Johnston, *The Austrian Mind: An Intellectual and Social History 1848–1938* (Berkeley and Los Angeles, 1972). An admirable book showing how a monographic study can illuminate general intellectual history is Peter Jelavich, *Munich and Theatrical Modernism: Politics, Playwriting and Performance, 1890–1914* (Cambridge, Mass., 1985).

# Index